# THE BURGESS BOOK OF LIES

# THE
# BURGESS
# BOOK
## of
# LIES

ADRIAN & ALAN
## BURGESS

THE
MOUNTAINEERS

Published by
The Mountaineers
1001 SW Klickitat Way, Suite 201
Seattle, WA 98134

First cloth edition published 1994 by Cloudcap
First paper edition published 1998 by The Mountaineers, second printing 2001

Published simultaneously in Great Britain by Cordee, 3a DeMontfort Street, Leicester, England, LE1 7HD

Manufactured in the United States of America

Cover design by Jennifer Shontz

Cover photograph: *Alan and Adrian Burgess,* by Kinde Nebeker

**Library of Congress Cataloging-in-Publication Data available.**

♻ Printed on recycled paper

# TO OUR MUM AND DAD

JOYCE ELLISON KNIGHT
&
GEORGE GEOFFREY BURGESS
of Holmfirth, Yorkshire, England


*They watched us leave for our first climb*
*and have cheered us on  ever since.*

# Acknowledgments

Telling stories to friends around campfires, in bars or in crowded base camp tents has never been difficult for either of us. The truth is that we revel in the act of entertainment and its capacity for forging tight bonds between storytellers and listeners. However, writing down those tales was another matter.

Most of the credit for this book must go to our many, many friends who have jogged oxygen-starved brain cells into recall. Chuck Masters read our drivel and was honest: "Lads, tell it like it happened, not like your English teacher would want to hear it." So we tried.

People like Geoff Birtles (*High* magazine) and Jim Curran (*High Living*) caught us elaborating our stories fantastically, and they snapped us back to gritty reality. California filmmaker and scriptwriter Jim McEachen told us more effective ways of telling stories that we'd told him many times before. Lorna kept a job while Adrian tapped out words on the computer, and then while we went to China to climb K2, she oversaw the pulling together of the book with our publisher John Pollock, editor Wayne Johnson and proofreader Craig Wicklund.

The main thanks, however, should go to the many people who have come together to shape our lives—and this story. We especially thank those who held regular jobs so that civilization, as we know it, didn't fall apart while we went climbing.

# CONTENTS

**1:** BEGINNINGS     **13**

**2:** EARLY ALPS: THE WILD YEARS     **37**

**3:** HOODS IN THE WOODS     **67**

**4:** TO THE HIMALAYA     **69**

**5:** A BRAWL & A QUICK CLIMB     **89**

**6:** CENTRAL PILLAR OF FRÊNEY     **95**

**7:** DAVI     **103**

**8:** CANADA: THE FALLING CORNICE     **116**

**9:** ALPS: SUMMER OF 1975     **125**

**10:** MCKINLEY: CASSIN SPUR     **131**

**11:** FITZROY     **149**

**12:** A 'STING' & HUASCARAN NORTE     **163**

**13:** LOGAN: SOUTH BUTTRESS     **177**

**14:** LES DROITES: A SHORT WALK WITH DOUG SCOTT     **209**

**15:** EVEREST IN WINTER     **217**

**16:** DHAULAGIRI     **245**

**17:** FOXHUNTS & DEBUTANTE BALLS     **273**

**18:** ANNAPURNA IV: A TALE OF THREE ICE CAVES     **279**

**19:** EXPEDITIONS: LARGE/SMALL     **299**

**20:** THE DOGS OF KATHMANDU     **307**

**21:** CHO OYU     **315**

**22:** K2: 1986     **321**

**23:** The Journey — 356

**24:** Lhotse Shar: A Time of Questioning — 363

**25:** Dream of Tibet — 375

**26:** Strife on the Strip — 381

**27:** Everest 1989: The Last Three Days — 385

**28:** Death of a Sherpa: To a Lost Friend — 405

**29:** The Winds of Manaslu — 413

**30:** Sherpa Friends — 421

**31:** Alone & Alive — 431

**32:** Climbing Thoughts — 441

**Epilogue:** Dispatches from K2 — 447

# THE BURGESS BOOK OF LIES

# CHAPTER
## *1*

**BEGINNINGS**

BY ADRIAN

I'm sitting in bright sunshine atop a gritstone bluff—Laddow Rocks. It's the summer of 1990 and I've just returned from Nanga Parbat, an 8,126-meter peak in Pakistan, where storms and heavy snowfall prevented us from reaching the summit. But that seems an age ago. The present feels very real. The Yorkshire sun is warm and relaxing to my body, but my mind is churning with memories. Twenty-eight years ago, I sat in this same place, amid swirling mist while safe-guarding Al up the last twenty feet of Long Climb. Our rope then was made of sisal.

Today as I soloed up the first slab and then the final crack, it was almost as if I was on the first ascent. The holds covered in green lichen showed no evidence of other ascents, yet somewhere in my sub-conscious I remembered the moves. Lush green grass grew on the ledges and white splotches of "cuckoo spit" peppered the long stalks. Every-thing was pristine. Where climbers once had wandered all over the but-tresses and slabs, there now was no human sign. Nature had reclaimed her prize.

As I sat there, my mind drifting back a quarter century, there came a slow, heavy feeling of loss. People no longer respected this proud and noble cliff. They had abandoned it for places nearer the road: places where the "technical move" was everything and aura nothing. I looked down my sport-clad tights to my technical-climbing slippers. Yes, things sure have changed. The popular modern crags now would be interlaced with rope and colored Lycra, with chalk dust filling the air. But, for me, this cliff will always hold a special place, because here there were beginnings.

Holmfirth is a small town of large stone houses nestled together on the steep sides of the Holme Valley. Its isolated nature comes from being landlocked on the north and south by green rolling pastures, and to the west are the Pennine moors, once called the backbone of En-gland. The river Holme is an east-flowing beck, a rib stretching out from the spine of the peat wastelands. Soft water, together with the local sheep, drew a woolen industry into the valley. Large mills, the tallest buildings around, were attached to the river's gently curving banks. When Alan and I were growing up, surrounded by products of the Industrial Revolution, the river used to change color a number of times a day. Blood-red faded to pink, then a splash of blue turned ev-erything purple. The poisonous dyes, gross products of man's igno-rance, killed everything in their way. By now, foreign competition has closed most of the mills, and the river is free once more.

To two twelve-year-old identical-twin boys, all these things did not pass unnoticed. Indeed, they were normal; we had lived with them all our lives. But we also knew secrets. We knew where the water bubbled clean and fresh-tasting, where trout hid under gently overhanging banks and, more important, where no one else ever went. Upstream the river narrowed, subdivided many times, winding brooks draining the acidic peat bogs. In 1960, we knew many of these places. On Saturdays, we walked, jogged and ran carefree among the tufts of cotton grass; wove around, over and through soggy marshes, slippery trenches and narrow, incised valleys. We followed the rough gritstone enclosure walls up onto the moors, broke off and headed for miles toward the jumbled outlines of "standing stones," drunken sentries in the middle of nowhere. Scraggly, lean-faced sheep started at the passing of two identically dressed figures: flannel trousers were tucked into grey woolen stockings; brightly-colored, hand-knitted chunky sweaters covered lean frames. Both lads wore old ex-army boots that were slimy with brown evil-smelling peat.With increasing maturity, we roamed farther afield; to the south were Bleaklow and Kinderscout, vast open landscapes bisected by cloughs. We learned the names that added so much to the character of the surroundings: Featherbed Moss, Black Hill and Chew Valley. We also learned how to use maps so we could find our way in the Pennine mist and rain. Due to the high precipitation in these areas, we often arrived home soaked to the skin and covered with mud—but filled with an inexplicable happiness.

We were the best of friends, often relying on each other in small practical and psychological ways. Because we had always had each other, we were not independent individuals, yet we did not need others. We tried to involve our school friends but frequently received some excuse or other regarding homework or family commitment. Although we continued to encourage others, we were probably happier when there were only the two of us, perfectly matched in pace and speed, dashing headlong across some soggy, beautifully intriguing moor. At school we were restless pupils who preferred to throw our boundless energies into cross-country running, swimming or athletics. Nevertheless, our teachers at grammar school were determined to fill our heads with information and squeeze us through examinations.

One wet, dreary day in the local library, when cold, damp fog rolled in off the moors and people huddled around their warm coal fires, we discovered a small, thin, grey guidebook to Laddow Rocks. It detailed many different ways to scale the rocks, complete with line drawings. We remembered the familiar name and recalled walking beneath the weathered buttress. Then they had simply been rocks, the same as many others standing guard over the dozens of valleys in the region. But the book turned them into something quite different. They became a promise of future challenges; after all, there had to be people who climbed those rocks. The guidebook spoke a different language: words like *buttress, cracks* and *chimneys* cropped up time after time. *Lie-backs, jams* and *holds* were ways of solving the problems. All these ideas caught and colored our imaginations. I can't remember how many times we studied that book in our school lessons. Its pocket-size allowed it to be concealed comfortably inside a history or geography text book, while the boring old teachers droned on and on. Then we discovered yet another book by J.E.B. Wright, which showed the climbing techniques of using one's hands and feet in a succession of moves and using a rope as a safeguard. We studied it more intensely than we ever had any schoolbook.

One Saturday morning, two fourteen-year-old schoolboys made their way over familiar paths to the base of Laddow Rocks. One of them carried a short coil of sisal rope, and the other kept burying his nose in a book, the way tourists do when visiting some ancient monument. There was a sense of urgent excitement in the air; if there had been any sheep around, which there were not, they would have sensed that something was going to happen. We sought to identify the different climbs and select one that looked feasible, although we were in no position to judge other than by sheer instinct. That day we learned what it was like to balance upwards on worn, rounded holds, then link those actions into moves and watch the ground grow farther away. Any one move was not desperately difficult, but when they were all linked together, the whole became something totally different. It was like magic. The rocks seemed impossibly difficult, yet we looked back and realized we had just climbed them. We had never felt anything so exciting, so thrilling. It was as if we had broken some rules, done something dangerous and got away with it. Somewhere deep inside there was an intense pleasure that felt good and right. We had rekindled innate feelings given us by our ape-like ancestors. Something had clicked.

During those early days we affirmed our reliance on each other, each never doubting the other's ability to hold a fall or provide moral assistance. However, this bonding process made us less able to relate to other people, and its legacy still crops up occasionally today.

For our fifteenth birthday we opted to buy our first climbing rope. The 120-foot, green-flecked, hawser-laid nylon rope was our first serious statement that we intended to continue climbing. Considering the amount of equipment people use today, we were ill-prepared. But blissful ignorance can lead a long way. We spent a week in the Lake District where we experimented with the complexities of multi-pitch climbs, where the ground was left far behind and a tangled rope or flawed judgment could end in serious injury. Route-finding became a necessity, or we could stray onto climbs that were beyond our limited experience.

I well remember the time I stood looking up a greasy Lakeland crag whose buttresses disappeared in the swirling mists. Alan was sure he could see the way ahead, a series of gashes and polished knobs weeping moisture from the typical 99 percent Cumbrian humidity. When we returned home, we were two very dirty urchins. Slime and mud covered our faces, jackets and boots, but our smiles went from ear to ear. This was the life!

Many school kids scam a day off school by feigning sickness and the like, but for us it wasn't as easy. What teacher would believe we were both sick together? We had to figure out another way of gaining extra climbing days. On Friday afternoons, we'd be expected to play soccer or some such game, unless we joined the cross-country team. Once on the team, we could run out of the school grounds and into the surrounding countryside. Then, minutes later when the locker room was empty, we'd return, pack our gear and be on the crags within the hour.

One such afternoon the grey mists were typically swirling around Dovestones Edge. Al climbed up to an overhanging bottomless chimney and there threaded a sling around a big old chunk of gritstone. That would be his protection for the difficult moves ahead. Standing motionless at the bottom, I was cold even though I wore two woolen sweaters and a cotton anorak I'd soaked in linseed oil. Thick leather-palmed gloves kept my hands warm enough. "How's it goin', kid?" I shouted. I couldn't see him but could hear a lot of grunting as he squeezed himself upwards. He must be nearing the top. Then, without warning, a dark shadow spun out of the gloom. A huge tug lifted me off my feet towards the chockstone. Al finally came to rest feet five feet above the ground.

"Ugh! Me waist!" he said. "Let me down! Thanks, kid. It's too wet."

By then it was pouring rain.

A month later, when 1963 was almost over, we joined the local mountaineering club. The Phoenix Club met every Friday night in a Huddersfield pub. At fifteen, we were too young to drink beer legally, but with straight backs and heads held high, we bluffed our way through the smoky throng of gesticulating climbers. Noisy chatter absorbed us into the throng. We listened to tall stories of epic climbs and crag-bound nights out. Our eyes grew wide and our excitement mounted. Yes, that's what we wanted to do, too, no matter what it took!

Every weekend we'd climb into a different grimy van or ramshackle car, to be whisked away to places we'd never heard of, crags we'd never seen or pubs we'd never drunk in. It was frantic and intense, with all our energies directed towards bigger and steeper challenges.

At school our work was beginning to suffer. Essays were handed in late, often sloppy and rushed to meet some inexplicable deadline. Our attention was elsewhere. Guidebooks and climbing autobiographies were our textbooks: the Shakespeares and Donnes of our learning. We attended school as though it were a factory, with our real lives beginning on Friday nights.

One such night we were approached by a small, wiry character whom we had only seen and worshipped from a distance, never daring to think we would ever climb with him. John Stanger was one of the best and most respected climbers of the group. His twenty-two years seemed to put him a whole generation above us, and his fearful reputation as a hard-climbing fanatic secured him the image of a demigod. How could we turn down the opportunity to tie into a rope with him? That same weekend we were to learn what an excellent teacher he was: patient and thoughtful, yet absolutely demanding of our efforts. We must have passed the test, because for weekend after weekend our threesome developed our skills from Derbyshire to the Lakes and back to Wales. John's old grey Austin van carried us everywhere. We were undaunted by misfortune or by bad weather, always bending our plans to suit the occasion.

John was a difficult person to get to know, and even after weeks of climbing with him, we still didn't learn how he made a living. "It's to do with telephones, lads," he'd say, making it seem mysterious and special. Then there was the way he never answered a question directly. It would always be, "if you like," or "maybe we should." To find out details of climbs was nigh impossible. He'd answer, "follow ya nose" or "hard enough" or "maybe you should try it." That he was intense and introverted didn't affect Al or me. The main thing was that he could climb, and do it well.

One fine Friday evening in early spring we set out for the Lake District. The previous week had been very dry, and by our reckoning, Scafell Crag would be dry enough so that we could climb its historic Central Buttress route. As usual, John was pushing the old rust-flecked van to its limits. It would lurch dangerously on almost every bend, causing Al and me to look on in terror, helplessly. John's face strained in concentration while he fought the wheel, a nervous laugh escaping his lips after particularly close calls. The roads were narrow and twisting with sudden right-angle bends or tight hump-backed bridges, and John knew every single one. Passing places were carefully learned and not an opportunity was lost. He'd pull out from behind some slower car, and we'd begin to edge past it with the next blind bend rushing towards us. Split-second timing was everything. His hips pushed forward, rhythmically urging the van onward.

We were taking a short cut around Ambleside, the picturesque gateway town to the Lake District, when disaster struck. An oncoming car went out of control on a tight bend and smacked into us, virtually head-on. My feet came magically up to the dash to soften my own impact. There was another smash and the lights went out. But at least we stopped. Somehow we'd demolished a farm gate and were surrounded by cow pasture. After exchanging names and addresses with the other driver, we turned our attention to our vehicle. The door was in a mangled state with its entire side caved in. One light worked. John pronounced it driveable, so off we drove into the night. At a very steep hill called Hard Knott, Alan and I pushed while the sick engine poured out black oil fumes. Finally we coasted down the other side, grabbed our climbing gear and began walking. It was near midnight when we lay down by the side of a bubbling brook to sleep for a few hours.

Who said the climb would be dry? An ugly water mark seeped out of the flake crack that was the crux of the route. Undeterred, we began to climb. Stanger led while Al and I did the best we could in our big, heavy mountaineering boots. We tried to use tiny edges on the outside of the crack, but the water made everything greasy. When it came time to execute the famous lie-back, we needed to use twice as much strength as normal just to make our feet stick. We were still at the stage when we thought we could climb anything with the right amount of technique, and we scorned fancy rock-shoes because they made everthing easier. It was Stanger who suggested better footwear: "I think you've learned enough in those big boots. Maybe it's time to buy some 'magic boots'."

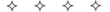

Back at school our teachers were beginning to wind us up toward our final O-level exams. Everyone told us just how important they were when looking for work, and even more important, they would allow us to continue our higher education. Great, just what we wanted . . . ! We felt ourselves locked into an institution where students were eager for their future to be at one of the great universities: Oxford or Cambridge. But our future was only as distant as the coming weekend, or if we really extended ourselves, to the Alps in some distant summer. The late spring weather was warm and balmy: perfect for climbing. But we were stuck indoors, listening to the drone of a teacher tell us how important Shakespeare's use of language was in *Henry IV, Part One*. Hell, Shakespeare didn't even know climbing existed, let alone do it!

At Whitsuntide all our friends, including Stanger, were spending a full week in the Lakes. We agonized as every day turned out warm and sunny. What would they be doing? Which crags would they be on? It became difficult to concentrate on the mass of old exam papers which lay strewn around the floor.

"Never again!" we swore. Indeed, it was the last time schooling got in the way.

That summer we went to Wales once the exams were over. Stanger was in the Alps, so we climbed as a twosome. We would set our hearts upon a route and then work up to that particular level of difficulty. It was an exhilarating time, slowly pushing our personal standards. And then pushing them again. At summer's end, our confidence had increased dramatically, and we felt as if we had grown.

More decisions needed making. Did we wish to continue our education? No. What then? We hadn't a clue. It was work or school. School or work. Not much of a choice. We'll go back to school.

We had done sufficiently well to be allowed to study for A-levels. These successes finally sucked us back into a system we had begun to dread. Luckily, school life improved, but Al and I were regarded as strange freaks for our climbing activities. None of our school friends could figure out what we did on the weekends. Our teachers even less so.

By this time we were living two completely different lives. There was the school life with people of our own age, and there was the climbing life with real adults in the real world. We'd show up on Monday mornings with enormous red weals on the backs of our hands and a distant, faraway look in our eyes: the glazed look of a person trying to hold onto a memory, a move, a passion. By the time Thursday arrived, our briefcases held more guidebooks and maps than textbooks.

During the winter early in 1966, cold, wet weather stopped us from regular free-climbing. The alternatives lay up the steep and over-hanging limestone cliffs found in the Yorkshire Dales and the Derbyshire Peak District. Here, artificial routes followed vague crack-lines by us-ing soft-steel pitons. This "dangle-and-whack" technique, as it was known by local climbers, was just that: while dangling from those of-ten insecure placements by using short stirrup-ladders, the climber then whacked home the next piton at arm's length and used it to make up-ward progress.

At first, this sort of climbing was desperately strenuous, and we tied ourselves, and our ropes, into tangled knots. We would use up so much energy that we often needed just to hang there, breath coming and going in great sighs, while the throbbing in our arms subsided. After more practice, our efficiency increased, and we became ambi-tious to do the harder routes. Time—or, more accurately, the lack of it—was always a problem with these climbs. The short winter days allowed no possibility for errors in judgment; it was common to see lights bobbing around high in the air, as friends attempted to rescue stranded climbers.

Because of this, we decided to experiment with a new idea. We felt that if we climbed together, rather than using the traditional meth-ods of belaying, we could avoid all these nocturnal epics. With sixty feet of rope between us, and a piton every four feet, it seemed we would be in no danger. If one piton pulled out there would always be plenty more to catch the fall. The most important rule was not to allow any slack to build up between leader and second. We were delighted with the result: no more need to stand around in the cold for ages while the leader sweated it out. But not all climbers thought we were sane, be-cause we'd broken with tradition, and we were too young to do that. We laughed at their comments. Why should we care? It was, in retrospect, a very safe system on routes where there were some good pitons spread out among the poorer ones. It wouldn't make sense on modern-day horrors in Yosemite, but a number of present-day top climbers use this system on speed ascents of routes like the Nose on El Capitan.

That spring we started to psych ourselves up for a first visit to the Alps. Summer was on its way and we could hardly wait. Every night after homework had quickly been put behind, out came the guide-books. There was one for the Dolomites of northern Italy, another for the Kaisergebirge of Austria and an outdated *Selected Climbs in the Mont Blanc Region*. Good photos were located in the autobiographies of pre- and post-war alpinists. Hermann Buhl captured our imaginations like no other person; he had soloed big climbs and had endured epics all over the Alps. We learned almost every paragraph by heart: "No need for pitons here. Up I go with the abyss ever deepening below me." Shudders of pure joy would flood our minds and bodies: "Just imagine all that rock. On and on, forever."

At seventeen years old, we held the belief that anything is possible. The barriers built up by life's conditioning did not exist. At that time we had not experienced the death of friends or had close calls ourselves. Though we had stretched our climbing limits, we'd always been taught by older club members to keep a safe margin in reserve to insulate us from accidents; to always be sure we could reverse even difficult moves or climb through a sequence to safer ground above. Even to this day on seriously big mountains, we hold onto this concept as a means of increasing our chances of survival.

Stanger, too, had a rare optimism, but when he saw the list of objectives we had compiled, I think even he thought we had gone over the top. Typically, he was not negative but commented: "Well, it's always better to have a long list than a short one."

One weekend in particular remains locked in my memory. The three of us set off for Snowdonia. John was in good driving form, and the number of nervous giggles came in direct proportion to the number of bends in the road. To save gas on long descents, he'd switch off the engine and coast. Faster and faster we'd go, clipping corners, screeching around others—all this in a van not known for its racing design.

As Capel Curig flashed by, the light began to fade, and the first drops of rain splattered across the windshield. For most travelers this would be a mere disappointment to see the weather changing. Not so for us. The reason: the headlights were still damaged from the accident a year before. Yes, they worked OK, at least until the first raindrops hit the bulbs. Then the night became as black as ever.

"Not to worry," said John. "Hold this flashlight out the window."

"Can you still see?"

"Sort of. Well, not very well—heh, heh!"

We were now descending into the windy Nant Gwynant Valley. There was a big drop-off to our right.

"John, I think you should slow down," I said. "Me 'and's freezin'."

The rain increased to a steady downpour.

"John . . . !"

I whipped my hand inside to avoid dropping the light. An empty silence. Then BANG!! A horrible scraping sound and we swerved across the road.

"What did you do that for?" asked John.

"John, me 'and's freezin'. Sorry. Go slow and I'll try again."

Next morning the sky was a heavy grey. Rain in the mountains, so off to

*Teenage Alan climbing in Wales*

the coast. There was a "secret" crag Stanger had seen a few weeks before. We went to look.

It could be seen easily from the road. Sharp, angular ribs jutted out above dark, flinty overhangs. There was not an obvious, climbable line on the whole cliff. I began to feel uneasy. Stanger was undeterred, so we scrambled up to the foot to get a closer look. I believe we might have gone away if a car had not shown up on the road below. People—obviously climbers: competition!—spilled out to examine both the crag and us. After a two-minute descent back to the road, we were proud owners of a route description called Hardd, scrawled onto the back of a speeding ticket. The others left, shaking their heads.

I tied myself to as many trees as I could find while John led off towards a rusty ring-piton. It was already steep but the rock began to bulge even more, forcing him left. He asked us to watch him. What did he think we were doing? Both of us were glued to his every move. It was John's way of saying he could fall. He managed to get himself past the first difficult moves to where retreat was nigh impossible and pro-tection distant. It seemed ages before he moved again. When he did, we knew that it was up—or off. It was up. He'd cracked it!

Then it was my turn. I felt uneasy because the rope was not

always going to be above me. If I fell, I would swing off into midair, dangling like a spider, but spiders have many arms if two get tired. Above the piton, I became horribly hunched up with my feet getting far too close to my hands. A back somersault was in the offing. My hands were beginning to sweat uncomfortably on an under-cling. A tiny, sloping foothold became the focal point of my world. I reached for it with my foot. It seemed out of reach. Retreat. Another try, toe drawing small circles in the air. I touched it but . . . oh, ho! I became desperate. My back ached. I willed more weight onto my outstretched foot, gently easing over onto it. Phew! The rest seemed easier with my veins full of adrenaline. What a position we were in, like eagles in an aerie!

The time drew nearer to our first alpine season, but our equipment was rudimentary, mostly ex-army stock. We had saved a little money from the one pound a month given to us by our dad. We went out in careful search of a real rucksack and a down jacket, both very expensive items. The Don Whillans Alpinist 'sac was the best we could find, and once we had a shiny red duvet jacket to match, we felt like kings: invincible!

The school year ended. One day later we were heading south in the old grey van, complete with new headlights. A box of tinned food lay packed in the rear. After all, who knew what those foreigners ate? The night ferry to Calais took only a couple of hours, but it was impossible to sleep because everyone around us was being sick. Once on dry land again, we set off, through Belgium, toward the German *autobahn*. We lumbered past Brussels—Bruxelles, it said on the map—at a steady 55 miles per hour. We were no longer involved in a three-hour dash to the Lake District; it was more like a marathon. Thankfully, there were no bends to challenge Stanger, and the driving became tedious.

Although I'd recently passed my driving test, Stanger was adamant that I didn't need to relieve him. It was easy driving, but we should have known he could have found a way to spice up the journey. The *autobahn* at that time had no speed limit. So just imagine the variety of cars, from rusting VWs to gleaming Porsches, all gunning the hell out of their engines in the equivalent of a lawless world. In the middle of it all, a rusting grey silhouette ambling along in the slow lane—the driver on the wrong side of the van, next to the curb.

Life would have been fine, and safe, if it hadn't been for those long uphill stretches and slow trucks. We'd sneak up to the rear of a laboring truck, like a dog stalking a moose.

John would ask: "Is it okay?"

A fair head would poke out the window, looking backward. "Wait. Ah . . . yes!"

And then we'd be in the danger zone, limping past a Mercedes truck pulling a trailer. Limping awfully slow, too, with John's hips working overtime to lift our speed half a mile an hour.

"Er, John. That car in the distance is coming up quite quick!"

What was once a dot had suddenly become a shape—in fact, a Porsche. There was the blaring of an alpine horn as we cut off the truck to let the missile by. Then there was the blaring of a deeper horn as the truck driver showed his disdain. Scientists say that molecules spin around in space without ever colliding. I'll bet the discoverer was a German.

Al has his face in the map.

"This town we keep seeing signs for, I can't find it."

"Not every town will be on the map, kid," Stanger says in his wisdom.

"Yeah, but this town of Ausfahrt must be big 'cause I've been seeing signs for it for the last half-hour."

Al shakes his head, and I listen to the conversation while half-asleep. We never do figure out the phantom city. A number of year later, I realize that in German *Ausfahrt* means "exit"!

We passed the Austrian border during the late afternoon. St. Johann in Tirol was next. It was very quiet in the late evening. By the time we had set up our two tents behind a large chalet, the setting sun was burning the West Pillar of the Predisthule a magnificent red.

The next morning we were up preparing our equipment before the sun rose. Our climb for the day would be on the East Face of the Fleishbank, which began from a glacier-sculptured hanging-valley a thousand feet above the valley floor. Because there was no English guidebook, we had only a photograph and a poor description of the route to guide us through the climb. It was pure joy to climb up the holds of solid, white limestone with the sun creeping down to meet us. The face was not vertical but rather a series of steep slabs separated by steeper corners.

There was a moment of confusion when I was asked to account for my ambiguous translation. I had stolen a huge fat German dictionary from the school library and, without previous knowledge of the language, translated the climbs we were interested in. It had consumed many long nights when I should have been doing homework, and this was the first test of my accuracy.

"Do I traverse thirty meters under an overhang or traverse thirty meters below an overhang?" John quizzed as he hung from a creaking piton, poised with his head pressed against a huge white roof.

"Well, it definitely goes left," I countered, stating the obvious. "I think you're too high. The traverse is at a lower level."

He half lowered and half climbed back down from the piton. A delicate task.

To Al, I whispered: "If he only knew how hard it was to figure out the descriptions. The bloody Krauts always stick the verb at the end of the sentence."

We were at the famous tension-traverse where a swing on the rope solved the problem. It was tremendous climbing. Never very difficult if we stayed on route, but always interesting. Then came the famous Dulfer Chimneys, named after Hans Dülfer, the first climber to make this route: a series of strenuous, overhanging cracks leading up to the summit. Because the climb was graded 5+ and not 6, we had decided it would be good training to climb it in our big mountain boots. This made the final cracks even more difficult. Our very first alpine climb was over. Nineteen years later, when I repeated the climb with my wife, I marveled at our audacity in thinking the climb too easy to use rock-shoes.

In the next week I grew to love the small alpine hamlets, with their colorful and sweet-smelling flower boxes; the cows, with large bells around their necks, grazing in the high alpine meadows; and the keen fragrance of pine in the warm afternoon air.

Another climb on the West Wall of the Maukspitze ended in an epic. First, the track shown on our map was nonexistent, and we finished by swinging branch to branch through steep, dense forest. When we succeeded in reaching the base of the wall, it was already four in the afternoon, but we began to climb anyway. It was hard. Steep, unprotected chimneys took us in four pitches to a small ledge where we would have to spend the night. It proved to be so small that we spent half of the time suspended from pitons. The next morning a wild thunderstorm brought hail and torrential rain down upon us. Tired from lack of sleep and physically stretched from the previous day, we began our descent. After two rappels [a *rappel* is a descent by a climber, as down the sheer face of a cliff, by means of a rope, usually doubled, that is secured above and arranged around the climber's waist so that the slide downward can be controlled] our ropes jammed and refused to pull down after us. We were in a small cave with water flowing down the ropes.

John rose to the occasion and with a grimace said: "I'll prusik back up the ropes and free them." [To *prusik* means to ascend a fixed rope using Prusik knots, which allow a smaller-diameter rope to slide easily along a larger-diameter rope but which lock in place when pressure is applied.]

Once on terra firma, we sped down through the high alpine meadows and into the dreaded forest. For hours we scrambled up and down, searching for a continuation to the trail. We were hopelessly lost, dog-tired. Small stars were beginning to dance at the edge of my vision.

It was John who refused to reascend: "I'm not climbing up one more time. We'll rappel."

Down we went, from stout tree to stout tree. How embarrassing to have to resort to that, but we were losing height. The last rappel landed us in the river. We were soaked to the skin and our hands bled. A crash of thunder reverberated around the peaks, and while we crawled on hands and knees up onto the road, giant hail peppered our hard hats. But we were safe.

I once read a gem of wisdom that you learn more on the climbs you don't get up than on the ones you do. If that's true, our education took a quantum leap that particular day. We'd never seen Stanger as tired. Nor had we ever had to dig as deep into ourselves to find the necessary energy. In a sense, we had come of age and felt more on a par with John that ever before.

Maybe it was as a result of the epic, maybe the need to separate ourselves from a bad memory or maybe the need for more adventure, but we decided to head for the Dolomites. A day's drive over the frontier and we were in the quaint Tirolean town of Bolzano. The weather was perfect again, so it was time for another climb.

The Roda di Vael has an uncompromisingly steep west face, which looks like it has been shaped by the single sweep of a giant sword. As we sweated up the steep track, the sun began to set. The face began to glow orange and gradually turned the reddest of reds. The Rotwand (*red wall*, in German) was welcoming us.

Alarming exposure is a unique feature of Dolomite climbs, where, looking between one's legs, the base of the cliff is always visible. The redder the rock, the steeper and looser it is. This Rotwand looked awfully steep to me, and we all were very impressed.

At the hut we met two Sheffield climbers who looked confident and relaxed. They were about John's age. Bob Dearman reminded me of a picture I'd seen of Jim Morrison of the rock group, The Doors, his face drawn and serious. Bob Toogood was quiet and let his friend do the talking.

"Three of you'll never do that route in a day," said Dearman. "We did it as a twosome and only just did it. And we're fast."

I barely slept. Even before the first pale light of dawn streaked the perfectly clear horizon, we were stumbling among boulders and scree towards the menacing dark shadow that was the face. An easy but loose chimney led to a huge flat terrace where we arranged our climbing equipment. Out of the packs came our thirty-five steel carabiners, which added another fifteen pounds to the leader's own weight, a severe penalty when hanging out backwards over thin air on finger-strength alone. [A *carabiner* is an oval metal ring with a snap link used to fasten a rope to a piton. A *piton* is a metal spike with a loop in one end; it can be driven into cracks in rocks or into ice and used to attach slings, etc., to the mountain.] Nowadays, the alloy carabiners are much lighter and allow greater freedom of movement. Although we carried no bivvy gear, one small pack contained a water-bottle and three grapefruits. [*Bivvy* is mountaineering slang for "bivouac," a planned or unplanned night on a mountain without tent or cave.]

John led off up a plumb vertical crack with rusty pitons every six feet or so. Sometimes he could free-climb by using only the rock holds, and at others he hung from the pitons. There was never a question of whether it was ethical to use these; alpinism had not reached this stage in its development, and an "anything-goes" attitude prevailed.

Then came three severely overhanging leads up the sharp edge of an enormous flake. John's body would hang bat-like against the grey morning sky, then would make a few moves and go limp once more.

"Take in. I'm resting," floated down to Alan and me. Then: "Slack! I'm going for it!"

His small silhouette began to crawl up out of sight. Our necks craned to see more, but the real messages came down the twin ropes. Small vibrations, a sudden jerk, then slack rope trickled down again. Each person displayed his own signature, his own personal energy— and his own doubts, too. We read them the way a blind person reads braille, through experience and sensitivity.

Alan sighed: "Phew! He's there!"

The rope had told him.

John's voice came next: "I'm safe."

We prepared to leave our minuscule stance. Where the flake ended there was nothing. No big, forceful feature to follow, only some expansion pitons sticking out of a nearly blank wall. I stepped from the security of the tiny ledge. My heart beat fast. My chest heaved. I tried to control the fear that rose toward my mouth. It was the most exposed place I had ever been. The grey scree [rock debris at the foot of a cliff] blurred somewhere off the point of my boot. I decided to look up instead, to focus my entire existence upon four square feet of coarse limestone. A narrow ledge appeared beneath sweaty palms. Then a cave the size of a refrigerator.

John giggled, "Nice, eh?" He knew I'd been scared, because so had he.

Above us, the rock looked more grey and solid. The Great Wall was the second crux of the climb, but with all the pitons in place, much of the sting had already been removed. They formed an iron pathway leading up into the blue sky, a reminder of hours of laborious "pegging."

"Let's climb together up these next few pitches, or else we'll all be hanging around for breakfast on these rusting pieces of iron," suggested Alan.

It was a good idea because it would also speed up our ascent and lessen our chances of becoming benighted. Memories of the short climbs in Derbyshire flooded back briefly, and we felt confident.

The sun-warmed rock slipped away into a land that was not ours. We looked upwards, thought upwards and climbed upwards. Speed was of utmost importance. It consumed all our efforts. Clip! Stand! Balance up the small metal rungs. Clip! Repeat!

Another cave came into view, but it had no floor, just a roof. We were swinging in our harnesses like children on a park swing. John complained of cramps in his hands, so Alan took over the lead. I was pretty tired, too, and so felt a great surge of pride as Alan swung up and out of view. After all, he was only seventeen and able to take over the lead on a notably difficult Dolomite climb. The next time we all regrouped, there was a big ledge, one that allowed us to hide from the terrific drop that had accompanied us all day. We were almost there.

"Hey, look what's here!" I shouted after finding a small metal sleeve jammed down behind a boulder. Inside, there was a registration book for recording the date of our climb. Pasted on the inside cover was a photo I immediately recognized. Herman Buhl! Our Super Hero! His face was drawn and haggard. I knew it had been taken after his solo first ascent of Nanga Parbat in 1953. He'd had a bivvy just below the summit, and it was no wonder he looked so worn out. The two modern-day first-ascensionists of the Rotwand, Brandler and Hasse, had obviously worshiped him the way we did. Sadly, he had fallen through a cornice while climbing in the Karakoram Mountains in Pakistan. We were amazed at how much Stanger looked like Buhl!

Even the last two pitches were steep, but the exposure had gone and we knew we had climbed the route. It was strange suddenly to be standing on flat ground. No pointed summit: only a pleasantly sloping shoulder of moss-covered limestone. Our timing was perfect. The light was beginning to fade, but it did not get dark until we had once again reached the mountain hut.

We took one last look up at the face and saw a tiny light twinkling and bobbing, caught in the vast expanse of rock. The two "boys" would spend the night propped in their small ladders until morning.

"Fast, but not fast enough," someone remarked.

An alpine season is not complete without a visit to the famous mountains of the Mont Blanc massif. For two days the van labored over steep alpine passes until finally a sign read "Chamonix: Mont Blanc." We had arrived. Compared with the last few weeks, the difference was remarkable. Climbers were everywhere. Tanned faces, bulging rucksacks and many, many different languages.

Ambling around the town, Alan and I felt insignificant and very inexperienced. We gazed wistfully at the bronzed arms and bulging shirts, certain that among those people were Bonattis and Rebuffats, all planning some super-desperate new route. We did not recognize the pseudo-French climbers who paraded themselves on the main thoroughfares. But overweight Parisian tourists were awestruck by such masculine animals.

The town lay in the shadow of such a vast array of spectacular granite spires that everything else seemed unimportant.

"Hell, everything's so big. What's that bloody mountain there?"

"The Dru. The guidebook says the West Face has only been climbed a few times."

The 3,500-foot sweep of vertical granite could be used as an ad for laxatives. The British super-climbers, Joe Brown and Don Whillans, had made the second ascent in a day and a half and had completely blown away the French alpine elite.

No wonder. What can *we* do?

We spent a couple of hours finding our bearings. An unusual caution caught us in its grip. These were *very big* mountains!

It seemed as though all the British we spoke to had done the West Face of the Point Albert, so we decided to climb it, too. It looked tiny next to all the other spires but would give us a measure of our abilities.We found the climb easy compared to the Dolomites, yet it was given a high grade in the guidebook. However, the amount of walking necessary before we could actually get to grips with climbing was something we were unaccustomed to. The scale was so huge that it was easy to underestimate distances, and we heard stories of climbers getting benighted on the easiest of routes.

After only one week, it was John who suggested a move to the southern side of the range. He had made arrangements to meet a very experienced climber, Brian Thompson, in Courmayeur. This necessitated a trip through the Mont Blanc tunnel into Italy. For Alan and me, this presented a major problem, as all the climbs in Italy tended to be longer and more difficult, and we were not sure if our experience was sufficient to cope with them. In retrospect, I can see that John wanted to distance himself from us just enough to force us out onto our own so that he could try something more ambitious that we didn't have the experience for. Anyway, he had the van, and it was better to follow him than be stranded in Chamonix.

While we were pitching our tent on a bed of dry pine needles beneath resin-scented pines, Al summed up our thoughts: "This is a much cleaner place than Chamonix. Not a turd to be seen, and no crowds either."

He was right. The place was idyllic, except for one thing. About a hundred yards away, behind a stand of evergreens, there was a tight bend in the road. Every car that screeched around it felt compelled to blare its horn. Welcome to Italy!

We selected a large lichen-coated rock and stared up in awe at the mountains. Our guidebook listed very few climbs on this side of Mont Blanc, presumably because no one from Britain had made many ascents here. The vast scale of everything made us wary, overawed by glistening, crawling ridges and massive granite buttresses that appeared nearer to heaven than to earth. We had to find something. It was our first real chance to prove we could climb without Stanger, and we should grasp the opportunity.

First, we would ascend by cable-car to the Torino hut; from there, several shorter one-day climbs were possible. After all, we had so little experience in judging weather and route conditions that we felt it would be foolhardy to venture too far too fast. After five days we had made two reasonable climbs: the South Face of the Dent du Géant—a short but technical rock-climb—and the North Face of the Tour Ronde. The latter had been our very first alpine ice climb and a real eye-opener. Our antiquated crampons [spiked plates attatched to boots] and ice-axes were not up to that kind of route and didn't provide us with a safe purchase on the ice. Our feet skated and slipped and forced us into cutting a few steps. The axes bounced off the hardest green ice, while the disconcerting sweep below our feet did nothing to calm our minds. Still, elated by our successes, we returned to the valley to plan another climb.

"What do you think we should do next?" I asked Alan.

"Something good and bigger than before."

"Not a lot of choice, is there?"

"You know, I've been watching people up on the Noire," Al ventured. "It looks good. I think we could do it."

" 'One of the most beautiful climbs in the range of Mont Blanc'," I read aloud from the guidebook. "Think we could do it?"

"Yeah. Why not?" he said. "We've done harder single pitches while in the Dollies" (referring to the Rotwand).

The Aiguille Noire de Peutery began almost in the campsite. From our perspective, it hung over the entire valley, a sky-piercing granite tooth bristling with towers—or *gendarmes*, as the French call them. We reached a decision; we would try to climb the South Ridge. Then the weather turned bad with a vengeance. A thunderstorm, drawing power from the hot southern plains, released its fury on the surrounding peaks. Giant fingers of energy burst out of a coal-black sky. Bolts of pure light danced from tower to tower, arcing down the line of our next route. We sat in the tent doorway, transfixed by the display of power. What if we had been up there? Sheets of cold rain beat on the tent while we tried to sleep. We knew there were climbers up there. What would it be like? We fell asleep wondering, our warm sleeping bags providing safe places to retreat into.

✧    ✧    ✧    ✧

The grass looked so green in the sharp morning air. A gentle stillness seemed to waft across the newly cleansed campsite. Yet, high above us, beneath a sky of pure blue, people were struggling for their lives. Rumors circulated: many dead, struck by lightning; others badly burned and waiting to be rescued. A dragonfly of a helicopter hummed above the ridge on missions of mercy. It was difficult to believe that anything could possibly be bad on such a perfect day, but the papers were full of bad news. How could climbing be about dying? It seemed absurd, something very new to our experience. Climbing had always been about living, unique in what it gave.

"I think we should take a sleeping bag" was how Alan saw the danger. I agreed. With warm bivvy gear, we ought to be able to survive many days of storm.

"No bivvying on top of towers either," I said, adding weight to our decision to go onto the route despite what had happened.

"We should go straightaway before other storms get a chance to build up," Alan concluded. We left the same afternoon.

Two friends asked if they could join us. We saw no problem in that, especially as four ought to be stronger than two. Walking up the winding trail was sheer joy. Alpine flowers bloomed from almost every crevice. Small trickles of water had turned into respectable waterfalls in the aftermath of the storm. Their miniature arcs reflected diamonds of light. Life felt good, real.

We were not alone. Other parties had similar plans, and we could see them up ahead of us. If they were competent, we would have no problems, but if not, they would almost certainly affect our progress the next day. It is not always easy to pass a slower group on a technical climb because there is often only one way. So it requires the sanction of both parties working in cooperation.

Dawn light filtered through the blue nylon of my sleeping bag and brought me out of a deep sleep. We had overslept. The colored dots that were climbers were shouting out climbing commands far above. There was not much time for eating. All we ate was a chocolate biscuit washed down with water.

The initial climbing was only a scramble, and we chose not to rope up. The chase was on and the competition inviting. When we caught up with one party, we found an alternative route around them. They were having problems with a tangled rope.

The rapid movement quickly warmed us up so that we were

traveling at full bore. When we turned a corner and discovered a party of four British climbers whom we knew, we halted politely in our tracks. They were older and more distinguished than us; they were in the celebrated Alpine Climbing Group. A lady climber was struggling to follow her husband up a steep step in the ridge. She had got herself into a bit of a mess while trying to rush and had forgotten to unclip the rope from a piton. Every time she tried to step up, her husband attempted to help her with the rope but ended up pulling her down instead. Patient communication broke down into screaming and swearing from her. Alan and I pretended to admire the view to hide our embarrassment.

They allowed us to pass them with cheerful encouragement. We realized that they would descend when we heard their doubts and lack of conviction. Soon we arrived upon the Welsenbach Tower, which the guidebook stated was the point of no return. Old rusting tin cans littered popular bivouac sites, but Alan thought this an unhealthy place to sleep.

"If ya got caught in a storm up here, ya'd fry like a piece of bacon," he said. This was where many of the casualties from the last storm had spent their final hours.

A long rappel into a narrow col [a narrow gap or pass in a mountainous ridge] was our statement that retreat was no longer to be considered. The weather was set fair, the rock warm and friendly, and our spirits soaring. There were too many pitons to be able to use all of them, but if the weather were to change and snow to fall, we had no doubt that they would permit our escape. Our friends had dropped behind and, as we carried only one stove, we decided to wait for them. An Italian pair passed us while we waited. Then we caught up with them and passed them again. A friendly race ensued, but we were beginning to get in each other's way. The stances were small and we were too many. At one such place, I took off my pack and then found there was no place to hang it. Then I did something I would never have done before. I grinned at the friendly fellow, looked him straight in the eyes, and clipped my pack onto his waist belt.

"Don't worry, mate," I said. "I'll soon be out of here."

His eyes widened in astonishment. Not a word was said.

Above, we cleared off rocks from a comfortable ledge and spent the evening looking at the alpenglow on the Gran Paradiso. When we awoke, the sun was already high in the eastern sky. After two hours' climbing, we reached the summit, with its lightning-scarred statue of the Madonna glinting in the warm light.

Our climb was over, our holiday at an end. That September we celebrated our eighteenth birthday. I'd been driving for one year; it had been three years since we'd first walked into the Clarence pub to join the Phoenix Climbing Club; and just over four years since that fateful day at Laddow Rocks. Stanger remarked that he wasn't sure if it was a good idea to begin climbing so young, as it might take over our lives.

Well, insight is a wonderful thing.

# CHAPTER
## 2

## EARLY ALPS: THE WILD YEARS

BY ALAN

After the alpine season of 1966, school could never be the same. Sitting in a hot, stuffy classroom and struggling with economic geography and the nuances of Shakespeare, it was too easy to stare through a misted window and dissolve . . . to reappear high on a Dolomite wall or an icy north face. The future was as far ahead as the next weekend, and lunchtimes were spent thumbing through climbing guidebooks. Invariably, Monday mornings found us with hands grazed and torn from a viciously steep gritstone crack, forearms and shoulders aching from the latest "extreme."

The secure prospect of another year in school did not conceal doubts about the future. We both were gravitating toward a teacher-training course in physical education, especially if we were accepted at

Chester College of Education, only a couple of hours drive from the climbing in Snowdonia.

Life was acceptable, each weekend's climbing balancing five days of academic boredom. We had few school friends; they lacked the color and experience of our older climbing companions. We had not discovered the delights of female distraction, so we single-mindedly pursued our rock-climbing passion, to the detriment of homework and examinations. It was not surprising that we were less than perfect students.

We scraped through our examinations and were accepted into Chester College. That summer we took jobs as climbing instructors at an outdoor-education establishment in north Yorkshire. Working at Beverly Park gave us enough funds to buy a small van, and it introduced us to a sport that would take on more significance later: Girls!

Loaded with the basic academic materials for our college course and an unreasonable amount of climbing hardware, we arrived at the steps of the somewhat conservative Chester College. We quickly established our priorities by seeking out fellow climbers from the college mountaineering club.

The academic year passed slowly, but we developed an interest in gymnastics and physiology; both disciplines appeared helpful in climbing. We socialized very little with most of our fellow students, whose interests were more in the direction of soccer, rugby and cricket. With one or two close climbing friends, we'd leave soon after lectures on a Friday afternoon and drive to Snowdonia, the Lake District or Derbyshire. We traveled in our small van, camped out regardless of bad weather and cooked all our meals over a small kerosene stove. We attempted climbs even if hampered by heavy rain, and we were never satisfied unless challenged to the edge of our ability.

One incident demonstrates our single-minded attitude toward our sport. We were in the Llanberis Pass of Snowdonia, the rain was lashing at the crags, and no other people were out climbing. Three of us sat huddled in our steamy van: engine silent, wind buffeting, rain splatting against the windshield. Above, dominating the road, Dinas Cromlech soared to the clouds: malevolent and black. Splitting the sheer rock walls was a corner, like an open book cleft it in two. Climbers knew it as Cenotaph Corner, and it had a reputation for steep, sustained difficulty. We had climbed it previously in dry conditions and knew it to be well protected and easily within our capabilities.

Given those weather conditions today, we would go for a run

or head for the pub. But in those days we needed to be heroes, to take sword and lance in hand and ride forward into danger to slay the mythic dragon—which was within ourselves. To wait for another day was unthinkable. With the dragon ever-present, action—hard and immediate— was the only solution. So we climbed the loose scree below the crag, no longer seeing it as just another rock-climb but as a voyage into a living legend. By challenging the very flesh of that inert cleft, we could partake of the myth ourselves.

After a rope-length of easier climbing, we crouched below the corner, already soaked to the skin through our canvas jackets. The corner ran vertically over our heads, and a torrent of water sluiced down the narrow fissure. I agreed to give it the first try. Tying onto two thick hawsers of nylon and carrying a selection of machine nuts, drilled out and threaded onto nylon-rope slings, I started up the rock. I worked my way slowly upwards, straddling the corner, and by fixing protection every six feet or so, I knew I would come to no real harm even if I should slip from the slimy green holds. Aid shouted encouragement through the wind, as I looked down between spread-eagled legs, with water streaming down my arms and back. The holds were sometimes sharp, square-cut and secure and, in places, offered space for three fingertips, while others were sloping or narrow cracks where two fingers were inserted vertically and twisted cruelly for support.

At 100 feet, I approached the crux of the climb. I was shaking hard with cold, and my fingers were slowly losing all feeling. A decision had to be made quickly: to continue up or to escape down. Suddenly the situation was taken out of my hands. My corduroy pants, rain-saturated and heavy, slid down around my knees! I kicked them free. Aid lowered me down, and we retreated to the climbers' cafe in Llanberis village. The climb was not completed, but the dragon, if not completely slain, had been driven away for that day.

As summer approached, we were drawn to the guidebooks of Mont Blanc and the Alps. We had saved hard from our college grants, sometimes at the expense of course textbooks, and we would be traveling as cheaply as possible. Amos, a climbing friend from Huddersfield, would join us. He was a big man, a few years older than us. He played rugby and climbed only in the summertime, when he went to the Alps. He had a robust, rather vulgar sense of humor and great physical strength.

He became our self-appointed mentor for the summer. His death a few years later, while he was descending the Matterhorn, came as a great shock to us. He had seemed indestructible.

Driving down the long, empty roads of France, with the van loaded with English tinned food, we laughed at Amos's wild stories and spoke of outrageous climbing plans. I'm sure Amos thought us quite naive.

"After a training climb, to get fit, we could do the Walker Spur or the North Face of the Dru," Aid asserted. "They'll be quite long, but I don't reckon they're that 'ard, especially if they're dry."

"Which route d'ya think first then?" I asked. Amos remained silent.

"Oh, somat short but technical, like South Face o' Midi," said Aid. "Gets us 'igh enough, but can be done in a day."

"That'd cost us a *télépherique* ticket," I replied. "Mebbe a route on l'M'd be cheaper, cuz we could walk t' bottom o' route."

"It's not 'igh enough, though," countered Aid. "We want t' get up t' 13,000 feet t' get fit."

Amos cautiously suggested: "Well, lads, if we took a week's food up to a hut, we could do a few shorter routes and see what the weather's up to."

He didn't want to squash our enthusiasm but probably felt it better to see how we climbed together and what we were capable of.

We drove directly to Chamonix, and went to the Biolay campsite in the woods behind the town, the traditional place for British alpinists. There were already many tents, vans and plastic cook-shelters scattered throughout the forest. We set up our two tents alongside a Czechoslovakian group. In the steady alpine mist and rain, the campsite was a dank, dripping place. Water had to be carried from the railway station fifteen minutes away. There were no toilet facilities, except the sheltered woods, and it took a brave man to wander there barefoot or at night.

The climbers of the Biolay were a hard-bitten crew, more resembling a band of brigands resting between forays than the elite of British alpinism. Any crime was defensible if it provided an opportunity for the next hard climb. The Biolay bunch raided supermarkets, looted wine from the back of hotels and jumped the rack-and-pinion railway that led up to the peaks. Local vegetable gardens rarely grew to maturity.

In the evenings most climbers drifted down to the Bar National to sip a glass of *vin ordinaire* or split a bottle of Alsace beer and discuss the weather and the next climb. The bar owner, Maurice, was a half-blind ex-colonel in the French army, who had a special affection for the British climbing characters who frequented his bar year after year. He understood well enough what a lawless bunch they were, but over the years he had come to appreciate their passion for hard climbing. He had known many who did not return.

Men with scraped fists and sunburned faces spoke of epic ascents and stormy retreats from mountains with names that lingered fearfully on the tongues of these alpine veterans. Legends of British climbing sat hunched over half-empty bottles of "Old Guides," while novices whispered their names and were careful not to stumble against their chairs. Names like Frêney Pillar and the Droites Direct caused conversation to hush respectfully as these mythological hardmen spoke in tense, understated dialect.

"Aye, lad," eavesdroppers heard, "there was a rock the size of a minivan . . . just missed us . . . cut the rope . . . wha' wi' no stove we 'ad to eat snow . . . ah, not that bad . . . ."

Aid and I listened in wonder, little thinking that we might already be as strong as those characters, only younger and less experienced.

We had heard of a climb on the Grand Capucin, an 1,800-foot smooth granite pillar. When Walter Bonatti first climbed it by its overhanging East Face, his ascent was considered a breakthrough in boldness and technique. Today there are many hard technical free-climbs on the pillar. Climbers arrive from the nearby Torino hut, equipped with lightweight rock slippers and sophisticated protection equipment. They carry tiny day-packs, climb quickly and rarely need to spend the night out. In 1968, alpinists climbed in mountain boots and frequently carried bivouac equipment, which caused them to move more slowly and therefore use the equipment they were carrying. Climbers now avoid storms, but in those days, we often had to sit them out. Finishing a climb while enveloped in swirling snow and howling wind was all part of the game.

We reached the foot of the pillar by taking a cable car to 13,000 feet and then traversing glaciers and snow fields through thigh-deep snow. A steep snow-gully ran for 400 feet to the start of the steep rock.

While we traversed slabs to a low rock cave, an unnerving boom echoed around the mountain walls, and an avalanche crashed down the gully, the debris spewing far out onto the glacier. We stared numbly at one another, an unspoken understanding of a near-miss.

It was already mid-afternoon and beginning to snow lightly, so we dug the snow out of the cave, settled into down jackets and made tea on our small stove. Later that afternoon, a couple of Italian climbers arrived and  moved past to minuscule ledges above, securing their lead position for the next day.

In those days before the advent of Gore-Tex and fiber fleeces, bivouacs were times for reflection and often suffering. We used light-weight down jackets to the waist and a short down-filled sleeping bag— a so-called "elephant's foot"— from feet to waist. If one was lucky, it didn't leave too large a cold spot around the midriff. We laid a large nylon bag on the snow to sleep on, and if it snowed, we pulled the bag over our heads. Sleeping in this "Zardsky" sac was a mixture of claustrophobic nightmares and partial suffocation. To light a gasoline stove and cook in the damn thing was like cooking dinner around a diesel truck's exhaust pipe. The condensation soaked our gear and froze into a crackling suit of armor. Our boots, wet from the deep slog across the glacier, became like frozen logs.

Nights began by lingering and ended with a slow, dragging breaking of dawn. One story I always felt sympathy with dealt with a couple of alpinists crouching and shivering in their bivouac as they waited out the night. Stoically suffering the tremors that tormented their shaking bodies, they waited for the pale light of dawn. The sky flickered on the horizon, and a faint beam of light streaked the distant peaks. Their hopes soared as the flickering swelled into light—and the moon rose. It was still six hours to daybreak!

That morning on the Capucin was not too bad as frigid awakenings go. At least we were on an east face, and the sun struck us early. We munched on chocolate bars and drank hot tea, savoring each warming mouthful, before uncoiling our rope and preparing to climb.

The first few hundred feet were up vertical shallow corners and cracks, not too difficult but unnerving with our clumsy frozen boots and numbed fingers. There is nothing quite like the exquisite pain experienced as one hangs from a piton, gasping clouds of frosty breath while cold, swollen fingers fill with hot blood, bringing nauseous waves of rising vomit, slowly ebbing to hands glowing with a steady throb of heat. Truly the agony and the ecstasy!

The sun rose, the rock steepened, and the ground crept further away below our heels. We attached rope slings to the fixed pitons as the face leaned outward. At one small stance that was the size and shape of a broken dinner plate, I was attached to a single four-inch blade of steel alloy. It had been driven into a vertical crack above my head, and like a romantic lover with a beautiful woman, I gave it 100 percent of my hope and trust. I tied myself to it and ran the rope, clipped through its eye with a steel snap-link, downward into the abyss where my brother was swarming through a series of overhanging flakes. A muffled cry and then a throaty curse swept upward as the rope went taut and then surged down like an angry reptile. I grabbed at the rope. It stopped. The piton held. A crash from the glacier and the smell of sulfur confirmed Aid's comment:

"I pulled up on a block the size of a minivan! The bloody thing came off! Lucky it didn't cut the rope!"

"Ya O.K.?"

"Could be worse. Could be down there!" He glanced backward over his shoulder.

"D'ya fancy leading the next pitch?" I was shaking now, after the surge of adrenaline.

"Give us a break, man. I'm a bit shook up. Couldn't you do it?"

"Lucky this peg held, eh? Should get easier higher up." Optimism said more in hope than fact.

It was almost dark when we pulled onto a sloping rock terrace almost on the top of the pillar. Mouths parched and hands torn by the rough granite, we prepared for another vigil, only this time a warm glow of achievement and muscular fatigue flowed through us. The challenge of the ascent had been faced and won. Danger was virtually over. Tomorrow was another day.

I lounged in a half-dream—comfortable, soft. Too warm, suspiciously warm.

"Aid. It's snowing."

"Yeah." Muffled. Unconcerned.

"No wind, though. Suppose it's O.K."

"Yeah."

Can't do anything about it anyway. Why worry?

Calm, gentle greyness: a watery dawn with snowflakes the size of thumbnails did not inspire fear. We only had to find the anchor points to rappel from, and the weather would clear as we got lower. We pulled on our oiled cloth jackets over eiderdown jackets—and looked like replicas of the Michelin Man. We prepared to climb.

The easy slabs of yesterday gave us tiptoe balances, and gloves scraped for incut flakes. We climbed up the final slabs.

This peak was a free-standing 1,800-foot rock pinnacle, which was joined to the main mountain mass at a narrow col. We were atop the huge pinnacle, and the mountain soared behind us.

To get to the only way down, we had to find the 300-foot vertical drop that hit the narrow col, which had steep gullies on each side of it. It was absolutely crucial to be correct in making the two rappels down onto the notch. If you missed the col, the vertical drop became at least a thousand feet on each side. It was vital to be able to see exactly what we were rappelling onto.

As we traversed around the summit ledges, we found old pitons and old slings that looked like rappel slings. We caught up with the two Italian guys who had passed us the day before and who had bivouacked on the summit. They were looking for the same slings and were as confused as we were about the route.

In those days, we didn't have anything like figure-of-eight descenders [a double-loop alloy device used to provide friction and absorb heat during a rappel]. We just had simple rappelling rope that we wore over our shoulders and wrapped round our body. We got the two 250-foot ropes tied together, threw them down the face into the mist and started to rappel down. It was a boiling sea of mist, and snowflakes the size of quarters were falling.

I rappelled down 150 feet and came to a small ledge and a rock-spike about the size of a man's fist. I put some half-inch nylon tape behind it, clipped myself onto it and shouted to Adrian: "O.K., come on down."

He came down, and then the two Italians followed him. We pulled the rappel ropes down behind us, which meant that all four of us were now hanging on this tiny ledge. Down below, it dropped vertically and overhanging. But we were confident because the guidebook said it was one long rappel. We should easily reach the notch, the col, within the next 150 feet.

I threw our climbing ropes down again. It was fortunate, as it turned out, that I also took the Italians' ropes as an additional safety rope. As Adrian pays out the rope—which was around his waist and he was belayed [secured by a rope] to the rock-spike—I go into the mist.

I'm hanging free, not touching the rock. I've got on a pack that weighs more than twenty pounds and it's pulling me over backwards. I've got on thick woolen gloves, the rope's icy, and I'm sliding down and down, thinking that sometime soon I must reach the notch.

Then I look down. The wind has blown away some of the cloud below me, and I can see the place where I should be. The notch is 150 feet over to one side!

Where I'm rappelling is down an overhanging rock wall. There's no way I can reach a ledge. This means I have to get back up the rope. Aid is standing on the ledge, belaying me around his waist. I'm hanging about 50 feet down, twisting and spinning, feet not touching rock.

I think: Holy shit! I better get back up! I'm in the wrong place!

I was scared, because we didn't have jumars or anything for getting back up the rope in those days. [A jumar is a device that slides easily up a rope and locks when downward pressure is applied.]

I think: What am I gonna do here?

I'm hanging on and I'm spinning around. And I'm tired! With my thick woolen gloves and ice on the rope, I'm having to keep a tight grasp on the rope to stop slipping further down. What I've got is an aid-sling—etrier they call it—around my shoulders. So I unclip this thing and put the carabiner over the knot in the safety rope.

Quickly I shout up to Adrian: "Hang onto the rope! Hold the safety rope!"

The wind's blowing my words away. I'm getting really tired. So I put my foot into the sling, stand up and transfer my weight off of the rappel rope and onto the safety rope. That pulls Aid off the ledge and turns him upside down and leaves him hanging on the belay. When that happens, he lets me go, lets the rope slip as I suddenly put all my weight onto it. And I go horizontal—spinning, falling.

I think: this is it!

I'm falling, spinning!

It lasts only a split-second, of course, because Adrian holds me just before I drop off the end of the rappel rope. There I am, literally hanging on the edge. And I'm so tired.

I think: I'm dead, gone!

I see the whole gully below me and clouds swirling around and snowing. I'm turned upside down, still hanging free. I'm spinning around on the end of the rope.

The Italians helped Aid back up on the ledge and, thank goodness, they'd grabbed the end of the safety rope and blocked it directly over the rock-spike.

So then, I've got a problem. I'm hanging there, and I have to get back up a hundred and fifty feet of overhanging rock. I didn't have any pressure slings or anything like that for getting back up the rope. By this time, Adrian obviously knew what was happening and realized I wasn't on a ledge.

All of them were paying close attention to what was going on. I had all the rope attached to me. If I lost the rope, *they* weren't going anywhere!

So then I thought: O.K, pull! I'll try to go hand over hand up the double rappel rope with these thick icy gloves, and Adrian can block me with the safely rope as I pull myself up. So I start doing that. Well, if you've ever tried to pull yourself hand over hand up a gymnasium rope, which is the width of your ankle, then sometime try to do it on a rope that's the thickness of your thumb, and do it wearing a rucksack and thick woolen gloves and with ice on the rope.

I make ten feet up the rope and I'm shot! I can't pull up any more! So I rock forwards with my feet in the etrier-sling on the safety rope and just hang there. I'm only attached by a waist belt, and I'm trying to keep in balance without strangling myself on that belt. (I didn't have a full harness then, like we have nowadays.)

So I'm hanging on the end of a rope, hunched over it so that my weight is taken partially on my feet. The rope is taut. It feels like a steel cable. I'm not pulling up any more. I'm too tired.

Then suddenly the rope just keeps coming up six inches at a time. I'm gradually being pulled up the overhanging rock. I imagine the three of them have some system of pulling me, and they're starting to bring me up. I start to get closer to the edge of the overhang. Then I get my feet back onto rock, so I can again start to take some of the weight onto my feet.

Then another twenty feet higher and I look up and I'm almost back at the ledge. I see Adrian's face. It's bright red! He's leaning over and pulling on the rope with his bare hands. He's pulling and straining, and every time he pulls, the two Italians block the safety rope behind the rock-spike. So it was Adrian alone who pulled me back up!

Well, can you imagine how I felt when I arrived on this tiny ledge that now seemed the size of a football field? I'm exhausted. We kind of hung there to get our bearings.

All I can say is: "Well, guys, it's not down there! It's across to our right!"

We're in the middle of these rock slabs. We have to get across 150 feet to the right of these slabs and then make another rappel to the point where we want to be. By this time, I was out of it and too tired, so it was someone else's turn to make decisions. We know where we should be, but how are we going to do it?

The Italians led off across with their safety rope and their climbing rope. Adrian followed and I came across last. From that point on, it was easy. It was a straightforward rappel down to the little notch col.

In another couple of hours, we were rappelling down a fifty- or sixty-degree snow gully, where a lot of the weight could be taken on our feet. Two or three hours later, we were back on the glacier.

I was feeling: "Wow! I'm really lucky to be alive!"

In 1968, during our second alpine season, the climbers we met were mainly British or French, but there were also Czechoslovakians, Dutch, Poles and occasionally a few Americans. The most important fact about the campsites in the forests behind Chamonix is that they were free. The people there were not wealthy—mostly young climbers trying to make a few hundred dollars last the whole alpine season from June through August.

If you were in these woods behind Chamonix from the middle to the end of June, you'd see vans with British registration plates creeping up into the woods. You'd see many vans. There were Austin minivans and Morris One-Thousand vans—not flashy cars: no Porsches!—and old Ford transit vans like Econolines, all loaded to the gills with English tinned food, climbing equipment and old tents.

The vans carried itinerant climbers. Some of them had real jobs and were there on two weeks' holiday, but most of them were people who had at least a month, many of them taking three months. A lot were unemployed. They'd stashed their vans full of food from England. They understood English food and were distrustful of French food and French culture. With little money, they'd show up and live for free in the woods.

Chamonix is not the driest place in the world. Camping there in the forest, even in the summertime, can be a very wet experience. The amount of climbing you can do there is relative to how well you can read the weather. Storms come blasting in off the Atlantic and hit the Mont Blanc massif, so timing when to do the climbs is dependent on the weather. That's all the conversation around the campsite: "When is the weather going to come good? How many days is it going to last?"

The small tents at the campsites were barely sufficient to survive in. So within their first two or three days, people went down into Chamonix or the villages just south of Chamonix to look for big sheets of plastic at construction sites. With this plastic, they'd build lean-tos and put together shelters to act as kitchens for the whole season: temporary shelters for the summer. People slept in tents but hung out under these plastic shelters. With little money to spend, they couldn't hang out all day in the Chamonix bars, where it was nice and warm and dry. They'd go from plastic shelter to plastic shelter, drinking tea and talking about climbs with friends.

When nighttime came, the scams started. They mainly involved getting food. Someone might know of an ice-cream machine that would be unattended after midnight, and a substantial quantity of ice cream could be released from it. Someone else might know where red-wine crates were stashed out in back of a hotel. A guard dog was there, and you had to get past the dog without waking it up.

In Chamonix, there was an outdoor glass-fronted rotisserie where a dozen whole chickens would be turning on the spit. You could see the chickens turning slowly, roasting and smelling delicious. One time the sight and smell were just too much for a character known as Daniel Boone. He whipped open the glass door of the rotisserie and grabbed half a dozen spitted chickens—in broad daylight and right in front of the shopowner—and ran off down the street. He just assumed that no one would pursue him. And no one did. So people didn't starve.

French bread is always very fresh, so every morning people would go down to the pastry shops, the *patisseries*, to get French bread. French *patisseries* have shelves in the front window that overlooks the sidewalk, and these shelves are filled with wonderful-smelling *gateaux*—big cakes. We could never afford those, not even one slice.

The scam was to work in pairs. There was a big fat lady in one of the stores. One person—the decoy—would go in and ask to buy a loaf of bread, a *pan longue*. As the lady put the *pan longue* on the countertop, the decoy would put out the money but "accidentally" flip one of the francs so that it fell on the floor behind the counter. This fat lady was not very mobile and a little slow, and she'd wearily bend over to pick up the franc. At which point, the accomplice—the fox—would sneak into the shop, rip a *gateau* from the window shelf and be away before the fat woman straightened up. So she gained one franc and lost 40! Then the climbers would go to a cafe and share the loot, this treasured *gateau*.

At the Bar National, where we were allowed to eat the *gateau* (because that was where we'd bring our own food sometimes), Maurice, the owner, came over to our table one day. A lady was sitting next to us and buying us coffee because we'd got the *gateau*. Maurice said, in French: "Oh, nice *gateau*." And the lady said: "It's their birthday." And Maurice said: "Yes, every day is their birthday!"

Outside Chamonix, directly above the village, is a beautiful needle-sharp spike called the Aiguille de Dru (*Aiguille* is French for needle). It has a North Face that's 3,000 feet high, with a classic mixed rock-and-ice climb that was within our abilities. The Aiguille de Dru is an historical mountain, because each generation attempts to put up a climb that makes a statement for that generation. As techniques and equipment improved, the climbing grew harder and harder. No climber could sit in one of Chamonix's outdoor cafes and look up at the granite spire of the Aiguille de Dru without dreaming of climbing it.

The North Face is one of earliest, and yet most classical, ways of climbing the peak. You can see halfway up the ice field, and with your naked eye, you can trace the line of the North Face, winding its way from the lower cracked granite slabs through the barriers of icy chimneys and gullys to the fine old, steep, cracked upper buttresses. The North Face was a wonder. We decided to try it.

Normally it took people more than one day to climb the North Face. In those days with the equipment we had, if you climbed it in one day, you'd usually bivouac very close to the summit on easier ground. The next day, you'd traverse round and rappel down the other side of the mountain, down a much easier descent route. The idea was to try to climb the peak quickly so that, if the weather changed during the night-time, you wouldn't be caught in the steep technical difficulties of the upper part of the climb. You'd have them behind you.

And that's more or less what happened to us.

Part of the journey to the foot of the climb involved a steep glacial moraine. To get up to there, you could wind up 2,500 feet of steep trail through a pine forest, which took probably two or three hours. If you had the money, you could buy a ticket on a rack-and-pinion railway. Unfortunately, that cost a good deal of francs and was beyond the pocket of most of the young climbers.

However, we had another method. After the railway leaves the station in Chamonix, there's a brief time before it enters a tunnel into the mountain. It slowly works its way out of the station and up into the forest. We'd hide behind trees in the forest, with packs on our backs and all ready to go. As the train came past, and before it had time to build much speed, we'd quickly spring out of the forest, leap toward the track, jump and grab one of the train handles and hang on. Then before the train could go into the tunnel and sweep us off, we'd whip open the door and dive inside. We had to do all this without being seen, so while the conductor was in the front of the train checking tickets, we'd jump on the back.

For this particular climb, we hid in the forest and successfully leaped onto the train and got a free ride up to the head of the railway. From the station, it was another three or four hours crossing the glacier, and then a steep climb up a tenuous lateral moraine up to a bivouac on some big boulders at the foot of the North Face. As Adrian and I approached this bivouac, we saw that a number of other people—mainly French and German climbers—were also bivouacking at the foot of the face, intending to do the same climb that we'd planned for the following day.

In those days, there was a certain animosity and competitiveness toward some of the other climbers, because by most standards, British climbers were technically very competent and yet had little big-mountain alpine experience. The French climbers had lots of mountain experience, having the Alps in their own backyard, but then they were technically fairly incompetent. (This is definitely not true today.) The last thing we wanted was to get stuck behind some slower-moving groups of French or German climbers.

We planned to leave before them in the dark, by head-torch. That way, we'd get ahead of them. We intended to get up about three in the morning, but we overslept. By the time we were ready and had made tea in the morning, we saw a stream of head-torches, French and

German, leading up to the foot of the face. Maybe half a dozen parties were ahead of us. We were at the back of the queue!

Fumbling around and rushing up the trail, crossing the bergschrund [the void between a rock face and the top of a glacier] at the foot of the face, we began to solo and climb up toward the first series of icy rocks. We realized now that we might have to bivouac on the face if these climbers in front of us started to go really slowly. Somehow we had to work a system of passing them. In the Alps, there's a kind of protocol: you ask for permission to pass. But if it's a rock-climbing pitch—if a guy's got his hands in a hand-jam crack—it's pretty difficult for you to get your hands in right alongside and climb round him. So passing is done on the ledges, when they're belaying.

On some of the easier rocks lower down, we had a system worked out. Adrian would lead off up and get in front of some of the people. Then we'd have two or three parties between Adrian and me. But everyone would start to climb again, and I couldn't come up behind him. So we'd still be behind the whole group.

We somehow had to rush past them all, all at one time. But for us to pass, we needed them to stop. So on the next pitch, I ran out as much rope as I possibly could and passed the whole group again. I kept on moving and started to bring the rope in for Adrian to climb. But Adrian found that the other leaders were also starting to climb, and he couldn't get round them. So he decided what he would do to give him a few minutes respite. Out of sight round a corner of rock, he tied a big overhand knot in all of their ropes. The knot then jammed up in their carabiners, and there was confusion—in French and German—between the leader and his second: "What's happening? Give me more rope! The rope's jammed!" By the time they discovered the overhand knot in their ropes, Adrian had managed to pass. We were in front of all of them!

Looming overhead was the first of the steeper technical pitches. It looked as though there had been some recent rockfall in the region. Adrian led off up this very loose section and anchored on about a hundred feet up. Some slack loops in the rope hooked over a rock pinnacle, and when Adrian pulled, it dislodged. A pinnacle the size of a medium-sized cow started to fall outwards. I threw myself into the back of a chimney crack. The huge boulder bounced past, cut our climbing rope and exploded straight over the heads of all the other climbers. All the way down you could hear the crash of rock: *Achtung! Achtung!*—just passing the German group. *Attention! Attention!*—just passing the

French group. Finally, a huge crash and the smell of sulfur as the boulder ground itself into the rocks at the foot of the face. Then silence.

Following that, there were shouts up. Obviously they wondered what had happened. They didn't know if we'd knocked that rock off or if it had fallen naturally. One of our climbing ropes had been cut (we had two of them; we were climbing in double ropes). I quickly climbed up to join Adrian and we held a discussion. Should we continue or not? With one rope, we could certainly climb up. That was not going to be a problem. But the second rope being cut would cause a problem on some of the long rappels of the descent route. And if the weather changed and we had to come back down this same North Face route, we would need the ability of long rappels that two ropes provide.

The exploding boulders had probably cut some of the other people's ropes below us. They, too, were having many discussions. We decided to continue, but the rest of the groups, obviously shaken by this experience and not wanting to have it repeated, decided either that it was too dangerous to continue or they didn't have any rope. They all began to descend. So now there were just the two of us on the North Face.

The climbing was magnificent. One of us would lead five or six rope-lengths, then we'd switch and the other would lead. The feeling of climbing quickly and confidently, racing rope-length after rope-length up the face, was exhilarating. We made a commitment to go using one rope, the possible afternoon rainstorms were accepted, and we were racing for the top. Later that afternoon we emerged on the rocky summit: a climber's dream peak.

This is a story of a Scotsman. At some point, he'd made the big mistake of taking too literally the idea of living on the cheap. On the way back from the bar at about one in the morning, we'd all seen the bakers working early, pounding dough and mixing up the bread, with hot ovens steaming.

One night the Scotsman sees this pile of bread at the bakery. Everybody's working, and it's dark. And he's drunk. So he collects huge armfuls of bread and fills his pack up. Somebody must have seen him. He staggers back to the campsite, about half a mile up the valley. He puts the bread in his tent, punches up his sleeping bag, collapses and passes out.

Next morning he's awakened by a tapping on his tent and shouts: "Monsieur! Monsieur! Monsieur!" So he looks out of the tent and says: "Ay, what's up, Jimmy?"

"This is the police," comes the answer. "We understand that someone in this campsite stole bread from the baker's shop last night."

And this Scotsman says: "I dunno what you're talkin' about. What bread?"

And there he was—lying in the middle of all the bread!

So they carted him away. He had to go down to the police station and get himself photographed.

The technique the police used with some of these miscreants was to take the shopkeepers down to the police station to see if they could recognize photographs of the various individuals. Sometimes the police would bring shopkeepers to the campsite and walk them around to see if they could identify anyone.

One day a black van showed up at the campsite. Out jumped all these gendarmes, some armed with submachine guns. They spread out all around the campsite, creating a barrier so that no one could escape. Then an officer came into the center of the campsite and said: "O.K., we'd like to take photgraphs of everyone." Everyone was, of course, "completely innocent," so they could barely refuse.

Outside our plastic shelter in this camp, we had a beautiful white plastic table with a Cinzano umbrella and a series of chairs that we had "liberated" from outside a cafe. Our area was next to that of some rather well known establishment-types of the British climbing scene.

The cops lined us all up. It was like a group photograph at a wedding. They were going take this big shot. Just the baddest people suddenly had to get up to the bathroom or somewhere. We were trying to shade our faces, hide our faces. A lot of sweaty foreheads were being wiped at the moment the shutter was about to click.

The establishment-types just thought it was a real hoot because, of course, they *were* innocent!

The Biolay campsite was a little too close to town for many of the residents of Chamonix. The poor guy down by the railway station who grew lettuces and radishes—well, his lettuces never survived. On the way back from the bar at night, everybody would just pick a lettuce. *Salade Anglaise!*

So the French tried to move us out of Biolay. They did that easily—just by trying to charge money. (It was, you see, illegal to camp there.) Everybody moved about three miles out of town up the valley toward Argentiere; we went into a field the size of a football field next to the river. It was owned by Monsieur Snell, who also owned the local climbing shop in town. I think the police agreed to it. They wanted all the thugs in the same area!

Finally, the Chamonix police decided to get the climbers removed. The townspeople were sick of being marauded by these English guys, so the cops found a reason to remove us: lack of sanitary toilet facilities. There was only an old toilet hanging over a torrential glacial river. There was a walkway out to the toilet, which was just a hole in the bottom of the toilet shed. The whole thing was held together and secured by a cable from the roof of the shed back into a tree.

We wanted to take responsibility, establish the campsite and rebuild the toilet. We went around and actually raised some money for the project. But first of all, we had to tear the old thing down. As a lady was entering the toilet for the final time before it going to be reconstructed, we decided that this was the appropriate time for demolition. Half a dozen of us swung on the supporting cable, and the toilet rocked like a taxi with a burst tire, careening backwards and forwards across the river. Eventually it actually jumped off the foundation and flooded inside. The girl came shrieking and screaming and leaping outside.

The toilet was rebuilt, and people managed to stay on that campsite for a few more years. It satisfied the police—the hygiene and so on.

In 1970, we thought Chamonix was getting a little crowded, and it was dirty and rainy. We figured the weather was generally a little better on the Italian side of Mont Blanc. By hitchhiking through the Mont Blanc tunnel, we could get into the beautiful twin valleys of Val Veni and Val Ferret on the south side of Mont Blanc. There you could go up the small side roads into the forest, and you didn't have any problems at all. The Italians were far more amenable to people camping in their forest than the French were.

So we moved to the south side of Mont Blanc. The weather also wasn't very good there, and I had some other considerations. One was an attractive slender girl from college whom I'd not managed to sleep with. She was hitchhiking out with a girlfriend of hers to meet me. We were waiting for some good weather so we could do a big climb on the Pillars of Brouillard (*brouillard* means mist) on the Italian side. The weather was never really good enough to do that.

We'd just finished a climb, on which we met a guy named Jeff. We'd done a great ice-route together, the Route Major. Everything went smoothly. It was one of those climbs you did mostly in the dark, crossing dangerous terrain. Technically it was not really hard, but it went over the top of Mont Blanc.

When we got back in the valley, I kept an ear open for my girlfriend (I'll call her Lynn). She finally showed up and stayed three or four days. During that time, Aid checked out the weather forecast several times every day. The girls saw that we obviously were far more interested in climbing than in spending time with them. Well, what were they going to do? They set their eyes on the resort of Portofino, the millionaires' yachting paradise on the Italian Riviera. So they left to hitchhike down there.

A couple of days later, Jeff and I thought: "We're just sitting here in the rain! Maybe *we* should hitchhike down to Portofino for a few days and come back when the weather picks up."

In that kind of situation, the sooner you leave, the sooner you're back. Adrian had a hard time with that and certainly wasn't going to lend me our van to drive down so we could chase girls on the Italian Riviera. So Jeff and I had to come up with another scheme. Hitchhiking for males in Italy—unless you're in drag and wearing high-heeled shoes—is a no-goer. We'd spend the rest of the holiday trying to get 200 miles.

So we worked out a scheme to "borrow" a car. Jeff and I looked for our transport down to Portofino. We felt we needed a car that would not embarrass us in the presence of the ladies in this particular resort. We spotted a red Alfa-Romeo. What's more, this Alfa-Romeo was also susceptible to our bent-spoon-and-fork technique of entering a window without damaging the vehicle. Not only did we know the location of the vehicle—it sat in the same place every day for a week—but it also was accessible to our hot-wiring technique. So we went around with empty gasoline containers and "collected" gas with a can and a pipe and stored it.

The plan for the grand finale was to "collect" the car around midnight, figuring that we had at least six hours of fast driving before it ever could be reported "borrowed." We were not going to use the *autostrada,* which were controlled toll highways. It might have been suspicious to have two men with northern-England accents in an Alfa-Romeo with Italian license plates. So we decided to take the back roads.

That was the plan. But all plans are fallible. At the appointed hour, our blood was running high, our pulses pounding. But the Alfa was gone! For the first time in seven days, it was gone!

However, parked next to where it usually was, there was an old Austin A-40 with Italian registration. It was the car version of the first van we came to the Alps in—in 1966. It was very easy to open and start up. The plan was set! We had to go! So we "collected" the Austin, took it to the campsite, filled up its tank, and took off by the back roads, heading south to the Italian Riviera.

We bypassed some of the towns. At about three in the morning, we came to a little town. I have no recollection of its name, but I'll never forget the town itself. Its main street was stone cobbles. There were balconies three stories high hanging out on each side. There were signs for bakers and butchers and little stores, little wine bars. Everything was closed, black.

We were driving down this cobbled street and suddenly Jeff said: "Oooh!"

He drove to the side of the street and stopped. Under the hood, there were wires that bypassed the ignition circuit and were connected by crocodile clips. We thought one of them had vibrated off. Jeff climbs out and flips up the hood. I'm in the back seat of the car, and all I can see is Jeff fiddling around under the hood. At that moment, round the corner from a side street, on an old Italian bicycle, comes a *carabiniere,* a cop. He approaches and I'm thinking: "Oh, shit! Italian plates on the car! The cop's going to ask Jeff what the problem is! And Jeff's going to speak in English! Then the cop'll ask him more questions...!" The whole thing flickered through my mind. Later when I spoke to Jeff, it turns out he was thinking exactly the same thing.

The policeman approaches, props his bicycle against the wall and asks Jeff: "What's the problem?" Jeff mutters, shrugs and points down at the carburetor. At that point, the *carabiniere* leans forward to help—and Jeff shuts his head in the hood! We ran for it, ran to escape! What else could we do?

Luckily, the cop didn't end up being hurt and he continued cycling up the street. He never stopped. Jeff raced around, pulled his pack out of the car and said: "I'm sure it's the gas gauge! I'm sure we're out of gas!" The gas gauge showed half-full, but we realized it was broken. We pulled out the crocodile clips, slammed down the hood and headed out of town.

When we reached the edge of town, we stopped, and I said: "Wow! Well, nobody's going to report the car 'taken'—it was 'missing, traveling.' It was just a trick. It just went out for a ride without its owner!"

We were thinking about how we were going to get to Portofino, which was still a hour's drive away. And, more important, how were we going to meet the girls? On the outskirts of the town, there was a three-story apartment house, and outside it was parked a Lancia Flavia! The Lancia is a rather sedate-looking car, but it has five gears and can do 120 miles an hour. We thought this could be the vehicle! It was the *only* vehicle around! Fairly easily, our "key" opened the door. We were inside, but we didn't want to start up the engine outside the apartment building. So I went round in back and started to push, with Jeff driving. I pushed it out, and it started down a hill with me on the back bumper.

In his excitement, Jeff suddenly starts driving on the left-hand side of the road, as he would in England. Around the corner whips this huge tanker truck. We didn't have lights on, of course. The truck bears down on us, blaring its alpine horn, and all the while, we're thinking: "No! No!" Whew! It misses us, and we get to the bottom of the hill, where Jeff pulls into a parking lot.

"That was close!" he says.

"Yeah!" I say. "You were driving on the wrong side of the road!"

Now that little hair-raising episode was over, I went to the front of the car and said to Jeff: "I'll get the hood up. You look around inside the car for some kind of hood release." So Jeff leans inside forward of the driver's seat to feel around on the floor for the release. Suddenly there's this blast of an Italian alpine horn! Immediately, he's out of the car and we're both over a wall!

I ask him: "What the hell was that? An alarm or what?"

"No," he says, "I brushed the horn with my shoulder."

We moved cautiously back to the Lancia. Its dashboard panel looked like the cockpit of a DC-10, with so many dials and digital stuff that we couldn't make it out. So we gave up, walked up the road and started hitchhiking. We were picked up by a truck. So rather than arriving in Portofino in an Alfa-Romeo or a Lancia, we entered it hitchhiking in a truck. And that's why, I'm convinced, I never ever did sleep with Lynn.

Later in 1970, I ended up with a real job. While Adrian was still freelancing, doing a number of jobs and sometimes guiding for the army, I had a job at a mountain school in North Wales, Snowdonia. This gave me enough financial security to buy a big red motorbike: a Norton 750cc Commando. It would do 120 miles an hour and compensated me for missing climbing.

Meanwhile, Adrian had gone to the Alps that winter with Bob Shaw, a stocky black-curly-haired Derbyshire guy. Aid had also gone out to the Alps earlier than I could in the summer. I could only get six weeks off in the summer of '71, but Aid had gone out again for a full three-month season. I was in Wales when I got a postcard from Aid that said something like this: "Just done the second ascent of the Red Pillar of Brouillard."

It was first climbed 13 years before by a top Italian alpinist, Walter Bonatti. It's a 2,000-foot red-granite pillar set in one of the most remote regions of Mont Blanc. It was a real coup just to repeat the route. But to put up a direct, harder, rock-climbing style to it! You can imagine how I felt. That's where I wanted to be. And what was I doing? Walking schoolchildren around the Welsh hills in the rain!

But at least I did have a motorbike, and I was doing a lot of rock-climbing on the weekends. On the bottom floor of the old residential school, I had a room that saw . . . a number of visitors—I was living my kicks some other way. But come summer, I intended to meet Adrian and Bob out in Courmayeur on the south side of Mont Blanc and join up with them to do some climbing. I'd also agreed to meet the peerless Dan Boone.

To help pay for gas to the Alps, I was to give an ex-girlfriend from Chester (I'll call her Susan) a ride out on the back of the motorbike. The time to leave came. On a motorbike, you don't have much room for equipment. So I put one pack on my back, one on my chest and one on the back of Susan, and off we went. I drove nonstop to Chamonix, then went through the Mont Blanc tunnel and met Adrian in Val Ferret, a beautiful valley of flowers and trees—and no people, not like France.

After I arrived, we had to decide which climbs to do. We made a couple of attempts on some unclimbed sides of the Grandes Jorasses. Adrian and I eventually climbed the Pointe Gugliermina, and Bob Shaw soloed it just behind us. It was a fun climb, even though technically it was graded fairly extreme. It went very straightforwardly, and we climbed it in a day. Then we looked for something else to do. Because the weather was bad around the whole Mont Blanc area, Adrian and Bob went off to the Swiss Alps to do some rock-climbing, and I went with Dan Boone to the Italian Dolomites.

Dan and I took the Norton 750 across the northern Italian plains to the Dolomites. In those days, you didn't have to wear a helmet, and I remember doing 90-100 miles an hour, chasing Italian cars. And then we were winding up these steep passes in the Dolomites, some of them with more than fifty tight U-turns.

Dan had climbed a lot in the western Alps, and he was a very accomplished rock-climber. He'd had a couple of epics, retreating while his friends had got frostbitten. He'd had another on the Central Pillar of Frêney, which at the time was a climb we'd not done; it's similar to the Pillar of Brouillard. Dan had a major retreat on it the previous year and only just escaped with his life.

He refused to climb in rock-climbing shoes. He would only climb in double-boots. He had a pair of big leather double-boots for *gymnastic* rock-climbing in the Dolomites! I realized this was going to be a problem. So we decided we had to find him a pair of boots in Cortina d'Ampezzo, a major center in the Dolomites. I wouldn't buy him boots, and Dan thought he didn't have the money.

I didn't want to be involved in any hit-and-run thievery, so outside the store I told Dan that if he was going to steal climbing shoes, I was not going to go in with him. I'd wait outside. So Dan disappeared into a store that sold leather goods as well as shoes. When I saw him about half an hour later, he was smiling broadly.

"O.K., Dan, got yourself some boots?" I said. I wasn't going to ask anything about how he got them or how much he paid.

He smiled and said: "No, I didn't get any boots but, hey, I got this great pair of leather trousers!"

As we walked past the front of the shop, I saw that the plaster model in the shop window was no longer wearing trousers!

Eventually Dan did find a pair of shoes, and we climbed the

South Pillar of Marmolata, a 2,500-foot pillar rated Grade 6. We managed to climb it in a day. It was first climbed sometime in the late Twenties or early Thirties. It's known because at the top it has a big icy couloir, a gully with overhangs. A number of people had died when they couldn't get around those icy overhangs. We climbed it very quickly.

All I can say about Dolomite climbing is that it is incredibly steep, but the climbing is not desperately hard. By American standards now, if you're climbing 5.9 or 5.10, you can do all kinds of impressive climbs in the Dolomites where you get into overhanging rock situations that you would never get on any other kind of rock.

Returning to Courmayeur, we had one small epic as we were coming out of the mountains and negotiating about fifty hairpin turns. At one point, the motorbike suddenly lurched across the road. I thought I'd just blown out the back tire. I pulled over and found out what had happened: Dan had fallen asleep on the back of the motorbike and rocked all his weight over to one side. If you do that on a motorbike, it changes the steering.

When we drove back into the campsite to meet up with Adrian and Bob, I thought that traveling with Dan Boone had been like traveling with a time-bomb. You never knew quite when it was going to go off.

The Alpine season of 1972 was probably the best season we'd had. It brought us some recognition as British alpinists. There were about 20 British climbers doing top-standard climbs, and our climbs were as good as any being done by them.

At the same time, equipment was improving. Technical ice-climbing equipment made at least a small step forward. Curved ice-tools were available, so you didn't have to cut steps going up ice faces. Crampons were the same as they'd always been, but hand-tools—the things that connected your hands to, say, 70-degree ice—were better. In the old days, we had to cut steps with the ice-axe and then put our toes in them and thus create a staircase of holes to climb up. With these new curved ice-tools, you could hit them into the ice and pull on them. They were a major reason we managed to do some of the ice-climbs we did in 1972.

By that time, a pattern was forming of what a three- or four-month alpine season consisted of. We would be rock-climbing in England in the spring. Then we'd go directly to the eastern Alps—the

Kaisergebirge or the Dolomites, where the summer season started earlier. The climbs there were not as serious in terms of objective danger—glaciers, rockfall and storms—and they were usually one-day rock-climbs. And yet they were technically difficult: steep, overhanging, sustained rock-climbs. It was a great place to train, to get into the swing for doing longer climbs. In England in the spring, the longest climbs were only a few hundred feet long. But then we could go to the eastern Alps—the limestone Alps—and train on longer climbs. After that, we could move over to the Swiss region.

In 1972, that's exactly what we did. We started out in the Kaisergebirge of Austria and did some great Grade-6 rock climbs. Then we moved to the Swiss Alps, to the Lauterbrunnen Valley. It was famous for the Lauterbrunnen North Face: a series of big north-face ice-climbs. In June, the conditions were good. You had good snow cover, and if you were lucky, maybe you'd find that these long, hard ice-climbs had all the loose rocks frozen into them. You could just kick steps of snow. As it happens, it never works out completely like that, but that was something we always hoped for.

In June, Adrian and I camped in the Lauterbrunnen Valley at a place called Stechelberg. First, we wanted to do a training climb. We chose the Ebnefluh, which is a 2,000- foot snow-ice slope. The climb started from the Rottal hut, which was 5,000 feet above the valley. We carried big packs up to this hut of the Swiss Alpine Club. There was no warden there, but there were beds and blankets and a little wood-burning stove. We took our own stove—sometimes gas, sometimes kerosene—and cooked our own food. As we were approaching the hut, we saw footprints in the snow and two other people way up ahead of us. We wondered who they were and thought maybe they were going to do the same climb as ourselves. From a distance, I could see that one of the guys had an ice-axe on the back of his pack. It looked steeply curved. That meant a technical ice-climber, somebody who probably was going to do a hard climb, somebody who knew that conditions in the early season could be good.

When we caught these people up, we found out they were Rab Carrington and Alan Rouse. So we all hung out together in the hut. We didn't really know them that well then. We were kind of acquaintances. They were going to try a new climb on the North Face of the Gletscherwand (it means "glacier wall" in German). Later that season they actually did the climb, but this time they were just trying it.

The next morning we all left at the same time, around three in the morning. We climbed the Ebnefluh with a couple of other climbers: an American named Gary and a young French-speaking Swiss boy named Marcel.

At the top of the Ebnefluh, where most people traverse out to the right and climb snow and ice around the corner, there was a big, steep, green headwall, probably 75 degrees. It was a wild pitch to climb, with the whole wall below us. But we decided to try to climb it.

Adrian led the first pitch. It was 150 feet of green ice. He used the new curved Chouinard ice-tools. He'd cut a small notch above his head, about three inches wide and three inches long. Then using the ice-tool, he'd crampon up until his foot was in the notch. This meant he actually got to rest in a little foothold once every eight feet. That was the technique we used on really steep ice.

That season I didn't have a good pair of climbing boots. At a party a couple of years before, Adrian had burned down the apartment in Chester, and my French technical-climbing boots had gone up in smoke. So I bought a pair of boots for five pounds and had an extra pair of steel shanks put in them, but they still were not good technical-climbing boots. I had a hard time on the steep ice, because my calf muscles had to make up for the rigid boot and the rigid crampons that people now use. I never get calf-strain nowadays, but in those days it was a major problem.

After finishing the Ebnefluh climb, we came down to a hut, which had a summer quarters and winter quarters. There was no warden there. We spent the first night in the winter quarters, which were dark, dingy and cold. Then we found that with a piece of bent wire and a little ingenuity, we could enter the warm atmosphere of the summer quarters, which had *kirsch* and considerable amounts of Swiss food. We thought this was a good place to rest up, rather than going straight down to the valley.

We searched the hut, looking mainly for food and beverages. We found the hut warden's revolver: a Luger or something. It wasn't loaded, but I hid it in case the warden should suddenly show up uninvited and head for his pistol and kick us out at gunpoint.

It was early in the season, and snow almost covered the hut. When you approached the hut, you actually walked on its corrugated iron roof. The second night we spent there, I heard the clank! clank! clank! of crampons walking on the corrugated iron. And I thought: Oh, oh! The warden! As it was the beginning of the season, it would have been natural for him to come and check his hut.

What would we say to a Swiss warden? We were basically living free in his private hut. Actually, we'd already arranged what we would do, but I don't think we seriously believed it ever was going to be necessary. I stood behind the door at the entrance way with a snow-shovel. I stepped out like a cricketer about to hit a homerun.

Then I saw that the person coming toward me was Rab Carrington! Rab's eyes grew to the size of ashtrays, as he saw I was about to plant him with a shovel. We welcomed Rab and Alan Rouse inside and took them into the luxury interior of our establishment. We stayed there a couple of nights before we all descended together.

We went back into the valley and camped at Stechelberg. By this time we were friends with Rab and Al. We got to know them in the hut and during the walk down. The British guidebook said that the area's hardest climb—pure ice-climbing—was the Direct on the Face of the Gletscherwand. We really wanted to do that climb. It was a dangerous route, because you climbed for at least half of it under big ice-cliffs, and occasionally a big chunk of ice would break off. One of the safe ways of doing this climb was to move quickly. This meant you needed good conditions and equipment you could move quickly on. It was the new curved ice-climbing gear that enabled us to do that. If we'd had to cut steps up all the way, it would have taken too long. The guidebook said it took two days. We climbed it in 18 hours.

We started out by head-torch and climbed up the lower sections. The middle section was steep ice, about 80 degrees. The boots I had—those things I'd bought for five pounds—were bending, and they got wet. Adrian had lightweight double-leather boots. When we pulled up just below the top of the face, we bivouacked in the lower lip of the crevasse. We didn't have sleeping bags. We sat on the ice, using our packs for insulation. It was a cold night.

In the morning, my boots were frozen hard. I took a vaso-dilator pill that makes the blood rush to your feet and hands. I stuffed my feet into the frozen-solid boots, and the blood pulsing around in my feet eventually thawed the boots out.

That morning, we climbed the face and were really happy. We had about 500 feet of snow-slopes, with quite deep snow—knee-deep snow at about 45 degrees—up to the summit ridge.

We descended down to one of the Swiss railway stations, called the Jungfraujoch. It was the end of the rack-and-pinion railway that ran up inside the north face of the Eiger and up to the Jungfrau col. We got down there about mid-afternoon.

Adrian pulled out his guide *carnet*—his little book with his photo in it—and I had his guide badge stuck on my jacket. I went in first to try to buy a ticket at the guide discount rate all the way back down to Grindelwald. The ticket-seller refused me. He asked for the *carnet,* the book. I said I'd left it down in the valley because I got it wet. He still wouldn't give me a discount price, so I had to pay full price. Then Adrian came in with his *carnet* and bought himself a discount ticket. What we didn't know is that the ticket-seller had figured out immediately that we were using one guide's *carnet,* and he radioed to the station ahead where the train came out of the tunnel on the Eiger.

I went in the station there to try to buy the second half of the ticket to Grindelwald, and that's when we realized that the guy had phoned through with his warning. So Adrian got to ride down for about two or three dollars, but the ticket-seller was going to charge me something like fifty dollars.

Adrian got on the train, and I became vindictive about all this. I ran down the trail and put big rocks between the rails, so that the driver would have to keep stopping and climbing out to remove them. That would slow him down a lot. So Adrian wasn't down much faster than I was.

Then we moved to Chamonix and set up camp in Snell's Field. It was like going home, because we felt confident about that area by now. We were already fit, having done a couple of good climbs. Like successful alpinists in the '70s, we'd got the rock-climbing skills; we'd got the new ice-climbing tools and some practice using them; and we were starting to get better weather-forecasting in Chamonix. That was crucial, because there are so many different kinds of climbs, depending on what the weather is. Some of them are purely ice-climbs; you climb mainly at night and finish by six in the morning. Some are rock-climbs, very long, serious climbs that require an overnight bivouac. And some are rock-climbs that you can do in a day.

The improvement in weather-forecasting in '72 meant that we could plan much better. The weather forecast would say: "Tomorrow there will be afternoon thunderstorms." Then we knew what kind of a climb to look for. We knew for some of them that we had to get up to the hut by night. You could leave the hut at midnight, do an ice-climb by torchlight, be up over the summit by midday, and be back down before the storm hit in the afternoon. Or you could choose a short rock-climb, so you'd be up and over the top before the storm came. Ice-climbs were generally done better at the end of June and in July. In August, when the thunderstorms built up more, the ice-climbs were drier and you got falling rocks.

We chose to do the West Face of the Petites Jorasses as one of the first climbs we did when we got to Chamonix. It used to be considered a full-day's rock-climb; many people  spent a bivouac on it. But we thought that by carrying little equipment and climbing quickly, we could probably do the thing between six and eight hours. Which is exactly what we did.

Five or six years before, people considered this a major climb, but we were now looking at it as a less serious climb. It was a 2,500-foot rock-climb, which started up a huge inside-corner dihedral, climbed over a series of roofs with a few pitons, up a diagonal crack and then up the final slabs. If you got caught on the upper slabs in the afternoon thunderstorms, we'd heard rumors that it would totally ice up. We knew some very good climbers who'd been turned back because of ice on those upper slabs. We climbed it in about seven hours, so that wasn't a problem. After we finished the climb, there were a few rappels down on the Italian side of the pillar, and we were back in the hut just as the afternoon thunderstorm started.

We did our next climb—the 2,500-foot North Face of Aiguille de Leschaux—in a similar way. It consisted of a big ice-slope on the lower part of the face and mixed climbing in the middle part; we could do all of that in the dark. At the top there was steep rock. By starting in the dark and by traveling super-light, we managed to reach the top of the face in half a day, and we were back in the hut by the time that afternoon's thunderstorm hit. In climbing the ice face, we hadn't noticed the bergschrund because it was pretty well snowed over, so when we thought we were at the bottom of the ice face, we actually were halfway up the face.

We had a list of climbs ready to go, depending on what the weather looked like. If it looked as though there were going to be two or three days of great weather, we did have other climbs: the bigger challenges like the Frêney Pillar, the North Face of the Droites. That's the kinds of climbs we were hoping to do.

We were not the only people who were doing hard climbs in Chamonix. There was a small-knit group of good climbers, and some of them were very colorful.

Peter Minks, a Liverpuddlian, was two years older than us. He was a plumber-electrician. He was an excellent climber who was waiting to solo the North Face of the Grandes Jorasses; he was also waiting to do the Frêney Pillar. And there were Cliff Phillips, a wiry little guy from Wales who was soloing hard rock-climbs, and Eric Jones, a tall, broad Welshman who was later to solo the North Faces of the Eiger, the Walker Spur and the Grandes Jorrases.

I hate lists of the top climbs. But if I was asked to say what those climbs were, I would have said the Frênay Pillar, the North Face of the Droites, the Walker Spur, the Direct on the West Face of the Dru, the Eckpfeiler Buttress on Mont Blanc, the Brouillard Pillars.

Peter Minks soloed the Walker Spur brilliantly in a day. At the same time, Rouse and Carrington, who were also climbing the Walker Spur, were bivouacked on a ledge just below the top.

In those days, if the weather was good enough to do a big climb, there would always be more than one party on it. There were some Japanese guys bivouacked above Alan and Rab. As the two of them were melting snow, they heard WHOOOSH! and looked up—it was a falling Japanese body! One of the Japanese had slipped higher up and come falling down. Rab said: "A wee Nip in the air!" A hard-core Scotsman!

# CHAPTER
## 3

## HOODS IN THE WOODS

BY ADRIAN

After wishing Al good luck in Chamonix, I headed back to England in a friend's car. I hate work at the best of times, and so it was sobering to have a teaching job all ready and waiting. I had to present myself before the school's headmaster a couple of days before the term began. Old college friends were to let me stay with them for a while, so at least I didn't need to hunt for somewhere to live.

The school was in Ellesmere Port, a dirty Merseyside town that sported a car factory and an oil refinery. The children, products of awful surroundings and equally poor home environments, were a motley crew of petty criminals. Many of the older boys could barely be contained in a classroom, and it was my job to redirect their endless energies away from crime and into various outdoor activities. Cat-burglars into rock-climbers, so to speak. Like me, they were pleased to get out into the fresh air, but I doubt it changed many lives—it might have made them safer while robbing tall buildings. If I left them on their own for even a moment, they would be breaking into cars, robbing the local post office or fighting among themselves. Occasionally I would have to use my own strong-arm-of-the-law to keep them in line, but generally the threat of a violent shaking was sufficient to tame them momentarily.

There was one time when I took a group of fifteen-year-olds to the local ice rink. They were being well-behaved for a change when into the changing rooms stumbled one of my charges, blood bubbling out of his nose.

"What happened?" I demanded sharply.

"Taylor!" is all he said.

I knew the culprit was a year older than the class with me, and I figured he must be playing truant. Sure enough, when I walked out onto the ice, there he was, surrounded by a group of admirers. As I approached, a gap opened to allow me passage. Thinking he was only going to get a reprimand, he stood defiantly still, chin jutting forward. A perfect target for a fast uppercut! His feet left the ice as his body spun backwards in a ten-foot arc. Without missing a stride, I took a firm twist of his long hair and dragged him across the ice as a cave man would drag a hunk of meat. Within minutes I had him into the manager's office to report the incident.

Later when I related the events to the headmaster, I received a handshake and a big grin.

"Well done, Mr. Burgess!" he said. "That boy is a complete pest!"

# CHAPTER
## 4

# TO THE HIMALAYA

BY ADRIAN

A l returned from France after climbing the Central Pillar of Frêney. I had to eat my heart out. He related the experience in such detail and with such zest that it was easy to imagine being there with him.

His story of the descent off Mont Blanc in a whiteout was a classic. He and his partner, Alan Dewison, were carefully desending the series of broad ridges that lead down toward the Goûter Hut. They could see, at best, fifty feet but knew the way from previous occasions. Sometimes they would go too far to the right, correct themselves by retracing a few steps, then continue once more. Then through the swirling mist and lightly falling snow came an unmistakable "Cooowee. Cooowee." Next from a completely different direction came the reply

"Cooowee. Cooowee." They stood still and listened.

Grey shadows began to emerge out of the white from all sides. Lost climbers who barely had the experience to be on the mountain during good clear weather were lost and wandering in circles. Tired females staggered behind bewildered boyfriends, ropes snagging and catching between their feet. Fathers led sons and mothers toward the shadows.

Everyone asked Al the same question: "Which way to the Gouter Hut?"

The image of fifteen people all following in Al's trail left me laughing in amazement.

"I felt like the bloody Pied Piper out there in the snow," Al giggled, "and wondered if I should lead them all to a crevasse."

Such flair did not exist in the people I met in my day-to-day teaching position. There were a few brighter than others, but most were boring. For them, tedium was normal and routine preferable.

Al and I found a small, cheap apartment that was little more than an extension built onto someone's home. It was the first place we'd ever rented. It had one large bed, a couch, a bathroom, a small kitchen and a TV, which we never watched. Alan got the best deal. As he explained, "Your girlfriend doesn't live in Chester and mine does. I obviously need the bed more than you." I took the couch.

As it was three miles from the center of Chester, I either used the public bus, walked or begged a ride on the back of Al's big red Norton motorbike. His petite blonde girlfriend, Daphne, frequently would be sandwiched between us. With my arms reaching around Daphne to grip Alan's waist, it looked like our two bodies had six legs.

We had learned the trick to finding teaching positions in this region, and Al quickly put it into practice. He went to the worst area of the worst town and then to the worst school and said to the headmaster: "I would like a job in your school." The bemused gentleman sputtered out a brief response: "What on earth for?"

At the time, the education minister in Britain was no other than Margaret Thatcher. She and a bunch of her cronies had come up with the perfect answer to unemployment in the United Kingdom: "Keep them at school." And that's what they did, much to the dread of most teachers, who were looking forward to seeing the backs of their oldest, most uncontrollable pupils. Being forced to remain in school for another year against their will created havoc in the schools.

That's where Al and I came in. We promised to control the

scourge—to take them out into the mountains and let them try to smash up rocks instead of classrooms. One teacher snidely remarked that breaking rocks in the mountains would be good practice for when they were doing the same at Dartmoor Prison. Teachers are so career-minded.

So Al found himself teaching in a nearby school. The methods he employed were daring, if a little innovative. First, he painted the inside of all the classroom windows black: "So they couldn't look out and get distracted." Then he'd take a record player into the classroom and put on something good and loud, like Jimi Hendrix or Frank Zappa: "So they couldn't speak to each other. And anyway, that's how they live at home." Finally, he'd have them clean his motorbike. And so it was, that after three years of careful training in physical education, he finally threw away the rule book and did things his own way.

It's always difficult to assess what kind of influence we exerted over those kids. Teachers come and teachers go. Money's earned and money's spent. It was about ten years later, when I was already living in the States, that I received a letter from one of the boys, though by that time he was a man. He'd found my address through the Alpine Club and wanted to thank me for the help I'd given him so many years ago. By the time I'd finished his letter, my eyes were moist and I had the sniffles. He went on to say that he kept an eye on the climbing magazines and knew what I'd been up to, and that his little daughter climbed, too.

British winters are notoriously wet and cold, while British climbers are notoriously rugged and thick-skinned. How else would the sport survive? Driving up to Derbyshire on Al's Norton was bone-chilling; the crags just about the same. But the pub—ah, yes, the pub. A roaring fire, steaming clothes, and bluish fog of cigarette smoke and cold beer. (Why the hell *cold* beer I've no idea.) Pubs are the places where dreams are made and sometimes enacted, where new climbs are planned and past ones relived.

Evenings come quickly at that time of year, so we'd always be snooping around for a party, and there were plenty about. The best ones were undoubtedly put on by the Alpine Climbing Group, which always seemed to get banned from returning to the same hotel. That's why they were the best. They were wild and the beer flowed fast. I have images of Alex MacIntyre being swung around by his curly mop—

courtesy of Don Whillans. Brian Hall once let the air out of the tires of a police car but then was chased by Derbyshire's champion sprinter—who happened to be a cop. Not Brian's best night.

British cop cars didn't carry foot-pumps, and letting the air out of their tires gave all the drunks time to drive away. I remember bespectacled, long-haired Doug Scott standing next to sport-jacketed Chris Bonington, both commiserating with a cop who had flat tires. Doug said, "I don't know why you're so concerned, youth. They're only flat on the bottom."

Most good ideas come up in the pub. At least, they always seem to be good at the time. Every climber knows that any plan hatched after a few bevies can be scrapped without too much loss of face. They always start the same way: "One of these days we'll have to. . . ." And that's how the Manikarin Spire expedition began.

I don't know how we happened on the full-page photograph in *Mountain Magazine*. Maybe it was the bold sweep of granite that first turned our heads, or maybe it was the word "unclimbed." Most likely it was both. Manikarin Spire had a mystical ring to it. The fact that it lay in India made it doubly inviting.

The photographer was Fred Harper of Glenmore Lodge in Scotland. His reply to my inquiry went something like this: "Dear Adrian, the Manikarin Spire is over 2,000 feet high and reminds me of Yosemite. We climbed the Southwest Ridge of nearby Ali Rattna Tibba, and the West Face of that mountain is also unclimbed. It would take even good Scottish climbers at least four days to climb it. Let me know how you get on. Fred."

"What's this 'good Scottish climber' shit about?" said Al. "You'd think they invented ice-climbing."

Over a midday pint in a Buxton pub, the decision was made. The Manikarin Spire Expedition would drive overland to India during the spring of 1973. Overnight our lives became frantic. During the day our teaching posts absorbed large amounts of time and energy. In the evenings we were busy typing letters to manufacturers of food and equipment. This was something completely new to us. We needed donations, and many people responded with samples and best wishes. The most common reply went something like this: "We get so many requests . . . I am sorry to have to inform you . . . good luck in your venture."

Bob Toogood was an accomplished auto mechanic. His main task was to seek out a suitable vehicle that would survive the 14,000-

mile journey. Bob Dearman approached a bank to see how we could pay for it—no mean feat because we didn't have much money. Suprisingly, Midland Bank of Chester took an interest, gave us a free loan and some cash as well.

I still had to obtain a leave of absence from my work. If necessary, I was prepared to resign my post. The headmaster was a good man, who knew of my passion for the mountains and the energy I brought to his pupils. Not only did he give me a whole term's leave, but he sought to have me paid in my absence. I could barely believe it to be true. He had only one request: "On your return, please tell the children what it's like to drive to India and back in order to climb a mountain."

In early April we began our long journey east. We were now six people, having been joined by two college friends, Tim and Steve. Our van was a Ford Transit with two sets of rear wheels and leaf-springs that sagged from being heavily overloaded. Inside there were boxes and boxes of food for the mountain, food for the journey, climbing gear and camping gear. Nothing could be left behind. Our destination: the Kulu Valley in Himachal Pradesh Province, northern India.

We were tightly packed inside the van. Three sat up front and three sat behind on seats fashioned from boxes. Only the two Bobs, Al and I were allowed to drive because we were the owners. From the beginning, we decided on two basic rules for travel: the maximum speed should not exceed fifty miles per hour, and we should not drive for more than two hours apiece. The idea was to get there in one piece without crashing. As you can imagine, there was quite a lot of back-seat driving.

On the third night, we met our first major hazard—a snow-storm while crossing a high Austrian pass. Windshield wipers struggled frantically to chase away fat snow flakes. Visibility was down to forty feet as we slid and slithered over six inches of hard-packed snow. A strained silence settled over us. Our entire project rested on my driving skills and a whole lot of luck—with more emphasis on the luck. Night caught us still on the road with our headlights reflecting off the swirling flakes. By the time we'd driven out of the storm, my nerves were raw and ragged, and I gladly handed over the wheel to Alan. Somehow we survived and crossed into Yugoslavia and warmer weather.

The road we took ran spine-like down the middle of the country, which seemed to be one long succession of fields and farmland. Compared with Austria, the place looked like a third-world country, with run-down farmhouses and horse-drawn ploughs tilling the land.

Our route then lay across the northern part of Greece. The sun shone down with Mediterranean benevolence. Eucalyptus trees cast their scent into the warm morning air, and the Rolling Stones' "Sympathy for the Devil" blasted out of the van windows. The sea sparkled blue, flecked with white tips of gentle surf. We were on our way and we were happy.

Soon we were on the outskirts of Istanbul, the old Turkish port and the last city of Europe. We waited in a line of cars, all bound for a ferry that would take us across the Bosporus Sea and into Asia. An official-looking guy approached us. He signaled me to give up the driver's seat so that he could drive. Thinking he was going to load us onto the ferry, I acquiesced. We slowly circled the parking area in first gear and returned to our original position. Then he hopped out, nodded appreciatively and walked away. I've no idea who he was. Maybe he was thinking of buying a Ford Transit van and needed a test drive. Suddenly, I had this awful realization of how naive we really were.

We drove from six in the morning until about nine at night. Sometimes we would be able to pitch our tents, and other times we would sleep by the side of the van. While camping somewhere in central Turkey, we found ourselves in the middle of a spring blizzard. Three feet of snow fell overnight, taking us completely by suprise. A grey dawn caught us running around half- naked, dressed only in tee-shirts, sandals and shorts. All the warm gear was packed away. So much for the well-prepared mountaineers.

Our passage from eastern Turkey into Iran was the first time we had to use a special bond for the van. The *Carnet de Passage* was a guarantee that we would not sell our vehicle while in Iran. The theory was that if the car did not leave the country again, the government could claim a fine from our bank. We drove into a kind of compound, surrounded by high walls and with a collection of dirty shacks in the middle. The first buildings were the Turkish customs sheds. A man dressed in flowing robes waved us past while a second checked our passports. Then it was on over to the Iranian side.

First, we had our visas checked. I handed over a wad of passports, each with an immigration form. An official put them on his desk, dealt with two or three of them and stopped as a young boy entered with a pot of tea. I was made to wait until he'd had his tea break, and then he dealt with the others. When he handed me back only five passports, I had to remind him of the one he'd dropped. He returned the final passport with a bored expression, a wave of his hand and a yawn.

The next hurdle was the bond for the van. Officials pointed me first to one shed and then to another. Why did I have to show a yellow-fever certificate in order to clear the bond? It was a classic run-around. In one dark and airless office, an unshaven and thoroughly disreputable character stamped a few documents and, while poised to hand them back, said in lilting English, "You wish to change money?" There was a certain pressure to his question.

"Yes, some." I was prepared to play the game.

He reached beneath his desk to a hidden switch and suddenly the room was bathed in light.

"Not the first time this has happened," I thought.

His long, thin fingers counted out fifty pounds' worth of Iranian rials faster than a Las Vegas gambler. I left with my documents. Finally, when they couldn't think of anything else for us to do, we were allowed to proceed through the far gate of the compound and make our escape.

From then on, we decided to use another border-crossing tactic. Ten minutes before any border, we'd stop, shave, put on white shirt and tie and then continue. It was a raving success. We were viewed as important business people and were brought to the front of every queue, given chairs to sit on and tea to sip, often under the irate gaze of dust-covered hippies who were also heading east.

The heat shimmered on the tarmac, the harsh glare straining our eyes. At the side of the road were burned-out wrecks of trucks and cars: blackened carnage from someone's carelessness. There was one bus flipped on its roof and another sliced in half, seats scattered everywhere. Oncoming buses grew increasingly aggressive and frequently forced us off the road and onto the gravel shoulder.

In eastern Iran a truck that had been following us for some time chose to pass us on a blind bend. He cut back in too early, and we were forced to swerve dangerously near to the edge of a cliff. Alan cursed him roundly and then rummaged in the back of the van. He found what he was searching for and with a malevolent grin loaded up our emergency flare-gun. We gave chase as in some Bonnie-and-Clyde movie; the only thing missing was the music. A red flare shot over the top of the cab and exploded before the wild-eyed driver, causing his truck to sway and lurch down the hill. A cheer rang out from the van. That would teach the bastard!

The road deteriorated to a rutted track immediatly before the Afghan border. We crawled along, weaving around potholes the size of bomb craters, ever conscious that a broken axle or leaf-spring would be a total disaster for the expedition. When we finally crept into the town of Herat, it was dark. There were no street lights, so we drove slowly down the narrow, winding lanes. Cloak-wrapped figures moved stealthily along the edges of our vision. They carried barely visible lanterns with gnarled hands and I'm sure that many held knives. There was absolutely no way we were stopping for questions. As we rounded a bend in the street, a hand-painted sign swung from the lower branches of a tree as gnarled as Adam: "Green Hotel Tourist Inn." Safe at last!

An old man opened a gate for us to drive inside the grounds, and we parked beneath a walnut tree. The hotel itself was a filthy warren of adobe-style rooms with simple wood-framed beds without mattresses. The sweet smell of burning hashish drifted from the kitchens. We decided it would be more pleasant to camp in the garden where we could be close to all our equipment.

Herat was a fascinating place, but the tall, dark, Aryan-featured Afghans were intimidating to us. They had a way of visibly sizing us up for what we were worth. The town dated back to biblical times. It was from here that Abraham's sons embarked on their journey to Egypt in search of Joseph.

We spent an hour visiting the local bazaar. Tables were laid out along the edges of the main street. Upon them were sheepskin coats mixed with hats made from wolf's fur and piles of broad sandals made from old car tires. It was soon time to leave, as we needed to drive to Kandahar that same day. There were no other safe towns nearer.

We were driving southeasterly on a road made from concrete slabs. Our van's tires made a low but regular drumming sound as they passed over the sealed edges of the slabs, inducing a hypnotic lethargy in the heat of the day. We had learned that this road was built by Russian engineers using techniques similar to those Hitler's minions had employed in building the *autobahns*. History was to show that roads of this type were suitable for tank travel, and maybe this is what the Russians really had in mind because they invaded the country seven years later.

I lay on top of our roof-rack watching the scorched countryside blaze by. The rushing hot air felt as though it were coming from a furnace, and inside the van the rest of the lads were baking. There wasn't a lot to see, even from the roof. An occasional cluster of mud houses could be seen at a distance, but we never passed through anything we could call a village, even though their names appeared on our maps.

Sometime during the fiery afternoon, we reached a wide slug-gish river. Everyone piled out of the van, I slid off of the roof, and it became a race for the brown waters. We must have looked like a bunch of basking hippos. From nowhere, a group of kids showed up to stare at the "whiteys." They plunged in and swam around us with great glee, but when one started to make crude suggestions regarding Tim's be-hind, we decided to leave.

The van, too, had needed the chance to cool. The temperature gauge had been hovering at the overheating stage for hour upon hour. Bob Toogood explained that the engine fan simply was not large enough to cope with such a hot climate. For days we had been forced to keep the heater on at maximum, and it was beginning to drive all of us crazy.

We reached Kandahar as night fell and found a tourist hotel. It had been such an exhausting day that we all collapsed onto beds under large swirling ceiling fans. As I stared through half-glazed eyes at the grinding, swirling machinery, I voiced a thought to Al: "Do ya think these things ever fall from the ceiling?" There were pieces of plaster lying about on the floor. "They look real heavy."

"Don't worry, lad," Al responded. "Castration shouldn't worry you for a couple of months at least."

The next morning we rose early to try and beat the heat, but Al and Dearman had a mission. They wanted to buy a gun. It would be much safer, they explained, if we could protect ourselves and our equip-ment. Into the bazaar they skulked, to be swallowed up by a swirling mass of cloaks and colors. While we waited, we watched people going about their daily lives. They moved with a purpose through the narrow streets. Merchants shouted out their "deals" for the day. Chador-clad groups of women moved more slowly, examining mechandise with talon-like fingers. Their age and appearance was anyone's guess, hid as they were beneath grey and black cloaks.

An hour passed, and the two adventurers returned packing a small hand gun. Stamped upon the side were three words: "Mad in Englad." I couldn't help but laugh at the absurdity. Were we supposed to use this gadget against the weaponry I'd seen slung around the shoul-ders of many of the men? I asked to see the bullets. Al showed me a box of shells of various sizes.

"Some should work," he said.

So the "marksman" would be playing Russian roulette with the equivalent of a pea-shooter. It wasn't going to be me. With an "armed escort," we set off for Kabul, the Afghan capital.

The road had been built by Americans and was surfaced with black asphalt. Walt Disney himself could not have built a better roller-coaster. After a couple of hours, we came upon a small lake. I suggested we test the range of our newly acquired weapon by firing it across the surface of the lake. Al slipped a shell into the breach and fired. BANG!! The bullet landed fifty yards out into the water.

"That would have hurt." A knowledgeable comment.

The next try wasn't quite as effective. Plewwt!! The bullet landed six feet from Al's feet. A tiny puff of dust popped from the desert floor.

"That would have hurt, too," I opined. "They would have split their sides laughing."

We continued on our way. The days were becoming unbearably hot, and the overloaded van began overheating after only a few miles. Finally, we had no choice but to stop and wait for the cool of evening. Consequently, when we arrived in Kabul, it was 1 a.m. As we drove around the deserted streets looking for a hotel or camping place, we came upon a large forecourt of cobbled stones. Over by a large gate a lone sentry stood quietly alert.

"Aid, nip over and ask that bloke where the nearest hotel is," said Al. I ambled toward him and tried a slightly exaggerated "Excuse me . . . ."

He snapped to red-alert and I found myself looking down a very ugly gunbarrel. I stopped dead (in my tracks, that is), opened my palms and slowly turned around.

"That guy isn't very friendly," I said to the lads.

It was the king's palace, and as he was deposed a few months later, I suppose the guard had good reason to be jumpy.

Wandering around the bazaars of Kabul was both exciting and insightful. Women wore the chador and men huge knives. Bob and I went in search of a large fan to see if we could overcome the heating problem. Meanwhile, Al set off for the infamous "money market" where we'd heard we could buy Indian and Pakistani rupees at black-market prices.

We returned to the van to find Dearman agitated and alarmed. While he'd been sitting in the van, a local bandit had jumped up onto the roof-rack and begun to cut away at the protective tarp with a large knife. Bob had leapt out with the pistol at the ready. For a moment they had glared at each other before the guy ran away. All that within fifty yards of a policeman.

In the afternoon we headed off toward the Khyber Pass and Pakistan. The road wound down through a deep gorge where the silver thread of a river glinted up temptingly. At one bend in the road, we parked the van and scurried down to a series of deep pools for a cooling dip. It was wonderfully refreshing after the sticky heat of the van. I can't help wondering what the passing busloads of Afghan travelers thought when they saw the semi-naked antics of the "Manikarin Spire Swimming and Sunbathing Expedition."

By evening we steered the van into the protective compound of the Gulshan Hotel in the town of Jalalabad. This was the last place in Afghanistan before the Pakistan border. The proprietor welcomed us with the grace of a Shakespearian actor: "What would you like? We have beer, whiskey, hashish. All is yours."

We dined on shish kebabs, fries and fantastic bread, all of which was spread out beneath a canopy of fruit trees. The local policeman squatted on the veranda with a huge hubble-bubble pipe before him. He looked vaguely like a short, plump Aladdin while he huffed and puffed to get the genii from the bottle. The sweet smell of hashish filled the warm night air.

The next day we entered Pakistan, bought a ticket for the crossing of the Khyber and set off up into what would be better named "No Man's Land." Though the pass is geographically within Pakistan, it is a lawless place filled with feuding Patans. Children threw rocks at the van while tall, handsome men looked on in amusement. They all carried heavy rifles and wore double bandoliers full of shells.

"The little bastards will smash the windshield," growled Al. He opened a pack of cigarettes we'd been using to cheer up customs men. Every time he saw adolescent hands raised in attack, he'd toss a couple of cigarettes out  the window. Stones would fall and the kids would scuffle in the dirt, while the van remained intact. Years later a guy told me that when he drove Mercedes cars from Germany to India to sell them, he'd cover the entire body with Styrofoam for protection.

The new fan solved the overheating problem, and at last we could switch off the heater. We cruised easily downhill into Peshawar and continued towards the old cantonment city of Rawalpindi. It was here that we learned we would need a special road permit to cross into India. The war between Pakistan and India had just ended, and the border was  open only on Wednesday mornings. The day was Thursday, so we had almost a week to wait.

We decided to head out to a nearby reservoir, Rawal Dam, away from the noise, dirt and constant jostle of Rawalpindi. The few days spent there were pleasant and relaxing. We swam, ate and sunbathed. During one very hot afternoon, I lay in the shade of the van reading a book. Suddenly, gunfire seemed to be going off all around us. I rolled sideways under the van. Visions of armed bandits flashed across my mind. We were about to be robbed!

Silence returned. Al walked over to the van and gingerly lifted out our box of amunition.

"The bullets got too hot and some blew up," he said, grinning. "So much for home-made shells."

A few days later we were on our way again towards Lahore and the Indian border. Driving had never been particularly easy since we left Austria, but now it was downright dangerous. Multi-colored trucks edged past us, horns blaring. Oncoming vehicles seemed to ignore our presence, forcing us to pull off the road or meet them head-on. The road leading to the border had two lanes, narrow and full of bicycles. I wove carefully around the bikes, passed through Pakistani immigration and pulled into the Indian customs area.

A large fat woman who seemed to be directing operations was downright unfriendly. Scowling, she snarled, "Have you any Indian rupees, guns or hashish? If you do, you will go to jail!"

She had us begin unloading the van. I had hidden the money we bought in Kabul, and Al had passed the gun to some travelers who had already been checked. Luckily we had so many things to empty that she soon became bored and left us alone.

We soon reached the border town of Amritsar: in India!

Travelers soon learn that there is very little privacy in Asia. There are so many people! Many live in lean-to shelters or, if they are lucky, in crowded rooms. When they see a Westerner, they are often curious to the point of rudeness.

As we were driving along, the muffler suddenly dropped onto the road with a grating of metal on stone. We pulled off into a seemingly quiet grove of trees. While Bob set about fixing the problem, I watched the empty horizon turn into specks of people, getting bigger by the minute. Bicycles stopped, people stared, chattering in Punjabi. Before long, a large crowd had formed. Some just watched, others gave advice and everyone tried to see what we had inside the van. Finally, the problem was fixed and we set off into the evening—and our last night on the road.

The Kulu Valley is in the foothills of the Himalayas, and with

*Van repair attracts a crowd in India*

the increased height the climate became cooler and more pleasant. There was very little traffic as we drove north along a narrow single-lane road. Orchards and fruit groves lined the road. Adults and children alike waved good-naturedly. A sign reading "Johnson's Orchard" marked the spot where we pulled off the road and parked beneath apple trees. We had arrived!

Five days later we stood outside the government rest house in a small village called Jari. It had rained in the night, and fine droplets of water hung suspended in the early morning light while mist clung to hollows down by the river. We were awaiting our porters who would help carry thirty-two loads of food and climbing gear up to a basecamp.

This was the first time we'd hired such people, so we didn't really know what to expect. At 8 a.m., they began to arrive. Stocky, dark-haired and downright savage-looking, they were dressed in jute wraps, coarse homespun jackets and flat felt hats.

"Are we really going to hand over all our possessions to this bunch of ragamuffins?" Dearman asked.

"Let's spread out among them so they can't pinch anything," Al replied.

We need not have worried. These people were steadfastly honest and actually believed *we* were the barbarians. They were from Mallana village, where we would spend the first night. Their religion, a mix between animism and Brahmanism, was unique in the region, and they felt their blood was as blue as it gets.

Following the rushing torrent of the Mallana Nulla, we climbed out of the valley heat, past red and white rhododendrons and huge jagged boulders coated with emerald moss. Though the trail was pleasantly shaded, we were carrying too much personal equipment and sweated a great deal. In late afternoon we followed a switchback trail that wound steeply up for a thousand feet to a cluster of wooden houses.

A tall, gangly village policeman came forward to greet us. He explained in halting English that we were welcome to be his guests that night and that we were considered too low caste to stay anywhere else. He explained that he was not from this village as he led us, in pouring rain, towards his home.

Next morning we followed a paved footpath of polished stone through the village and into a deciduous wood beyond. Off to the right and 2,000 feet below, the glacial torrent boiled and foamed. The spring snows were obviously melting fast.

Just before evening we left the trees behind and entered an area of high pasture, flecked with the green of new spring grass. Crocuses poked out from the moist soil, and the first alpine flowers were beginning to show. After a night in tents, while the porters huddled in small circles, we set off to reach our proposed basecamp at 12,000 feet. The flattened grass showed that the snow was not long gone, and we set up camp close to the snowline in a hummocky meadow.

We needed to pay the porters for their work so they could get back to their village before dark. Each one was handed a bunch of rupees and each face lit up with glee. Most of them couldn't count the money we gave them, and they had to trust us as much as we'd had to trust them. Mountains have a way of helping forge bonds, and this had taken only three days. Off they bounded and we were left alone to complete a job we had travelled 7,000 miles for.

We could not see the Manikarin Spire from basecamp; it was set back at the head of a small hanging glaciated valley. Over the next few days, we investigated the approach beneath the huge West Face of Ali Rattna Tibba and through a small icefall.

When we finally saw Manikarin Spire, Al summed up our collective disappointment: "It's not even as big as the Grand Cap!"—a rock tower near Chamonix. It was only about 1,500 feet high. Although imposing, it was hardly worth the effort we'd expended to get there.

Back in base camp, we had some decisions to make. Should we continue with our original project, despite its being a thousand feet smaller than expected, or maybe find another objective? Al and I were attracted to the West Face of Ali Rattna Tibba, but the two Bobs were a little hesitant. However, we convinced them once we explained that we could always try the Spire after climbing the West Face.

Ali Rattna Tibba is a little over 18,000 feet, but its West Face drops 4,500 feet from its perfect summit. It is a mountaineer's mountain, perfectly pyramidal and steep on all sides. Its clean granite, cut across by steep ice-bands, promised exciting climbing, and we thought we had spotted a route that would allow us to link the ice together by a series of tilted ramps. As the weather was nowhere near settled enough for us to attempt the face, we decided to observe it for a few days to see where the avalanches funneled and how much rockfall we could pick out. In the Alps, the guidebooks would help explain some of the objective hazards, but on a new and unknown face, we had to learn everything for ourselves. We didn't want to blow our chances—or our brains out—by being too eager.

It was the third of June when we felt ready to make an attempt. For a few days the weather had been reasonably clear, and the West Face had shed its excess snow while still leaving enough white ice to climb. We left base camp in the evening and bivvied that night beneath the face. Sitting out on the glacier, we craned our necks for a final check of the climb. Once we were on the face, we wouldn't always be able to see the correct line the route would take. We needed to memorize as much as possible beforehand.

The first part could be climbed in the dark as it was only a forty-five degree snow-slope. Then a snow-ramp led up to the right into some chimneys. The summit headwall held secrets we could no longer see, and I knew we'd have to use all our energies to escape the wall.

While we were sitting there, the sun set on the summit pyramid. Yellows deepened to gold, then to orange and finally the tip glowed deep-red and was gone. The cold came immediately.

We started up before dawn. Climbing in the dark can be fun, but my rucksack felt heavy and the altitude added an extra leaden feeling to already aching calf muscles. Our world extended to the fading limit of the headlamp's beam. As we were climbing unroped, we could stick close together, and somehow this made me feel more confident, less alone.

"How's it goin'?"

"I'm sweatin' like crazy."

"Yeah. I'm hot, too. Can you see the others?"

"They're about three-hundred feet down."

The slope had narrowed into a gully, and we were on our front points. A fall would be fatal, but the ice was good and solid. We felt secure. Soon we arrived at a small level col where we stopped to rope up and wait for it to grow light. The climbing became serious immediately as I climbed towards the blue bulge of a frozen waterfall. It was the key to the lower section of the face and led up into a long diagonal snow-ramp, the one so obvious from the glacier. Al had a piton belay when I left him.

I tried to tighten my mind in concentration, ready for the immediate difficulties. As I gained ground, my breathing turned heavy and strained. Suddenly the ice became thin and rotten. My ice-hammer sliced through the rotten surface and then bounced off the underlying rock. I needed more security. There was a thin, ice-choked crack I'd uncovered about nose height. I tapped a soft-steel piton into it, clipped the rope and relaxed for a moment.

It never ceases to amaze me how at one moment one can be puffing and blowing and looking at a forty-foot fall, scared shitless. Then in goes a piton and the world looks perfect again. With increased confidence, I happily ran out all the rope and anchored myself to a pointed rock-spike protruding from the snow. Al joined me while trailing a rope down to the two Bobs. There was no point in asking them to re-take the risks I had. They could do the same thing for us up higher.

I continued in the lead, climbing up the right-hand edge of the snow-ramp. Even though the ramp was a hundred-and-fifty- feet wide, I wilted at the idea of blazing up the center. It looked exposed to rockfall, and so I crept up carefully next to the rock. I could also find solid rock anchors rather than just an ice-axe stuck into soggy snow.

I knew what was happening when I heard the familiar buzzing. The falling stones sounded like a nearby helicopter. We dove for cover, pressing our bodies into the rocky depressions. Shrapnel burst overhead, leaving the familiar smell of sulphur. Other rocks spun off down the ramp, leaving intermittent slashes where they'd bounced. It was midday, and we were forced to stop climbing and look around for a place to spend the night.

As we scraped at the snow beneath our feet we quickly came to hard, brittle ice. For more than two hours we hacked and scraped away until we had a small ledge to sit on. Every few minutes another rocky salvo would scream overhead and interrupt our labors. By seven that evening, the face fortunately had begun to freeze again. The stonefall ceased, and our taut nerves could relax. We made soup, followed by sweet tea and chocolate bars. It had been a tiring and nerve-wracking day, and despite warm down jackets and lightweight sleeping bags, it took a while before our bodies relaxed enough to accept sleep.

The morning light held a bluish tinge: the sort that has reflected off cold snow. My blood felt thick and my muscles sluggish—all the normal feelings after a bivvy, but just a little bit more than normal. At least the snow was hard and perfect for climbing. I cramponed diagonally up leftward across the ramp to where dark granite swept overhead. Then we were able to follow the natural curvature of the gully until it halted abruptly beneath a frozen waterfall of green ice. Bob Dearman took an exploratory look around the corner. There was a squeal and he came flying into view. He'd taken an exploratory dive off some steep rock.

Al handed me his rope and set off up the steep ice. "Keep a good watch on me, will ya, kid?"—his only comment to show that things had taken a step up in levels of seriousness. We could see for only a hundred feet because an evil-looking bluish ice-bulge blocked out everything else. Al climbed carefully towards it, his breathing labored and his 'sac visibly dragging him backwards. Beneath the bulge, he fought to get in an ice-screw and shouted down: "Lower me off. I'm buggered."

Down he came with a grunt and a curse: "The bloody 'sac was dragging me off. You finish it, will ya?" We changed places and it was my turn.

Non-climbers might wonder at procedures in a situation such as this. How are decisions made in extreme circumstances? Who decides who will do what? Well, it's both simple and complex at the same time. Survival is the goal. The number-one objective is to escape the mountain. Notice I didn't say: to complete the climb. That was the objective when we began the climb, but life quickly becomes basic. The only way to escape is to work as a team. Al had been temporarily beaten back, but he'd already given me a head start by getting up to the bulge. I had to complete the pitch to satisfy objective number-one. It didn't matter who led the pitch just as long as someone did. This was not the time to build up one's ego, but the time to allow two egos to escape.

I left the pack with Al while he gave me a tight rope back up to his high point. It felt like a difficult Scottish ice-climb, steep and serious. I pondered for a moment how they would rescue me if I were to fall and injure myself. It seemed that the possibility of a fall was high. I couldn't see around the bulging blue ice as it forced me to lean out backwards with a lot of weight on my forearms. With ice-hammer planted firmly at head level, I locked off a bent left arm, hanging from it while I replaced the ice-axe at full stretch above the overhang. Trusting most of my weight to this, I then leaned back gently—oh, so gently—and tapped crampon points into the brittle outer lip of ice. A quick plea for it to hold, another heave, another thwack with my hammer and, shaking slightly, I balanced past the main difficulty. A scary glance down past aching feet showed three huddled figures, with the ramp flowing white below them. Sometimes waiting in silence is worse than being in the heat of the action.

I lashed myself to a big old rock spike, hauled up my bag and then belayed Al. His face was all smiles as he led up a series of bubbly ice-bulges. Beyond, we could see a shallow, steep rock chimney with ice flowing down the back. The difficulties had returned.

Al began climbing a hand-sized crack to the left of the main chimney. The afternoon heat had begun to melt some of the ice, and large chunks banged and clattered past him. He climbed using a mixture of free and aid techniques. The ring of steel on steel echoed around us. Before long, the rock steepened sufficiently to force him to use more and more pitons until he finally stopped twenty feet below an exit leading to the upper snow-band. There was no ledge, and so he hung with his feet braced in etriers.

"Keep your crampons on, Aid," he bellowed down to me. "You'll need them higher up."

I passed him carefully, crampons grating and scratching on the rock, their steel points flashing like knives.

"Watch my bloody leg, will ya?" Al pleaded. "Whatever you do, don't come off and land on me."

First, I used some jammed nuts and stood in aid slings; then a rock pin followed by a long U-shaped ice-piton squeezed into a narrow crack. A one-inch thick plaque of ice draped over the final bulge. I eased my body up to make myself as tall as possible, sank my axe into the ice and then began to step out of the aid sling.

"Shit! It's tangled on my crampon!" I couldn't move up or down.

"Hold it together, kid," shouted Al, watching my crampons.

I managed to kick free of the sling, but the extra effort was draining my arms. It was either up or off. I pulled on the axe, planted the hammer, pulled again. My whole weight was on a piece of ice so thin it should have broken. Crampons found the ice at the same time the axe thunked solidly into the snow above. I was safe. It seemed ages before I stopped shaking and caught my breath. I needed some strong, solid anchors for the other three to jumar on. I scouted a band of rock. Two fantastic pins hummed out their safety as I pounded them home.

Night was almost upon us as I began the next lead. The snow angled up at between forty-five and fifty degrees, and I could kick big steps. There was nowhere to go where there might be a ledge. I stopped, dug out a platform two feet across, sat in it like the seat of a car, and brought Al up to me.

"Not much 'ere, lad, but it's all there is," I told Al quietly, trying to sound positive about the whole affair. We scratched around in the dark, trying to make bigger platforms but kept on hitting the underlying granite slabs. Our sole anchors were two axes, each planted halfway to the hilt. Pretty pathetic security.

Seated next to Al, I dozed lightly with my head resting on his cushioned shoulder. He was the sentinel who made sure we didn't fall off the ledge. Later when I awoke, he slouched across my knees. In this way our night passed without incident.

We were off again in the grey light of dawn. There was a new urgency to escape the face. After the snow-band, the rocks steepened again. Al was leading a horrible-looking crack that wouldn't have been out of place on our local gritstone crags.

"Watch me!" he shouted.

What did he think I was doing—sleeping?

He slid ten feet back down the crack and landed on his feet. My heart was pounding, but all he could do was laugh. He was really going for it today.

A hairline crack traversed out onto a huge prow, like the bow of a ship. Al sank a pin and out he swung. I do believe he was enjoying himself, but he was scaring me. The sun crept down to meet him, a brilliant red figure poised up on the edge. Then he dissappeared around a corner, and the rope trailed slowly out.

A shout from above echoed out: "We're out, out, out!"

I grinned at Bob Toogood: "I'll drop you a rope down. There's no point in you lads having to repeat those antics."

Al was sitting in a rocky alcove, a kind of grinning gnome. "One more pitch and that's it, lad," he said.

The summit was the size of a table. We took photos but didn't linger. Our bodies felt heavy. We were dehydrated and tired. The tension of the past days had drained us. The South Face was all soggy snow and falling rocks. Water poured off the slabs, and we lapped at it like overheated dogs.

# CHAPTER
## 5

## A BRAWL & A QUICK CLIMB

BY ADRIAN

A white skullcap of cloud sat atop the summit of Monte Bianco, promising a storm within twelve hours. Inside the van, it was hot as we drove north to the Mont Blanc tunnel. Destination: Chamonix.

"Ten days isn't bad from India to Cham," said Al, lying in the now almost empty belly of the van, naked to the waist and bronzed as a California surfer.

"Only two breakdowns in seven thousand miles. Could have been worse I suppose," said Bob Toogood as he steered the van aound around a confused Fiat.

"Bloody Eye-tyes!" he snapped.

"I can't believe Dearman couldn't hear that bloody drumming

of the wheel bearing," I complained. "It overheated so much that the nut welded to the stub-axle."

"He'll be with his wife tonight, so all's well," said Bob, who had suggested dropping his partner off at the Milan airport as we drove by. It was a good idea. Dearman's homesickness had begun to get on all our nerves.

Late-afternoon light filtered down through tall pines as we bumped along the potholed track that led to the campsite— Snell's Field. Water splashed up from muddy puddles and the grass looked extra-green and lush. The season had begun wet.

We searched for a patch of high ground near one corner of the field and pitched our large French-style frame tent. There were a few orange Vangos and a couple of Black's tents all shrouded in plastic with dirty pans collecting flies and dirt.

Days passed and storm after storm battered the high mountains. The snowline crept down into the trees while we shuffled from cafe to cafe, searching for a warm place to hang out. A thousand feet above our heads a white blanket of cloud merged with dripping pines. No one was climbing.

"I wish you lads had been in the Alpenstock last night," Bob said one morning. "The bastard waiters beat up a Manchester lad pretty bad. He'd only pinched a candy from off the bar. They were in a bloody ugly mood."

"Well, just maybe we should all go down there tonight and show them some manners," said Al, warming to the idea. "Shouldn't be that hard to get through to them. Tell the Aussies tonight's the night for culture."

The Alpenstock Drugstore doesn't sell drugs—of any kind. It's a bar-cum-cafe where you can buy a sandwich for an extortionate price, a *cafe au lait* for almost the same and a beer at twice British prices. It has a jukebox playing the latest in hip French tunes, and English vies with French for the dominant language.

We were seated next to Pete Minks, a well-known Liverpudlian climber and brawler, and Eric Jones, a mild-mannered Welshman, and his girlfriend. Stories were being swapped and beer being drunk. In order to build up a bit of tension with the proprietor and his waiters, we'd been playing the "twenty-centime game." This involved going to the bathroom and switching the light off so that a twenty-centime coin could be placed in the light-bulb socket. The next time someone switched on the light it shorted out the circuit and blew out all the lights in the bar. It can be a useful trick to swipe a bottle of liquor off the bar if you "happen" to be standing there when the lights go off.

However, that particular night we would use the blackout to casually toss an ashtray over the bar and smash a few glasses. The temperature was rising, and I checked the Aussies. They'd all come equipped with big mountain boots. It was obvious they weren't going to be running anywhere. The management was becoming frustrated because they couldn't actually catch anyone doing wrong. We grinned and kept on the pyschological pressure.

About midnight we'd just got another set of drinks when the manager came over to our table with a large leather bullwhip gripped tightly in his meaty red hands. Without warning, he cracked it down on an empty table behind us.

"Drink up!" he bawled in French. He looked ugly—and clearly felt powerful.

No one gave him a second glance, but muscles began to tighten ever so slightly. He felt he was being ignored, and so he shouted again and went to take Minks's glass. Pete was more than ready. He splashed beer into the guy's face and brought up a chair to protect himself from the whip. They both stood, alert, facing off.

I glanced to the bar, thirty feet away, and saw a waiter running to the phone. He was going to call the cops. I needed to stop him. Without thinking I picked up a heavy steel chair and hurled it over the bar. The guy collapsed, phone in hand. For one second I stood there, feeling that maybe I'd just done something really stupid. The door was a long way away.

Then the silence snapped with an almighty roar. The monster had broken free. The air was full of projectiles: more chairs, potted plants, glasses. The sign boards at the bar collapsed onto ducking waiters. I noticed one of the Aussies smacking off light stands with a chair. Bulbs popped, bottles exploded and the huge bar mirror shattered. Then we were climbing out the large windows into the cool Chamonix night.

Laughter filled the air: nervous energy expelled. In the space of two minutes, the entire bar was wrecked. It had been a good night. And not one climber had been hurt.

Later in the season, with the weather improving, we began to make plans. Bob Shaw came over from England, and we hoped to make a threesome on the North Face of Les Droites. As the climb was still regarded as difficult in those days, we knew we'd need some fine, settled weather.

The old rustic Refuge d'Argentière had been dismantled earlier that year, and in its place a huge tourist "show-hut" was being constructed. The workmen building the new place lived in two small wooden shacks nearby. We slept in the four-foot crawl space under one of the shacks.

Our arrival was accompanied by approaching bad weather. Wispy tendrils of white cloud clung to western summits while the temperature dropped and the air filled with the expectant odour of rain. Our sleeping mats were unfurled; a brew of tea placed on the stove; and we munched on some bread and cheese. Then the rain began: a deluge, actually. Sheets of water cascaded down the side of the hut and flowed over the ground. We crouched in our small space, trying to stay away from the edges where water splashed at us. It was more than disgruntling to be huddled beneath a shack like some wild animals. It was very annoying.

Above us, laughter—French peasant laughter—rang out in the night. They were having a merry old time. The bastards! We decided we deserved more. Al had an idea.

"They must keep all that wine stored somewhere," he said. "I'm going out to find some."

He slunk off into the night, the idea of theft a justifiable retribution. After ten minutes we heard a soft hiss: "Psst! Here, lads! Grab these, will you?" Four bottles of red wine were thrust into the light.

"Good man! I doubt we'll be going anywhere tomorrow in this stuff," I said, nodding toward a flash of lightning.

"Great. Let's make some *glühwein*," suggested Bob.

Hot wine tasted good in those circumstances and helped numb the discomfort. Bob's wit increased by the cupful until he had us all rolling around in stitches. He told us of his days as a driver for a funeral parlor.

". . . And on hot stormy, summer nights they'd go out and pop all the bloated stomachs with a knife," he explained.

"They can't just go stabbing them, can they?" said Al.

"Course they can. Can't have 'em blowing up, can you? Shit everywhere!"

As the evening progressed, we added less water and more sugar to the wine: a potent mix.

"Getting in and out of those tiny Derbyshire cottages was pretty difficult with a stiff," said Bob, "especially as one of the guys had a club foot and could barely climb up the stairs."

Bob was warming to his tale: "They'd strap 'em to a board and throw a sheet over 'em and then try and get to the hearse–where I was–without the neighbors seeing. Once an arm fell out and dangled there for all to see. They nearly got fired for that. Aye, driving that final taxi was something else. Shop talk gets a bit distasteful."

The patter of rain retreated into the distance. We slept. I woke up at midnight and had to relieve myself. I felt drunk and heady. Looking across at the towering north walls–Droites, Courtes and Triolet–I realized the stars were out. The weather had cleared and we were too wrecked to climb. I crawled back into my bag and didn't awake until the sun had been up for hours.

"That was a bit of a screw-up, don't you think?" said Al, sitting in the sun and making a drink.

"My mouth tastes like the bottom of a parrot's cage," I said, holding my head. "I think the Droites will be out of condition after yesterday."

"Seeing as we've no food left, I think I'll run back down to Argentiere and buy some more," said Al. "Then I'll get the cable car back up and be back here by the afternoon. How's that sound?"

He was soon a dot in the distance. About two that afternoon we saw him reappear: a red figure holding two grocery bags with long loaves of French bread sticking out and no bit of climbing gear. He was casually walking up the glacier looking like a tourist who got lost at the check-out.

"I got some strange looks at the *télépherique* station. They wondered where the hell I was going carrying these," he said, laughing as he put down the bags. "Let's do the Courturier Couloir tomorrow. It's in pretty good condition." [A couloir is a steep gully.]

He had a point. We should make use of the good weather, even if we didn't climb our primary objective. The Courturier Couloir lay up the north face of the Aiguille Verte and was a straightforward ice-climb of fifty to fifty-five degrees and about 2,500 feet high. It was a good classic climb.

Daybreak caught us still approaching the open ice slope. Tiny specks of light, made by other climbers' headlamps, flickered a thousand feet above us. They had begun very early indeed. Our 'sacs were quite big and heavy with all our bivvy gear, but we decided not to rope up until we felt it was really necessary.

"Let's solo up and see if we can't pass all those others," suggested Bob, who was becoming competitive.

We all warmed to the idea. It would be fun to cruise past them, a casual *Bonjour!* here and *Grüss Gott!* there. We set off with crampons crunching through hard snow and ice axes thudding into perfect névé [granulated snow that accumulates at the top of a glacier].

The first party we passed grunted in French. We sped on silently. The second group was more friendly: *"Salute!" "Bonjour!"*

The next group looked familiar: tatty clothes and Troll harnesses. They were English. We knew them.

"What are you buggers doing here?" they asked. "Thought you were on the Droites."

"We had a severe encounter with red wine and the Droites are not in condition."

"Are you going to put a rope on like sensible people ?"

"Don't think so. Want to get to Cham for lunch." A hint of one-upmanship.

"Well, if you fall off, do you mind doing it to one side so you won't skittle us off?"

"Don't worry, youth. Time to go!"

We set off again with exaggerated speed. In less than three hours, we sat on the summit. The peaks were quiet and peaceful and surrounded by a serene stillness. The entire Mont Blanc range lay before us, glowing in the morning sun. Down there, the world was still sleeping. Such beauty silenced even our exuberant threesome. We crouched there in awe.

Bob finally broke the spell: "Let's get back to Cham before some bugger runs off with our women. I need to get laid."

# CHAPTER
## 6

## CENTRAL PILLAR OF FRÊNEY

BY ADRIAN

The summer of 1973 was almost over when we returned to Chamonix from ten sun-soaked days on the French Riviera. There'd been hot sand, cheap wine and two particularly charming French girls. We put all that behind us and returned to our large tent in Snell's camping field. It had rained most of the time we'd been away, so there wasn't even a need to feel guilty about not climbing.

A burly Yorkshire character came over to greet us: "How ya doin', kid?"

John Barker was on his annual vacation and was looking for someone to climb with. We'd known him for a number of years and had met him at various cliffs throughout Britain but had never tied onto a rope with him. He was built like a professional wrestler, all muscles with a chest as broad as a barn door. He was also known to be very "punchy," and I doubt he ever lost a battle.

"Hey, John," I said. "What's the British police force going to do while you're on holiday?" He was the only cop I knew.

"I've just left, kid—too corrupt," he replied. "I'm looking for someone to do a big route with. What are you doing?"

Over the next couple of days, we formulated a plan. Al wished to repeat Bob Shaw's and my route on the Red Pillar of Brouillard, and Rab Carrington would go with him. I decided to go to the Central Pillar of Frêney with John, and with us would be Bob Shaw, who would climb with Dave Knowles.

We'd met Dave for the first time that summer. He lived in Glencoe, Scotland, and despite his heavy Lancashire accent, he pretended to be Scottish. He'd climbed the North Face of the Eiger the previous year and so was well qualified to tackle one of the most difficult and remote climbs on Mont Blanc.

Our ragtag foursome took over some empty berths in a tin icebox of a hut balanced precariously over the Brenva Glacier. The weather was fine, and the hut began to fill up with other climbers quite rapidly. It was the departure point for all the climbs on the Brenva Face, and we could easily trace the lines of a couple of routes we'd already done three or four years before.

While putting together a thin, watery vegetable gruel, I heard a scuffle next door in the dormitory. Oh, oh ! Where's  John?

The answer came a few minutes later when a shaken Frenchman crept in with sleeping bag wrapped around his shoulders. Evidently he'd tried to move into our bunks.

I turned to Bob and said: "Nice having a cop around for evictions, isn't it?" Our sleeping places were assured.

At midnight, we groped our way down onto the glacier, with help from dim flashlights and a brighter moon. First we had to walk across the glacier to a small pass, cross it and climb down to beneath the hanging seracs of the Brenva and Eckpfieler Faces. It was no wonder the place had an evil reputation. If one ice-cliff collapsed, we would all be finished. Blocks of blue ice lay scattered across our route. Time to run. We stumbled, slipped and staggered over blocks the size of refrigerators until we finally reached safety.

Above us , a 1,500-foot gully led to Col Peuterey and steepened towards mid-height. When I arrived at a 15-foot step, Dave was searching around by his feet.

"Damn!" he said. "A crampon's come off."

"Put it back on then," I said.

"It's not 'ere," he responded. "Must have come off lower down. Funny I never felt it 'appen."

I thought of his old leather straps and the filed-down stubs that acted as points. Strange that one of the best Scottish ice climbers should have such worn-out gear. Or was it?

I shrugged and said: "Just climb with one. I'll cut you some nicks for your left foot."

We pressed on, Dave hopping nicely.

Dawn crept slowly into the eastern sky just as we emerged from the gully. The 2,000-foot Central Pillar began to reflect  light, turning cracks and buttresses into one glowing monolith.

Yorkshire hope began to mix with Scottish understatement:

"It's in the bag!"

"Up by midday, Jimmy!"

"In the Bar Nash by tonight!"

It was easy to be glib in good weather, but I'd already been halfway up the pillar with Al and we'd spent a solid 18 hours getting down in a horrible snowstorm. During an early attempt, the famous Walter Bonatti nearly died there. His good friend, Oggioni, did, along with three Frenchmen.

Dave was still crampon-limping up ice that had reached fifty degrees, and there was still no mention of a rope.  Whether it was because of pride or skill, I was impressed.

I began to get out the rope where ice turned into rock and the pillar began. I turned to Dave and joked: "Only one crampon to carry now. Lucky bugger!"

Unexpectedly, there came a crash from above. An icicle had melted off an overhang much higher and out of sight.

"Here comes the ice, but where's the Scotch?" I heard someone say.

There was a crunch, followed by a WHOOMPH! and then: "The bloody rope's cut!"

Bob stood nursing the remains of one of his ropes. The longer piece was only 70 feet. I looked at John, jerked my head skyward and said to Bob: "Just climb on a shorter length. If you need to rappel, you can use ours."

We were committed to the climb and to each other. It was great rock-climbing. There were big cracks, thin cracks: all sizes stretched out overhead. It was intoxicating and addictive. A lie-back flake followed a hand-crack. Then somewhere along the vertical road was an overhang with pins to clip. Icicles hung from the lip, so I snapped one off to suck on.

An occasional pin showed up to signpost the way, but we were too absorbed in the climbing to care much about protection. Our 'sacs were not too heavy: just a few items of bivvy gear, a stove and a bit of food. My single-leather boots tiptoed nicely on the granite crystals and when thrust firmly into cracks seemed to stick there as if by magic. The sheer joy of uncluttered movement held our interest while we ran out rope-length after rope-length. Bob and Dave were having to belay in the most awkward places because of their short rope, but they were climbing well and smoothly.

By late afternoon, I belayed beneath a nasty-looking overhanging squeeze-chimney. Our British guidebook said it was the key to the middle part of the pillar. Bob thought he could see another way, a steep slab with pins for protection. Faced with a crack or face-climbing, I immediately reverted to my gritstone apprenticeship and chose the chimney. Don Whillans had climbed it during the first ascent, and I could imagine his short, powerful figure climbing it with grace and dexterity. My ascent was thuggish and fast as the rays lengthened and the light started to go. I was on a ledge, not overwhelmingly large but a bit like an old truck seat, though not as soft.

We all squeezed on the ledge and began to make tea.

"Ugh! What's that floating in your tea, John ?"

"Me teef."

"I didn't know you had false teeth. Put 'em back! It's bloody revolting!"

"What happens when you get cold? Do they rattle?"

Despite the seriousness of our position, the teasing went on. Everyone was the brunt of one joke or another.

It felt strange to be sitting alongside Bob, yet not climbing with him. He'd become a great friend over the years and was one of the few people, except Al, I'd climbed with in the Alps. We'd gone through a lot together. I remembered the hilarious time we drove from Chamonix to the Bregalia, climbed the Cengalo North Pillar in four and a half hours and drove back again without paying a penny for gas. We siphoned it out of parked cars along the way. In a way, the Frêney Pillar should have been ours together, though I certainly didn't hold that against either John or Dave. It was just the way it had worked out.

Only street people and climbers know what it feels like to wake up so stiff with cold that it's easy to believe there is a sun-god. So when all we saw were clouds, we not only felt cheated but scared, too.

"Perhaps we should go down?" said a voice from beneath a down jacket.

I snapped fully awake and said: "No, up is the only way out. I've done the descent before. I'm not doing it again."

I felt confident in our ability to escape, no matter what happened. The clouds crowded in, and it began to snow. There were four inches of fresh snow on my pack before it stopped and a weak sun broke through. I sighed with relief. We still had a few more hours before I knew it would return.

The most difficult climbing was above us on the Candle: a compact monolith with few cracks and awesome exposure. Luckily, most of the pins were already there, and we could pull on them for aid.

Bob was up above, standing in a sling attached to a drilled-out plumber's-nut. I was preparing to make a pendulum across to Dave's stance when there was a scream: "Ah-h-h!" Arms, legs and pack came flying towards me. I ducked instinctively and found myself looking into Bob's relieved face.

"You okay?" I asked.

"The nut pulled out," he said and swung back up to join Dave, who was distraught.

"My bloody 'sac's gone!" wailed Dave. "The rope snatched it from behind the flake. My bivvy gear, ice-axe, camera—everything!"

I estimated that the whole shabby lot wouldn't have fetched more than ten pounds at a junk sale, but at that point, high on the south face of Europe's highest mountain, they were priceless.

"Now you'll really be able to move, without a 'sac and all," I said, trying to sound positive. But I thought about the storm.

"Too right, Jimmy, I'm off," said Dave, his adrenaline putting him in top gear. They slowly pulled away from us.

When I swung around a corner into a bottomless dihedral, I remembered a story from the first ascent. Don Whillans had tried to free-climb the corner, found himself unable to take a hand off to place protection, decided to keep climbing and had fallen seventy feet from the narrow, overhanging chimney I could see above me.

"The bloody nerve," I whispered to the pin that supported my weight, "to throw yourself at a pitch like this."

I could look between my feet and see the glacier far, far below.

I was absorbed in the interesting climbing, but my real concern was the clouds rising from the valley.

"Okay, John. Come on up. I'm there."

I stood on top of the Candle. The rock-climbing was over, and snowflakes floated down from the surrounding cloud. We were on the highest lightning rod in Europe when a BOOM! echoed from the west.

"Oh, shit! Please be quick!" I prayed to John.

We still had 800 feet to the ridge and then Mont Blanc de Courmayeur. And then Col Major. And then the real summit. And then. And then . . . .

On the small pass between the pillar and the main face, John tightened his hood around his face.

"Aid, you know those pills you carry?" he said, referring to some amphetamines I keep in my first-aid kit. "Well I think I'd like to try some."

A policeman making a decision. The highest drug-deal in Europe taking place. A pill for speed. Some speed for life. Some life in a pill . . . .

"Oh, stop it, Aid," I said to myself. "Get moving before we freeze!"

My thoughts were beginning to wander. We were wallowing in snow up to our crotches, without anchors while clouds wrapped us in cotton-wool. I couldn't see more than a few feet, but when the wind suddenly hit me in the face, I knew we'd reached the ridge. I tried to remember the way from two years before when Bob and I had traversed the Brouillard Ridge, from the top of the pillar Alan was now climbing.

"Hell," I thought, "I hope Al's not at the lower end of the ridge right now."

We flogged our way past some rocky pinnacles, dark shadowy fins at the edge of our visibility. Soon after, the ground beneath my feet sloped gently downhill. We must have crossed Mont Blanc de Courmayeur and be heading for Col Major. I'd exited from the Brenva Face once at that point, but then it had been perfectly clear.

"How do you know where we're going?" said John, panting as he followed my steps.

"Up," I gasped, saving my breath for step-kicking.

"Eh?"

"The summit is the highest thing around here. So we must keep going up."

I re-examined my altimeter to make sure we were gaining height. I stopped at one point and, turning to John, I warned him: "Make sure there's no slack in the rope, because Geoff Tabner fell into a crevasse around here after we did Route Major."

We didn't need to intensify the epic we were having by holding crevasse-rescue practice. Then, as if by magic, I trod on a piece of frosted orange peel. The snow felt more solid under foot. We were on the summit!

My nylon jacket seemed to be doing funny things. I blinked to clear the ice from my lashes. No, there really were bluish flames dancing on my jacket's shiny surface. I imagined myself a Christmas pudding covered in brandy—sort of glowing. An electrical charge was building to a dangerous degree, and we were likely to be the next strike point.

"Move, John! Move!" I shouted. "We're going to get hit!"

I glanced over my shoulder to see why the rope had come tight. John was on his hands and knees. What on earth was he looking for just when we needed to get the hell off the summit?

"John," I bellowed. "What have you lost? Man, it's going to strike us!"

I tugged at the rope, a vision of charred flesh adding strength to my arm.

"He's lost his marbles," I thought. "Here am I on Europe's highest summit about to get a thunderbolt up the wazzu, while John pretends to be a dog."

"Urg-g-g!" Not a bark but a stream of vomit spat out into the snow. I coiled up the rope as I went to his side.

"You okay?" A dumb question. He obviously wasn't.

A monstrous crash of thunder boomed out of the clouds. My sphincter almost gave up the ghost as I fought to maintain control.

"Let's go, kid!"

John staggered to his feet, and I coaxed him to slide down the descent on his back.

"Faster, man! Faster! I've got ya!"

Down we went. Stumbling and sliding as steps broke and slabs of fresh snow avalanched into the abyss. Each step made was one nearer to life, a life I knew I really wanted to keep. The Bosses Arête is the easiest way up Mont Blanc, but it still has some awesome drops off its flanks. Not that we could see anything. Our world existed of twenty feet of swirling snow. The ridge curved down for six hundred feet to a tin bivvy hut where  Bob was calling out into the storm: "Ai-i-i-d!"

The call came over and over again, whipping around the ridges to be finally consumed by clouds.

"I thought you'd had it, youth," he said as he finally clasped my shoulder and began to untie the icy rope from John's harness. "We've been here a couple of hours. The hut's packed to the gills 'cause of the storm."

"It takes more than a wee storm to finish me off," I said, grinning and grateful for my friend's concern. I added mischievously: "Besides, all those lads in the campsite would be trying to steal my girlfriend . . . ."

# CHAPTER
## 7

## DAVI

BY ADRIAN

There are times in life when you meet a person who forever changes your outlook. The mingling of adventures and experiences with such a person allows no retreat. For us, that person was Davi Vevar.

It was difficult to believe that anyone could be so crazy. We constantly found ourselves trying to protect him from himself. He would sit on the branch of his life and hack at it while daring the ground to come up and get him. All of this helped us to feel pretty normal by comparison.

Davi (DAH-vee) was the delinquent son of a Welsh parson and a year or so younger than us. While Al and I were living in Chester, he was attending Chester College. He was a wild man, both in appearance and actions. I first met him as I was about to enter a party, and he materialized out of a dark November night and stopped me.

"That will be a quid to help pay for the keg," he said. "The ladies get in free."

He was dressed in a dark-grey trench coat with a woolen hat covering most of his black, curly "Hendrix-style" hair. His heavy Welsh accent was gruff and intimidating. I paid up.

"Ta very much," he said and melted back into the night.

He didn't climb but he liked the parties, and that's how our lives became entwined. We'd climb all day and Davi would watch from the safety of a can of ale. Then one day the inevitable demand: "Take me on a climb." Al roped him up and away they went.

There were no easy beginnings for Davi. He wouldn't have entertained the idea of an easy climb. The climb was called Tensor and difficult enough for Al to treat it with respect. It starts in an exposed position a hundred feet off the ground, and the first moves are a trying traverse left underneath overhangs. Then it weaves through the overhangs to the top of the cliff.

Davi took one bold step left, promptly fell off, swung out like a spider on a thread and shouted up to Al: "A've lost me fags!" He began to climb hand-over-hand up the single rope, a large loop of slack building up the farther he climbed.

"Don't do that, Davi! You'll fall!" I bellowed up. But it was too late. He was moving as fast as a rat up a flue. When he reached a pin, he swung up on it, sheer terror giving him untold strength, and Al took in all the slack. Davi had become a climber.

He had so much natural finger-strength (I suspect from crushing empty beer cans), combined with a fearlessness bordering on crazy, that he quickly fitted into the mold of a climber.

One day he came up with a crazy scheme to visit an old girlfriend in the south of France. We'd drive the thousand miles each way. Al and I would climb, and he would . . . well, he wouldn't climb. All this would happen in the space of six days. He thought we were crazy for even going along with him.

We were heading south on the *autoroute*, Davi at the helm. A thick mist had cut visibility to a hundred yards, but that didn't stop him driving at eighty miles an hour. What scared me was the way he was trying, at the same time, to mix himself a gin-and-tonic between his knees. The small hole in the can of tonic kept missing the large neck of the gin bottle, but he persevered unswervingly—literally. I shut my eyes and tried to sleep.

The week was almost over, and we'd all had our own brand of fun. I counted the cash in the communal purse.

"Davi, where's all the money gone?" I asked. "There's only ten francs left."

"We spent it all on wine. Don't you remember ?" He paused to consider the honour at stake, and added: "Don't worry, Aid. I'll borrow some from Noelle (his girlfriend)."

What little money we borrowed—well, had been given—had run out by the time we were north of Paris. It was midnight when we pulled into a gas station and began pumping gas. A sleepy attendant ambled towards us as I zeroed the pump, smiled and pretended I was just beginning.

"*Combien franc de gasoline*?" I asked. "How much gas?" he asked back. I stuck up two fingers. He stared at me in disbelief. I'd asked for half a pint. Then we were on our way to the night ferry and another scam.

"Davi, we don't have enough money for three tickets," I said. "You'll have to hide in the back."

We covered him with sleeping bags and junk.

"Stay still, Davi, we're almost at the ticket office."

He was wriggling about, and the whole pile of junk was moving.

"Turn the fucking heater off! I'm frying!" was his muffled answer, followed by a string of Welsh curses.

"Davi, stay still! The customs people are there, too. We're going to have to smuggle you in."

We had taken a step from a small crime to a critical one. Smuggling people into England is taken very seriously. We made it safely on board and prowled the decks looking for food.

"I'm so hungry I could eat a horse between two mattresses," I growled.

"How about a protein roll?" asked Davi.

"What's that? Where is it?"

"Up in the lifeboat. Won't be a minute."

He began climbing up the superstructure in the pitch-black night, the flitting shadow of a cat-burglar.

A whisper came down out of the swinging hull: "Aid, catch!"

A package flew through the air and was under my jacket within a second. He clambered back down. Mission completed. The three of us grouped in the corner of the well-lit bar, saliva building in our mouths. I slowly brought the package out into the light and let out a moan: "Davi, it's a hank of fucking rope!"

When I moved into his rented townhouse, I could hardly believe the mess. Books and climbing gear lay strewn in every room. The first night I laid out my sleeping pad among the jumble and swore that things would have to change. To get Davi to clean the place up was a major step forward, though his motives were different than mine.

"The chicks'll love a clean place, eh, Aid?" he said.

I didn't tell him they might not wish to share the place with me as well, because we both slept in the one room.

He was teaching biology at a nearby school, while I taught outdoor education at another. Some of my plans involved taking eight children up to Scotland to climb some snow gullies and do some winter hill-walking. Davi wanted to come but first had to figure out how to get time off work. The morning we were due to leave, he went into school as usual but with a crazy plan in mind. He put on a tie around his neck next to his skin. Then he dressed normally in a white shirt and second tie. Just before going to report sick to the headmaster, he tightened the first tie to a point of near-strangulation. His face turned bright red and his eyes almost leapt from their sockets. All the veins in his neck and face dilated. The headmaster thought he was about to have a heart attack and sent him home immediately. And that's how Davi first went to Scotland.

That week was the first time he'd climbed on snow and ice and was as strenuous a time as he'd had in the mountains. However, it was after the day's efforts that the fun really began for him. He would sit by the open coal fire in the Glencoe bunkhouse and relate story after story to open-mouthed teenagers. He became their Superman, their Robin Hood and their Rambo. But never their saint. Enamoured by his wildness, they decided to play a prank on him. While he lay on his bunk, they held him down and cocooned him with a climbing rope–strapped him to his bed. Davi played the game and allowed it to happen. After he'd twisted and writhed to free himself, he set out on the chase. He found them safely locked in the mini-bus, jeering at him through the windows.

By this time I'd joined in the chase and decided I'd flush them out. With a butane-gas stove in hand, I casually poked the burner head through an open window and turned on the gas. Every head turned to watch. Noses began to twitch. Some clever joker began to open windows. Oxygen began to mix with the butane. They thought they'd won. Fingers pointed in glee. I showed them my final card–a cigarette lighter held ready by the hissing jet. The doors burst open and Davi grabbed the culprits.

When he began to tie their hands together, they relaxed. After all, it was all in fun. Wasn't it . . . ? When he led two of them like mellow ponies to the back of the van, they raised their heads in suspicion. I herded the rest of the kids into the bus and Davi, giving the two boys twenty feet of slack rope, tied it off to the back seat. We were ready to go for a run. Or should I say, they were.

I drove very slowly out onto the narrow lane, around the winding corners–four miles per hour. Davi stood on the tailgate like a fisherman with a delicate catch. The boys were striding out well. Long loping gaits showed power and confidence. Half a mile later their expressions were not quite so confident. How much farther was this going to go on?

Davi was shouting instructions to me: "Ease off a bit, Aid. We don't want them coming down with 'road rash,' do we?"

Deep laughter roared out from the rear of the bus. Suddenly, horror of horrors, the local cop car emerged from a shaded bend up ahead.

"Shit! Stop!"

I slowed to a careful halt while Davi put his arms around the two runners and drew them towards the van. The bobbies were smiling. I gave them a wave. They returned it and went on their way.

About that time Davi met a girl who owned a Morgan sports car. She was gracious enough to let Davi drive it, and he liked to go fast, very fast. We'd flash off down to Wales in a little over an hour, climb all day and burn back again. I have a vivid recollection of being a passenger in the roaring machine with my behind little more than nine inches from the passing road. The long hood that stretched out before me looked like it was taking aim at the oncoming traffic circle. Would we make it? We were doing a hundred and twenty! The smell of burning oil and the trembling of the whole frame had me speechless, when Davi growls out: "Just like a fucking Spitfire, Aid!"

He loved to point out to other riders a couple of marks on the dash. He called them "Aid's teeth marks!"

During this time, the Chester constabulary received orders to trail Davi and observe his movements. He must have unknowingly led them a fine chase, he in the Morgan and they in their small underpowered minivans. It all began in a Cheshire country pub, full of white-shirted Chester businessmen. Davi's girlfriend, Sean, had a large, aging St. Bernard dog who suffered from an arthritic hip. She'd been injecting the poor animal with a morphine derivative and had forgotten to throw away the syringe. A few beers down the line, Davi had begun to use it to squirt beer at unsuspecting locals. For him it had been clean fun and harmless enough. He'd dumped the syringe in an ashtray when he left, and the suspicious publican took it to the police.

From then on, the wonderfully ingenious minds that run the long arm of British law had decided that Davi was dealing in drugs obtained through his girlfriend's father, who was a doctor. He fit their profile so closely that he had to be guilty. Wild curly hair; an obvious disregard for authority; a penchant for parties; loud music and friends with long hair. Plus, how could a lowly teacher afford a flashy sports car? One summer evening Davi left his girlfriend at her parents and headed home, his hair blowing in the wind as he tore, carefree, along the winding country lanes. He was having fun. Unbeknownst to him, the cops thought no one in their right minds would ever drive like that, unless they were carrying a load of drugs.

He pulled into his driveway and found Al Rouse, Brian Hall and Daphne all using an overhanging balcony to train on pullups and other climbing moves. Five minutes later three strangers, one a woman, walked purposely towards them, following an overly eager Alsatian dog.

"Who you looking for?" asked someone.

"Get inside! Police!" was the response. One pulled a gun.

They were all taken inside and told to strip naked while the officers searched for needle marks and other signs of drug addiction. Davi stood sheepishly, dressed in only his girlfriend's underwear. The cop wondered what kind of person stood before him. Davi explained: "Must have grabbed me girlfriend's undies by mistake this morning."

After the embarrassingly obvious blunder, the cops left. Even the dog had its tail between its legs.

To report Davi's conversations fully is not easy. He had spoken only the Welsh language until age eight and so brought a completely different slant to the English he spoke. I never knew a person who could fit so many four-letter words into one sentence. He'd slip two between article and subject, then one for the verb and another one to qualify it and likewise for the object. All this with the sing-song lilt of the Gaelic.

He was becoming an accomplished climber, and to some degree this kept him out of trouble. He poured his vast energies onto the rock, but you still couldn't keep him out of the pub in the evenings. I remember returning to the house one night after all the pubs had closed and Davi was starving. He would often forget to eat because he'd be so busy just doing . . . something.

The cupboard held a couple of slices of stale bread, a blob of butter and nothing else. Imagine my surprise when I see him scouting out for anything edible and his gaze stops at a friend's tropical-fish tank. Inspired by the wriggling and darting goldfish, his hand dips quickly and comes up with a prize. Onto the toast and under the grill it goes. There's a scream as his girlfriend comes in and snatches it off, to plop it back into the water. It sank.

In those days the Chester party scene was pretty active. We'd often meet in some classic old Cheshire country pub before going out on the town for the evening. When Sean invited a group of us back to a birthday party at her parents' home, we gladly accepted. It would naturally be a posh affair and so an invitation meant we'd been accepted, even if it was on a trial basis, into the upper echelons of the local who's who.

As Davi perceived it: "The food'll be good, and they think climbers are exotic, so don't get caught scratching yer arse."

The evening passed with the chink of fine crystal and many a fine conversation about why we clung to greasy rock faces and endured nights out tied onto tiny ledges.

"Why do you do it?" was a common question, and one of us

would always answer something like: "Well, it seems to make all this," eyes dropped to an almost empty glass, then a pause, "so worthwhile." The host would then glimpse the dregs and scurry away to correct the balance. From the kitchen a *plop* reached trained ears, a satisfying sound.

After everyone had left, I asked Sean if she had a sleeping bag I could use. She told me her sister's room was empty and that the bed was big enough for me and Davi. She was playing it pretty cool in front of Dad.

"Fancy bedroom," I commented. "Where's her sister now?"

"Off visiting some rich boyfriend. She's going to get married in St. Paul's Cathedral in London."

I stood over a dressing table full of expensive-looking perfumes and deodorants.

"Fair number of smelling stuff here, Davi," I said.

"Yeah, look," he replied.

I turned my head into a fine spray of French perfume. He was using it like fly spray and I was the fly.

"Bastard! I'll smell like a Parisian hooker."

Come morning we sat in the airy country kitchen, warm coffee before us. Sean had left to make toast. Davi looked over at me with a slightly guilty expression.

"Fucking hell, Aid," he said. "I woke up last night and smelled that perfume. Didn't know where I was and thought you were Sean's sister. I caught myself just in time. Bloody embarrassing."

Davi seemed the most dangerous after the pub. On one occasion, we went back to his girlfriend's country cottage. He'd just bought a new chainsaw to help in his part-time firewood business and was anxious to show me see how it worked, so he fired it up with a deafening roar in the dining room. My memory flashed back to the movie, *The Texas Chainsaw Massacre*. In the next minute–after a "Watch this, Aid"–he raised the blade, shredding the wire and paper lamp shade, and continued to cut off a big chunk of the country-style dining table. His *girlfriend's* country-style dining table! Not long after, he lost the use of the Morgan car–and girlfriend, too.

Urged on by tales of fighting and plunder, he'd like to get into the occasional brawl to keep his hand in. One time in Glencoe we'd been out ice-climbing all day in nasty, snowy weather. The climbers' bar at the Clachaig Inn was elbow-to-elbow standing- room-only, with the faintly musty smell of sweat and drying clothes. Ian Nicholson, a giant of a man and local climbing expert, was behind the bar, collecting empty glasses at closing time. Al, Davi and I were nearby, finishing the dregs of a heavy beer. A young, leather-clad biker lass stepped up to the bar and demanded another beer in no polite fashion. When she was refused, she smashed a glass defiantly but had not counted on Ian's rapid reflexes. He has the largest hands I've ever seen and to have one of those clip a fast back-hander must have hurt.

Forward moved the boyfriend to avenge her pride, but quick as a flash, Al and I had his arms twisted in half-nelsons and he was thrown out the door.

We really didn't think too much about the incident until moments later the sea of bodies hurriedly parted to form a ten-foot-wide swath: we at one end and the bike-chain-swinging boyfriend at the other. Davi was primed. He, Al and I stood shoulder to shoulder while the guy advanced to the far side of a billiard table. Whack!! Down slammed the chain. Thick oil was imprinted on the green baize.

There was an explosion of action as Davi leapt the table before the guy could rearm. A bone-shattering crunch as fist met skull. We quickly followed as arms reached out to stop us. Davi was a blur of fists and ducking head as he guarded our backs. The next thing I knew, the bar was empty and we were all three stood there grinning in a pile of broken glass. The inn owner ushered us into a smaller, private bar.

"Keep ahold of that biker until the local police sergeant comes," he said and then turned to us. "And in the meantime, wot all ye be havin'?" he asked.

"Glen Morangie will go down just fine, thanks," said Al, ordering the first of many free Scotches.

I only ever climbed one alpine route with Davi, but it was a day to remember. He'd just returned from an attempt on the South Face of the Aiguille de Midi with an attractive girl called Muriel.

"There were too many people all over the route, Aid. Ropes crossing every which way," he said. However, I'd seen his pack before he'd left. He had so many bottles of wine and wedges of Camembert that I could see he had very different ideas about the climb than she.

We were hanging out in the Chamonix campground and Davi

had nothing to do. So I asked him: "Al, Bob Shaw and I are going up to do a rock route on the Forgotten Pillar on the Argentière. Do you want to come?" The route had had one ascent by a French friend, Georges Bettembourg. He was a great Chamonix climber and wanted us to confirm the difficulty of the climb.

The next day we roped up at the bottom of a thousand-foot pillar of beautiful granite. Though I normally climbed in boots, we'd all decided the Alps warranted using rock-shoes. From the beginning, the climbing was classic. There were thin cracks and delicate traverses, all at about 5.9 standard. Davi climbed quickly without bothering about much protection. It was a real pleasure to see him so at home and in perfect control. He'd not climbed many long routes and I remember him commenting, "Aid, it's much bigger than Tremadoc (a Welsh cliff)."

"Sure is, Davi."

"How we going to get down?" A crag rat's question.

"We'll rap back down."

We reached the top of the pillar at mid-afternoon. While I searched around for some good anchors, I heard Davi driving a pin.

"I'll rap from this, Aid." The rope was already threaded, and he was about to lean back on it.

"Wait a second, Davi! I want to test it," I said, pulling him back onto the ledge. I gave the pin a sharp tug downwards, and it dropped an inch in the crack.

"Oh, Davi," was all I could say. I quickly chose a fatter pin and pounded it home. Then I made a back-up anchor by slotting a small wired wedge into a constriction.

"O.K. Down ya go."

On a small ledge, Davi leaned out to look down a huge corner with two sets of overhangs. The exposure was extreme.

"There'd be nothing fucking left," he said.

"What?"

"If you fell. There'd be nothing fucking left."

"Shut up, Davi! You're getting me scared. You go first, but watch your head as you drop over the lip of the big roof."

I watched his yellow hard hat getting smaller.

CLUNK! His head connected with the rock.

"Fucking overhang!"

He never would pay attention.

Davi is constantly meeting life head-on without thought for the consequences. He's also very creative. He finally seduced his wife-to-be by climbing up the outside of her hotel with a bottle of champagne in hand, broke into her room and was sitting there, complete with cheesy grin, when she returned to her room.

When he married Gail, his life changed. Not that he wasn't still crazy, but now he mixed it with elegance. He would sip wine from the best crystal instead of a cup, eat steaks

*Davi and Gail*

from a plate rather than mashed potato from the electric kettle, and wait until nine-thirty before leaving for the pub instead of going at six.

He wished to introduce Gail to some of his climbing friends, and so together they went to a Christmas party being hosted by a North Wales climbing club. The gathering was held in a granite-block fortress of a hotel in some quaint Welsh village. Davi was on his best behaviour and even wore a suit given to him by Gail's first husband. The evening progressed with plenty of joviality, and Davi sank untold pints of the local brew. Then the happy couple retired to their room, which, as in many Welsh hotels, did not have its own bathroom. That facility lay just down the hallway. In the middle of the night, Davi awoke with stretched bladder and a desire to relieve himself. He groggily dragged himself out of bed and staggered in a befuddled state to the toilet. Then, during his return to their room, he miscounted the doorways, unknowingly got lost and entered another room. Settling himself beneath the warm sheets he was soon asleep, far into the Land of Nod.

Morning arrived with a rude awakening for Davi.

"What the hell are you doing here?" barked an angry guy, lying on his side in the other half of the bed, less than two feet from Davi's sleep-encrusted eyes. Davi awoke with a start, furious.

"What the fuck are *you* doing here?" said Davi. "Get out! Where's Gail? Hey, get lost, you faggot!"

"It's *you* who must leave. This is *my* room. I'm the hotel manager!"

"Ugh! What? Are you sure?" Davi was waking up fast. "Oh, sorry about that." Then Davi left, wrapped only in a towel.

One spring we decided to climb on the granite of the Cornish coast. There was a comfortable climbers' hut down there, but as we weren't members, we used names of people we knew who were. After a hard day's climbing, the evening lengthened into late night. Al Rouse showed us a climbing challenge which involved wriggling between the ceiling and a steel supporting girder. One by one we tried the problem and everybody was laughing at the efforts. It held quite a lot of danger because if you squeezed part of your shoulders through and then slipped, there was a high chance of snapping your neck. At this point we'd forgotten that people were trying to sleep upstairs.

Then Davi tried. Both shoulders were locked in between joists and his feet were swinging free when he decides: "A'm fuckin' stuck!" said from the depths of flattened lungs. We roared with laughter. Gail, dressed in the finest silk, began to look a bit worried.

"Don't be daft, Davi," she said. "You got in. You can get out."

"A tell ya, woman, A'm fuckin' stuck!"

Another roar of laughter. Then came a string of Welsh expletives that would have made his father blush, and he moved a few more inches through the gap. Finally, after another great heave, he was through and he swung down to the floor. The uproar was tremendous.

Then a man appeared at the door. "If you lot don't bloody shut up, there's going to be a big problem," he said. "A very big problem."

I could have guessed the next thing that would happen. Davi moved quickly to the door and began poking a straightened finger into the guy's chest.

"Don't ya come in here fuckin' shouting yer fuckin' abuse in front of my bloody wife or I'll fuckin' put you outside and lock the fuckin' door!" Davi looked terrifying. The man slunk away without another word.

Whenever we pass through England, we always look up Davi. He doesn't climb any more, now we're not around.

"It's just not the fuckin' same, Aid. All these poncy bastards dressed in their pink tights passin' 'round their diseases. They don't even like to fight . . . ."

Gail is just as beautiful as ever, and they have a young son called Jan. You can see he's proud of his dad, and I guess he's heard a lot of stories.

Sometimes, when Davi's had a couple of pints, you can spot a wistful look in his eyes. They tell of the past and think to the future. Who knows, maybe he'll climb again yet.

# *CHAPTER*
## *8*

## CANADA: THE FALLING CORNICE

BY ADRIAN

I had never before lived in a place as cold as Calgary. After our visit to the vertical deserts of California granite in Yosemite, the Canadian winter seemed doubly harsh. It was so cold even steam wouldn't rise. I looked out of our warm, centrally-heated apartment toward the city center and marveled at the way steam poured over the edge of fifty-story office buildings: steaming white waterfalls set against metallic-black glass. Brrr!

One day a dark-haired, wiry expatriate Scotsman, Bugs McKeith, approached Al and me.

"Are you boys interested in doing a few wee ice climbs around here?" he said.

"Yes," Al replied. "What mountain do you have in mind and what particular route? I'll check it out in the guidebook."

Bugs grinned. It was difficult to grasp what was going on behind his piercingly intense eyes.

"I don't think they'll be in the guidebook, lads," he said. "As for the name of the mountain, it's not important."

The climbs actually were frozen waterfalls found below treeline and often only twenty minutes walk from a good road. This was the new era of Canadian ice-climbing, and there were many slivers of ice to be climbed for the first time. Some of the more obvious climbs had already been made by a small band of expatriate British climbers who had made Calgary their home during the late Sixties. Bugs appeared to be the keenest of the band, and as we knew few climbers, it made sense to let him show us around.

The drive north from Banff toward Jasper follows a wild and often windswept road; it was not uncommon to see foxes and the occasional bear taking short cuts along the tarmac surface. From this road we made our first exploratory reconnaissances in search of ice. The surrounding rock was a poor quality limestone formed in steep bands separated by good ledges; this helped the ice form in tiers and so created the pitches of the climbs. One of the first we attempted looked like a curtain about two-hundred-feet high and often vertical.

"How the hell do you climb this stuff, Bugs?" was our first response. It looked so steep and brittle.

"A little bit of cunning and a fair amount of patience should work out best," he said evasively.

The cunning bit involved attaching short aid-slings to drooped-nosed ice-hammers known as "pterodactyls." These were tapped gingerly into the ice and acted somewhat like hooks. The patience involved Al and me, who had to wait a few hours in the cold shadow of the ice until Bugs had completed the first section. Then we would attach our jumar clamps onto the rope and climb it, removing any ice pitons that Bugs may have inserted to protect himself.

Al was jumaring gingerly over the final bulge when he blurted out: "Holy shit, man! The belay!"

Bugs had not been able to find a good anchor in the rock and so had tied off the rope to his ice-tools. The two short picks hooked into the ice were Al's sole attachment to the world of the living. Worse still, Bugs had untied from the rope, and so had no commitment to the belay. From then on, we kept a close watch on his handling of the rope.

Bugs named the route "Ice Nine" after a book he'd read (Kurt Vonnegut's "Cat's Cradle"). I reckoned that after that kind of rude introduction to Canadian ice, we ought to build up some experience on the oft-climbed easier routes. It just wasn't the same as the Scottish climbs we'd done.

Living in Canada was very different from England, as we kept being reminding. I remember a pleasant sunny afternoon in January when Al and I decided to walk to the nearest grocery store. Wearing only T-shirts, we walked the mile and a half to a huge supermarket. Snow lay piled where plows had pushed it to the curbside.

We entered the warm, fluorescent-lit Safeway and began our shopping. We weren't in a rush, just cruising around checking out all the shelves.

"Whoever in England would believe they have a whole aisle just for pet food?"

"Yeah. And a whole herd of cows wrapped up in the meat section. Cheap, too."

By the time we had walked around the huge interior, paid for the food and left with bags tucked under our arms, night had fallen. So had the temperature. Two shivering, semi-naked idiots wound their way through unfamiliar streets, looking for home. I couldn't believe it: we were lost! We quickly became desperate as the temperature dropped.

Then along came a familiar person – a guy who lived next door.

"Oh, man!" we pleaded though chattering teeth. "Where's the house?"

On another occasion I had arranged to climb with a girl whose living room floor we slept on for the night. I told her I would wake her with a bang on her bedroom door, except I actually said: "I'll knock you up in the morning."

Her eyes widened with surprise and then narrowed with defiance as she replied emphatically: "You sure as hell will not!"

One time Al and I helped pour concrete all day long. The concrete dust had a definite drying effect on our gullets. Little wonder, then, that we went along with the rest of the building crew to a local beer hall.

The Calgary bars were like huge school dining rooms: bare tables; simple, hard-backed chairs; and plenty of rules. Ah, yes, the rules: no singing, no dozing off and no walking about with a glass of beer in hand. It's a wonder they actually let you drink the damned beer. But that's all they wanted you to do: drink, drink and drink. Then when you'd got so drunk that you forgot the other rules, they'd kick you out to drive home.

All began well on that particular evening. We flushed out the concrete dust in the first ten minutes. In the next ten we swept away the hunger. After an hour we had consolidated all the camaraderie of the day. We were well on our way to solving a large number of the world's problems when Alan went to phone our girlfriends and see if they would like to join us.

They arrived at the same time a band began to play. Well, dancing makes one thirsty, so we drank a few more beers. It was about that time that we began to forget some of the rules. Daphne sat on Al's lap while holding a beer. Various people began to move from group to group with beers in hand. I later learned that the correct way to move a beer from one table to another was to ask the waitress to do it for you. With that kind of musical beers, a person could die of thirst.

From a corner of the room, a 300-pound gorilla, a bouncer, eyed us as potential troublemakers. A clever chap—because we were. Alan spotted him spotting us and decided that when the trouble began he would be sober. Al began to drink water.

Suddenly there was a crunch and a tinkle of breaking glass. Someone had accidentally knocked over a glass of beer. The trouble had begun. While a number of beer-bellied brutes moved in for the kill, Al edged towards the door and, before anyone could stop him, was baiting one of them: "Outside, Jimmy!"

The man was too stupidly confident to decline. As soon as they were away from the main crowd and in the glass foyer, a blur of concrete-coated knuckles played out a tattoo on the guy's chin. Down he went with Al astride his chest. The snap of a breaking arm must have told Al all he needed to know. A familiar form of rodeo for Calgary spectators.

I missed the next bit because of the tightly packed and swaying crowd. Al had gone and through the blur I heard someone say: "It was him that did the fighting." They were pointing at me!

Two bunches of bananas took a firm hold on my throat. Just before I was about to pass out, I saw my girlfriend dive at the guy. It must have looked like a terrier hanging onto an elephant, but it did give me a chance to duck and turn into the waiting arms of the police.

In the back of the police car, I tried to explain my innocence. There was no point in saying: "It was my twin brother." I could guess their response to that. Off to the "drunk tank" I went. Once behind bars,

I did the only thing I could. I lay out on the cold tiles and snored the night away. Alan, on the other hand, had a nice warm bed. He owed me one.

The New Year of 1975 neared as we began to make fresh climbing plans. A California climber, Charlie Porter, arrived in Calgary. He was well-known for his multiple-day climbs in Yosemite National Park—more precisely, on El Capitan. When he asked if he could accompany us on our ventures, we saw the obvious advantage of having a strong fourth climber in our group and agreed immediately. Bugs was less friendly toward him, and I suspected there would be some rivalry.

Our next objective was a long gully on the lower slopes of Cirrus Mountain. The climb began only minutes from the Banff-Jasper highway but looked as though it would take a number of days. Al and I knew very little of its history and really did not care. Even though it was unclimbed, it wasn't a mountaineering route and so held little attraction for us as a major ascent. This was not the case for Bugs, as we discovered in retrospect. For him every first ascent of these waterfalls was crucially important. We learned later that many other local climbers held the same view. This created a competition to which we twins were oblivious.

As we scrambled over short ice bulges to the start of the harder climbing, I began to realize the tremendous size and length of the climb compared with those we had previously done. A seventy-foot bulging step barred our way. I spotted a yellow line of rope hanging down from above.

"I wonder who's been up here before us?" I asked, without suspecting that Bugs knew exactly.

"Some other local lads tried it last week and came down," Bugs said. He didn't say that he knew they were on their way back soon and that's why we were there: to beat them to the climb.

Over the next few days, we began to work on the route, and work it turned out to be. We were not climbing quickly enough to ascend many pitches a day, so we would leave rope hanging down the pitches we had climbed to facilitate a rapid return to our high point.

The most interesting climbing came at the final 900-foot curtain of cascading ice. Except for two ledges, the place seemed horrifying, vertical and unlike anything we'd ever seen before. There was a small cave at the base of the pillar to which we would return each evening. I climbed with Charlie while Al roped up with Bugs. Each team took turns in the lead, while the others supported their efforts in whatever way they could.

I sensed an increasing friction between Charlie and Bugs and wished they'd be a bit less intense about the whole affair. Charlie did not trust the anchors that Bugs had placed. One morning, as Charlie swung up onto a fixed line, he turned to me and said: "If these anchors fail, put Bugs in hospital for me, will you?"

You could feel the tension. At times like these when the climb was steep and the ropes were beginning to freeze to the ice column, I wished we had more mutual trust, or else it would be better to descend.

Over the next few days, the four of us each led pitches that were as steep as anything we'd ever done before. I got the next-to-last pitch. Charlie was holding my rope while standing on a very large powder-covered ledge. If I fell, I knew the powder would serve as nothing more than a blanket to leap into before burying me like a shroud. I climbed carefully. At 70 feet I placed my first piece of protection—an ice-screw. Seven inches of metal seems really short when there's a potential seventy-foot plunge. I didn't feel too comfortable with that prospect but climbed on all the same, because that's all there was to do. Progress had become more a question of using the stupidly short ice-tools as attachment points for stirrups. It was a form of aid-climbing with which I did not feel at all familiar. It was very scary for a person like me who needs to feel in control of situations; my personality insists upon the balance of chance very much in favor of the player.

First I'd peck at the ice with the pick, each successive blow landing in the previous hole until enough of the tool was buried. Small cracks in the ice would "star" out from the hole, and if a blow was too heavy, the whole thing would shatter and fall away. This kind of performance had me in a state of mental revulsion. If I could have gone down to join Charlie in conciliation, I certainly would have. However, it was too late and I couldn't. And what's worse, he wouldn't have been conciliatory anyway.

I did the only thing I could and kept on stepping up toward a small ledge positioned to the right of the ice. When I finally arrived, it was only then that I could really assess some of the risks I'd taken: 150 feet with only two ice screws between me and a very hard landing. I wasn't at all sorry when we'd finished with that climb and could plan something in *real* mountains.

To climb in the Alps in winter was still a tough experience in 1974, but to climb in winter in the Canadian Rockies was almost unheard of. We began to relish a fresh challenge, an opportunity to do something no one had done before. With that    motivation, we decided to try the unclimbed North Couloir of Mount Kitchener. It was the kind of challenge we had begun to understand in the Alps, and as the weeks went by, it became more and more an obsession.

Looking back on this, it's clear that we had a dangerous mentality. When you allow little choice for opting out of a project, common sense often becomes obscured. Death is made of such inflexibility.

The North Couloir of Kitchener can be seen from the Banff-Jasper highway, so Al, Charlie and I drove up to take a look through a pair of binoculars. It was almost a relief to jump out of the freezing metal box that was Charlie's Volkswagen bus and into the dry cold air of the Rocky Mountain winter.

"Doesn't get much sun on it," observed Al, who stood shivering in a too-thin jacket.

"There shouldn't be any stonefall, either," I added, remembering a story I'd heard about a summer attempt that ended with ropes chopped from a constant barrage of stones.

It took us only a few days to dig a comfortable ice-cave at the base of the wall, but it snowed and we returned to the luxury of a wood-stove in a nearby youth hostel. Charlie was obviously not used to hanging around and waiting for his climbs to come into condition, or for weather to improve. His level of hyperactivity began to scratch at our nerves, and we sought to relax him.

"I've got an idea," whispered Al. "Have you got any of those sleeping tablets left?"

"You mean Valium? Yes, I have some. You're not going to . . . ." I knew he was.

"In his bedtime hot chocolate," Al giggled. So Charlie began to get a taste for longer sleeping hours, and we got the chance to continue ours.

The weather finally began to look better. Blue skies appeared when cold polar air pushed southward. Most of our food had been left in the ice cave, so our packs felt quite comfortable as we post-holed through fresh snow on our way for another attempt.

"You can see where the door to the cave used to be by the

shadow of the ice debris beneath it," Al pointed out as we approached the foot of the face. The recent snowfall had smoothed over all but vague traces of our past visit.

Looking up into the shadowed North Face, we watched powder slithering down in small rivulets. The final cornices jutted out alarmingly more than 4,000 feet overhead. [A cornice is an overhang of hard snow  and ice, created by the wind on the leeward side of a ridge.] Although I was wearing leather double-boots, I had to keep flexing and relaxing my toes to stimulate the flow of blood. Inside the cave it would be warm and secure, so we dug frantically to unearth the familiar cavern.

"Here's some old piss stains," Charlie said.

His deep voice and ice-rimed beard gave him the appearance of a Canadian grizzly. He lifted out a block of ice and looked into the spacious chamber. We all clambered in and set up "home" for the night.

While we melted ice for soup, we began to form a strategy for the climb. We had about a thousand feet of polypropylene yachting rope we'd fix above the cave. If that was successful, we  would dig a second cave where the ice steepened and changed color to a darker grey. Then we would pull up the rope and fix it above, giving us a jumping-off point for the narrow gully that slanted up to the cornice and the top. The last part would be very committing, and descent would not be easy. In this way we could lessen the number of nights out in the open. Our strength would probably only just last out the project, and it made sense to conserve warmth and energy for as long as we could.

The first couple of days went fine, but Alan suddenly began to get unmanageably cold feet. Whatever he did, his toes would remain numb, and he chose to forgo the route to save his toes.

"Good luck, lads," he said, his disappointment all too obvious.

I suddenly realized that if he didn't go, I didn't want to go either. But I couldn't let Charlie down at the eleventh hour. A real dilemma. My legs had lost their spring. My moist eyes felt cold, too.

Two days later I led around into the narrow gully that was the key to the top. The two ice-screws that anchored me were only part way in because the ice was too hard. Charlie arrived and laboriously placed a bolt in the rock of the gully wall. That made life more secure. He got a full rope-length above and repeated the bolting in friable orange rock. I joined him.

The black dragon of fear appeared in the back of my mind. Something was wrong. I looked around me, hoping for an answer. Nothing obvious. I don't know if it was because the gully was so narrow that it felt claustrophobic or because huge gobs of ice hung glued to the side walls. The place just felt dangerous.

It was dark and it was cold, but there was something more sinister, too. Suddenly, two of Charlie's ice picks broke. With the cold, the metal had become too brittle and the ice too hard. The feeling of impending doom rose into my throat.

"Maybe we should go down and replace the gear. If one more breaks, we're really in trouble." My voice boomed and echoed around the steep retaining walls. Charlie agreed and returned to join me.

I stomped my freezing feet as Charlie disappeared down the rappel rope and out of the gully's mouth. I followed, leaning backwards, my crampons biting well in the hard ice. I was still well above him when the whole mountain seemed to shudder under the shock wave of a sonic boom.

What was happening? When I looked up, I understood and nearly vomited with fright. The entire rim of cornice was tumbling down the gully, foaming, churning, rocks exploding outward.

"Christ! My ropes!" I thought.

The avalanche would cut my ropes that were still anchored within the cleft. Debris bounded and crashed a hundred feet to my left. I weighted my feet, leaned in and asked God not to kill me. Soon the yellow rope would snake down the ice, and I would fall with it. Fear petrified any further action.

It became quiet. Charlie shouted up. The rope remained in place, and I had my life. Very, very gently I half-climbed, half- rappelled down to him. Maybe only strands, possibly hairs, held me to the damned mountainside. It was the not knowing that was terrifying.

Al told me that he had watched it all, quite helpless, from the doorway of the cave. From his lower position, he could see the hole where the cornice had fractured. He did not know just how precarious my position had been, but he was very glad to see us when we staggered down the final slopes.

There was no way we would ever return.

# CHAPTER
## 9

## ALPS: SUMMER OF 1975

BY ALAN

After climbing Canadian waterfall-ice all winter, Aid, Daphne and I flew back to England on the first of April. Our plan was first to do rock-climbing in England. Then Daphne and I would travel in Paul Moores's Volkswagen Beetle and climb in the Dolomites, before meeting Aid and his French girlfriend in the Austrian Kaisergebirge. We were looking for steep rock-climbs.

The mountains around the Dolomites' center, Cortina D'Ampezzo, were still blanketed by winter snow, so we searched for a sunny, south-facing steep route to climb. On the huge face of Tofana di Rozes, there was a 2,000-foot pillar that seemed relatively snow-free. A knee-deep trudge in wet snow up an approach trail brought us to a hut.

Because it was early in the season, the warden was not there, and the hut was locked. In those days, trivialities like locks and bolts rarely deterred us. A skylight window gave me access to a fully provisioned bar and kitchen. I was holding a large glass of brandy when I opened the front door and invited Paul and Daphne to enter "our apartment." After preparing our equipment, Daphne and I settled into the warden's private room and his big old feather bed.

Before dawn the next morning, Paul and I left Daphne in the "apartment" and broke a trail to the foot of the face. The climb went smoothly up the steep limestone cracks and walls. There were two memorable sections: one was a very steep wall between two roofs where we had to belay, hanging in slings from old fixed pitons; the other was a huge chimney-crack that split the upper face.

Despite ice on the upper rocks, we climbed over the summit in early evening and began our descent. The slopes, which were normally scree, now were ice-slopes worthy of a Scottish ice-climb. Rather than fall trying to descend them in the dark, we spent the night sitting on our rucksacks. Our teeth chattered and the sweat of the day froze on our skin.

After arriving back at the hut, we decided to find another "private apartment." We moved to the Vajolet Towers, where we thought we could discover similar accommodations. We climbed a short Grade-4 route and did find another hut. Although the warden had hidden his stock of beer, we soon located it. After an hour of effort, a locked door opened and revealed the prize.

One morning we climbed a fine 800-foot face on one of the Sella Towers, and in the afternoon we drove over the Brenner Pass to the limestone Alps of the Kaisergebirge. During our first alpine season in 1966, we had been turned back from the Mauk West Wall, and now I hoped to complete it.

The hut at the foot of the wall gave Paul problems. With his tool-kit laid out neatly on a bench, he used a hacksaw blade in an unsuccessful attempt to open a window. Paul was reaching for the tool of last resort—an axe—when the hut-warden came over the brow of a hill. The warden saw Paul holding an axe, with me standing ready beside him, and he nervously opened the door for us. We climbed the Mauk West Wall without a problem.

We met Aid and Christine, and after saying goodbye to Paul, we set up our two small tents. In the following week, we climbed a difficult Grade-6 face. After that, it started to rain. We huddled for days in our leaking tents, with no money to eat in restaurants or take shelter in bars. Occasionally we'd hitchhike into nearby St. Johann and buy a meal of bread, soup and pasta. Then we'd return to the tents and resume our chatting and reading.

In the hope of finding better weather, we eventually caught the train to Grindelwald in the Swiss Oberland. We climbed the North Face of the Grosshorn in three hours and then spent more time sitting around in bad weather.

We took another train to Chamonix and went to the Biolay campground. Many of our climbing friends were there, and over bottles of cheap red wine, we discussed our plans. We wished to climb the very difficult and never-repeated route of Walter Bonatti on the Eckpfeiler Buttress of Mont Blanc. Bonatti first climbed the route in 1962 and claimed it was his most difficult mixed rock-and-ice climb; it was known to alpinists as the Bonatti-Zappelli route. Tut Braithwaite also wished to make the climb, and we agreed we should first make a training climb.

We went up to bivouac at the foot of the Mont Blanc face on the Aiguille Verte. We climbed it quickly and descended to Chamonix, intent on the Eckpfeiler Buttress. Tut was staying in the tent of Alex MacIntyre, whom he invited to join us.

In the Biolay campground at the time, there were a number of groups interested in the Bonatti-Zappelli, and competition was intense. We told everyone that we were going to climb the adjacent, often-ascended Cecchinel-Nominé Couloir. Only after we left the valley and were ready to start the climb did we let Alex in on our secret. Alex, who was rapidly making a reputation as a strong ice-climber, merely nodded in agreement.

The night before the climb, we stood outside the hut and examined our route. A steep narrow couloir led up to a rock barrier and then continued to the Peuterey Ridge, which led to the summit of Mont Blanc. The major danger was from the falling ice that threatened most of the route. To minimize this danger, we would climb unroped and at night to reach the safety provided by the sheltering rock barrier.

What scared us most was the idea of repeating one of Bonatti's hardest climbs. We wondered why no one had repeated his ascent in the thirteen years that had passed since his success, and we were prepared to believe the horror stories we had heard. Sometimes the psychological barriers surrounding a climb—and finding the nerve and willpower to overcome them—were the major problems.

Even with our relatively antique ice-climbing equipment, we completed the climb in ten hours. By midday we sat on the Peuterey Ridge brewing tea over our small stove.

After we returned to the valley, we found that Paul Moores had arrived from England. Together we quickly made plans to climb the North Face of the Grandes Jorasses. This face used to be considered one of the most difficult in the Alps, but as time passed and more accurate information became available, the Walker and Croz Spurs were climbed regularly and therefore had lost a good deal of their earlier reputation. Our projected route was on a third spur to the right of the face, which led to the Pointe Margherita; it had been climbed only twice.

At least half of the climbing problems around Mont Blanc are caused by rapid changes in the weather. To be caught high on an alpine mixed-face in the middle of a snowstorm, without the possibility of descending and with avalanches sweeping down, means almost certain death.

The face we had chosen proved very steep and serious, with much loose high-angle rock and very few resting places. We bivouacked on a precarious snow-ridge 2,500 feet up and reached the summit early the next day.

The weather was still holding, so after only one day's rest, Aid and I returned to the foot of the North Face of the Droites. A few years before, Reinhold Messner, a brilliant Tyrolean climber, had scaled a rock pillar on the North Face. His climb had never been repeated. We decided to try.

At one point on the pillar, we lost the route. Rather than making a traverse to avoid difficulties, I got myself committed on a vertical loose wall. While I was clearing ice from rock to reach better holds, a column of ice four-feet high and two-feet thick came away in my hands and threatened to pry me from the rock. I glanced down at Aid and saw he was badly anchored on the wall below. I knew I dared not fall.

Before my strength evaporated, I quickly took my ice-hammer and gently chipped away at the block, letting the pieces fall away between my legs. A wicked snowstorm caught us on the final slopes, but it did not stop us from successfully completing the climb.

Chamonix was crowded with climbers sitting out the rainstorms. We accepted an invitation from Alex to go to the Dolomites in his group's big old van. Alex, Jan, Blond Nick and Black Nick, Daphne, Christine, Aid and I formed a group that hurtled along the Italian *autostrada* intent on fun. We all did some Dolomite rock-climbs.

During a rest spell in Venice, an incident spiced up the trip. One evening we had all finished eating a series of pizzas. We gave Jan our *lire* to pay the check and left the restaurant. Jan was reluctant to part with any of our meager cash, so he boldly walked right past the cash desk. Quickly a couple of white-aproned waiters pursued him, and soon we all were being chased through Venice's dark narrow streets.

We came to the end of one street and were faced with the murky waters of the Grand Canal. Aid and I looked at one another and, in instant agreement, turned to fight rather than launch ourselves into the dark rat-infested waters.

Blond Nick quickly stripped and, holding his clothes above his head, started to swim the hundred yards to the oppposite bank. When he crawled out at the far side, he was dripping with slime. He approached a solitary girl to ask directions. He was  surprised when she screamed and ran away.

Aid and I escaped without incident. Our pursuers had more common sense than courage.

Another alpine season was over. We returned to England, where Aid went to a teaching job and I went to work in Snowdonia as a "sinker" in the bottom of a 700-foot-deep hydro shaft.

# CHAPTER
## *10*

## McKINLEY: Cassin Spur

BY ADRIAN

I glanced down the row of defendants alongside me: Paul Moores, Don Whillans, Tut Braithwaite, brother Al, "Binks" Blackie and John Howard. They all looked sober and apprehensive as they faced the lady judge from the confines of the jury box.

She went down the line, asking each of us in turn: "Have you ever been in trouble with the law before?"

To a person, everyone tried to look as innocent as possible as they answered: "Oh, no, ma'am. Never."

Don Whillans had recently been in the world press after it took five British constables to pin him down in the rear of a cop car after he'd been caught driving while drunk. Even he said: "Oh, no, ma'am. Never."

She listened to the policeman as he explained the circumstances of the arrest.

"Madam," he began, "five hundred cans of beer were stolen from the Talkeetna Hotel, and I interviewed three witnessess. One, who was the owner, said that these people were seen loading the cargo into the back of their pickup truck. The stolen beer was recovered the next morning at the time of the arrest. One beer can was missing."

"What happened to that can?" she asked.

"I was thirsty after the night before, ma'am," said Don, in a Lancashire accent as broad as his body. "I paid for it later."

His head hung slightly forward, maybe in shame but more likely to hide his laughing.

"Are there any more details I should be made aware of?" the judge asked.

Our uniformed captor stepped forward: "Ma'am, I would like to put on the record that I have never before arrested such a group of likable and polite individuals. They had just finished a big climb on McKinley and had let their hair down—a little too far. I ask you take this into consideration."

We'd obviously done a good job of brown-nosing. Innocence beamed from every set of our shiny cheeks.

The judge, *our* judge, turned to pull down a big black book, heavy with the weight of the law. She flipped through its pages and then demonstrated the power of the word.

"For a theft of five hundred dollars," she said, "the crime is considered grand larceny, the punishment for which is between one year and five years in prison, or one thousand to five thousand dollars in fines."

You could have heard a pin drop. Our faces paled at the information. This was serious stuff.

She flipped more pages, stroked them flat and continued: "If we divide the total theft by the eight of you, we can call this crime a misdemeanor."

Heads raised a few degrees in hope. Thank goodness it was only a misdemeanor. Wasn't that like a speeding ticket?

"The maximum sentence for this is one year in jail or one thousand dollars," she continued and paused to glance down at us, sitting quietly like "Seven Not-So-Wise Monkeys."

"However," she continued, playing us as if she were an expert fly-fisherwomen, "the minimum sentence is thirty days in jail—"

Our hopes were bobbing up and down like a float on her line.

"—and the minimum fine is twenty-five dollars each."

Her gavel came down like an auctioneer's hammer. Twenty-five dollars it was! Gone to the lowest bidder!

Later she showed us around the jail. If deterence was ever supposed to work, it certainly did then. For an hour or so, at least.

Charlie Porter was the first person we knew who spoke of the Cassin Spur on McKinley. He reckoned it was one of the best plums in North America if climbed "alpine-style": that is, from bottom to top without to-ing and fro-ing on fixed lines. The three previous expeditions had approached this giant 9,000-foot face as they would a Himalayan climb, with reels of fixed line and big support teams.

The famous Italian mountaineer, Riccardo Cassin, put together the team that made the first ascent, and he called it one of his best climbs. Considering that he'd made numerous first ascents in the Alps, including the Walker Spur on the Grande Jorasses, this meant something to those of us who also sought to climb the route.

Al and I mentioned the route to Tut Braithwaite and Paul Moores, and when I showed them a photo, they were hooked. Their enthusiasm was best described by Tut: "Nine thousand vertical feet is higher than the Southwest Face on Everest, and we all thought that was big." He'd just returned from playing a major part in a successful expedition led by Bonington. That had been a large and complicated affair, and he looked forward to a more-climbing-less-planning type of trip.

For Paul Moores, it would be the highest mountain he'd ever been on, and for us twins, it would about match the elevations we'd reached after Ali Rattna Tibba, on a quick foray to Indrasan. However, McKinley is much more massive and serious.

Tut phoned us at our dad's house and said: "Don Whillans asked me the other night if he could come along on the trip. I told him he'd have to ask you lads, as it's your trip."

Whillans was one of the most famous mountaineers in the world, and even though Tut said he'd "gone to seed" a bit, who were we to judge?

I replied to Tut: "He could go on the West Rib with other friends of ours. I think he might be a bit slow to climb with us four. Anyway, tell him to give us a call."

I hoped I hadn't sounded arrogant, but Tut had seemed to agree. Don's phone call came, and a day later so did he.

"Eh, lads, Don Whillans," he said. "Nice to meet ya." He had a heavy Lancashire accent with a flat tone to it.

As he stood in the low Victorian doorway, I could see that he wouldn't have to duck to get inside, but he might have to turn sideways. He was huge. No wonder he was such a formidable brawler. We'd read all there was to read on the man—and there

*Don Whillans*

was a lot. He was built like the wrestlers you see on TV, but shorter.

"Come on in! I'm the twins' dad, Geoff. Would you like a beer?"

To ask Don if he wants a free beer is like asking Don Juan if he wants a woman. I hoped dad was prepared to accept a severe trouncing of his home-brew stock. Dad was more excited than we were to have this great person in his house. I wondered what dad would say when Don sat on one of his chairs and broke it. After a couple of ales, which helped dissolve my nervousness, we settled down to business.

Don opened: "Ah get the feeling you boys think ah'm a bit outta shape for't Cassin route." He followed this with a steady quaff so his glass could be refilled. "An' ya might be right at that. What's this other job ya got in store for me?"

"The West Rib is a good-looking route," said Al, pointing to a photo. "Three of our friends are going to do that at the same time. You could join them."

"I'd be quite 'appy wi' that," said Don. "I like to get into the mountains still, even though I'm sorta retired." He patted his tummy with pride.

As the evening progressed, the open, good-natured person that was Don came across. He didn't have the reputed aggressive primadonna personality of his youth, but was a much mellowed individual who felt comfortable with himself in the wisdom of later years. (A quick calculation tells me he then was about my age now: forty-five. Gulp!)

Another evening when we were packing some gear to ship to Vancouver so we could save money, Don arrived to help down some beer and pack his own aluminum trunk. He came through the door with: "Are we packing or supping?" He knew dad would have the bottomless barrel ready and didn't want to disappoint him. Upstairs we opened his load to try to make it lighter.

"We have to fly it onto the glacier, Don," I said, sifting through his gear. "There's too much here. Do you really need this tin mirror? You won't be shaving will you?"

"Ah, lads," he breathed out gently. "This has been on every expedition with me. But I suppose I don't need it."

He slipped it into his pocket. The next time I saw it was on the glacier. Here was a man who could be sentimental and we, at twenty-eight years, could not see it.

We struggled and squeezed, pulled and pushed, and still the lid of the aluminum truck wouldn't shut. Don stood by, regally sipping his pint. I wonder now what he thought of us.

He took a step forward and said: "Ya need a bit of weight, lads." Double-entendre at its best. He stepped up onto the trunk, and it snapped to with the finality of an elephant stepping on a mouse. Don could always be counted on to come up with an answer to any problem, but he never came forward until perfect timing could add extra clout to his solution. It was uncanny.

Toward the end of May, Al, Binks and I flew to Vancouver to drive all our gear up the Alaskan Highway with John and Bob. I had a last-minute call from Doug Scott, who told me he'd just climbed a new route on the South Face of McKinley with Dougal Haston.

"We left the Cassin for you lads," he quipped.

It was hard to believe the sudden interest in McKinley. Most British climbers knew very little about the mountain, and here were two trips going to climb the south face within the space of weeks.

Doug continued: "While we were on the face, we left a tent at the bottom with some heavy camera lenses in it, and with all the snow-fall we lost the lot. Can you keep an eye open for it?"

"Yeah, sure. Have you got any tips you can give me about climbing on the mountain?"

"It was really cold, youth. Take an extra sweater."

We drove for a week up the gravel-and-mud road of the Alaskan Highway. It reminded me of the pictures I'd see on TV of big international car rallies. Enormous logging trucks heading south splattered layers of mud across our windshield. Each vehicle fought to keep wheels in the parallel ruts. We bounced and rolled on foam mattresses laid out in the back of the truck while the Canadian forests slid by. Finally we arrived in Anchorage and collected Paul, Tut and Don from the airport.

Halfway to the small village of Talkeetna, we stopped off at a bar to have a quick beer and stretch our legs. It was a rustic wooden building right out of the Wild West. After one beer, we were ready to continue our journey, but the barman had other ideas. He began ringing a large bell and shouting: "Happy Hour! Happy Hour!"

We looked at each other with guarded suspicion. They didn't do that in English pubs.

"Half price beer from now on!" he bellowed.

They certainly didn't do that in English pubs. We stayed. We probably stayed too long. Cowboy music wailed out, and we tapped our feet to the rhythm. We were all together and we were on our way to McKinley. All cares left behind in England—a long way away.

It was time to be on the road again. Someone scooped a string of bottles off the bar as we left and the party continued in the truck.

"Hey, turn up the sound," someone shouted.

"Don't hog the whiskey," said another.

Thank goodness England was a long way away.

All gear was loaded aboard two single-engine Cessnas, and we climbed aboard, dressed in heavy boots and pile clothing. Don was the only exception. He was dressed in his city clothes: cotton shirt, flannel pants and suede shoes. He had a sleeping bag tucked under one arm, and he looked like a commuter who'd lost his briefcase. Later he would step out onto the expansive Kahiltna Glacier at 7,000 feet dressed exactly like he was.

Over the next few days, we began to ferry loads up toward the mountain. There were climbers bustling about everywhere, most heading up the normal route of the West Buttress. While they chose to rise at dawn and carry their equipment in the heat of the day, we decided the cool of the Alaskan night was the best time. The snow then was iron-hard, and we could escape the painful frying effects of the sun.

The first time I saw the south face with the dramatic sweep of the Cassin Spur in highlighted detail, it looked enormous. The mountain appeared to float overhead, despite being a long day's walk away. We could easily make out the large hanging snowfield, the two rock bands and the final buttresses of rock interspersed with snow.

" 'Ave ya 'eard them lot over there? They're sayin' prayers," said Don.

He pointed to a group of elderly Americans all sitting down to eat dinner together. They were trying to be the oldest group ever to climb the mountain, and I'd seen them looking askance at Don as he strolled about, dressed only in a transparently thin one-piece silk suit, his Lancashire manhood plainly visible.

Our external-frame tents were very strong but somewhat cramped for glacial living. Paul, who was six inches taller than the rest of us, complained about being wedged tightly inside.

Tut, on the other hand, quoted Monty Python: "Luxury! When I grew up, we used to live in a shoe box."

From then on, whenever someone complained there would be a roaring chorus: "Luxury! When I was a lad . . . ."

After a few days we moved up into the branch of the Kahiltna below our respective climb. We selected a small site beneath a stable-looking ice-cliff that backed onto a deep crevasse. Though we were still an hour from the beginning of the climb, we were adequately protected from avalanches coming off the face.

No sooner had we erected the tents than thin veils of high cirrus swept across the sun. The sky was filled with circular rainbows, and a long, thin plume bannered the summit. Things looked bad. By morning it was snowing heavily.

A day passed and we became restless. It was hot and stifling inside the tents. Outside, visibility was down to a few hundred yards. Al and I decided to build an igloo so we could cook more comfortably and all be together.

"You know how to build one?" I asked Al, suspecting he didn't.

"I once read in a book . . . ," he began.

"Luxury!" The others were listening.

An Eskimo would have been ashamed, but a Plains Indian would have been proud, because our igloo looked like a teepee. Nevertheless, it served its purpose well.

In the late afternoon of the third day, a low growl rumbled down out of the mist. A gigantic mass of snow began to pour down the southwest face, left of our route. It billowed out and rolled over itself in its urgency to expand. Down it came, past the base of the Japanese Couloir and onto the glacier a mile away. We watched and still it came on, unstoppable. Then we were scrambling, with half-laced boots, towards the igloo. A hissing, swishing sound filled the air outside as four inches of powder plastered tents and igloo. The crevasse behind camp swallowed most of it.

Once the air cleared, we searched the base of the route for the tent belonging to some Americans we knew were there. Surely they'd been swept away. Even the vacuum created by such an avalanche would have been enough to pull the tent from its platform. No, it was still there, and small black dots were moving around outside it. The Americans later told us they were terrified and just lay there waiting to be annihilated. Although I've since seen many immense avalanches in the Himalaya, they never cease to stir up a feeling of overwhelming power and helplessness deep down in the pit of the stomach. They are the one thing that puts the size of a mountain into perspective.

It doesn't take many days of being confined in a tent before a certain lethargy sets in. Mealtimes were the only thing by which to measure the passage of time. Between them, we'd lie comatose, or occasionally we'd read for a while. I'd already finished Al's *Carpetbaggers,* and my book, *Demian* by Herman Hesse, was far too heavy reading for the circumstances.

"Trying to be too intellectual, youth," teased Al. "Good ol' sex and adventure is what you need up here."

What we *really* needed was good weather. During the afternoon of the fifth day, the cloud that had blended rock-buttress into snow-slope and ice-cliff into crevasse  began to dissolve. Stray snowflakes twirled into sparkling diamonds against a backdrop of hazy blue. It could be the break we'd been waiting for.

"Let's put eight days' food together, just in case," someone suggested. We crawled from the tents and stretched our bed-sore limbs. The temperature had dropped, an encouraging sign. On a stamped-out platform we laid out our precious packages, and the decision-making began. How much soup? How many chocolate bars? Each of our two teams made up its own bag and then compared it to the other's. We didn't want one team to have too much while the other had too little. That would have created a difference in speed between us, with the lighter load moving faster. Conversely, we didn't want anyone going too light and then having to rely on the others to feed them if we got caught in a storm.

It was the 21st of June 1976, pre-dawn and cold, very cold. The Alaskan sky held a glimmer of light. We ate some granola with hot milk and then began to dimantle the tents. Carefully, but with numb fingers, we packed everything we'd need into our packs and tested the weights carefully. Al and I had an agreement. We'd each test both our packs a number of times and then agree on the heaviest. Some weight would be unloaded into the other, and we'd continue testing until we agreed they were similar.

I put the finishing touches to my overboots and crampons and said to Tut: "Are you lads almost ready?" They were.

A clip of ice-pitons swung from the outside of my pack. I took them, screwed the clip into the ice-cliff and said to Al: "We don't need these 'cause everything will be snow." He agreed.

At that moment, a thought hit me, but I quickly buried it. If we disappeared on the mountain, those screws would be the last hint of where we'd gone.

An hour later we'd crossed the glistening white carpet of the upper Kahiltna, woven our way between chunks of avalanche debris and arrived at the base of the route. The Japanese Couloir swept up-wards for 1,500 feet to the crest of the ridge. Steep rocky walls hemmed in a sheet of ice like some great ravine pitched up at an angle of fifty-five degrees. A yellow trail of rope disappeared upwards: the Americans' rope.

"Do you think it'll be safe enough to use?" I asked, thinking how much time it would save if we could use it.

"It should be, but as we don't know who they are, be careful," answered someone as I put a hand on it. I decided to use my axe as well. I rammed into the snow and it felt solid.

I was glad we were finally getting to grips with the climb. Sitting and looking from a distance at a mountain as big as McKinley tends to undermine confidence and determination. There are too many "What ifs . . .?" to comprehend. Action has its own way of clearing the mind.

As I climbed, I thought of how strong our team really was. Tut was without question one of the best British alpinists ever. Because he didn't write in the magazines, his name was never in the spotlight like some, but every year he'd add another dozen big alpine climbs to his experience. On Everest it was he and Escourt who broke through the crux rock-band. We'd known him for almost a decade—since we were kids, in fact. He'd often show up at the same crag where we were, and he'd climb some desperate route. In the Alps, too, he'd nearly always be around. The previous year we'd done some routes together and the final one—the Eckpfieler's Bonatti-Zappelli, along with Alex MacIntyre—showed just how confident he was on steep ice.

My thoughts were broken by the arrival of a small col and a heart-stopping drop-off on the far side. I'd reached the ridge. Above, the crest of the snow ridge continued after a short rock step. After my breathing became normal again, I continued up.

I'd known Paul Moores for a shorter time but had climbed with him more than with Tut. He was now twenty-four and worked as chief instructor at an army climbing center near Glencoe in Scotland. His boyish face belied what a crazy devil he could sometimes be. Just before he came on the trip, he married an attractive girl from Somerset; Roz would have to possess the patience of an angel. Rumor had it that the night before his wedding he was seen swinging naked from the signboard of a cozy rural inn,"The Singing Cock." Because of his tall broad build, he found rock gymnastics less interesting than long runouts with his weight on his feet. His ice-climbing skills were superb.

I looked down now and could see my friends climbing steadily up. Everyone looked solid and confident. The ridge above was easing, and I was tempted to rush to see more new ground. Then the day was suddenly over. A huge flat shoulder of snow the size of a tennis court came into view. I looked at my watch. I'd been climbing for four hours. I stepped up toward two yellow tents, and an American accent greeted me: "Hi! How many are you?"

"Four. They'll be here in a minute," I panted. I dumped my pack in the snow, sat on it and tried not to look too tired in front of those strangers.

"I dropped my camera," a tall blond guy said. "Did you see it? It was a Leica."

"No, but I wasn't looking," I replied. "Sorry, mate."

Al arrived and I broke off the conversation to go and get a shovel from him to begin the tent platform. He handed me the stove at the same time, and its loud roar made a comforting sound while we worked on the ledge. We were thirsty and knew it was important to drink a lot to offset our day's work.

The afternoon passed lazily with us lying on top of our sleeping bags. There was the occasional banter with the others, but we were too involved in tending to our nutritional needs to think of much else.

We didn't spend much time with the American team. It was years later, when I was living in Boulder, Colorado, that I came across two of that team's members, Brad and Dick, and learned what strong climbers they were. Later we climbed together in the Himalaya.

By six the next morning, we were on our way up the Cassin Icefield. Once again the cold was so intense that my feet began to go numb almost immediately. I kept wiggling my toes, but they were becoming painful. I was forced to stop in the middle of the slope and loosen my boots. To do this I needed to take off my heavy outer mitts, and suddenly my fingers were numb, too. Panic surged through me as I zipped up the neoprene overboot and rammed my hands under my armpits. "I feel sick," I murmured. Vomit rose in my throat, and I fought to keep it back.

The others had begun to traverse to the right and a steep rock corner. It was time to put on a rope. The rock was of a good-quality granite with solid cracks. In the angle of the corner, a generous smear of ice caked everything. The best way to climb it with a heavy pack was to stem across the corner with the hands while crampons teetered in the ice. Tut made it look quite easy, but I wasn't fooled. He had a way of making every difficulty work with and for him, like a tai-chi master. It was every bit as hard as I'd expected. We were engrossed in the so-called First Rock Step.

A small, awkward chimney had to be exited on its right wall, and we were back on snow. The sun had come around enough to warm up my blue nylon suit. Without warning, a drifting patch of cloud homed in on us and the occasional snowflake fell. In the mist above me, I could see dark shapes moving around, looking for the tent platforms we'd read about. Beyond them was an immense formless bulk, which had to be the Second Rock Barrier.

"What's that like up there?" Al yelled to Tut, who was balancing around with tent poles in hand.

"I think it's big enough for the tent," replied Tut. "If I put it up, I'm hoping Paul will sleep on the outside."

"Luxury!" whooped Al. "When I was a lad, I slept in the bottom of a pool."

Al and I made a similar platform ten feet below them. It was precarious work with a big, black drop-off to the right and a grey drop below us. We were at a height of about 16,000 feet. More than half of the face was beneath us.

Once in the tent, angry devils began to kick at the back of my brain. I lay and waited for them to stop. But they were having too much fun, so they continued.

"Do you think I might have edema?" I groaned to Al, who was busy making soup. "I've never had a headache this bad, ever."

"Don't worry, lad. It'll go. It's just the hard work today. You take it easy and I'll do the cooking."

Thank goodness I could rely on Al to take care of everything while I lay there feeling like death. All afternoon I lay still, half in and half out of sleep. Sometimes my daydreams would become sleep-dreams, but I always had tightness across the forehead. The fear that I might be dying haunted me.

Specifically, I was afraid of cerebral edema (or *oedema*, as we learned to spell it in England). Edema is a frightening condition, an abnormal accumulation of fluid in body tissues. In pulmonary edema, the air sacs of the lungs become waterlogged; the result is drowning. Cerebral edema is excess fluid in the brain; it can be lethal.

A thought would come to mind, and my brain would begin to spin it around and twist it into something else until I no longer knew what I thought. Al cared for me and forced me to eat and drink.

The next morning was a bad one. The headache was still there, and it was snowing, too. We decided to stay where we were rather than flounder around in the snow. I was relieved I'd get a chance to recover. By mid-afternoon I felt better and thrust my head out into the crisp air. Disintegrating clouds swirled around the rocks, and behind there was a hint of blue.

"Tomorrow should be good," I called up to the others.

"Just as well," Paul called down, " 'cause Tut's farts are stinking us out up here."

"Luxury! When I was a lad, we didn't have freeze-dried foods."

The storm passed, leaving an inch or more of powder on all the rocks. When we began to climb, the buttress above our heads looked dark and uninviting, and icicles hung from every small overhang. By traversing a rope-length to the left, we found that a hidden rocky corner sliced though most of it. The holds sloped outward and down; crampons grated on stone; lungs gasped at the fresh morning air. At the top, I stopped to take a photo of Tut. He had a big smile and was obviously enjoying himself.

"How's the head this morning?" he inquired as he moved alongside me.

I told him I was fine.

"I don't get them these days," he said, "unless I drink too much wine." He grinned. Having him around was comforting.

Paul and Al came past and relieved us of trail-breaking, and I cruised in their steps.

Paul appeared to be going strong, plugging away relentlessly. He climbed almost every day while working for the army as a civilian. When I asked him about this, he smiled and said: "I used to be in the army as a boy-soldier but had to leave when we were caught with someone else's Mini-Cooper in the middle of a plowed field."

I never did learn the full details, but I knew he liked to drive fast cars. Over the years I've watched his cars go from hot VW's through various souped-up Fords to a Cosworth—a formula-one racing engine placed in a fairly standard-looking body.

The snow-slope continued for at least another 300 feet, and then the angle began to ease back and we all stopped beneath a small outcropping of rock. I dumped my pack heavily into the snow and turned to the others.

"I've still got a mass of food in my 'sac," I said, "and I don't want to haul it all the way up the hill if we don't need it. I think we could unload stuff here."

Everyone agreed. While we went through our packs, a brew was put on the stove. A hopeful enthusiasm radiated through our idle chatter. If the weather stayed good, we could hope to finish the climb by the end of the next day. We were so far up the climb that to descend was almost unthinkable, and by dropping off excess food, we were making a strong statement of commitment to the summit.

Off to the southwest, Mount Foraker rose from a sea of cloud, an icy island floating and shimmering in the sun. We were already higher than its summit. That knowledge kept us pressing forward.

A big open snow-slope rose up to our right. This was our route. At first we climbed without ropes, but with all the fresh snow around, we became cautious of possible avalanches and decided to tie in. After a thousand feet, we found ourselves on the edge of a huge couloir: the one that Doug Scott and Dougal Haston had climbed. It looked straightforward, but if it were ever to avalanche, it would be a monstrous one. Climbing its left side was a little steeper as we headed for some rocks and ultimately the ridge.

I shivered as I huddled in cold, blue-edged shadows. We all agreed that there were possible tent platforms tucked into the lee of the ridge, but they were covered in hard blue ice.

"Time to start hacking," said Al, voicing our thoughts.

At 17,000 feet, it was hard work, but a good night's rest was worth it. Everyone worked hard, chopping and whacking with axes blazing. An hour later, the MSR stove was roaring out its happy tune, and we lay resting and dreaming of the summit.

This time it was Al who complained of headaches, and it was I who tried to convince him they would pass, though I had no reason to believe this. If any of our group became sick at such a critical point, we were in serious trouble. Maybe we should have spent more time acclimatizing on the normal route. Nowadays that's what people do, and it's probably stopped a lot of epics from developing.

Throughout the night, Al's groans kept me awake. He told me the pain was so excruciating he could hardly see. By dawn he had drifted off into a more comfortable sleep, and when I looked out of the tent, I knew we weren't going anywhere. A strong gale blasted the ridge above, swirling snow about the tents. If it persisted for many days, we were in trouble, what with all our extra food a thousand feet lower. On the other hand, it would give Al a chance to recover.

"I feel hungry again, kid," Al finally said. "Most of the pain's gone." His face had perked up a hundred percent.

"That's great, lad," I replied, "but we'd better eat carefully, in case this storm persists."

Although there was a lot of wind, not much fresh snow fell, and this led us to hope the storm would be short-lived. By late afternoon the sky began to clear.

Tut shouted across to us: "We should eat something and then begin to get ready to move. It never gets totally dark and we can climb through the night. How's Al?"

"Al's okay again," I yelled back. "Just a few more brain cells down the drain. We can be ready by seven."

I set off first, dressed in all my clothes, plus a down jacket and pants. Rime clung to the rock like sequins on a ballroom gown. Once on the ridge, the first part was almost hiking around a few pinnacles with heavy, drifted snow. Climbing unroped, I moved out left onto steeper ground, trying to avoid the hard labor of trail-breaking.

WHOOMPH! An avalanche triggered under my feet, and I leapt back, startled. Tut found me wide-eyed and shaken.

"Bloody hell, man!" he said. "See that slab that's cut loose? I was just on it!"

We roped up. I felt strong and continued plugging a trail with Tut moving up easily behind me. Paul and Al were roped and following in the rear. After two hours, the ground began to steepen and the route wove through rocks. We decided to stop and make a drink. The stove purred, and we each sat facing out and down into the dusk. The isolation was supreme but we all felt the closeness of the summit.

I dumped some orange powder into tepid water—too much I discovered when I took a sip—and passed it around. No one else seemed to notice how acid it tasted, but I began to feel very strange. Then, suddenly, I almost vomited. I stood hunched, arms hugging my stomach, trying to belch but I couldn't. My legs turned weak and I had to sit back in the snow. All my energy seemed to have left me. I was numb with disbelief. How could it happen so quickly? Could I make the summit at all?

Al tied on with Tut, and they began again. Rope-length followed rope-length, while Paul and I trailed more slowly. He had begun to tire, too, but forced himself forwards; years of climbing experience took over to enable him to survive. Climbing in the half-light, bone-weary from altitude and the long night, my mind drifted in and out of a dream-like state. Nothing seemed harsh any more, and the only reality were the boot prints left by Al and Tut. I sat with my back against a rock pinnacle while hauling in the rope to Paul. For the first time that night, I felt comfortable and just a little sleepy. Paul arrived and slumped down with a thud. I shook my head to drive away the fatigue.

"Must keep going, lad," I croaked and set off again.

The rocks lay wrapped in soft shadows with silvery tongues of snow linking the route together. A short snow-filled gully had steps disappearing upwards. I sensed the top was near. Excitement rose in me, and I began to move more quickly. I felt the rope to Paul come tight. I'd forgotten about him. I waited. Then we climbed together into a bright but heatless sun.

Tut and Al were already there, grinning and with rime and snot frozen in their beards.

"How you feeling, boys?" Al asked.

"Good, now we're up," I said. "Where's the top?"

The main summit was a few minutes higher, but the snow was crisp and firm—easy climbing. We reached the summit at 5:30 a.m. Lying in the snow was the frozen body of a sparrow. Someone had

*Tut, Paul and Adrian on the summit of McKinley*

carried it and placed it on the highest tip. It served as both an offering and a warning: "Nothing can live up here!"

We turned and headed down. Though tired, we found descending easy after our long night of uphill struggle. The further we descended, the thicker the air became and the faster we could move. At Denali Pass, we walked into an expedition's high camp where people were milling around, watching our progress.

Someone came forward with questions: "Where've you come from? What route have you done?"

"The Cassin. Finished it this morning." Our pride must have been unmistakable.

Someone brought a drink forward for us to share. They were nice people, but we were not yet ready to give up on our tight-knit team. Feeling overwhelmed by the size of their group, we prefered to leave and pretend we still had the mountain to ourselves.

However, that concept was  shattered as we continued. Other climbers were struggling up the slope to the pass. Small circular, red sleds swung from their waists, each with a pack strapped to them.

"They don't even follow the trail you break," said Tut, staring with disbelief at the fiasco being enacted. "It'd drive me crazy having one of them swinging around,"

We were back in the land of conformity without question. Our climb was definitely over.

That afternoon we walked into our old camp at the junction of the Kahiltna Glacier. We'd already descended 11,000 feet. The air tasted thick and warm, and each of us slept well into the next morning.

A day later we were lounging in the sun back at the airstrip. Don's group hadn't returned, but we decided to wait for them in case there were any problems.

"Are you waiting for your friends?" asked a tall, friendly American. "I saw them coming down yesterday. One's a short fat man, right?"

"I wouldn't let him hear you say that, old pal," I said. "That's Don Whillans."

The guy's jaw sagged and he returned to his tent.

Later, "a short fat man" came into view. His opening comment was typical: "Aay! They let anybody into the mountains nowadays!"

He was grinning broadly. It was great to see him. Later the others arrived, and we sat around, steadily circulating a bottle of Scotch. Don sat on a wooden crate with his short legs swinging and a broken ski held vertically in his right hand.

A young Japanese woman came hesitantly to our laughing group, holding a familiar Whillans' Harness in one hand.

"Excuse me, please," she stuttered and blushed as all eyes turned to her. "Is Mr. Whillans here, please? He make autograph, please?"

Don grinned, took her pen and said: "You 'ave good taste, lass." We all roared. She looked both alarmed and proud.

Suddenly a crashing roar boomed across the glacier from Mount Hunter. Everyone turned to watch as a giant avalanche swept the steep face. White clouds swelled and rolled across the ice.

Don's voice broke the spell: "Ay, we'll just let that one through." He pushed the broken ski forward as if it were an avalanche-release control lever. I thought: That Japanese woman may just kiss his feet!

Not long after that, the Cessna picked us up. Later when it finally rolled to a halt on the dirt strip, we jumped out, dragging packs as we went. Everything was piled in a heap, and we barely broke stride before heading to the Talkeetna Hotel for a beer.

Too many beers.

A day later we were in court.

# CHAPTER
## *11*

## FITZROY

BY ADRIAN

Construction work in Calgary slowed down with the first winter snows. It was reason enough to pack in the grueling work that had consumed me for the past ten weeks. By working under the name of "Mike," I'd managed to save up quite a stash of dollars, but even the climbing friends I worked with had begun to call me Mike all the time, and I was beginning to feel like two persons.

My French girlfriend, Christine, was working in a local restaurant and she, too, was winding up her job and preparing for our next adventure to South America. Al and Daphne were in similar circumstances in the nearby town of Canmore. Soon they came staggering through our doorway, loaded with climbing and camping gear.

"We're all ready to go then—travelers' checks, passports and all this bloody lot," said Al, letting the equipment crash to the floor. "So what time does this Greyhound bus leave then?"

"Eight tomorrow morning," I told him. I'd asked my dad to buy four one-week "Runaround" tickets in England at the modest price of seventy dollars each. That gave us time to travel to Miami to take a flight to Buenos Aires.

Five days later we were seated aboard a Pan Am jet, exhausted.

"Some trip, that," said Al, "and I reckon we spent as much on food as we did on the bus ticket."

"Yeah, four days and four nights is a quick way to see a lot of America," I responded. "I think we should fly back."

The rest of our group was awaiting us at the home of Argentinian climber, Hector Vietes. Alan Rouse was climbing with Rab Carrington, and Sue Carrington accompanied them. Brian Hall was teamed up with John Whittle, and then there were the four of us. We were not a structured expedition, just a group of friends climbing whatever took our fancy.

Rouse characterized the group: "We can call it the 'Climbers, Wives and Girlfriends Expedition,' and those climbers that don't have either needn't look too long around here."

In the two days we stayed in B.A., as we now called it, we saw little of the everyday kind of person. Rather, we met climbers and friends of Hector who spoke English and were very hospitable to us. There was a feeling of "nakedness" about not being able to communicate with people in their own language. Christine, a linguistics wizard, tried to teach me the rudiments.

"*Es muy caliente*—it's very 'ot," she taught me in her best English, twisted by my own Yorkshire accent.

"Couldn't I just wipe me brow?" I asked. I wasn't a very good pupil.

"What about *tengo sed*—I'm thirsty," she countered. She had a French accent, but barely.

"Couldn't I just say *cerveza*?"

"Aid! It's just as well mountains don't talk."

"*Speak*," I corrected her smugly.

We flew to Rio Gallegos on an Aerolinas Argentinas jet. Judging by its forty-five-degree approach to the ground, it was piloted by a retired air-force warrior. I thought we were going to be killed before we even reached Fitzroy.

"Don't worry, Aid," said Rouse, who had noticed my pallor. "They come in so steep because of the strong winds. Didn't you ever read any of St. Exupery's books about flying mail to Chile? They took off, flew west for four hours and landed farther east than when they began."

"Pretty windy," said Al.

"Al's good at logic," said Daphne, rolling her eyes.

Once on the ground, we all loaded our huge packs into various taxis and set off for "downtown" Rio Gallegos to meet one of Hector's friends. Our cluster of taxis deposited us outside the man's locked home. As we sat on our bags, we could never have anticipated what happened next.

An army truck rolled around the corner, followed by a number of tightly packed military jeeps. The convoy screeched to a tire-searing halt, and camouflaged bodies spewed out onto the road. My mind moved quickly, but my body showed the relaxation of an innocent tourist.

"Just don't do anything fast," I hissed to anyone who cared to listen. "The bastards are carrying enough arms to blow us from here to B.A. and back again."

A machine gun mounted in the back of the truck swayed to and fro between the hands of an eighteen-year-old with an apparent IQ of eighty and testosterone level of 200 percent. We remained motionless, arms by our sides until rough hands turned us toward a nearby wall, raised our arms and spread our legs. We were searched for weapons and then asked us to open our bags.

"Fitzroy!" I said, holding up a rope. "*Andinistas*! Climbing!"

I looked like I was involving them in a game of charades. As the words sank home, they relaxed and lowered their gun barrels.

"*Ah, Andinistas*! *Fitzroy*!" And they left. Just like that.

"They all have to complete a training course in the Fitzroy Park and so know enough about climbing," explained Rab.

"Bloody hell!" said Al. "The lad who frisked me was trembling. I was scared his gun would go off by accident."

Complete with red bandana, Al could have been a stand-in for Che Guevara, if his hair was black. "I think they thought we were terrorists," he said.

After an overnight ride in the back of a construction truck, we arrived at our Fitzroy Park destination on the 24th of November. During the last few hours of the drive, we'd been served a brilliant view of the entire mountain range. Fitzroy stood out the tallest, like a giant shark's fin surrounded by the equally impressive pinnacles of Poincenot and Guillaumet. Off to the left was the Cerro Torre group. Here were some of the most famous mountains in the world, and we were to try to climb them. I felt dwarfed.

Then the days began to pass—too quickly and with no climbing. The weather would swing from blue skies to heavy snow within hours. Large lenticular clouds, looking like extraterrestrial battleships, drifted in from the west. Our camp in the trees was a small, cozy A-frame shelter made out of plastic sheet and logs; it was comfortable enough, but it soon became boring. We were slowly learning the need for great patience in Patagonian climbing.

Before we could get to the foot of Fitzroy, we had to ascend to Col Superior, a journey that could take anywhere between three and six hours, depending on whether the snow was frozen. Then came a couple of miles up a gently rising plateau to the base of a thousand-foot-high couloir. We found old fixed rope in the bed of the gully and rearranged it for our own use. It helped to speed up our ascent, but still the weather would change before we could get our teeth into the real climbing.

Soon it was six weeks after our arrival in the area, and we'd hardly had any opportunity to climb. Two South African climbers, Dave and Tony, arrived at our camp, intent on the same route. Spurred on by their enthusiasm, we were soon at the base of the difficult rock-climbing in appalling weather. While they sat in the open wrapped in a thin bivvy sheet, Al and I dug into the snow-slope like hyperactive terriers.

"Damn!" I cursed. "The snow is only five feet thick, and then it's hard ice."

"Cut sideways just beneath the surface," yelled Al, the wind whipping his words away as soon as they formed. I dug and scraped. Then Al took over until there was enough of a hole for us both to squeeze into. At least we were out of the gale. Methodically we hacked at the black-ice. If we could carve out a narrow shelf, there would be space for us to lie head-to-foot. To say it was claustrophobic would be an understatement. It was more like two people sharing the same coffin.

The morning of the 6th of January arrived without any respite from the weather. Strong winds blasted spindrift into a maelstrom of spinning white. At one point, Al went out to relieve himself and was gone about ten minutes. I was beginning to get worried when his frosted beard burst through the entrance hole.

"Phew! I'd lost the entrance," he said, wriggling back into the womb of the cave. "It's desperate out there. Can't see a thing. My eyelids are freezing together. There's no way we can descend now. It's too bad. The others must have left at first light."

Our second night passed with the knowledge that we had to force a way down the next day. We made some hot chocolate and stuffed our damp sleeping bags into our packs. The Great Escape was about to begin. Next, we roped up and set off down. We carefully retraced our steps to the top of the gully, stopping only to catch our breaths before launching off down the fixed ropes. Once on the plateau, our real problems began. The snow was so deep that we sank in up to our armpits. We were wallowing in the stuff, and visibility was down to about fifty feet.

"We'll have to swim through it!" Al groaned.

"Look, I've got a compass," I said, waving it in my hand like a gambler with an ace. "At least we can go in a straight line. I hate the thought of getting lost and having to swim more than we need to."

We set off, roped together, swimming and crawling along the surface like two turtles lost on the open sea. It would have been funny if our situation hadn't been so serious. All the crevasses were snowed over, and neither of us could have stopped a fall. After about three hours we finally recognized the shape of a black rock – one that was slightly above Col Superior. We'd made it! Three hours later we staggered into the campsite drenched to the skin.

That epic showed us the need for a good ice-cave, well supplied with food and fuel, at the base of the difficult sections. If we could base ourselves there instead of in the trees, we would save precious time and maybe be able to use the rare and desperately short periods of fine weather. Dave's friend returned home to South Africa, and as we found Dave's easy-going but focused attitude very attractive, we asked him to join us. Climbing as a threesome would be slightly slower, but we could often climb together and the added strength of three would offset the difference.

More than a month passed. Every morning we'd get up at 2 o'clock, go to the cook-shelter, make tea and check the weather. There would be no decisions made from the warmth of a sleeping bag, where it's easy to dismiss a chance through laziness. The routine was tedious, but it kept us directed toward the mountain.

What I did not see was the effect it was having on my relationship with Christine. She was always being put into second place by the mountain. It was always "Fitzroy, Fitzroy." I ought to have known better, but I was blinded by my desire to stand on Fitzroy's summit.

By the 22nd of February, we had dug a comfortable ice-cave near the coffin of our previous one. We'd also had a few near-successes. Twice we nearly reached the summit before being driven back by horrible weather.

Our food was almost finished, too. While I baked some fresh bread, ready for our next attempt, Al disappeared into the forest, brandishing a long knife. There were a number of flocks of half-wild sheep on a nearby hill, and Al was the Stone-Age carnivore. By late afternoon the bread was ready, and Al strode gleefully into camp.

"Bopped one on the head with a stone, then slit its throat. A pretty one, too," he added. Daphne's eyes narrowed.

During a brief clearing in the weather, we hauled the bread and roast mutton back up to the cave. Almost immediately the clouds closed in again. The famous Patagonian winds began, and we sealed up the entrance with blocks of ice. Even deep inside the snow, we could hear the persistent drone and howl of the gale, like a toothache that' always there, always nagging.

Our small barometer began to show the pressure sinking by one point per hour. We had learned to rely on barometric pressure as a sure sign of deteriorating or improving weather.

Al summed up our feelings, locked away inside the ice: "It's like being inside a bloody aircraft, trying to land in poor visibility. First we go up, then we go down."

It was like that for seven days. If we were in any danger, it was of getting bed sores. Then at my hundredth examination of the pressure gauge, I noticed a steady improvement.

"The pressure has gone up a couple of points in the last two hours," I reported. "That's the first time in a week. Maybe we'll soon get a chance."

The next morning confirmed my hopes. Every hour the pressure climbed another point. It was finally happening. We were going to get a chance to climb.

"Let's have a big breakfast and start getting ready," suggested Al. "We could climb up to that ledge below the big corner this afternoon and be in a position to reach the top tomorrow if the weather holds."

He was right. We had to create our own luck. To wait even a moment would diminish our chances.

I kicked out the blocks that sealed the cave entrance and peered out into the frigid air. Clouds still swirled all around the peaks, but there was a hint of blue in the west. We would be setting out before the weather was fine, but we had to trust our gut feelings.

By one in the afternoon, we were ready to begin the snow traverse across and up to Col Sylla. The route was first climbed by an American group, whose most famous member was Yvon Chouinard. They had employed aid-climbing skills learned in Yosemite to over-come some of the difficulties, and it had taken cunning route-finding to link it all together. This is, however, slower than free-climbing, and we reckoned from our previous attempts that we could climb it all without pulling on a single pin. The route had been climbed twice since the first; the mountain, eight times. The route is said to be one of the most exposed on Fitzroy. Winds blast across it laterally; there is no lee-side to hide in. This increases the "hunted feeling" once the weather turns foul.

Once on the col, we tied into the rope. My feet were freezing in my single-leather boots, and I danced around like a crazed punk to get the blood flowing. The weather was improving by the minute, but it was bitterly cold in the shade. We knew that by climbing upwards we'd reach the sun. A flake-crack curved overhead, breaking through an overhang rimed with hoar frost. Small delicate snow-flowers grew from the grey granite.

Al set off, half lie-backing, half jamming his way upward. He climbed quickly before his hands froze, but by the time he reached a ledge they were numb. We could hear his stifled cries as the blood returned. Next we traversed left across snowy ledges and into the sun. Life seemed suddenly brighter.

Above was one of the scariest leads of the climb. I'd led it first, and Al had, too, on the second attempt.

"Dave, how about you having a go this time?" I said.

"I think it's a bit drier than before," I added to make sure he couldn't refuse.

The pitch began as a corner with a smear of ice flowing down the inside. Where this petered out, the crack became blind and refused to accept even a pin. A little higher I'd discovered a hairline crack for a thin knife-blade pin. It was all there was to protect the bold moves ahead. The crack suddenly widened so much that it was too difficult to jam, necessitating some tricky lie-back motions before the shoulder, and then the whole body could be wedged inside. When I'd led it, there had been ice inside the crack, and my feet were in danger of skating off.

Dave climbed it well and with the precision that was to make him one of Canada's finest alpinists when he moved to Calgary years later. Al and I spent no time repeating his actions. We jumared the rope.

In order to maintain a rapid pace, the leader would climb on two ropes and then bring up the other two climbers simultaneously. By this means, we reached a small ledge tucked beneath an overhanging wall two hours before darkness. We knew we could reach the summit the next day if the weather held, and if it didn't, we wouldn't have as far to descend. While we made some soup and later some tea, I found myself casting anxious glances toward the icecap to look for any suspicious clouds or haze. There was none.

That night it felt much colder than I would have expected at the relatively modest height of 11,000 feet, but the air was still and we had warm sleeping bags. At the first hint of dawn, we began to organize our gear. Al made the first observation of the weather.

"You know," he said, "there's a slight hint of cloudy haze covering the sky. What do you think?"

"It's definitely going to change, but the pressure is steady," said I, the guardian of our weather station.

"We can begin climbing, and if it turns bad we can always turn around," added Dave.

We all agreed. That was the only logical decision. What was left unsaid was that we would push the attempt to the maximum before giving up. We were going for it!

Al stemmed and jammed his way up a steep corner, his movements fluid and fast.

"He's certainly in overdrive this morning," I said to Dave. "Let's get after him."

I looked at the sky and noticed that the cloud had increased, but said nothing. I wanted this climb!

We chased each other around to the left, and I was in the lead when I had to halt abruptly. Before me flared an iced-up crack requiring care and a good belay.

"Watch me carefully!" I yelled back to Al, and set off. Once the crack was beneath me, there was a steep wall with small, sharp edges. I tiptoed carefully, so full of concentration that I found myself enjoying the situation. Gone were the worries of weather and storm. I felt I was really living.

Soon we were on a ridge that had a number of towers either to traverse around or climb direct. The previous storm had blasted atmospheric ice onto the windward side, and it was like climbing through a garden of snow flowers. At the base of the last tower, I stood beneath an imposing corner with a crack in the back. It was fine climbing but steepened abruptly so that I was forced to climb out to the right and into a wide crack stuffed full of ice crystals.

"This is hard and unprotected!" I shouted down, knowing that if I fell, it would be a sixty-foot whipper.

"Go for it, kid! I've got ya!" yelled Al.

His confidence poured into me and I set off—jamming boots, scraping hands, wedging elbows: anything that would allow me to make progress. Halfway up, I realized I was not just fighting for the top but for my very existence. It was so strenuous and I was generating so much heat that I could scrape away ice crystals with bare hands and not feel the cold. Winded, I hauled myself over the top and set an anchor.

I was forced to pull on my jacket hood to protect me from the stinging wind. By the time the others stood with me side by side, we had to shout to make ourselves heard. We could see the summit, about five hundred feet up to our right. Very near. Almost teasing us.

Dave led out horizontally across an easy ridge, the rope drawn in a tight, humming arc. Should we be there? Should we begin the descent immediately while we still could? We answered the questions by quickly following Dave. There was still time—if we hurried. A short rappel led to snow-covered ledges and the beginning of the final climb over mixed rock and ice. Quickly strapping on crampons, we retied the rope and began climbing.

Our route information said the final slope took an hour. In our circumstances, that seemed an eternity, but we had to take the chance. A succession of snow patches linked together with steeper bits of hard bubble-ice made us earn our progress. The fear of an impending epic pumped adrenaline into our veins as we panted up the remaining feet.

Half an hour after donning crampons, we stood on the summit. To the west, the sky was as grey as a Manchester November morning.

We were on top of Fitzroy! At precisely the moment a Patagonian Roarer was about to begin!

"Let's get the hell outta here!" screamed Al. We began the descent without looking back.

As we raced down across the traverse of the towers and began the rappels, I began chuckling to myself. We had got away with it! We were going to get down! Looking back up to the ridge, I could see the wind whipping ice-crystals out into the atmosphere. It was chasing us down, but it wasn't going to win. We'd barely stolen the summit!

One rappel above the col, Dave leaned back to begin his descent. As he weighted the rope, I saw the knot begin to unravel in the thin cord sling. It popped, I grabbed. He stood there for one suspended moment, balanced between toppling backwards and rocking forwards. The moment seemed to go on and on. I held tight. He came back into the rock. We replaced the rogue sling and continued on down.

The wind roared through the narrow pass, funneled and compressed beyond its original power, but we were almost at the cave. The dragon had lost the chase. As darkness fell, I struck a match and lit a candle. The warm yellow glow flickered as it illuminated our temporary home. Outside the dragon roared, frustrated and hungry.

Standing among the wind-stunted trees back in camp, we looked up toward the mountain, but the storm had swallowed it. We had to spend two nights in the cave before we could escape down.

I was sick of the mountain, and I had something else on my mind. Christine had told me she was leaving. She'd had enough of waiting around for someone who barely seemed to acknowledge her presence. It seemed unreal, as though it were happening to someone else. In fact, as I thought about it more and more, it seemed as unreal as the summit itself. I had not meant to be unkind or obsessive, but I wasn't accustomed to failing to climb a route I had my mind on. And that had seemed a real possibility. I became very unhappy and begged her to stay with me, but she had already made up her mind.

Suddenly, the mountain and the summit seemed a waste. I'd wasted my time and squandered a relationship. The summit wasn't worth it. I wanted to turn back the clock, to be given a second chance. But it was too late. We all returned to Buenos Aires, and Christine said goodbye.

The delights of returning to a big city—with all its good food, wine and plentiful beer—were dimmed for me by Christine's departure. Hector was a generous and warmhearted man who instigated parties and outings to entertain us. The other four climbers had also had successes. Brian and John had made the first ascent of Cerro Stanhardt, and Rab and Rouse had made a new route on Poincenot. We all had reason to celebrate, and celebrate we did. Probably too much. Well, a lot anyway.

In Rouse I found the perfect "partner in crime." I was now single and so was he—if 10,000 miles of separation from a girlfriend could create that classification.

Buenos Aires is a city not unlike Paris. The middle classes are well-educated and elegant. There are classy restaurants, sidewalk cafes, hip discothèques and all kinds of clubs and music joints. Long-legged, narrow-waisted Latin women strolled the fashionable streets. Their high cheek-boned faces framed by jet black hair had Rouse and I gawking and stumbling in our tracks. He, the Cambridge graduate, could already speak some Spanish and seemed to pick it up as fast as I picked up burrs when hiking. He had access to the women's charms. I didn't. This would have to change.

For the first time in seven years, I sat at a table and studied. I set myself a target of committing ten words a day to memory. I seemed to remember, somewhere in a hazy past, that Christine had told me you could speak a Latin language if you knew three hundred words. But it was important to know which three hundred. I wished she was there to tell me. But then, remembering my motives, I shook my head with a sigh and bent to my studies. I would figure it out myself. I thought of the lines I would need, the questions I would ask. Then I practiced them all morning.

Come afternoon, I'd stroll the streets with Rouse, drink a couple of beers at a street cafe and generally try out any new words I'd recently learned. Slowly, the essentials were becoming fixed in my memory. What was it Christine had said? You need to forget a word twelve times before you can remember it. Well, I'm not sure the statistics were drawn up from a pool of thirty-year-old climbing bums, but I did forget them a lot—and somehow remembered them, after all.

My brother and Daphne had just returned from the nearby coastal resort of Mar del Plata. She was a sun worshiper, so Al had suggested a few days lying on a nice beach. As she came into the room, Daphne's petite frame didn't look any more tanned than when she left.

"You wouldn't believe it, Aid," she said, shaking her head. "It was bloody freezing! We sat in deck-chairs on the deserted beach, wrapped in down jackets while the wind blew sand in our faces. Nobody goes there at this time of year. It was like Blackpool in January. Al just sat there oblivious to it and read his book."

I laughed, remembering the time he took her out to dinner on her birthday. She dressed in a cocktail dress, and he made phone reservations. When they got there, they discovered the place was a dive with plastic-covered tables. But they sat there alone and ate dinner.

We'd been in Buenos Aires for a couple of weeks when a well-known Yosemite climber, Jim Bridwell, arrived at Hector's place. Though we'd met him briefly while in Fitzroy Park, we still had to get to know him. He was a few years older than I, with broad, muscular chest and huge biceps. It was his first real climbing trip away from Yosemite, so he was only just learning to orient himself outside of a place in which he was king.

He held up a letter from a Yosemite friend and said: "I can't believe what's happened up in the valley. The first time I leave, and everybody hits the jackpot."

He shook his head as he told me how back-country skiers had found a crashed light-aircraft packed with bales of marijuana. All his climbing friends suddenly took up skiing and carried out packs full of the stuff before the FBI could cordon off the wreck.

"I could be rich," he lamented. "Everybody has new cars and the latest sound systems, and I'm stuck down here."

Rouse and I said we had a treatment for his ills. We took him out on the town.

By this time, we'd struck up associations with a number of different women. There were daytime ones and nighttime ones, depending on their work and when they had free time. We were always free to roam the city in hedonistic fashion. Evening activities in the city always began much later than we were used to. Eating dinner at ten was not unusual, and then there were movies, discos and early-morning music dives to visit.

Jim fit in well with our lifestyle, being a party animal at heart. Never a day began without the first rays of dawn illuminating our return to Hector's home.

I remember one morning when we found ourselves locked out, standing on the deserted cobbled street with three amiable companions. We banged on the door but no one came.

**Twin on gritstone quarry climb,** *circa* **1963**

*ABOVE:* **Twins climbing on gritstone:** *circa* **1963**

✦ ✦ ✦ ✦

*BELOW:* **Holmfirth, Yorkshire—the twins' hometown.**

"Bugs" McKeith on "Ice Nine": 1974

*ABOVE:* **Alan and Bob Shaw near summit of Aiguille Verte.**

✧ ✧ ✧ ✧

*BELOW:* **West Face of Ali Rattna Tibba.**

**North Face of Le Triolet: the route the twins climbed in 1968.**

*ABOVE:* **Fitzroy and neighboring peaks.** *Photo by Marie-Christine Lacroix*

*BELOW:* **Huandoy Peaks seen from last bivouac on Huascaran Norte.**

**Traversing steep slope on Huascaran Norte.** *Photo by Brian Hall*

**Doug Scott on Les Droites after ascent of Northeast Spur.**

"What we going to do?" I said, looking at Jim.

One of the girls answered: "You are climbers, yes?"

She pointed at the high brick wall which had small edges and ripples built into it. It was like Jane telling Tarzan what to do.

Jim attacked the wall as if his manhood were at stake. I stared up at his diminishing figure and glanced nervously around. If a police car were to come around the corner, they'd probably shoot him first and ask questions later. I could imagine the headlines: "Famous American Climber Shot While Breaking into Buenos Aires Home as Friends Watch."

Six weeks after we returned from Patagonia, Rouse and I set off by train to catch up with the rest of our group, who had gone on ahead to Bolivia. We'd had a lot of fun, made a lot of friends and learned some Spanish. How could anyone say we'd wasted our time?

# *CHAPTER*
## *12*

# A 'STING' & HUASCARAN NORTE

BY ADRIAN

After the long journey from La Paz, it was refreshing to spend a few days wandering the streets of Lima. One afternoon a Dutch couple explained to Al and me how they had been the target of a money-changing con. We listened closely, to learn as much as possible so it wouldn't happen to us.

A Peruvian had approached them on the street and led them to a building where he said his boss would change the money. He took their dollars, walked into an office—and never reappeared.

"When we looked through the door," they said, "it was a fire escape!"

We sympathized with them: "Yes, the world is full of treachery."

Soon thereafter, a guy came up to us on the street: "You want to change money? I can give you the best price. Ninety-eight *soles* for one dollar."

I looked at Al. The price was too high to be real, and therefore it could be . . . .

"Yes," said Al quickly. I caught a knowing glance from him. The double-con was on.

Sure enough, the guy said he had to go tell his boss we were coming, and we arranged to meet him in one hour.

"I can't believe we're so lucky," laughed Al. "We'll go along with his tale right up to the last minute—and then we'll rob them! Ha! They'll probably be loaded from robbing all the other tourists."

I'd always wanted to pull a "sting" like this one, and we'd be teaching them a lesson, too—a nice piece of justification.

The guy showed up, presumably after warning his accomplice. He led us to an office building. Inside, a corridor was lined with green doors, and at the far end there was one more. He went to that one and knocked. A voice on the far side told him to enter.

Al and I looked at each other and gave a vigorous "thumbs-up." We were both trembling with excitement. It would be any moment now.

The guy returned to us and asked to see the hundred-dollar bill. We handed it to him. And then we quickly took it back. Each of us twisted one of his arms up his back and propelled him ahead of us through the door—just in case there was a knife awaiting us.

The accomplice looked horrified, with mouth and eyes wide open. But not for long. He took off up the fire escape with Al snapping at his heels. It was time to give a few lessons to the guy I held. He wriggled and squirmed but didn't dodge any of my blows. He was getting noisy—screaming, actually—and collapsed into a wailing heap at my feet. Al returned empty-handed.

"The bastard got away," he said, looking disappointed. "The fire-escape door locks from the other side."

Suddenly the corridor was full of people coming out of the other offices. All were shouting and looking at the crumpled, sobbing pile.

"This could get nasty," I whispered to Al. "Let me deal with it."

I moved forward to use my Spanish: *"Nosomos agentes especial por la proteccion de la gentes de Los Estados Unidos. Documentes por favor."* I told them we were American police agents!

That changed things quickly. I think it wasn't unusual to see long-haired agents working over somebody or other. We scanned their I.D. cards once we'd lined them up against the wall. Everything seemed to be in order, so we briskly walked away with the clicking heels of officialdom. Once out in the fresh air, we burst out laughing. We were free, but as Al summed up: "We didn't get the money!"

Dawn had just arrived as the public overnight bus from Lima rumbled down the main street of Huaraz. This tiny Andean town is one of the main bases for climbing in the Cordillera Blanca. In some ways, it's the Peruvian version of Chamonix. There were four of us: Al and Daphne, Brian Hall and I. We hauled our oversized luggage off the roof of the bus and headed for a five-story bulding a hundred yards away.

"The guy in Lima told us to find Pepe at the Hotel Barcelona," said Al, "and that's obviously it. He said it was the highest building in Huaraz."

It was the only building of its size left standing after a major earthquake ten years before. Pepe was its vivacious owner.

"Welcome! Welcome!" he said, smiling. "You want go to fifth floor? That is where all climbers go."

He led us up a steep, narrow stairway to a large, well-lit room with mattresses set out on the floor. It reminded me of the sleeping arrangements of alpine huts. We dumped our loads and turned to Pepe.

"Where can we get some breakfast?" we asked.

"I will show you," he replied cheerfully. "Come!"

From then on, he was our personal guide to Huaraz, its cafes and its night spots. I think he was rather bored with small- town life, so when foreigners arrived at his hotel, he reveled in giving them all his attentions.

One night he took us to a dimly-lit discothèque called Los Scorpios. After my eyes adjusted to the dark, I could see that we were the only gringos in the place. Most of the other occupants were local village girls, dressed in cotton skirts a mite too short and wearing rouge and lipstick a mite too red.

I turned to Brian and, with a grin, said: "Hey, man, I think he's brought us to the local whorehouse. What do you think?"

"I think Los Scorpios is a good name for this place," Brian replied. "God only knows what these girls are carrying."

"You wish to dance?" asked Pepe as he waved over a gaggle of hip-swaying señoritas. With a laugh that was maybe a touch too innocent, he added: "They know rock 'n' roll, salsa . . . . They know many things."

"I'll bet they do," I answered. "I think we'll just listen to the music for a while, have one drink and then maybe see what else the nightlife of Huaraz has to offer."

I looked over at Daphne who had hold of Al's hand. He wasn't going anywhere.

The climb we wished to attempt was on the North Face of Huascaran Norte, the lower of the twin summits of Huascaran. Still, it was 21,500 feet high, and we knew very little about it, except that Dave Cheesemond had suggested it as a worthy climb. Pepe took me to see a friend he thought might help. Sure enough, the man had a copy of the French climbing magazine *La Montagne*. In it was a description of the first ascent and some photographs.

As far as my limited French allowed, I understood that there had been only one ascent, in 1966. Robert Paragot had led a team of twelve top French alpinists to the face. They had seiged it with fixed rope and a lot of equipment. By systematically fixing rope on the entire route, they could ascend or descend at will, and after their success, they could escape the mountain by their way of ascent. One person had been killed during the descent, and that cast a shadow on one of the most difficult climbs in the Andes.

"I wonder why it hasn't been repeated?" asked Al.

"Probably because the style they used is now outdated, and no one has tried it alpine-style," explained Brian.

"We should do it," I said. It was the unanimous opinion.

Although we had all the necessary equipment, one thing was lacking: a stove. Our MSR stove had blocked up with soot from using unclean fuel in Bolivia. Al decided to clean it by cutting the fuel line— a butchering job because it ruined the stove. We finally obtained a small Primus stove that operated on kerosene and decided to make do with it. What a mistake! Epics, tragedies and disasters often begin well before the actual event, and although it's easy to learn by hindsight, we should have been learning from experience.

I cannot remember why we decided to take only four days' supply of food, but that was probably all we felt we could carry because we didn't have any special freeze-dried foods, just packets of soup from local shops.

Once everything was packed away in our 'sacs, we jumped aboard a truck that took us up the dirt road to Lake Llanganuco. We pitched our one tent in a peaceful meadow by the lake. Daphne had come with us, but would go no higher. A couple of hundred yards away, a large French expedition, led by the famous René Desmaison, was busy laying seige to the rock face of Huandoy Sur. They were a big group with many tents and all the trappings money could buy. We felt very small and insignificant by comparison, yet deep inside us there was a certain pride. We didn't need that glamour.

Next morning Al said his goodbyes to Daphne, and the three of us labored up grassy slopes and scree towards the North Face. We planned to spend a few days acclimatizing ourselves near the snow line before continuing.

It was three hours before dawn when we left a pleasant bivvy and climbed up onto a heavily crevassed glacier that protected access to the face itself. As we zigzagged around deep holes, our headlamp beams helped us avoid dropping into the crevasses. Suddenly we reached a dead end, where hundred-foot-high ice cliffs barred our way. My pack felt heavy, but worry weighed me down more.

"I hate wandering around, lost in shit like this," I said. "We must find a way soon."

By slowly backtracking, our headlamps throwing laser-like beams up into sinister overhangs, we saw a slight possibility. A buttress of snow leaned against part of the cliff and even though it was steep, it wasn't overhanging. Up we went, the increasing drop almost invisible because of the dark.

We broke through and escaped onto a flat snowfield with the huge face before us, though we could only see only the lower portion. Solving that first problem gave us a needed boost.

I knew that the sequence of difficulties on a climb is like walking down a corridor full of doors that are stiff and hard to open. You push and push and suddenly the door swings free, and you hurtle towards the next one with added momentum. Then it doesn't pay to look back because you instinctively know the door you just burst through has closed tighter than ever. Now we would have to push very hard.

As the sky began to lighten in the east, we dug into our packs for extra climbing gear. Brian led off up brittle, slaty rock that was thinly smeared with dabs of ice and covered in places by rotten snow. It looked steep and insecure, and Brian was making a lot of grunting noises. However, the rope paid out slowly, and no problem held him up for long. He'd been climbing on Scottish ice for many winters before coming here, and now his skill was paying off. When Al and I joined him, he was balanced safely on a small snow platform with his ice-axe as the sole belay.

Neither Al nor I had ever climbed with Brian before. We'd bouldered on the same problems during evening workout sessions and even lived in the same house, but we'd never tied onto the same rope. This didn't worry us in the least, though, because his reputation went before him. He'd climbed a number of important alpine routes in the middle of winter and was a close climbing friend of Al Rouse. All ample qualifications.

We were in a narrow ice-fluting with high walls that kept out any sun. I continued by kicking steps in snow for another rope-length and pushed in my axe as a belay. As we had only one snow-picket, we'd try to use it to strengthen the main belay, but often found that our anchors were mainly psychological.

Again, Brian led out toward the sunlit ridge above. The snow was deep and unstable. He would thrust his arms horizontally into the snow and then try to wriggle his feet higher, often sliding back down again. As a last resort, he took a small shovel and attacked the slope with vigor. Over an hour passed before we heared the familiar cry: "Come on up!"

He'd managed to dig a vertical trough up through the snow and had reached the first good belay of the climb. Some of our tension eased with this knowledge. The route continued along a narrow ridge crenelated by dark, rocky towers and caps of white snow. We climbed first to the right and then to the left, trying to avoid the most obvious difficulties until the light began to fade. We cleared two small rock ledges of snow and rubble and settled down for the night.

My throat felt like dry sandpaper from not drinking all day, and my shoulders ached from the heavy pack. Also the increase in altitude made my head buzz. I could see by the weary looks on my companions' faces that they felt about the same. Once we had the stove melting snow, we sat back and waited and waited. It was taking forever to turn the snow into liquid, let alone bring it to a boil. By the time we'd all had a drink of soup and tea, it was already eleven.

"If we don't get enough liquid tonight, it could be disastrous higher on the climb," said Al, stating what was on all our minds.

"Maybe we should just rest here tomorrow so we can re-hydrate," I suggested. "At least we wouldn't be in as much danger as having to do the same higher up."

So it was agreed. The next day we'd rest, drink and recover from our long first day.The whole of that rest day we sat around and melted water in the sun. We didn't need to use as much fuel because we'd found small dripping icicles off to one side of the ledges. However, we needed to conserve our food for the days ahead, so we ate sparingly.

"Good job I've got a bit of my 'spare tire' left," joked Brian, who sometimes carried extra weight in England but looked as fit as a butcher's dog. Both Al and I were quite skinny despite all the meals we'd put away in the cities. Even normally, we had a hard time putting on weight.

Day Three began as the first milky light of dawn filtered across the face. I tried to make light of our position and sang out: "Hi-ho, hi-ho, it's off to work we go . . . ."

First we climbed up onto a snow ridge and then followed that until it merged into the rock above. The friable brown rock was too steep to climb, so we moved diagonally up to the right beneath large icicles that were obviously going to crash down once the sun hit them. Al then led out right and up onto a steep ice-face. It was real climbing, like you'd find on a difficult alpine route. After a while, Al's shout drifted down to us to say he was safe. Up we went, one at a time, to join him on a tiny rock ledge.

"Good lead, lad," I panted. "Where the hell does it go now?"

"Up this shitty rock onto that ice and then up to that rock buttress."

It looked hard and, given the weight of our packs, strenuous, too. Brian offered to take the lead. I was glad because I was feeling light-headed and none too brave. He balanced up the horizontally seamed shale. Crampons grated and scraped as he inched upwards. He appeared to be having difficulty reaching solid ice, and there was no protection. Al and I stared at each other and then at the belay. The tension built.

"I don't know if this pin will hold a long fall," whispered Al so that Brian wouldn't be distracted. "It's okay to stop us falling off this ledge, but if he comes hurtling down . . . ." His words trailed off into the unspoken prospect of flying down the face. It was enough to make you want to vomit.

Then the pregnant silence was broken by the sound of steel on steel and the THUNK of an ice peg being driven. We relaxed and breathed again. Slowly, Brian made his way up the grey ice until he reached some reddish rock. He'd used up all the rope. He shouted down that he was securely tied on.

When it was my turn, I tiptoed up the rock toward the ice. It felt very insecure because I couldn't tell if my crampons were going to skate off the rock. Then, after a long, tantalizing reach, I planted an axe into solid ice with a heavy, swinging blow.

I've heard people describe ice-climbing as a "vertical dance." Images of ballet and neat, tiny steps come to mind. Well, when you're on grey stone-scared ice at an altitude of over 19,000 feet with a heavy pack increasing the gravitational pull, ice-climbing is nearer to a "vertical grunt." Calf muscles begin to scream "STOP!" and the effort of gasping and panting brings a myriad of stars into the corner of one's vision.

Although the climbing was physically stressful, it provided its own release. Watching did not. Watching gave you time to realize where you were, how big the climb was and what might happen if someone took a big fall. However, we slowly began to accept all the danger and let it melt into our consciousness so that we no longer worried about it.

When we were all together again, we still had time to consider what an airy place we were in. The ice dropped away over cliffs so that we could only see the glacier far below.

"We need to find somewhere to spend the night before too long," said Al, craning his neck to examine the cliffs above.

I couldn't see anything that resembled even the tiniest ledge. The route followed a steep ramp up and across an imposing shattered wall that had ice bulging out over it. After we moved a couple of more rope-lengths, the sun began to set. Brian waved towards a small ridge of snow off route and up to the right

"Not a palace," he said, "but maybe . . . ."

"We could probably squeeze onto that if we had to."

"We have no choice."

By digging and scraping at the snow, we widened it enough for two people, but it was tight. Al and I hunched gratefully onto it, though we could not straighten out our legs. Brian scratched around immediately below us and appeared comfortable, with his feet in his pack and sleeping bag up to his armpits.

"This bloody stove is no use at all," growled Al as he fought to increase the flame.

I wanted to say: "I know, but some stupid bugger busted the other one." In my fatigue, I looked for someone to blame.

Without a good stove, we were becoming dehydrated. This drained us of essential energy, so we climbed more slowly. That meant spending more nights on the wall and more dehydration. A dangerous cycle. The only answer was to climb up and out—escape. A descent was nigh impossible. We didn't have enough gear. Besides, many of the anchors were too bad for rappelling.

Al and I snapped at each other:

"Don't push me!"

"I'm not! It's you who's got more room!"

"Can't you stay still?"

"My legs are cramping!"

All night, we fought for a tiny piece more of the ledge. The fatigue was making us irritable. Tempers simmered. Yet we needed to remain a strong unit. Our very existence demanded it, but our animal instincts were rising almost beyond control.

A night of repressed anger gave way to a morning with very little joy. We left without even a drink. Al led.

"That was the shittiest night I've ever spent," I said to Brian. "We must find something better tonight, or I'll be totally buggered."

The climbing became absorbing from the start. We could see short stretches of very old white rope—left over from the first ascent— emerging and disappearing from beneath the ice. At least it showed we were on the correct route. After a number of pitches on horrible rock, a flinty bulge of overhanging stone, glued together with bluish-white ice, made us halt and take stock of our courage.

Al worked his way through the roofs and into a chimney above. It reminded me of the analogy I'd heard about climbing up a hundred-foot-high filing cabinet: "If anything pulls out, just slide it back in again."

We were climbing like automatons, with the sole thought of reaching a good ledge and making something to drink. Most of our conversations had dried up with the spittle in our mouths. A heavy fatigue hung over us, but we refused to give in to it. To do so would be the end of everything, for all of us. We each had a responsibility to the group. Ever so slowly we gained ground.

By early afternoon, the angle had eased back and small ledges could be seen up to the right: a perfect place to stop early and slake our raging thirsts. Every ledge was narrow but long enough for one person to lie down on. My ledge sloped outwards and was only two-and-a-half-feet wide. Some construction work was necessary. Meanwhile, Al sat patiently as he attended the malfunctioning stove.

"I've had better service from an Istanbul hooker," he snarled, holding the pot expectantly. At least we had all afternoon to melt some snow.

It was the first reasonable night I'd had on the climb, and though I can't say I felt fresh, I did offer to do some leading the following day. There were some chimneys and shallow gullies that helped us to gain height quickly. Al and Brian climbed together while seconding, and this also helped our speed.

We had been on the climb for five days and were beginning to feel the first pangs of serious hunger, so we did what all deprived people do: we made plans for the future.

"We can buy a roast chicken each when we get down," dreamed Al.

"Yes," I added, "and piles of chips in that greasy restaurant."

From then on, whenever things got tough we'd shout across acres of rock to each other: "Just think of the roast chicken!"

We'd been so absorbed with the climbing that when we found ourselves surrounded by mist, it startled us, like coming out of a day-dream. There was snow in the air, too. Could it be a change in the weather or just afternoon cloud? We hoped the latter, because a major storm would probably stop us from climbing. We'd be stuck on the wall. No place to go. The consequences were obvious.

Brian led off up into the cloud. It was a straightforward snow slope, and the rope ran out fast. We tied on another when it had all been used, so that he could climb three hundred feet before stopping. When we joined him, wet snow had begun to pile up on his pack.

"I think we should stop now before we get too wet," he ssaid, "because we can pitch the tent if we kick out a ledge here."

He was right. The slope steepened up above, and anyway we couldn't see where we were going. Dense clouds swirled, hiding everything around us and heightening our feeling of isolation.

Al crouched in a corner of our small tent, his jacket hood pulled over a woolen hat. He said: "I'm thinking about that roast chicken, lads, but it's not giving me any warmth."

I emptied out my small nylon food bag. There were two chocolate bars, some soup, a small bag of sugar and a few tea bags.

"That's all I've got left," I said. "What about you?"

They also were almost out, and we'd been on half-rations as it was. Stretched out in my thickly-quilted sleeping bag, I still felt cold as my body fought to maintain a critical level of heat. It was probably converting its last ounces of fat into energy. Outside, the sky began to clear as the day ended.

"Tomorrow should be fine," said Brian, poking his nose through a gap in the door.

With that knowledge, maybe I'd sleep a little easier.

In the morning, grey clouds still swirled around us as we packed up the tent and shouldered our packs.

"Maybe we'll reach the top today," I suggested, trying to bring our minds together for a common goal, even though I knew it wasn't really necessary. We all wanted to escape this face as soon as we could.

*Alan on Huascaran Norte*

Once more Brian led off into the mist, and by the time he reached a belay, he had been absorbed by the cloud. Another rope-length and still another took us to the base of some very steep, compact rock. We could no longer ascend. We looked around, peering through the mist for a solution. Ice slopes slipped away to left and right. It was eerie.

"Over there to the left," said Al, pointing at a narrow snow-band sandwiched between granite bluffs. "That's the beginning of the big traverse. We're a bit too high. You rappel down first, Aid."

Using one rope as a rappel and the other for safety I lowered myself down to the left.

"Man," I said, cringing, "if those ice screws come out we'll all be off, big-time."

I tried to make myself as light as possible. It wasn't as easy as it first appeared, because we needed to get to a point so far left it was more like a pendulum. After sixty feet, I set an ice- screw and, with my rope through a carabiner, I began to lean again, crampons set in hard ice to push me sideways. After repeating the maneuver with another screw, I reached the base of the sought-after snow-band.

"Come on down, and I'll pull you across," I shouted, "Please be careful!"

Before Al began the next pitch, I stared anxiously at our anchor of two screws. We were three people and three packs, all hanging from those screws like kids on a swing set. I shook my head to clear the image. This was no place for doubt. We were too close to the edge. At a small yet comfortable rock ledge, Al brought us across.

"I can see the way up over rock to the base of the final corner," he exclaimed. "We'll have to bivvy soon. Let's hope there's a ledge up there."

The rock glowed bright orange just before it abandoned us to the frigid night. Brian and I sat side by side with feet in packs to stop us slipping off the ledge. I looked up to Al who had fashioned himself an eagle's aerie.

"Are you comfortable up there, kid?" I asked.

"There's bloody water dripping onto me, and it's freezing as soon as it touches my jacket," he replied. "I can't believe it's doing this. When you've got some tea, can you pass some up to me?"

This was before Gore-Tex, and the thought of being drenched to the skin was unthinkable. I perched the stupid stove between Brian and me, with a single, large crystal holding its foot in place. I thought of how people always speak of roaring stoves and looked at our pathetic machine. The purr it made wouldn't even scare a tabby cat. I suppressed an angry urge to toss the thing down the mountain and be done with it. But the parallel to our own demise was too obvious.

It was a long night of constant sliding off and tensing back onto the sloping ledge. Maybe I occasionally dozed, but it was never anything significant. I tried thinking about a girl I'd met in Buenos Aires. What did she look like? Could I remember? Memories were clouded, and her face blended with others I'd known. Then I tried to remember the names of others I'd met during my life. It was my own way of "counting sheep," but it didn't put me to sleep. However, it did increase the will to escape the damned mountain and return to some real living.

Before dawn, we were stomping our feet to warm them, impatient to begin. The rock was immediately steep, but Al attacked it with vigor. The nature of the rock had changed and become more solid.

"Go for it, kid." I shouted up. "Think of the roast chicken."

He had begun to lie-back up a crack set in an open book-like corner. It looked impressive. Then he dissappeared from view. The rope paid out slowly.

"Come on!" echoed from above.

"It gets a bit easier now," Al reasured me, when I passed him to climb a series of snowy corners. I didn't share his optimism, because the cliff bulged out above our heads in a final grey bastion with a creamy white cap of ice draped over it.

A couple of rope-lengths later, the temperature suddenly dropped. Mist obscured the sun. Each of us dove into packs to find our down jackets. We had reached the "sting in the tail." It was as though the mountain needed us to reconfirm our commitment to life, our desire for freedom.

Al demonstrated his resolve by taking off his pack for the first time on the whole climb.

"I'll haul it after me," he said. "This is too overhanging."

First he stemmed, with arching back, up a bulging corner. A rusty pin beckoned to him tantalizingly. His outstretched arm waved a carabiner towards it, but he needed to raise his feet higher. His whole body hung suspended over the vast exposure of the entire face. Mist swirled like white dragons protecting the dark battlements of metamorphosed granite. They would not let him escape easily.

He clipped the pin. His cleated boot soles tiptoed up, stopped, shuffled about and stopped again. The rope moved out.

We heard an "Ahhh!" Silence. Then an alarmed voice: "The pin just dropped! Watch me!"

He'd pulled on an ancient pin that suddenly threatened to "ping" out. We could hear the ring of steel on steel as he replaced it. Then we heard: "Okay, I'm going to stand in it."

The tension built while I paid out the rope. A fall at this stage could result in an injury that would be difficult to deal with. We waited, shivering slightly as the wind picked up. The ring of more hammering told us he was up.

Brian and Al were on miniscule ledges when I joined them.

"You get the ice, Aid," directed Al, who had every reason to feel pleased with himself.

I studied the seventy feet of steep ice at their backs and moved gingerly towards it. Under normal alpine conditions, I would have front-pointed it without cutting a single step, but there was no way I could do it with my legs feeling as they did.

"I'll have to cut steps," I told them, "but I'll do it."

I swung the adze time after time. Small holds appeared, and I stood in them before repeating the exercise. For me, it was a final act of desperation to be rid of the wall once and for all. I gasped and I swung. Stepped and then gasped. Slowly the angle eased. Looking down on the others all I could see were two huddled figures. And beyond, mist.

Then it was easy. I could walk. The rope came tight, and I slumped in the snow. We were there! My head spun. I was in a daze. A small voice told me we would live.

When the others arrived, a slap on the shoulder and a hand-shake said it all: "We're up!"

When we finally reached the valley with the glow of success erasing many of the recent ordeals, Al and I were busy planning a harder and more difficult climb. We asked Brian to come with us, but he declined. He decided to return to England.

He reasoned: "You two just can't keep on doing harder and harder routes without something going wrong. Anyway, how could we better the climb we've just done ?"

# CHAPTER
## 13

## LOGAN: SOUTH BUTTRESS

BY ALAN

I said to my brother: "Hey, Aid, Lauchlan and Elzinga have asked me if I want to go to Logan. They want to try the route they failed on last year. Whaddya think?"

"Is that the same route that Dick Renshaw and his buddy tried the other year and failed on at some horrendous corner covered in ice?" responded Adrian. "It sounded hard. Who else is going, besides Lauchlan and Elzinga?"

"Ray Jotterand," I said. "He's the guy that did the Upper Weeping Wall ice, that new Grade-6—300 feet of vertical ice. He's obviously good, but I don't know how he is on alpine stuff."

We were both getting around to the same question: How strong and competent were the climbers who'd invited me? I'd climbed with

John Lauchlan when I first came to Canada five years earlier. He was then in his late teens, a talented young Canadian climber beginning to make a reputation for himself. We climbed a number of hard, long rock-climbs in the Bugaboos, culminating in an eight-hour ascent of the Beckey-Chouinard Pillar on the South Howser Tower—a climb that takes most people two days. In that type of technical climb, John was fast and competent. Since then, he'd done a number of hard alpine climbs with Jim Elzinga, his regular climbing partner.

Jim was a completely different kind of climber. While John was lightly built and very intense, Jim was well over six feet tall and weighed almost 200 pounds. John was a successful rock-gymnast; Jim, with huge legs and powerful shoulders, was built like a Swedish logger.

"They're very competitive," said Aid, "and I bet they'd like to burn you off if they could. Would you have to climb with Jotterand?"

He touched on my real doubts. Would we be climbing as two separate teams of two? Or would we operate as one team of four, helping each other conserve strength with one common goal?

"We'd have to work as a team," I said. "Otherwise, *no one* will climb it. It's more a matter of how much the competition would get in the way. I'd like to do a big climb. It feels like ages since I've stretched myself."

I knew Aid would have to stay behind and work in construction, and I knew he would be thinking of me every day as he pounded nails.

"Think carefully, lad," he concluded.

One problem weighing on me was leaving Daphne behind for a month. During the previous winter, we'd been through some rocky times. Having done little climbing, I'd been bored, and I'd been caught having an affair with a woman I cared little for. I had risked Daphne's and my relationship, more for the risk itself than anything else. I enjoyed living on the edge and had confused my rebellious attitude toward mountains with a feeling of being trapped. I had selfishly ignored Daphne's feelings and made our relationship a testing ground, rather than keeping those passions where they really belonged: in the mountains.

We had put our relationship back together, and I felt guilty at even thinking of going away for a while. But when Daphne encouraged me to go, I phoned Ray Jotterand and told him I was on. The team met in Lauchlan's house and pored over maps and photographs.

"This is where we got to last year," said John, pointing out locations on a photograph. "This band of rock is where I fell from and screwed up my ankle. It's lucky we had a radio with us. The chopper winched us off from this snow terrace."

"How do we get to the face?" I asked. "Do we fly into a glacier someplace or do we walk in?" As the team's latest addition, I was completely ignorant of the route.

I did know that Mount Logan was in the Yukon and was the highest peak in Canada. At 19,850 feet, it was nearly as high as Denali (McKinley) in Alaska, but being situated closer to the ocean, it had more ferocious weather. The 10,000-foot Southwest Face had been climbed only once by a route known as the Hummingbird Ridge. It had been climbed using siege tactics and fixed ropes: a style that allowed for a safe escape if anything went wrong.

What my teammates were suggesting was that we be set down at the foot of a face that had already repelled strong teams—with twelve days' food, no walkie-talkies and insufficient equipment to retreat down the face if we could not climb it. It was a bold plan, ten years ahead of its time for a face of this difficulty.

"We either fly by light plane to land on this flat glacier here," said John, as he pointed on a map spread on the table, "or we get a chopper to drop us off all the way up near the bergschrund, right under the face. If we have to climb up from the glacier to the face, there's some danger from avalanches. Last year we saw some big woofers come down and sweep across this bit here. We'll have to play it by ear."

On the far side of the mountain there was a high-altitude research station where John's girlfriend, Judy, was working. The plan was to have our skis dropped there by the light plane that supplied the place. After the climb, we'd ski the easier side of the mountain, down a glacier known as the King Trench Route, and then we'd be airlifted out by a small Cessna.

We discussed what food and equipment to take, opting for twelve days' supplies and the lightest gear we could muster. We would begin the ascent with fifty-pound packs; that would be heavy at first but would become lighter as we climbed higher. If the climb took longer than twelve days, we would be in serious trouble. We would not have sufficient technical hardware to rappel back down the face. The only way out would be over the summit and down to the research station.

At the beginning of May, we flew to Kluane Lake, a small town in the Yukon Territory, and set up a small camp to wait for the weather to clear. The mountain was eighty miles away and part of a weather system different from that at Kluane Lake. We had to wait until both places had clear weather before the plane or helicopter could ferry us to the mountain.

We camped on the edge of the lake and every morning checked with the Park Service for the weather forecast. Hanging around waiting for the weather to clear was hard on the nerves, creating tension in our small group.

"The weather looks better this morning," said John. "I think we should try to fly."

"Yeah, maybe we should just go," I agreed. "This waiting is getting to be a drag. I don't know how long I can hang around. I promised my wife I wouldn't be away for more than three weeks."

Ray was more nervous about the climb than he was prepared to say openly. He knew we had resources for only one attempt. If we flew to the peak and couldn't land, our money would be finished and with it our chances.

"But what's the point of getting to the face and not being able to climb?" I asked. "If the weather is marginal higher up, we would just waste our food supplies and blow our chances."

I was taking the role of the conservative partner in this debate, but I also thought that John was exploiting his role of pushy young hardman, liking the image but safe in the knowledge that I would veto any overenthusiastic, hare-brained decisions.

Jim was reflective and seemed to weigh the various arguments openly and honestly. He appeared older and more mature than I expected, balancing the different sides of our debate carefully before giving his opinion.

"I think everyone's points are well-made," he said. "We don't want to go too early and waste our attempt, but at some point we're going to have to take a chance. We'll never know for sure what the weather will do."

After we had waited ten days, the weather cleared at about eleven one morning. John returned from the charter office and said: "okay We're on our way! Let's get the gear together. What are you going to wear, Al? We'll be landing on the glacier."

"Full gear, I suppose: boots, windsuit, harness, the lot," I replied. "We don't know if there'll be crevasses when we climb out of the plane. We may have to rope up immediately. Remember that guy on the winter McKinley trip. He jumped out of the plane straight down a hole. Spoilt his day. Killed him."

We were cocky and full of optimism.

An hour later Jim and I were jammed into a light plane with big packs stored behind us. John and Ray were to follow by helicopter and get dropped off at the foot of the face. The chopper then would fly down to the main glacier where we would have landed and would take us up to join John and Ray. We were aware that the vagaries of weather could change our plans, and we made sure that we were never separated from our own personal gear and food. It would not be pleasant to spend nights out on the arctic tundra without tents, sleeping bags or food.

We had a feeling of emptiness as the chopper pulled away, the roar of its engines becoming fainter and fainter.

There we were: a group of four, surrounded by equipment and dwarfed by the huge South Wall of Logan rearing up behind us. The sudden decision to go after all the waiting, the scramble for the chopper and the instant loneliness: all accentuated our feelings of vulnerability.

It was hot. The snow basin acted as a huge reflector and turned the glacier into an oven. Above us, a wide couloir climbed more than a thousand feet, and we needed to move away from the danger of rockfall. Under packs that weighed more than fifty pounds, we labored up the lower slopes to some small snow ledges protected from above by rock cliffs.

We spent the early afternoon digging and leveling the ledges, putting up tents and melting snow to make tea and juice. We had hardly spoken of the face above, but as the afternoon cooled and the sun lowered over the ocean to the west, our minds turned to the climb.

"Tomorrow looks okay," I said to Jim. "Up the couloir, I suppose. But where do we go at the top of it? Can you see the rock corner from here?"

"There's a campsite out left at the top of this gully," he said. "We can either stay a little below the top, where there are bigger ledges, or go higher to the foot of the Renshaw Corner. That's the steep rock-and-ice corner that stopped the first team that tried it. You can't really see it from here, but you can see where we got to last year—above those ice cliffs way up higher. Tomorrow will be a long day. We should get some rest."

Sleeping at near-arctic latitudes in May is difficult. It barely gets dark. I pulled a headband over my eyes to simulate darkness and settled down to sleep. We were only at 9,000 feet, and my sleeping bag was far too hot. I sweated, tossing around uncomfortably. Excitement and trepidation made deep sleep impossible.

"Time to go, Ray," I said. "The snow's frozen hard. We need to move before the sun hits this gully."

I was stuffing equipment into my pack and looking upwards with that excited, nervous feeling I get of the unknown.

"Looks like we don't need the rope at first," said Ray, fixing his crampons to his double-leather mountaineering boots. "You can start if you like."

Mornings on a mountain have the same kind of chaos that most people experience on their way to work. Stumbling around with a coffee in one hand, trying not to forget anything. Fitting crampons onto boots. Stashing spare gloves in front pockets and a bar of candy in an inside pocket. Water-bottle filled for the day.

Starting slowly but aware of how fast everyone else was moving, I followed the line of steps. John was already ahead, kicking into the frozen surface, two kicks to a step, efficient and confident. Following a line of footholds is always less strenuous than making them, and we all caught up with John, moving in a silent line behind him. Later we switched leads, spelling one another. The couloir narrowed, steepened and then unfolded before us like the train of a bride's dress. We approached a narrowing area as the first golden streaks of light appeared overhead.

My pack was heavy, and I felt hot. Sweat cooling uncomfortably on my skin made me irritable. We were climbing a little too quickly for a climb that would take more than a week. Panting freely with legs that ached, I wondered how everyone else was feeling.

If I'd been with Aid, I'd have expressed my opinion: "Slow down, ya fucker! We'll burn ourselves out at this rate!"

But with this team, I did not have that closeness, and I held my tongue. Frustration was rising in me, as I grew aware of my own ego-driven image. These guys had been climbing ice all winter, while I had been pounding nails on a construction site. I felt they were probably more tuned and technically efficient than I was. In reality, we were all trying to establish ourselves within the group, to create our own niches of recognition. But a huge pack has an amazing ability to bring everyone's skills down to one common denominator: fatigue.

We arrived at a series of ledges in the upper reaches of the colouir and erected our tents. As we melted snow for juice, we could clearly see the Renshaw Corner, a shallow corner-crack leading for three hundred feet out of the upper right-hand side of the gully. It was coated in ice and powder snow, and I understood why other teams had great difficulty there.

"It's still early enough to fix a couple of ropes up on the corner if we want," I said. "Maybe Ray and I should go light, with only enough gear for the job. It'll give us a good start tomorrow."

The corner had quite a reputation, and I wanted to lead a few pitches, to climb with Ray and to establish myself as a technically competent team member.

Ray was enthusiastic: "Great! We can take two extra ropes to fix. It'll be good to climb without these big packs."

Quickly sorting through slings, carabiners, ice-screws and rock-pitons, we kicked steps easily to the base of the corner. The first rope-length climbed more steeply, mainly on ice with the occasional rock step, to a point where the corner reared upwards and overhung, a black bulge casting a shadow down the corner.

"Shall I lead up this pitch?" asked Ray. "You can have first go at the bulge."

"Sure!" I replied. I was excited get my teeth into some steep ground, and this pitch had quite the reputation.

Ray led upwards, his ice-tools biting firmly as he swung from the shoulder.

"Good ice here," he called back. "Steeper than it looks. I can't get any screws in, though. This powder-snow gets in the way. Won't support my weight."

"Try and get a good anchor up in the corner, maybe a rock peg," I replied. "You're doing fine!"

Ray disappeared over a short rocky crag. Traces of powder drifted into the air, and a light wind blew small clouds of snow in a

curving arc before it slid hissing into the lower gully. The sharp reso-
nant ping of steel on steel told me Ray was driving in an anchor. A
pause and then the rope came tight.

"Okay, Al, come on up," he shouted. "I've got a good pin into a
solid crack up here. The corner above looks great."

Following the steps in the ice, I arrived to find Ray lodged
securely on a small ice ledge, a broad grin displaying satisfaction and
confidence.

"Well led, Ray!" I said. "Steeper than it looked. Whaddya think
of the bulge?"

"Looks hard," he replied. "I can see why they made such a fuss
over it. I think John climbed around it last year by some ice on the
right."

I realized John had not given me all the information, perhaps
hoping I would fail on the bulge. It gave me a strange feeling to think
that there was unspoken competition within the group. The wall itself
was challenging enough without adding the risks of a divided team. I
thought back to the conversation I'd had with Aid and wondered what
he would do. But this was not the time to divide my attention. I decided
to give the bulge all my effort and concentration.

"Watch the rope, Ray," I cautioned. "If I come off, I don't want
any more slack than nec essary. I'll try and get some protection before
the hard part, though I doubt that an ice-piton would stop me much."

Placing the ice-tools firmly above my head, I moved up, slowly
but positively, kicking the crampon's front points firmly into the blue
ice. Legs slightly splayed for stability, I replaced the tools higher and
repeated the movements. I scanned the corner above, trying to get a
feel for the difficulty and for the possibility of placing a piton. My feet
searched for slight easings in the ice: a place to kick my boot sideways,
a flake of rock to place a toe on, while my ice-tools explored the glazed
surface to seek a weakness. A firm swing from the shoulder and
THUNK!—the tool set firmly. I relaxed my shoulders and arms, letting
the blood flow to fingers cramped by the strain. I breathed deeply, gathered courage and stepped upwards.

"It's not so bad," I called back. "A few more feet and I can get
a rock-pin into the crack where the ice thins out. Just watch me. Don't
let the rope drag."

A little more and I could rest in a small niche against the rock.
I took a rock-piton and placed it halfway in a narrow horizontal crack.
Freeing one ice-tool, I tapped gently at the head of the piton and felt it

bite into the crack. As I swung harder, it produced a higher note and began to "sing." A few more blows and I clipped the rope into it with a carabiner.

"I'm in! Amazing what a solid pin does for your nerves," I called down to Ray. "It looks better than I expected. The ice is quite thick until the bulge, but I can use rock holds and stem around it. I'm moving up."

Working one foot up onto the left wall, I pressed on the opposite wall with my right hand. I could then move my right foot a little higher onto a small notch, and in a wide stemming position, I levered upwards. Crampon spikes grated scarily on the small rocky protuberances, but held. I dared not reach too high with my hands lest it force my boots to slip. With patience, I arrived below the crucial bulge. My body was calm and relaxed, but my heart hammered with a sharp sense of loneness that threatened to dislodge me.

The problem revealed itself. While my ice-tools could be securely placed on and above the bulge of thick blue ice, my feet would lack any significant purchase.

"It looks hard for about six feet, and then lays back," I shouted to Ray. "If I come off, I'll slam into this side wall. So watch the rope!"

Knowing that to hesitate would cost me strength, I stemmed up the corner and swung an ice-tool into the ice above the bulge. My left hand held a rock-flake and allowed me to lean outwards to get a better view. The tool bounced off the ice, and I tried again. I needed a really good placement, one that would support my whole body-weight. On the third blow, it held firm, and I let go of the flake and my right arm took most of the weight. I quickly brought my left arm into a position from under the bulge and tried to flick the other tool into the ice. My right arm was locked bent, straining to hold until at last the other tool held and I pulled on it to rest. Committed to move up or fall, I drew my crampons up onto the rock, locked off on my right arm and released the other tool. Everything depended on speed. I could feel my feet begining to slip and knew that my one arm could hold only briefly. A desperate swing with the free tool into the ice above, a violent pull with both arms and I had a cramponed toe biting into the ice on the lip of the bulge. A second boot followed, and with straightened legs, I regained balance.

The rest of the pitch was easier. It led onto lower-angled snowslopes near the crest of an icy rib. I anchored the rope and brought Ray up.

"Good lead, Al!" he cheered. "I can see why people had such trouble before. A couple of inches less ice and it would be impossible. Let's fix these ropes and head off down. My throat's dry and I need some food."

That night in our small tent, Ray and I basked in our success, drawn closer by our shared risk. Ray voiced some of his fears.

"You know, Al, when we talked of this climb back in Cal-gary, I didn't know whether to come along or not," he said. "I've never done a climb of this length. Two days on a route is one thing, but two weeks— or however long it will take—that's a completely different kind of commitment. I didn't know about John and Jim. They always climb together, and I wasn't sure what would happen if things got tough. Would I get ditched or left? You and your brother don't exactly have a reputation for tolerance, what with all the fights I hear about. But now I'm glad I came."

"I know what you mean," I said. "I usually climb with Aid on anything that's really serious. I wasn't sure how the team would work out. I know John's very competitive, but I know my instinct for survival is very strong. I don't intend to die on this face."

The next morning we worked our way back up the fixed lines to our high point. John and Jim took over the lead. John would lead a rope-length and anchor the rope, and we would climb up it, using ascending devices. When he was leading, John would dump his pack with Jim, and we would take turns carrying it up for him, sometimes returning to the last anchor to retrieve it. In this way we slowly progressed. Icy traverse followed steep ribs of snow, leading to the base of a vertical ice-cliff.

"I remember this from last year," said John, taking more ice-screws in preparation for the steep pitch. "It's above here we get onto the big plateau, the place the chopper lifted us from."

"It doesn't look very far, though, maybe eighty feet at most, and the ice looks good," I commented. "It looks as though you can follow that ice chimney for a little way before getting out onto the face."

I sensed I was deliberately playing the pitch down, just as John was building it up. It did look steep, and the blue ice looked dense and uncompromising.

"Away you go then," I added. "Put plenty of protection in. We don't want any accidents."

While John was working his way up the ice, I looked back down the face. We had made good progress, but the weight of the packs was slowing us down. We could expect to spend at least another five days on the face. Would the weather hold? Would there be difficulties above that would prove insurmountable?

Commitment and risk: how did these elements of everyday life affect our behavior? Here the facts were simple. We committed ourselves to the project, and knowing the odds, we took the risk. How we performed in the face of the difficulties, how we behaved with our fears surrounding us: that was the point of being here. To know directly how we reacted: that was the quest.

But even here, where the truths were simple, our egos struggled to maintain our identities. We wanted to be seen as strong, to be known as skilled, to fulfill our own self-images, to be a hero in the face of danger. What is courage? Is it in facing the dangers of steep ice boldly and swiftly? Or is it in how you behave when you have no choice and your fear is at its greatest? During the next days, I would ponder these questions many times.

John climbed skillfully up the blue-ice wall. This was his kind of ground, the place he excelled. As streaks of sunlight and shadow reflected from the corners and ice-ribs, John's silhouette disappeared onto easier terrain.

"Come on up," came John's voice faintly. "The rope's tied off. This is the camp."

Rather than re-climb the pitch, we attached ascenders to the fixed line and used these. I came last, carrying John's pack as well as my own. I was impressed by the steepness. The ice was not the usual texture but was hard and brittle, splintering when crampons were kicked into it.

I heaved myself over the lip onto a plateau of snow the size of a basketball court. After the steepness below, it seemed a haven of security and comfort. We took off the rope and wandered freely—unfettered, secure and relaxed, once again in the land of the horizontal. We pitched the tents, melted snow for soup and tea and lounged as if on vacation. The tension of the vertical world eased from taut, knotted muscles. The arctic sun scorched the snow, the easier slopes reflecting mercilessly: a huge solar-oven sapping our energy and blistering our skin. Seeking protection, we threw sleeping bags over the tents. The sun lowered behind distant jagged crests, and we were bathed in alpine afterglow. Then the temperature dropped, and the ice began to crack in the cold of an arctic night.

Our tents were small, more the kind you would take on a week-end camping trip than to a huge alpine face. We had stripped them to a bare minimum, leaving behind the rain flys and tent stakes. Ray and I slept head to toe inside the gossamer-thin nylon, the light of an arctic night illuminating the deep sleep of fatigue.

The sun had climbed high over the eastern ranges by the time we had melted snow for hot chocolate and granola cereal.

"The face above is where I fell last year," John said from the other tent. "The chopper landed right here. What do you want to do today? I think we should take a rest day and maybe fix a little rope above."

"Good idea," replied Ray. "I feel tired after yesterday. Wouldn't mind a rest."

Ray looked comfortable, sitting with his sleeping bag pulled up around his waist and making a bowl of hot cereal rapidly disappear.

"Are you thinking to fix the rope?" he asked John.

"I don't know," came the reply. "I'm kinda nervous after falling last year. I suppose I could. At least I know where the route goes."

"I'd like to give it a go," I called to John. "We could both go and figure it out as we get to it—and take three or four ropes with us to fix. We can be back by midday and rest up this afternoon."

I wanted to see what the route above was like, although I was nervous at the thought of leading a pitch that John had fallen from. We packed light packs: a few ropes, ice-pitons, rock-pitons and snow-flukes, often called "dead men." Starting from the plateau, I led out over steep snow towards an easing in the ridge where I found an old length of yellow polypropylene, a reminder of last year's epic.

John came up, looking animated, and breathlessly declared his wishes: "I think I want to try to lead it again. It would be so easy to give it to you to do, but I'd never forgive myself for chickening out."

"Fine, no problem. Just take it easy and make sure you put some protection in. What held you last year?"

"A rock-pin. I fell on it twice."

John began to climb up along a short snow-crest, with the whole face dropping away to the left for more than 4,000 feet. Coming to a rock step after sixty feet, he placed a snow-fluke in the hope that it would slow him down in the event of a fall. The next thirty feet were the difficult sections, and I heard the high pitched ping-ping of a rock-piton being driven home.

"Watch the next bit," John called down. "I think the pin is okay"

"Take your time," I encouraged. "Clear the snow from the holds and don't trust the powder. I've got ya."

I tightened the grip on John's rope leading around my waist. I watched his movements with concern. He was clearing the powder from the rock with his hands, but his cramponed feet were trying to kick into the loose snow for support. He paused briefly, straightened his right leg, and then he was off—flying backwards. There was a sharp jolting tug on the rope and he stopped.

"What the fuck!" I snapped. "Get ya weight on ya feet before the pin comes out! What happened?"

"My feet slipped."

"I told ya not to trust that powder! Now be bloody careful and get up there! Don't ya dare start flying again!"

If the piton had pulled, John would have fallen directly toward me, ripping out the fluke and shooting down toward the glacier. I doubt I could have held him. I would have followed him, catapulting a short distance behind.

He started again, more carefully now, clearing the holds of powder and placing the crampon points delicately on the sloping edges. After twenty feet he placed another piton.

"How is it?" I asked.

"It's a horizontal blade," said John. "Not far in, but mechanically sound. Another ten feet and it gets easier."

"Okay. Take ya time. Make sure the anchor's good."

I felt myself stating the obvious. Of course, he should find a good anchor. Why would he accept a less than satisfactory one? If it had been Aid, I would not even have mentioned it, but then again if it had been Aid, he would not have been sloppy, taken chances and fallen off.

"Come on up," John's cry rang down.

I started to climb. It was straightforward to the rock, where it steepened. A slight tension gripped my stomach. I put my ice- tools away in holsters on my harness and, using woolen-gloved hands, felt for the holds. They were not deeply incut but flat and surprisingly large with a thin veneer of ice coating them. The wall was less than vertical, and I was able to stand in balance without too much effort. The secret to this type of terrain is to use your feet carefully and not take long steps; to choose intermediate holds for the feet; and to avoid pulling on the handholds, using them only for balance. The rock below me, I moved up to where John had two ice-pitons and a dubious rock-pin as anchor.

"Good lead!" I complimented. "I enjoyed that! Let's get back down to the tents for a brew." Tea is never far from the mind of an Englishman.

That afternoon, we lay in the heat of the tents, contemplating the upper half of the face. A short wall of ice separated us from an easier snowfield that steepened to a final narrow gully, blocked by a three-hundred-foot-high rock-barrier. The gully led out onto the final upper slopes of the mountain at 16,000 feet. With luck, it should take us no more than another three days.

We started late the next day, after lounging around eating and drinking most of the morning. Melting snow for cooking seemed to take forever, and we needed large quantities of fluids to maintain our hydration. Our packs were lighter now, and the thought of only a couple more nights before reaching the summit prompted us to keep only the bare minimum of resources and eat the rest. Lighter packs meant more speed, and speed meant greater safety.

Five days of good weather had passed, and a couple of more good days were all we could reasonably expect. If we could escape onto the easier upper slopes, we could probably dig a snow- cave to protect ourselves from any violent storms. To be caught on the steeper part of the face, with fresh snow-avalanches pouring around us, could be fatal.

It was past midday by the time we started up the fixed lines. John went first and I followed closely behind. At the top anchor we sorted the equipment, and I led off onto sixty-five-degree ice overlaid with two feet of powder-snow. I swept the snow away with both arms before I could plant ice-tools and step up onto the cleared ice. It was slow, strenuous work. I was fighting for each foot of height, breathing hard; I was like a vertical swimmer. After eighty feet, the ice steepened to a crest of rotten snow, unstable and dangerous, forcing me rightwards to firmer ground. I was amazed how powder this deep could still adhere to the underlying ice and was cautious should the whole slope decide to slide, taking me with it into the depths.

"John, I'm going to traverse round the corner," I called. "Then you won't be able to hear me. Let the rope run and when it comes tight, give me a few minutes to get a belay. Then come on up. I don't know how good the anchor will be, so take it steady."

The ice improved but the rope dragged with the sharp change of angle. Another thirty minutes passed before I crawled, hauling desperately, onto easier snowslopes. I anchored the rope to my ice-axe and using it as a handline worked my way back to a place where I could shout to John.

"Okay, John, it's tied off. Use a jumar and come on up."

A faint acknowledgment drifted up. I was surprised how warm it felt, even though it was almost midnight and as dark as it would get. The arctic sky shimered with a million points of light. Even this raw wildness was not frightening. I was lost in the immediacy of the beauty, not thinking of the future but reveling in the success and the wonder of now. It had been a difficult pitch, and my shoulders ached from the exertion. The warmth I had generated radiated through me, leaving a vibrant sense of well-being. We were on easier ground and finding tent platforms would be easy, a good night's sleep guaranteed.

One by one the team arrived and we sat in the stillness, not speaking much, feeling our sense of isolation.

"That was hard work with a big pack, especially that last traverse," Jim finally said. "I couldn't see my feet in the dark. All I could see was the big drop below as I climbed around the edge."

Jim's pack was even larger than mine; he was carrying some of John's gear. It was part of their silent agreement. John would lead the steeper, more technical ground if Jim would carry a heavier pack on the easier sections. On this face, I was never quite sure who was getting the best deal.

We split into our teams of two and quickly put up the tents, each person absorbed by his task and own thoughts. My mind was on sleep. A little to drink and a warm place to lie down was all I asked. Tomorrow would be another day and would come soon enough.

✧   ✧   ✧   ✧

I awakened warm and comfortable, with a slight stiffness of muscle. At my side, Ray was breathing slowly and evenly.

I lay silent for a few minutes and wrestled myself into a sitting position, surrounded by my down bag, only my head showing.

"Ray, we'd better get up," I said. "It's nine o'clock already. I'll get the stove going."

Outside the tent, I could now see more clearly where we had come from the previous night and where we had to go. We were at the foot of a huge ice-slope, almost 2,000 feet high, easier angled where we were camped, climbing more steeply above to end in a series of vertical rock-cliffs. Five hundred feet above was a vast black hole in the ice, forming what appeared to be a cave of some sort. Overhead, streaks of high cloud curled from the north, suggesting a change of weather, maybe a storm. I ducked inside the tent and sat next to Ray.

"We might get snow," I said. "Hard to say, though. Maybe the clouds will blow through. How're ya feeling?"

"Hungry," said Ray. "We hardly ate anything yesterday. My mouth feels raw, and I need something to drink. How does it look above? Can you see the top?"

"Not the top, but the next section looks easier. We'll figure out what to do when we talk to the others."

We drank hot chocolate and munched on granola bars. I wondered how Ray was holding up to the stresses of a multi-day climb.

"How many nights has it been now since the bergschrund?" I said. "Five, I think. I lose all sense of time on this thing. Part of it is 'cause it never gets dark for long. It'll be a few more days before we get off this face, that's for sure."

"I've never been on a climb this long before," said Ray, "especially when we don't know where we're going exactly, and there's no chance of getting back down. I hope my strength lasts. These big packs are desperate, and we barely get enough to eat."

Outside, I made a suggestion, not sure how it would go down: "Ya know, if these clouds bring a storm with them, we could be in trouble. If we get caught in the open without shelter from the wind, our tents could get shredded. Fresh snow on an open slope like this would be a real avalanche hazard. Maybe we should see if there's a cave up inside that ice."

I pointed to the black cavernous hole above us and continued: "If we could get the tents up inside that hole, we could at least wait and see what these clouds bring. And if it does suddenly storm, we'll be pretty safe in there."

John looked intense. He said: "Yes, we could do that, or we

could try and race the weather, although we don't know for sure if there is a storm on the way. We don't need another rest day, but that cave is worth a look."

It took us less than an hour to climb the easy slope to the entrance of the cavern. In the cave's center, its roof was more than thirty feet high. and its floor sloped gently back for fifty feet. Jagged flutings of green ice hung from the ceiling. The floor was covered with blocks of ice debris. A cold breeze blew throughout. It was austere and gloomy, not a welcoming place. But a snowstorm could not touch us if we camped deep inside. We agreed to put up the tents, make tea, and wait a short while to see what the weather would do.

Ray stared up at the cracked roof and gave voice to what all of us were thinking: "The less time we have to spend in here, the better I'll like it. Those chunks of ice up there could fall at any minute, and it's colder than hell. I'm shivering standing here. Let's get those tents up and get into our bags."

"He's right, Al," said Jim. "This is a nasty place, but I suppose at least it gives us some shelter. I hope this ice doesn't shift. There might even be a crevasse under this floor. We should stay only as long as necessary. Meanwhile, we'll keep a sharp eye on the weather."

The gloom and cold of our cavern affected everyone in a similar way. We spoke little.

Clouds blew up from the glacier surrounding the face. Steel-grey mist and a biting wind swept the slopes. I knew that we had made the correct decision to halt, but the sense that we had lost a day made me feel uneasy. How would this wasted time affect us higher up? Only time would tell.

The weather cleared by early morning, fortunately without depositing fresh snow. Kicking good steps in an easy snow- slope, we gained height quickly, reaching a steeper expanse of blue ice. Jim led off, the rope trailing from his waist.

"The ice is quite good here, only a few inches of snow on the surface," he said. "We should all move together when we can. Tie into the rope sixty feet behind me, and I'll put in ice screws for protection. John, you remove them as last man up."

It was a fast, if a little insecure, way to climb, with no room for a slip or fall. Should anyone make a mistake, we could all tumble together onto the meager ice-anchors. I felt increased respect for Jim as he kicked steadily upwards: this was terrain where his powerful legs gave good account. I panted to keep up, my pack straining its harness, calves burning to hold crampon points steady. By midday, we approached a rock buttress soaring into the mist like the prow of some ancient vessel. A light snow fell, and we gathered on narrow ice steps to review our position.

"Looks like we'll have to stop here," said Jim. "We can't be sure we'll find a place on that buttress to put up the tents. If we chop the ice here, we might just make a ledge big enough."

"I'm quite tired," said Ray. "I don't know if it's the altitude or lack of food, but a rest would be fine by me."

He was struggling to take off his pack, tangling the straps with some slings and climbing hardware.

"Here, let me give ya a hand with that," I said. "Don't drop it or we're in real trouble. Put it down here and clip it onto ya ice-axe. We can dig a ledge out of this ice—it'll take a while but that's okay. I reckon we should dig two ledges, one here and one just below. Whaddya think, Jim?"

"Sure, you guys start there and we'll dig ours below," he replied. "This ice is soft enough for about three feet and then it turns to hard green. It looks fine, though."

After two hours of hard chopping with ice-axes, Ray and I had a platform almost big enough for a tent. Six feet down, Jim and John had cut a similar ledge. The tents would hang a few inches over the edge and we would have to tie onto the rope to prevent sliding outwards, but it would work.

The cloud had risen, cutting out the sun and swirling far down the face. Flurries of fine snowflakes dusted tents and jackets, and equipment that was hung from ice-screws frosted over.

Looming overhead, the granite slabs took on the personality of fearful darkness. Scarred by eons of rockfall and fractured by the frosts of time, they held promise of escape. Beyond them, the face eased to summit slopes. We were close, but we were still outside a door locked firmly, sealed by nature itself. Only by our will to survive, facing whatever lay ahead—our trembling fears tamed and transformed into action—could we hope to open that door. We were at a crucial turning point of the climb, both emotionally and physically.

✧   ✧   ✧   ✧

The cloud thickened. A biting wind blasted snow across the slabs, driving between the slope and the tent walls. Every hour we had to climb from the warmth of our down bags to dig away the drifts, disturbing our rest and chilling our fingers. The night darkened and the maelstrom howled. Inside our tent, we spoke of our fears.

"I wonder what our friends are doing in Calgary right now," said Ray. "It seems such a long way away. Sometimes even my girlfriend's face appears vague, and I can't hold the picture of her in my mind for very long. I'll be glad to get out of here. I think this climb was too big for me to be on. I feel I don't have the kind of strength it takes, not knowing what the route ahead is like, what will happen."

"Ah, nothing changes," I responded. "Aid will have had a six-pack of beer and be fast asleep. The alarm will wake him in the morning, and he'll pull on his construction clothes, drink coffee and go to work. When he's driving to work, he might wonder where we are, and he'll wish he was up here with us. If you think about it much, you weigh the choices, look at the options, and I'd still rather be here. One place is much the same as the next. At least here we're alive and warm—even if I could eat a bucketful of stew. If we don't get scared, it has a kind of magnificence. I know it's easy to get nervous wondering about tomorrow, but what strength we have—the four of us all working as a team—even if sometimes we get down on one another, we all know that without the efforts of everyone we'll never get out of here."

Then I changed the subject: "The tent wall's sagging again. It's your turn to do the digging. Less philosophy and more action! Out ya go!"

"Al, it's snowing like crazy out here. There's a foot of new snow." There was heavy panting and a muffled curse. "I almost dropped a glove . . . Oh, look out . . . ." Then silence.

"Ray! Ray, what's happened? Shi-i-i-t!!"

A wall of snow hit the tent wall and kept on pushing, pushing harder.

"I've been hit by an avalanche," I shouted. "The tent's about to break!"

"Al, are you okay? Quick! Is he buried? Get a knife! We'll have to cut the tent!" Jim's voice cut urgently through the sounds of chaos.

"It's okay, Jim, don't cut the tent!" I shouted. "I'm sitting up and the worst has gone. Wow! That was scary! What happened?"

"The snow on the slabs above avalanched," said Jim. "It's lucky there was only 150 feet of it, or it would have swept you away. The slide hit Ray while he was digging your tent out, but he was clipped onto the security rope. He slid twenty feet before the rope stopped him."

"I'll hold the tent up from the inside if ya can fix the poles," I said. "I think one's broken. What a bloody mess! Ray, where are ya? Can ya get behind the tent and dig away the snow? Let's get this sorted out quickly before all the gear gets wet and frozen. Brush away the snow from the ice-axes and crampons. Make sure everything is well clipped into the handline. It might avalanche again. Without gear, we're as good as dead."

It took more than an hour to salvage the wrecked tent and clean the snow inside it. There were three inches of powder over sleeping bags and sleeping pads that had to be cleared before we could rest. If the snow melted with our body heat, it would  soak our down-filled bags and turn them into useless frozen sacks. I had a new bag covered with the latest Gore-Tex fabric, which was revolutionizing outdoor gear. This nylon-based material claimed not only to be waterproof but to also to "breathe" and prevent the buildup of condensation. My bag was holding up to the abuse, but Ray's was beginning to freeze.

The remaining few hours of night passed slowly. We were restless and watchful for dangerous repeats. As the weak grey light of the arctic morning pierced the fragmented storm clouds, it ceased to snow. Exhausted but more secure, we fell into a deep sleep, waking in the late morning.

We were well-rested but felt the effects of our minimum rations. We cleared the debris from the previous night and hung ropes, ice-cased like steel hawsers, in the sun to dry. The day was already more than half gone, and a debate grew as to how to procede.

"Maybe it's better to spend another night here and start early tomorrow," I said. "We can fix the ropes on the rocky section this afternoon and at least avoid getting caught without ledges tonight. If we have to cut more tent platforms, it'll take most of the afternoon."

I argued for restraint, looking to Ray for support. He remained silent.

John spoke: "We've already wasted most of today. We should try to make up for lost time and see how far we can get. It must get easier above these rocks. I don't want to loose a foot of height once we've gained it."

Ray looked at his boots, and in a quiet, tired voice, stated what we already knew: "Whatever you guys decide is fine with me. I'm not feeling strong enough to lead anything, but I'll try to keep up as best as I can. I think I can jumar if you guys fix the rope. I just want to get off this damn face."

Jim supported John's argument for moving on immediately, with a vague reference to getting away from our present ledges in case it began to snow again. With more than slight misgivings, I packed my rucksack and sorted the climbing hardware, ready to go.

"Okay, lads, let's get going if we're going to," I said. "It's already getting colder. These ice-screws will work as anchors from here."

John volunteered to lead the first rope length up the slabs. He moved steadily, sometimes placing a rock-piton for safety, until he was high above our heads. Jim followed, while Ray and I stood shivering in the waning light and creeping cold. We flapped arms and stamped feet, wondering what was happening above. John had gone on, leaving Jim hanging on a small ledge in the middle of the face. There was little communication.

"How's it going, Jim?" I shouted, cupping my hands to my mouth. "What's it like? How far to easier ground?"

"I can't tell, Al. The rope is still going out. John must have seen a way to go."

"We're bloody freezing down here. It's going to be dark soon. Maybe you should fix the rope and come back to these ledges."

Jim was looking upwards and gave no sign of hearing me. An hour passed. Still nothing.

Then a shout from Jim: "Come on up! The rope's tied off!"

"This is bloody crazy," I muttered. "I hope he's found somewhere to put the tents. I'll go next, Ray, to see what they're up to."

The rock was so steep and seamed with ice-filled cracks that it became clear why it had taken John so long. He had done a good job leading it. I climbed up the rope using jumars and arrived at the first anchor-point. The rope once more ran up and slightly to the left: up the same compact slabs. My frustration eased with concentration and effort, and again I thought how John had done a really fine piece of climbing; this was the type of technical ground on which he excelled.

Out of the gloom, two figures emerged, huddled against the slope. Warmed by my efforts I climbed up the final twenty feet of rope.

"Good lead, John," I said. "Did you find a place to stop?"

"No," he said. "There's no ledge."

He and Jim were anchored on a 60-degree snow-slope, with the rest of the snow-gully stretching out behind them. The light was beginning to go, so it was difficult to see into the gully and below the rock. The slope just dropped away vertically.

There was absolutely nowhere to put up a tent. The temperature was starting to drop. There wasn't much darkness up there—only two or three hours a night—so we decided to cut small ledges in the snow, snow-pockets where we could sit. I hacked away and got out a ledge big enough to sit in. I was anchored to an ice-axe driven into the snow—not a very good anchor, not if you start falling.

It was so cold that I took off only my crampons, kept my boots and overboots on and got straight into my sleeping bag. I'd cut the ledge a little bit scooped so that I could put my sleeping bag down and not slide out of it; it was a little like a bucket-seat in a car. We didn't try to melt snow for tea or cook at all. We got some frozen chocolate bars out of our packs, stuck them inside our inside jackets, thawed them and ate them. And tried to rest.

That night the wind got up, and it started pouring snow. The storm was coming from above us down the narrow gully, and it kept sweeping around us, covering all our equipment. I'd taken off my crampons and hung them over my ice-axe. The rope, which was coiled at the side, was frozen in huge twisted white chunks of nylon.

It must have been about three in the morning—one of those mornings when you're so cold you don't want to move. The cold was a kind of inner-cold from lack of food and fluids; we were all a little dehydrated. It would have been easy to stay where we were. I poked my head out of my sleeping bag and looked around. The others were still wrapped up in their bags. There was no movement. I had the kind of feeling you have when you hear of four bodies being found months later and you wonder what happened. Didn't anyone move? Did they just continue lying there until it got colder and colder? And people froze.

The thought scared me. I've got to start moving! I realized I would warm up if I started to move. I stepped out of my sleeping bag, feeling wobbly. I didn't have my crampons on, so I had to be careful not to slip. I stuffed my sleeping bag into my pack. By now the packs were getting quite empty. We had hardly any food left—just a few soups and chocolate bars.

I bent over to put on my crampons and fasten the straps. It's important to be careful when you're putting on crampons in the morning. If you don't do it correctly, they'll fall off after five or ten minutes, and you have to stop to put them on again. It's possible you may even lose a crampon. I was focusing on making sure the crampons went on well. I couldn't do it with thick gloves. I had to take them off and use thin liner-mitts to tighten up the straps.

After about ten minutes of putting crampons on, I started to gather my other equipment. I was still wearing my harness from the day before. I shook ice off the rope and threaded it around and through my hands and let it run down the slope so that it wouldn't freeze into knots when I started to climb. I got my ice-axe and ice-hammers.

After I tied onto the rope and was ready to go, I saw that Jim and John still hadn't moved in their sleeping bags. I shouted at them: "Come on, guys! Get up! We've got to move!"

I knew we were in a vulnerable position. If it started to snow, the slopes above could avalanche down the gully. Ray was starting to move, and I began to climb up the slope by myself, just kicking steps, big steps.

I was not going too quickly, just trying to keep warm. I knew that if I just kept moving for half an hour, I would warm up. I looked down from 60 feet up, and there was no one holding my rope. I was soloing! I continued moving.

After about a hundred feet, I came to an ice-step that was only 10 or 12 feet tall, but it was more difficult. By this time, my feet were warm, and my whole body was starting to feel some heat. I spent about five minutes putting in an ice-screw, clipping a carabiner and slings into it, and then clipping myself onto it.

I shouted back down: "Hey, Ray! Grab hold the rope, will you? It's steep for about 10 or 12 feet. I'll belay just above here."

I started to enjoy the climbing. The axes were going in well. It felt exhilarating. We're going to climb out of it!

Maybe because I was warm, I began to feel better. I stepped up over the top section out onto the slope above and chopped a small ledge for my feet and put in two good ice-screws. As soon as I clipped into the ice-screws, I felt much safer and secure. Ray was now tied onto the rope below, which meant that he was also safe. I pulled the rope in directly to the carabiners and belayed him. He climbed up to me, stopping every 15 or 20 feet, bending over his pack and looking tired. I don't think he was tired from the effort of the climbing but from the lack of food and a very cold night. All three of the guys came up to me and clipped into the ice-screws. I continued on.

This went on for two more rope-lengths. On the third, I was halfway out and kicking. There was powder-snow over the ice. I was kicking my crampons in, but I felt they weren't biting into the ice correctly, I looked down and my left crampon was hanging from my boot.

I thought: "Oh, shit! I didn't put the crampon on right and it's fallen off."

Looking closer, I noticed that the part where the strap fastens had snapped, probably because of the cold. So here I was, trying to repair a crampon about 70 feet above my friends—and I had no anchors. I placed both ice-tools in, put in an ice-screw and brought up everyone else. I managed to repair my crampon by putting the straps underneath, around the bottom of the point.

To get to an easier snow-slope, we had to go up a 1,200-foot gully that began about 100 feet wide and narrowed to about 40 feet. After my crampon broke, I wasn't into leading, in case I got into a serious position.

None of us could afford a fall at this point. A fall would have been fatal for all of us. The anchors were not so good that they would have withstood someone falling 300 feet onto them.

We got into a sequence in which John led and Jim came second. I was third with my pack, and then I would go back down and jumar up again with John's pack. John was now the leader and I was kind of a mule. Jim was holding the rope for John. Ray was too tired to do much of anything. He could only just manage to get himself up to the anchor points.

John led out another five rope-lengths. We could feel the tension building, because as the gully narrowed, it steepened to about 65 degrees for the last 150 feet. The snow thinned out to green-blue ice with no snow cover. Any climber knows that this means he's about to reach the top. We were all starting to pull together.

When John was halfway up the final pitch, I shouted to him: "Go on, John! Great man! You're almost there!"

He ran the rope out and went out of sight. When someone goes out of sight on that kind of ground, you know that the ground has become easier. The angle has eased off. We heard him shout. We couldn't tell what he was saying, but we knew intuitively that he was there. He'd tied the rope off, and we all moved up on our jumar clamps. We moved up one at a time because we didn't know how good the anchor was. But we could sense that we were coming off the face now. We'd escaped!

When I jumared up, pulling out over the lip of the gully onto the glaciated easy slopes, I saw that we could put a tent up anywhere at that point. Even though the altitude was around 17,500 feet, we'd come up so slowly that we didn't really feel the exertion of altitude. What we felt was fatigue from lack of food and liquids.

We all shook hands and stood around, with the coils of rope at our feet. We started to giggle, stamped out a ledge and put up the tent. We started our stoves and put snowballs into the snow-melt cups. We each had just one more cartridge for the stove.

The sun came over the southern horizon, and it started to warm up. We could feel the sun soaking into our bodies and we started to feel warmth. It wasn't warmth from moving around and climbing, but warmth just from the sun. We knew we were going to spend the rest of the afternoon there. We wanted to sleep. We all felt lethargic from lack of any real sleep. In past nights, we'd just dozed for a couple of hours, enduring those nights that seem never to end. Now we could stretch out full in our sleeping bags.

We could set out our wet sleeping bags, which were still snowy from the night before. The bags had been icing up from condensation, and we'd never had an opportunity to dry them. Now we could toss them over the tent and dry them out, which meant we could be insulated completely again. We could hydrate and even dry out the ropes.

We knew we could survive now.

We looked above us. The ridge continued to the Southwest Buttress. There were ill-defined and lower-angled snow-slopes. To the left, where we could see we'd have to go, there was a line of ice-cliffs we'd have to traverse around. There was also a large snow-basin, with the kind of angle you'd see in the upper part of a ski area.

The summit appeared to be a series of peaks, points on a ridge maybe 1,500 feet above us. We knew there was the main summit and subsidiary summits, most of which were only a few feet lower than the main summit.

Over to the left a little, I could see a pass. I figured that this was probably the pass that went directly down into the research station where

John's girlfriend, Judy, worked and where are our skis were. We knew that if we got there, we had complete security. There was a hut and tents. There were radios and a supply route served by a turbo-charged small aircraft.

We had started climbing at three that morning and came out just after midday. We rested and slept in the afternoon.

Evenings were completely light on the upper part of the mountain. Even when the sun went down, we still got light because we were so high on the mountain. We knew we could probably climb all night.

The slopes were easy now, and we weren't likely to fall off of them, if we could just figure out where we were going. We started to discuss which route we'd take.

Now that we were all safe, Jim and John were becoming kind of separate again. They gave indications that they wanted to go on alone, but I said it was important for the team to continue our drive to the summit. Although we were going to have to traverse left for four or five hundred yards, they wanted to come back above the ice cliffs. They felt this was the best continuation to the summit.

On the other hand, Ray and I just wanted to escape the mountain. Ray told me that he didn't know how much longer he could keep going. Some wispy clouds came over, and Ray said if the weather changed, he didn't know how much longer he would be able to survive. He felt it was very important for him to get down to the research station as fast as possible.

I was kind of split. I could see that to get to the bottom of the mountain was easy—we could almost walk down if we wanted to. I thought maybe I'd take Ray up to the pass where he could see the research station, and he could just walk down from there. Then I would climb up along the ridge to the summit. If John and Jim wanted to go their own route to the summit, that would also be fine.

We all started off roped together on the first section around the ice-cliffs. After about an hour and a half, we rounded the ice-cliffs and came out on a snow platform above them. At this point, Jim and John started to walk across a shelf of snow toward a snow-slope that looked as though it probably went up to the summit.

To the left was about 600 feet of snow that led to a small col. I started climbing up there, taking Ray up in steps. The climb was so easy that we just carried the ropes. I resented that Jim and John had started off, that they were so ambitious they apparently didn't care what happened to Ray. I suspect they knew I would take care of Ray anyway. They expected it of me.

At about 10 o'clock that evening, Ray and I arrived at the top of the col. Then I could see that we were, in fact, far away from the research station. It was way over to the left. But it turned out that the pass we'd come to was just below the summit, which was maybe twenty minutes' walk above the col. Jim and John had gone way over to the right, not on the summit ridge but on another ridge.

Ray and I left our packs on the little col and soloed in the most amazing light. It was eleven in the evening when we reached the summit. The sun was going down. The wind was whipping spindrift over the summit on across to the slope. Above our heads there was hardly any wind, but around our feet, legs and hips, there was about three feet of windswept powder.

The light and visual effects were amazing. The sunset light was reflected in the snow. We walked through purple, pink and red powder-snow, as our crampons bit into the firm crust. It was surreal. It was like a light-show. We just walked up to the summit. It was quite cold, but there was no strong wind—just a breeze whipping this very light powder-snow around our feet.

Then I remembered where I was. Ray was the photographer of the two of us, so I walked up to the summit and held my ice-axe up in the air for the classic summit pose. I remember that photograph. It has the purple and red light of the arctic sunset.

Ray came up to me and we hugged one another. Ray was overjoyed. He'd almost given up on the summit. He'd been convinced that, instead of going to the summit, he was going directly down to the research station. He was preparing himself for failure and shame and this jolt to his ego: he'd come so far and he'd failed to keep up with the rest of us. But now you could see that he was feeling stronger.

We looked around but could not see Jim and John. Later we heard that they'd traversed below. After we separated from them, they traversed off below this other rounded final reach. Jim had become quite sick from the altitude, and they'd had to camp and spend a wretched night there. They didn't arrive at the summit until the following evening.

We didn't know any of this at the time. We thought they were somewhere just below us. They obviously hadn't been here before us. There were no footsteps, no signs.

So we turned our back to the summit and started to plod down toward the research station. It was three or four miles away down an open basin: a sea of bluish snow and ice, easy to handle, not steep but a long way. After the first thousand feet of 35- or 40- degree slopes, we came onto an easier slope where we could have easily skied.

But I was breaking through to the mid-calf and knee on this crusty slope. I thought: "Yeah, that's all we need! We get to the summit, the research station is just below us, and I have to break trail! I just continually took steps. Crunch!—breaking through the crust—crunch! crunch! It took another three or four hours of trailbreaking before we got to the research center.

Everyone was asleep when we got there. We put our tent up and lay in it until about seven o'clock in the morning when people started to wake up. They invited us inside. Judy was there and she made tea for us. We lay around all afternoon, wondering where Jim and John were.

We kept asking Judy: "Have you seen them? Heard from them at all?"

They had binoculars at the research station, and we used them to scour the summit slopes. But there was no sign of climbers. About five or six o'clock that evening, we saw two dots appear on our trail, way up toward the summit. And it was Jim and John coming down. They arrived slowly. They looked very, very tired. They'd followed our broken trail. At least that helped them a little bit.

We were all at the research station. We were safe, but we still had to get off the mountain. To get down to the foot of the mountain, the normal route—the easiest on the mountain—is the King Trench Route. At the end of that route—at about 6,000 feet—there is a glaciated system where a light plane equipped with snow-skis can land. This is the base camp for that route.

To get to the summit from the King Trench Route, you have to cross an 18,000-foot pass, which separates the research station from the King Trench Route. So we had to climb back up about 1,000 feet and descend into the King Trench Route.

About noon the next day, we started to kick steps, carrying our skis back up the slope and over the pass to get to the King Trench Route. Well, irony of ironies! As we approached the top of the pass, a storm blew in! We were enveloped in cloud, unable to see either the research station or the King Trench Route.

So there we were—having escaped from a dangerous face and made the summit at 19,850 feet—now wrapped in cloud, spindrift and wind. It was hard to know even which way was down. We actually rappelled down, slowly. It was probably no more than 30 degrees of angle, but we couldn't tell because of the spindrift and bad visibility. It might have gone over a cliff—we couldn't tell. It was like those days when you're skiing easily, and suddenly you're crashing down because you have no perspective of where vertical is or where down is.

After two rappels down the hill, we got into a bit better visibility, but the conditions were desperate. We needed shelter. We desperately needed shelter to survive!

Our fingers and toes were freezing. We were badly prepared. We weren't mentally prepared for this kind of sting-in-the- tail. This was the sting, the *real* truth of the climb. The artificial truth was when we set ourselves against the difficulties of the mountain.

We're soft in confronting those difficulties. We're aware of how strong we are, how we fight the pitch, how we relate to our friends— all the things you do when you're on a face and in control. Then after the summit, after the prizes have been given out—suddenly, the sting-in-the-tail! The mountain turns round and shows you who you really are!

Now it's how you respond. This is the truth. It's nothing sexy and dramatic. There's nothing sensational that will go into climbing history and literature. There's nothing you can tell your friends about. There's no big trauma: just a storm on a mountain pass. And it's so powerful that you could die. You're not going to fall off, but you could freeze.

It showed who we really were, because we started to panic. We were racing around. We tried to get the tents out. I stabbed the skis into the snow. Don't lose any equipment! Don't let anything blow away—or we're dead! If a tent blows away, we're dead!

So I started to organize: "okay, guys, let's get the tent up! Let's get one tent up."

We unraveled the tent, and John dove inside it. His body weight held it down. He was just lying there inside, out of the wind. The rest of us were struggling to get poles up. Then Ray got inside. Then Jim and I erected poles to give the tent some structure. Then Jim got inside. The tent was up, but it needed to be secured.

I've got gloves on, ski goggles, down hood. I'm warm enough. I'm secure. And I know we could be here maybe for days. So the tent has to be secured. I went around and drove the ski tips into the snow to use them as tent stakes. Then I tied the tent down in as many places as I could. Everyone else was inside the tent. They're only tiny tents. Three people inside is pretty crowded. Then I ducked inside the tent myself.

The wind was 60 or 70 miles an hour, and it was coming in around the fabric. I looked at the stitching on the seams and thought: "This looks like a backpacking tent, not a mountain tent. I wonder if it'll hold. Wonder if it's going to shred."

We got into the tent around three o'clock in the afternoon. We sat for twelve hours in that tent. We talked about everything. We tried to melt some snow, but the stove was broken. We shared the final bits of chocolate bars. We realized we didn't know how long the storm would last. If it lasted a week, we'd come out emaciated, if we survived. Again there was the fear of the unknown. Yet we knew that back over the pass, which was only a few hundred feet above us, and straight down the research station had everything we needed to survive the storm.

We became divided on what to do. I thought John and Jim were maybe going to start down into the storm, down to the King Trench Route. We had no idea where we were going. We couldn't see! That was definitely not what I wanted to do. If I was going to use the last of my strength, it would be to go back over the pass to the research center. That was our security, if we really needed to go anywhere.

About midnight, I told them: "Look, I don't know what you guys are going to do, but tomorrow morning when it becomes light, I'm going to pack up and go up over that pass and back down to the research station. If you guys want to come with me, you can. I'll break trail. We can be roped together. I'm not going to start down into the glaciated system of the mountain when I have no idea of the layout of the land."

There was a silence. I'd given John an ultimatum. All during the climb, any decision I made John wanted to counter, to do something opposite. I don't remember the exact words of his response, but it was something like: "You'll leave us? You mean *you'd leave us?*"

I knew that Ray would come with me. He didn't give a damn: the guys had already left him once. Strangely enough, a few minutes later—as I felt calm, knowing that we were going back over the pass—the storm let up. At three o'clock when the arctic morning began to get lighter, the wind dropped completely. It was going to be a perfect day. The storm had blown itself out. There was no need to retreat.

We were spared again. But the storm had really put the cogs down again. I felt sad that I'd always had to try to resolve indecision and that finally I had to deliver an ultimatum. Then, within a half an hour, it wasn't necessary.

The weather broke and the rest of that day was easy—sometimes skiing, sometimes walking down. By four o'clock that afternoon, we were down at base camp of the King Trench Route with half a dozen other teams. Using someone else's radio, we contacted Kluane Lake for a flight out.

Once we were back down among other people, out came the egos. Everyone talked about the climb. The storm the night before and the fears we all faced: all that was swept under the table. The next day we flew to Kluane Lake.

The climb's media-event downside started there. John called his parents and friends in Calgary, who apparently relayed his story to radio and newspaper people.

I found out later that Adrian heard on the radio that Jim and John had reached the summit and that Ray and Alan hadn't. He told me he thought: "If my brother hasn't reached the summit, *where is he*?"

It was wrong for John to say that Ray and I hadn't finished the climb, to report that when he and Jim began up the final snow-slopes toward the summit of Logan, Ray and I had gone left up to the pass and hadn't finished the climb. The media echoed John's remarks.

When we got off the plane in Calgary, there were all these media people, apparently organized by John's friends. I hadn't had a shower or a shave or anything, but everyone else had tidied up. They must have known there was going to be a press conference, but I didn't know anything about it.

It was the usual kind of media stuff: How did you feel here? How did you feel there? And so on.

I called Adrian and told him to put a six-pack of Guinness in the fridge. In the phone booth next to me, I overheard John phoning his parents. I heard him say: "Yes, I led the hard pitches."

So we were, back in the land of super egos. The magic of the summit and the storm that had seemed the decisive sting-in-the-tail had been forgotten.

As a result of the climb, I gained a very close friend in Ray. This was in May of 1979. That fall, Daphne and I separated, and I felt myself very much alone that Christmas of '79 in Calgary. Ray kind of returned a favor and looked after me during the Christmas season.

Ray was killed the next spring in an avalanche while skiing in Europe. In the late winter of 1982, John died while trying to solo an ice-climb. So now there's only Jim and I alive from that group.

A lot has happened since then. I haven't seen Jim since probably 1989, when we met in the Everest area. We didn't talk about the Logan climb.

I'm not sure if it's been repeated since. I don't see why it shouldn't have been.

# *CHAPTER*
## *14*

LES DROITES: A SHORT WALK WITH DOUG SCOTT

BY ADRIAN

For a month, I sat in my small rented apartment and looked out over Mont Blanc, the Dru and all the Chamonix Aiguilles. My knee, swollen and useless, hurt every time I moved it. A torn medial ligament—a typical skiing injury—was taking a long time to heal.

In the afternoons I'd limp down the long hill to the Bar National, meet up with Al Rouse for a beer, go home, cook dinner and then meet up with friends again in the bar. Life was tedious and frustrating, especially as I was there to climb and the weather had been particularly fine.

It was the early days of 1980. My brother was working in a

climbing store in Calgary. He had written to tell me he also had torn a medial ligament while skiing: the knee opposite to mine.

Slowly, I began to recover and dare to make plans for climbing. I teamed up with a highly skilled British climber, Stevie Haston, to try a winter ascent of a rarely climbed route on the Triolet North Face— to the left of the Direct Route Al and I had climbed in 1975.

Stevie and I quickly climbed half the face and had to sit out a nasty snowstorm. During the night, I almost fell out of the pack I was standing in while adjusting my belay – there were no real ledges – and Stevie grabbed me at the last moment before I slid off down the precipice. We later retreated, but at least I knew my knee was strong enough to climb.

A week later I decided to climb the 3,000-foot-high Bonatti Pillar on the Dru with a young Scotsman. It was a grave miscalculation on my part, probably born of frustration caused by my injury. The young man was very enthusiastic but did not have the experience to tackle something as difficult as we planned. I was so confident of my own abilities that I ignored his. It wasn't until we had climbed the couloir to the foot of the pillar that he realized he was in well over his head and told me so. Luckily we were in a position to retreat without much trouble.

Later I had time to dwell on the implications of my enthusiasm. A few years earlier, a famous French guide had made a winter climb on the North Face of the Grande Jorasses with a younger, less experienced companion. The guide barely escaped with his life, leaving the young man dead from exhaustion. They spent too many freezing nights out in the open, and a sudden storm finalized the affair. I could have led the young Scotsman and myself into a similar situation.

Around the middle of March, Doug Scott showed up in Chamonix to take part in a French television documentary. He was keen to climb, and it was difficult to turn down the opportunity to climb with one of Britain's finest mountaineers.

"We could do either the Walker Spur (on the Grande Jorasses) or the Droites Spur," I suggested, going for the "big ones" without hesitation.

Doug scratched his chin through his thick, black beard and replied easily: "Let's do the Droites, youth. I've got plastic boots since I smashed my ankles on the Ogre, and they're better with crampons than for rock-climbing."

His long, unkempt hair and gold-rimmed spectacles made him look like a wise guru. In fact, he was that to me.

Doug was about five years older than I, but we had many friends in common. Bob Shaw was one of his proteges and Tut Braithwaite was a contemporary. He was the first Englishman to climb Everest (with the Scotsman Dougal Haston). I was proud to be able to climb with him.

We left the next morning and, after taking a cable car up to the Grande Montets, descended across the glacier to the new Argentiere hut. It was deserted.

"I'm surprised there's no one else here," I said to Doug as we stared out of the huge picture windows at the great north faces of the Droites, Courtes and Triolet.

This view is one of the most awesome in Europe, with the mountains so close and so steep that they overpower the imagination. By then I'd climbed every one of the faces by one route or another, and every time they had a different effect upon me. The first time was the Triolet, I was terrified. The second was with Bob Shaw on the Courtes in winter; I was still impressed. Each time afterwards, I gradually become more comfortable. But sitting opposite Doug, with our tiny stove purring away, I still felt the overwhelming power of the place.

The Northeast Spur of the Droites was one of the finest hard classic climbs of its day, and it still had had only two winter ascents. The 4,000-foot prow can best be described in three sections. First, a long snow-and-ice gully cuts through several rock bands on the left of the crest. Then the climb makes a series of heart-stopping traverses onto the bold sweep of the North Face, and it finally joins a tight-rope ridge before the summit. My imagination kept me turning fitfully for most of the night.

By the light of a flickering candle, I watched the gas stove heating our first pan of Ovaltine. It was eerie, just the two of us in such a large empty dining room. We mumbled the occasional unimportant comment.

Then Doug came up with something more profound: "If we were the last two people on earth, I wonder if we'd be doing this?"

It was too early in the morning for me to conceive an answer to that, and for a moment I suspected it was a precursor to a "cop out." I well understood the pre-dawn nervousness that always hits me before a big route and wondered if Doug was wrestling with his own. I needn't have worried, though. It was just his natural philosophical curiosity.

An hour later we were roping up beneath a steep ramp of snow, given substance by dawn's first light.

"You can do the first one, youth," Doug said, "and I'll do the second up into the gully." His confident face beamed beneath his old hard hat.

As we crossed snowed-up slabs, I could see that the first two pitches would be steep. I set off self-consciously, kicking with my feet and thwacking with my ice-tools. Doug would be watching me closely. I was acutely aware of that scrutiny. I didn't want to dither or hesitate while seeking a comfortable rhythm. I noticed the weight of my pack immediately as it tugged me backwards. It was an inevitable reality that in winter we needed a lot more warm equipment and food than in summer. I needed to adjust my balance with greater precision.

Once I'd run out all the 150 feet of rope, I lashed myself to a nearby rock-spike and brought up Doug. He moved up with measured ease and a big grin. Climbing is always easier than thinking about it. Once engrossed in the problems at hand, the needless worries of the night seem to dissolve with the stars.

At the top of an easier ice slope, we came across short, hard corners of rock, often coated in a film of polished water-ice. Slowly and with short, delicate steps, I inched up the first one, still wearing crampons. I couldn't afford to fall because I would slide, tumble and probably tear my recently-healed ligament. Studied caution was the order of the day.

When Doug was in the lead, I relaxed and let my mind wander. It had been eight years since I'd made my first alpine-winter climb on the Courtes. Then it had stretched us to our limits, what with poor and barely adequate equipment and our lack of knowledge of winter conditions. Compared with the present, I'd been ill-prepared. Now I wore a one-piece suit and had a sleeping bag sealed with Gore-Tex. My boots were warmer, though still of leather, and my ice-tools had a sophisticated curve that gripped the ice better.

All day we climbed. Toward dusk, we reached a fragile snow ridge on a narrow col.

"We could dig a platform here, Doug." I said.

"No," he replied. "We should keep climbing until it's dark."

I always have the fear of being caught out on a steep face with no ledge to sit on at night. Knowing that the chances of accidents increases at the end of long days, I like to stop with time to spare and not take the gamble of finding another ledge. However, Doug didn't wait to see if I agreed. He climbed up a long, steep corner on rock and I followed him in the gathering gloom. He stood on a small ledge.

"This is it, youth," he said. "Make yourself comfortable."

"Not a lot of room," I replied.

"There's a smaller ledge that you just passed," he said. "You can sleep there, and we'll both cook on this one."

He began to arrange the two-man bivvy tent. Once inside, with the stove melting ice, it was warmer. We sat back-to-back in silence, wrapped in our own thoughts. It had been a successful day, but there was still a long way to go. I glanced over my shoulder and saw him writing.

"What you writing, Doug?" I asked. I wondered if he was one of those people who kept a diary wherever they happen to be.

"To the wife, youth."

"What? Can't you write to her when we get back to Cham?"

"She keeps asking me what it's like on these climbs. So I thought I'd write it down now while I still remember. Here, pass your mug and drink this soup."

I smiled to myself, remembering how friends had told me that Doug could be a bit eccentric at times.

Later I carefully lowered myself down the rope to my allotted ledge. It was narrow, but by putting a sling of rope under my feet, behind my knees, around my waist and under my armpits, I couldn't roll sideways. Cocooned in my thick, down bag, I drifted into a heavy sleep.

The next morning by the time I'd packed my gear and was ready to climb, Doug had made a hot drink. I quickly gulped it down and said: "I'll be off!"

My crampons scraped on the solid grey granite. Soon we knew we had to leave the ridge and make a series of sweeping traverses onto the North Face. It was a daunting prospect. I'd felt quite safe on the crest, but the face spun giddily down for 2,000 feet. After one false start, we selected the correct point, and I tiptoed across patches of ice with my hands gripping the occasional rock. Once I'd made the commitment to begin, it was not as difficult as it looked. Many small spikes were hidden within the drapes of ice, and the trick was to figure out which were spikes and which were not. Then, with a quick chop of my axe at the correct place, a handhold would appear. We swung leads throughout the day. It was hard work, and without rigid crampons, my calves were feeling the strain.

"Are you okay, youth?" Doug asked. "Your face looks pinched."

"Yeah. I always look like this. It's just the cold," I said, hating the thought that I looked strained in front of Doug.

The days seemed too short. The light was already fading as I gathered some ice-screws from him and tied my pack off to his anchor.

"I'll pull my 'sac 'cause it's slowing me down so much," I said, "and we need to find somewhere to stop."

Without the pack, I felt freer and much stronger, and I could climb quicker. I headed up a narrow chute to where I hoped the face joined the ridge. I vaguely remembered being in the same place when Al and I had climbed the adjoining Messner Pillar five years earlier. Suddenly, I could see a huge pinnacle twenty feet above. By now it was dark. Very carefully, making sure I didn't trip over my own feet, I front-pointed toward it.

"Phew!" I said to myself. I flipped the rope over the back, tied myself securely to it and shouted down to Doug. My voice, small and insignificant, was almost lost among the acres of rock and ice: "You can jumar now! Tie on my 'sac!"

I began to haul in the red rope. The rope drag was terrible and gave way one foot at a time. I cursed my weakness at having taken off my pack. "I should have kept it on," I thought bitterly.

My hands ached and cramped as I hauled and hauled and hauled. Then I could hear Doug somewhere in the inky darkness: "Keep pulling, youth. The rope was twisted around the one I'm jumaring on."

The pack swung above him, and he had to keep dislodging it from fingers of rock. Soon we stood together, headlamp beams criss-crossing as we hunted for somewhere to spend the night.

"There you are, youth," Doug said. "On that rock."

A patch of ice clung to a sloping slab of rock. It looked improbable, but at least my belay was directly above. I began hacking carefully, trying to sculpt an inward-sloping dish. After half an hour, I had shaped a ledge eighteen inches wide and three feet long. That would work nicely if I hung my feet in my pack and used my sling-support system again.

Doug was over to my right and performing his own scratching motions into an ice slope, but I was so busy making sure I didn't drop my crampons or other precious gear that I didn't take much notice. Sometime late into the night, he passed me a drink. I had eaten a frozen can of tuna mixed with some mayonnaise but little else.

Once again I slept well and came awake slowly, with heavy lids. I could have slept more, but today was the day to escape. I'd slept with my boots on, loosened but still on my feet. It was something I would never normally do because they can restrict circulation and cause frostbite. But dropping them by accident in the dark would have been worse.

"Had a strange thing happen last night, youth," Doug said as he busied himself holding a pan of snow over the stove. "I dreamt that some friends were telling me off for not concentrating on small details. Then I woke up and decided to check my belay knot. I'd tied it but not clipped into it. You might have had to finish the climb on your own."

I thought about my dislike of night-climbing and setting up bivouacs in the dark.

It didn't take me long to get ready and set off up the ridge that led to the summit. A strong wind whipped powder across the ridge, stinging my bare cheeks and lifting the slack rope up into a curving arc. When I'd been here with Al, the weather had been socked-in, and it had been snowing. I tried to remember the line of the route but couldn't.

At one point I found myself wedged in a steep twelve-inch-wide crack. I knew I hadn't climbed it before, because it was the kind you never forget. It kept trying to spit me out. I fought it aggressively, unprotected but determined not to fall.

I was being driven into an irreversible corner. I made a final, wild lunge for the top. My crampons levered up on unseen crystals, while my gloved hands grabbed a rounded ledge. I had made it but what a stupid position to get myself into.

After that, the climbing became easier, and we climbed together up a final slope. Doug reached the rappel slings first and was able to look over the crest to the Grande Jorasses and farther toward Mont Blanc. The sky was blue, and all we had to do was descend.

# CHAPTER
## 15

## EVEREST IN WINTER

BY ADRIAN

A l Rouse could always be relied upon to have a crazy
scheme somewhere on the back burner. At the Bar National in Chamonix, he served up his latest one: "Aid, a few of
us have been talking about going to try Everest when we can get permission. Would you be interested in going?"

Then Al added the punch line, measured and slow but with his
typical boyish enthusiasm: "The Ministry (of Tourism in Nepal) have
said we can go next winter, and there's a slot open for the West Ridge.
There'd be no oxygen and no Sherpas."

He made his statement sound almost casual. I was flattered he
would ask me, and I was fool enough to agree. When I had a chance to
consider the challenges, I realized we'd taken on one hell of a task.

Everest had been climbed by its easiest route only once in winter. That expedition sported the cream of Polish Himalayan climbers in great numbers, and they used supplementary oxygen. I remember one of their comments that appeared in reports of their climb: "If it hadn't been Everest, we'd have given up really soon rather than risk our lives."

So now we were going to try the whole of the West Ridge, which had been climbed only once—by a forty-strong Yugoslav team. At that time, it was one of the most difficult climbs in the whole of the Himalaya. And we were to try in winter with only eight people! I suppose not using oxygen was just the topping on the cake. I should have said no, but I didn't have the experience then to know that. In a way, I suppose brother Alan and I were proud to be climbing alongside some of the best British climbers of the day: Joe Tasker, Paul Nunn, Brian Hall, John Porter, Dr. Pete Thexton and, of course, Al Rouse. We had a huge challenge and a strong team, and the adventure promised to be nothing short of wild.

As happens with this kind of venture, someone had to "sacrifice" his house to gear collection and packing. Paul Nunn was the victim. Goodness knows what his wife, Hilary, thought. But Paul's good-natured chuckle never stopped, despite mounds of clothing, climbing gear and paper wrappings piling up against every wall in his house. It was the kind of scene that keeps TV soap operas going for weeks, but this was real life.To cap it all, we were hoping to make a TV documentary, and a film crew of Allen Jewhurst (director), Mike Shrimpton (camera) and Graham Robinson (sound) joined our group. I wondered if they could even dream what they'd let themselves in for.

In early November, we all showed up at London's Heathrow International Airport. We had seventy large boxes of gear.

"How on earth are we going to get all this aboard for free?" I asked, looking at the mountain of gear.

"Because we have to, Aid," said Rouse. "We have some 'inside' help, and we don't have enough money to pay for it."

Cart-loads of our gear kept on disappearing down to the loading gate. I was impressed. Then there was an announcement that our flight would be delayed a half hour. Once in the air and bound for Delhi, India, Rouse came over and fed us a snippet of information.

"The flight was delayed because they had to unload someone

*Alan Rouse*

else's luggage so that ours would get on," he said, grinning. "Everything's working so far."

He spoke too soon. In every carefully planned scheme, there's always a hiccup. It came dressed in a smart blue uniform when we landed in Delhi.

"Oh, no, sir. It is quite impossible. The flight is full and you have very much baggage." An official of the Royal Nepalese Airline rocked his head from side to side with an idiotic smile that was meant to lessen the impact of his words. It didn't!

"Maybe tomorrow," he said, rocking his head again until I thought: "If he does that one more time, I'll pull it off his bloody shoulders."

"We'll have to split up," decided Rouse. "I'll go with as much luggage as I can get on and you can try again tomorrow." He disappeared through immigration.

"Nice bloody place to spend twenty-four hours," snarled Alan, looking at the dismal departure hall. "We'd better begin hassling them about our luggage now so they'll really want to get rid of us tomorrow."

"Cut up the foam mountain and let's make ourselves comfortable," I said, stripping the wrapping off a large coffin-shaped package that contained the expedition's supply of foam mattresses. We took turns guarding our equipment, all the while under the careful scrutiny of sly-faced janitors.

"Those buggers would really like to get their thieving little hands on that lot," Al said and nodded towards the janitors, who ducked their heads and pretended to go about their work.

In the morning, Pete Thexton sat up on his mattress, rubbed his eyes and cursed: "The bastards finally got something. My sneakers were by my head. Now they're gone and I never noticed."

"Yeah, that's how I lost my virginity," said Al, unable to resist teasing.

Later that day they promised to put all our gear on board, so we boarded the flight to Kathmandu. The weather was perfect as we flew east along the southern rim of the Himalayan Range. We passed Dhaulagiri, then Annapurna. Just before we landed, I thought I caught a glimpse of Everest, with a large wind-plume strung out from the summit.

Mike Shrimpton had twenty-five gleaming camera cases as part of his luggage. They contained film stock, movie cameras, lenses and tripods: everything necessary to make a full-length documentary. He carried a list of contents with lowered prices to show to the customs men. A man of great experience with third-world countries, he should have expected trouble. The silver boxes stood out like gold bullion at a garage sale, and Nepalese customs men are known to be as bent as a nine-dollar bill.

"Come back to get them tomorrow," a customs minion said with an evil smile.

"We wish to take them today."

"This is not possible," said another power-fed smile.

"Maybe there's a special tax?" I asked, suggesting a bribe.

"Maybe there will be tomorrow, sir."

"Look!" I said firmly. "Do you know that Prince Charles is in Kathmandu to go trekking?"

"Yes, sir. It is in all the papers."

"Well, we're supposed to be filming him *at the British Embassy!*" I emphasized the last words and continued: "We need the boxes, *now!*"

The custom man's face suddenly became more serious, and he stood an inch taller, hitting the five-foot mark. He said crisply: "You must take them immediately, sir. Welcome to Nepal!"

Kathmandu has many wonderful restaurants, with cuisine ranging from Chinese to American to Japanese and even Italian. Half-starved-looking trekkers and climbers can often be seen gorging themselves on piles of lasagna (vegetarian, of course) or miniature cairns of French fries (or chips, depending where you're from).

We had only two days left before we planned to depart for the mountains, and that gave us an excuse to gorge, too. There would be no rich food or Star Beer for two months, so we were determined to eat our fair share in the days that remained. We called it "The Camel Principle." Others may have called it gluttony.

Al and I followed our steak with cheesecake and apple pie. I think the steak must have been overly salty or we were overly thirsty, because we lost count of how many beers had been opened. K.C.'s Restaurant was packed with delirious Western tourists speaking at the top of their lungs while trying to compete with Dire Straits' "Romeo and Juliet." Allen Jewhurst, our East London film director, plunged into the throng dressed in red-rimmed black muscle-shirt and Indian-made sapphire-blue satin shorts. Tight satin shorts.

Three ebullient American women at a neighboring table were busy lacing their coffee with dark Nepali rum. They stared at the shorts and their eyes sparkled. Then the shameless comments began to flow: "Oh, nice color!" "Shiny, too!"

They didn't faze Allen one bit. He threw them a disarming smile, said something in Cockney, which I knew they couldn't understand. Within minutes he had squeezed in alongside them.

Al and I watched with predatory amusement. He was one and they were three. It was time to move over and get in on the action. We offered Allen a beer and followed it across to the other table. The girls were out of control, their laughter almost drowning out Dire Straits' explosive music. We began to explain why we were in Kathmandu, but they teased us and didn't believe that anyone would want to try to climb Everest in the middle of winter. They thought we were hoaxers, and not being shy, they told us so.

I noticed that one of the girls, Lorna, seemed to know more about climbing than the others. When I said we were attempting the West Ridge, she knew that the American 1963 expedition had climbed the upper section.

I learned that Lorna had rock-climbed in her native Colorado, and her visit to the Himalayas was part of a long-held dream. In fact, she and her friends had come directly to the restaurant from a ten-day trek. They hadn't had time to go to the bank for money, and they began "cruising" us to buy them a meal. We were pushovers, and the expedition footed the bill.

Lorna, a blue-eyed beauty with long, wild hair and suntanned cheeks, never seemed to stop laughing. Her quick wit and clever humor constantly threw out challenges. We parried as best we could, but these

*Nepalese village on the way to base camp*

were no doe-eyed, dreamy trekkers. Al was busy telling her bright-eyed friend how he was a photographer, and I could see that she indulged him without believing a word. If I'd been more sober, I'd have found it quite unsettling. The evening ended with an hilarious episode when too many people tried to climb into too few rickshaws.

The following morning, I met Lorna for breakfast at the Kathmandu Guest House. Over coffee I discovered she was to make a lone trek around the Annapurna Range and then go with her two friends to Bali.

She asked many questions about the forthcoming climb. How cold would it be? And what about the winds? Yet she didn't seem to think it a crazy or reckless venture. There was a certain gleam of close understanding between us which emboldened me to ask if she might, by chance, consider being here when I returned in February. She grinned, looked at the table to hide her thoughts from me and replied that she would like to visit the Everest region sometime during her travels. In the meantime, she would send me postcards from Bali to remind me of what I was missing in the way of warm beaches and fresh fish. I laughed. I already knew what I would be missing.

✧ ✧ ✧ ✧

As we hiked in bright sunshine from small village to tiny hamlet, it didn't feel as if we were going to attempt Everest in winter. Women threshed wheat and snotty-nosed children scuffled in the dirt. The porters carrying our equipment sweated up the hills and sang around their cooking fires in the cool of the evenings. Al and I often walked together, joking with the porters and occasionally trying to carry one of their loads with a tump-line. We soon came to the conclusion that the porters had very powerful necks.

It was the first time we'd ever trekked toward Everest, and every turn in the trail added a new experience and insight into how people lived. Though we climbers were having a relaxing time, the film crew was busy trying to capture our impressions and interactions. There were constant questions: "What do you feel about the coming climb? Do you think the team is a strong one? How do you expect the weather to be?" They were difficult questions to answer because the climb we were to attempt was outside our experience. When you got right down to it, the climb was outside all but a few climbers' experience. I preferred to keep an open mind on the many unknowns and enjoy the hiking. The mountain would be upon us soon enough.

A week into the trek most of the porters returned home. At the time I didn't question why and didn't interfere with Rouse, who seemed to have everything organized. Knowing what I do now, I suspect that our *sirdar*, a bit-too-flashy Sherpa called Dawa Balu, had stolen some of the porters' wages and they'd had enough. After we finally hired another group of porters, we were still fifteen short, so Al and I volunteered to come up with the last group a couple of days later.

As soon as our brilliant Sherpa cook, Wang Chup, had left with the main group, we realized our diet was going to change profoundly. Instead of the soup followed by cauliflower fritters, rice, dhal and canned meat, we ate rice, rice and more rice. Then we ate potatoes and rice.

I remember one night when the only shelter was a single- room hut in the middle of a dripping, Tolkien-like forest. It was the kind of place you'd normally pass by with a quick thought: "Hmm, I wonder where the pigs have gone?" But we rented it.

Al and I were wedged against a wall while a group of five porters—all sisters, cute and innocent—occupied the rest of the floor. We'd settled into our warm sleeping bags, with the girls whispering and giggling in the pitch black. Then it began. One of them made a rasping, gurgling sound as she drew phlegm up into her mouth. Splat! Something hit the wall above my head. The giggles got louder. "Ugh," I heard

Al mumble as he burrowed down into his sleeping bag. They were all at it, roaring and spitting. Splat! Splat! Splat! I covered my face in horror. Listening for more attacks, I slowly faded into sleep.

We joined up with Rouse in Namche Bazaar, the main Sherpa market town, and he led us for another hour up to Khunde, where the rest of the team was hanging out.

"Joe, Paul, John and Brian all flew into Lukla a few days ago," Rouse told us. "We're waiting for yaks to carry the gear the rest of the way to base camp."

The village of Khunde reminded me of a small Welsh village—minus the roads. The buildings were of neatly trimmed stone with either wood-shingle or tin roofs.

Joe lay out in the sun with a book. He told us of a recent dinner engagement in London: "Went to 10 Downing Street, lads. To see Maggie (Prime Minister Margaret Thatcher) and have dinner with the King and Queen of Nepal."

"Did they serve you *dhal bhat* (lentils and rice)?" Al joked.

"They wouldn't ask you to go, youth," Joe continued. "Couldn't trust you to behave."

Someone reminded Al of his behavior at the British Embassy reception in Kathmandu. While everyone was saying their polite farewells, Al could be seen at the far end of the lawn scooping glass after glass of wine from the tray of a mesmerized waiter.

The yaks arrived and we moved toward base camp. We were at over 12,000 feet and each day was quite short, partly because the yaks are slower than porters but also because we needed to acclimatize to the new elevations. In recent visits to the same area, I've always chosen to stay in the Sherpas' lodges where it's warm and cozy, but this time we camped out and stayed apart. This helped us to steer clear of the lung infections surrounding these places, but we missed out on seeing a lot of the local customs.

I spent one day walking with Joe, and as we were virtual strangers, we began to touch gently on climbing and our experiences. Our mutual respect held a certain dignity, which allowed us to explore each others' ideas and basic philosophies. He told me of his "near-misses" on K2 the previous summer and how he was avalanched in his tent and nearly suffocated at 26,000 feet. I listened to his stories with awe. I tended to be more cavalier in my general attitude towards the coming climb. The time would come when we needed to be more serious about the climbing, but I preferred to delay a little longer.

*Wind whips plume from Everest's summit*

It had been a dry autumn that year, and when we reached base camp on December 6th, there wasn't any snow on the ground. That first night it felt cold, very cold, but the air was still, and in my large A-frame tent I had the luxury of space and a super-warm sleeping bag.

Everest had looked big ever since I'd seen it a week previously, so when we actually arrived in base camp, I'd become accustomed to its bulk and grandeur. It was our proposed route that held my attention more than the mountain. It was long and parts of it were steep and unrelenting. The way to Camp 1 on the Lho La was up a granite cliff as big as most mountains in the Alps. In fact, the whole scale of things was so much bigger than I'd previously seen that I told myself to examine only one portion of the climb at any time and that would help keep my fears within bounds.

During one of the first nights, I awoke from heavy sleep to find I was being lifted off the ground and then dropped again, like a failed proponent of levitation. A sudden gale had swept down off the mountain, and I could hear a flapping of loose tarpaulins mixed with shouts and a roar as powerful as a jet engine. Snap! My tent poles broke and the tent shredded. My cry of "Oh, shit!" was lost in the wind. It seemed that everyone was stumbling around in the milky dawn light, grabbing guy-lines, ropes, rocks, anything to hold down the kitchen tent.

I lay for a moment, poised between half-consciousness and full-action, listening. It wasn't the surrounding wind and chaos I focused on but that background roar: an angry, warning roar unlike anything I'd ever heard before. A hungry, uncaged beast: it was the jet stream pushing through the pass 2,000 feet above us. It was to become our constant companion, but I'll never forget hearing it that first time.

The climb up to Lho La Pass began as a scramble up scree and then more solid bands of rock. The steeper climbing began with a short rappel into a snowy gully and then some smooth slabs for a few hundred feet. We needed to fix rope on all this section to ease our ascent to, and descent from, the pass.

We had no designated climbing partners but simply gravitated to whomever we felt like climbing with on any given day. It was natural that brother Al would join me and Joe for the first reconnaissance. The rocks we were climbing over were sharp and flinty and liable to abrade thin ropes, and we were forced to use fat eleven millimeter ones which were heavy to carry. As Al pointedly said, "Four of these fat bastards and me 'sac's full."

Because the weather was clear and sunny and because we were in the lee of the mountain out of the wind, our progress was fairly swift. John and Joe had completed a tricky traverse and reached the foot of a vertical tower almost three hundred feet high. The previous Yugoslav expedition had strung a caving ladder down the full length of this, and when Al returned from having led this section, he was extremely animated in his descriptions.

"You start with this overhanging corner," he said. "I daren't use the ladder 'cause the bloody thing may have come detached. So I get over the top of that and there's all these loose flakes. Oh-oh, I think, I'm going to crunch the lads below. Me lungs are bursting from hanging on, too. So I keep going, on up to a small ledge. On me way back down, I check out the ladder and drive some of the pins back in again. Somebody's tied old tin cans to the rungs so it's easier to get your feet into the rungs. Now it rattles and jangles like a herd of Swiss cows."

This became a landmark pitch on our climb. It's a pity it disappeared in 1982 when the whole tower fell over. It must have made one hell of a crash.

After ten days we arrived at the broad open plateau of the Lho La. The wind was not severe when I first arrived, but we had lived with the omnipresent roar and knew no tent could ever remain there. An ice cave was the obvious answer.

We dug a small passageway straight into the slope: big enough to allow a climber to enter at a stoop wearing all his down clothing but not so open that the storm could enter. After about six feet we sloped the tunnel upwards and entered another six feet. On either side of that section, we then opened up some sleeping platforms two or three feet off the ground so we could sit on the benches and have our feet in the corridor. A number of the team commented on the claustrophobic feeling they had of being entombed inside the snow, but once the winds began again with a vengeance, everyone was delighted with the results.

Down in base camp not all was running as smoothly as it should. Our *sirdar* had proved to be dishonest and unreliable. Some of the equipment had been "lost" during the approach. Though we couldn't prove it was his doing, he was the one ultimately responsible. Then there was the disruptive effect he had on the other Sherpas. He would sit around shouting orders, making personal demands and doing absolutely nothing himself. Finally our Nepali liaison officer fired him.

Our Sherpa cook staff also had many other problems unique to winter expeditions. They would go out to a small frozen pool and hack away at the ice until a basket was full of chunks and then carry it back to the kitchen for melting. There was no running water for miles. Then the kerosene began to separate in the cold and large amounts of wax clogged up our pressure stoves, causing them to flare up and go into "melt-down" as solder softened.

One time while sitting in the dining tent, I saw one of the cook-boys, like a movie stuntman, leap out of the cook tent with a full jerkin of gasoline. Flames belched from the spout as he ran away from the tents, blowing helplessly at the flames. Luckily for us—and him—the gas was so cold it didn't explode, and the flames were eventually doused.

All these problems added up to inadequate food and contaminated water, which meant that people were constantly sick. Then there was the super-dry cold air which irritated chests and invited pulmonary ailments. Al and I never suffered from this problem very much. I believe we had become accustomed to similar conditions while working in the Canadian winters.

Once the Lho La cave was established, people began carrying up food and rope so that we could work on the mountain above. It was exciting to be getting somewhere, and we could see the whole of the West Face and Ridge stretching up before us. This face was as complex and steep as many alpine North Faces, and because the wind had scoured it clean, it was almost devoid of the soft snow that helps speed up climbing. For a couple of days, John, Al and I worked fixing rope on the lower section.

From base camp we carefully watched through powerful lenses as Brian and Pete edged their way up ribbons of black, glassy water-ice. Brilliant climbing led them through bands of smooth granite and over a final overhang. They had cracked the crucial problem of the face. The psychological boost we all felt was immense. For Brian, who had been plagued by sickness, it must have been a strong affirmation that he was still climbing well.

That night the first of many storms pounded against the mountain. Climbers who were preparing to go relieve Brian, and Pete stayed in base camp. The roar of the wind was dampened by a heavy mantle of snow building up on our tents. Life turned to basics: eating, drinking and keeping warm. It began to look as if we were to have a white Christmas, so Brian radioed that they, too, were descending. It was depressing to have the weather foul us up when the teamwork and momentum had been building by the day. I just hoped it was not a serious turn for the worst because while we were achieving results everyone remained "psyched" and hopeful. Inactivity breeds its own cancerous restlessness, which can destroy the will to continue.

As evening light began to filter into the dining tent, Brian and Pete staggered into camp. Brian threw open the door and for a moment appeared like an apparition, covered in snow and with icicles hanging from his beard. His face was weather-beaten and grey.

"That was no fucking joke," he said, wearily dropping his axe and pack to the ground. "It's so bad up there I didn't know if I was going to get down. Halfway across that top snow slope, the wind was snatching my breath away so fiercely I dove my head into a crevasse to catch my breath. The wind actually lifted me up into the air. I was like a kite flying from the rope."

His eyes glittered like those of a madman as he continued: "All that snow on the loose rocks lower down had me tripping and falling, too. I'm knackered." The mountain had shown some of its armor.

Christmas Eve day dawned murky and drab, and since we were all together in base camp, we decided to celebrate the season and our achievements thus far. Mike Shrimpton wanted to film a "Christmas cameo" to send back in a news report. We all sat around outside the tents with large mugs of Scotch whiskey, telling tales and offering toasts to the camera.

Al felt he should get in the last word of Christian cheer in the movie. "Here's to all the men in bed with our women," he said. I noticed a few turned heads and worried faces, but the moment passed.

The long nights in base camp were taking some getting used to. We'd try to sit around the dining tent once the evening meal was over, but even wearing inordinate amounts of clothing was not enough. We'd still feel cold. I would slither into my down sleeping bag wearing eiderdown booties and gradually begin to get comfortable, but my feet remained icy cold. When I woke in the morning, it was the first thing I'd notice—cold feet. After weeks of this, I took it to mean two important facts. First, my red-cell count had increased sufficiently to partially restrict circulation. Second, my body was beginning to "run down" because of the combined effects of inadequate food, high altitude and the unrelenting battle against cold. Himalayan winter climbing was barely in its infancy, and we were learning all the time. I vowed to have a double-insulated dining tent and kerosene heaters on the next winter expedition—if I made it through the present one.

Then there were the psychological implications. Al Jewhurst came into the communal tent, shaking his head.

"I hardly slept at all last night," he said. "I think the L.O. (liaison officer) is losing his marbles." Al's tent was next to Mr. Singh's. He explained: "The L.O. spent all last night moaning. You know, he hasn't been out of his tent for three days."

"You're sure he wasn't praying?" I asked, aware that the climbers had been praying. "Do you think he's sick?"

"I think he's lonely, and I think the cold's driving him crazy," said Al. "If he was praying, it was for us to let him go home."

I was keen to get back to where the action was. So were Joe, Paul and the two Alans. The route up to Camp 1 was becoming more familiar, and we'd learned a few tricks about getting a heavy 'sac up the steep section. The bottom end of the safety rope was not attached to ropes lower down as was normally the case. We'd tie our pack onto the loose end and rest it on a ledge. Then we'd climb the overhanging caving ladder for a hundred feet and stop to haul up the bag. We just had to be careful the 'sac didn't tumble off the ledge or we'd look like a spider with a dumbbell tied to its waist.

A big advantage to living in an ice-cave is that we could begin to get ready in the mornings before it was light. In a tent there's always a heavy coating of frost that falls onto clothing and sleeping bags, and it makes early starts a real trial.

We left the cave as dawn was breaking and began the mile-long trudge across the Lho La to the foot of the face. Our beards became frozen with rime within half an hour, and people were too busy panting to speak. I clipped a jumar onto the first rope and began the long climb upwards. Kick, step. Kick, step. Stop, pant. Begin again. To vary the use of my leg muscles, I'd first face left and then change to face right. Then I'd face in and begin over again. It was monotonous, strenuous work. The only reward was being able to look down and see how far I'd climbed.

Paul and Joe were up ahead preparing to break new ground. I could see them crouching in a small cave while the wind tugged and flapped at their clothing. Paul had not been able to generate much warmth even when climbing, and he was shivering uncontrollably as I approached him.

"I think I'm going to have to go down while I still can." His words came out staccato and trembling. There wasn't much I could do for him except offer to take his place and hold the rope for Joe. I watched as he carefully descended. One careless slip or unmeasured movement while he bypassed the anchors and he would be dead. Our lives hung in the balance.

Joe led off round a corner and began climbing up snow- slopes, all the while angling in a rightward curving arc above vertical cliffs, which added to our feeling of exposure and vulnerability. Once I'd joined him, I was able to continue in the lead up some flakes of rock that stuck out like fins and provided great handholds. I enjoyed climbing with Joe because he was supremely confident, but there was more, too. Although he pushed himself hard, he never pushed others; that was for each individual to do for himself. It was as though we had a common understanding and respect for each other. I had sensed a competitiveness between him and others like Rouse and Paul Nunn, but with me he was not competitive. Certainly, he was ambitious but that was different. With me, he was supportive and a perfect companion, much as my brother had been over the years.

By the time we reached the foot of an open snowfield, it was time to return. The thought of darkness catching us out on such steep ground made us hurry down all the faster. As I rappelled down the ropes, I considered the problem of doing the same with frostbitten hands. It would be nigh impossible. There were too many complicated "change-overs" at anchor points on the fixed ropes. It didn't need the precise insight of a rocket scientist to figure out the seriousness of our position.

Paul, Brian, Pete and Al were all back at the cave when we ducked into the icy chamber. John had dumped a load of gear and descended, much to Joe's disappointment. He'd hoped that John would climb with my brother the next day and felt compelled to stand in for him. It appeared that with so many people up at the ice cave, John had been asked to forfeit his place at the front.

The next day while Al and Joe fixed more rope, Paul and Rouse carried up equipment in support. It was good that we were switching climbing partners a lot because it kept all of us committed to the climb. When John re-ascended, I met him outside the cave and said: "Me and you can fix tomorrow, if you like."

I'd spent a month in Poland with John, Al and Mick Geddes and appreciated John's climbing skills as well as his healthy sense of humor. He was a thoughtful person who often came up with poignant statements.

He once said to me: "You know, you and Al are quite different."

"Oh, yeah?"

"Yes. It seems as though you've always got the brain, and he's always looking for it."

Despite our enthusiasm to return to the front, the weather had other ideas. Cloud descended and the wind raged. John began to feel guilty at our inactivity and tried to convince me to climb despite the weather.

"We should be up there, Aid," he said. "Every rope-length counts."

"No bloody way I'm going up all those ropes in this storm," I said. "We wouldn't accomplish anything anyway. Just knacker ourselves for nothing."

Luckily, the following day dawned fine, or else I may have had to give in to John's demand for an epic. By eleven-thirty we were at the high point of the fixed ropes and rushing to fix more. The days never seemed long enough. John's figure crouched, silhouetted against the slope of sparkling crystals. White clouds of vapor spumed from his gasping lungs. He looked as if he was on fire. After three hundred feet, I led again and then he took over once more. We were heading toward some rocks that formed a low relief ridge on the mountainside. Hopefully we'd be able to put a camp there. Frustratingly short of our goal, we once more were forced to descend.

"It was a good day, man," I said, looking at John's frozen beard. "Tomorrow should see us at Camp 2."

When we eventually reached the crest, we could see down to base camp, where we knew the camera crew would be filming. On the crest's lee side were places where tents might survive; the snow was too hard and shallow for a cave. I needed a rest after the past few days, so I headed down to base camp.

The next few days served to illuminate a new set of problems in gaining height on the ridge. My brother and Paul had gone to Camp 2 and set up a small but strong box-tent. The weather had turned foul again but not sufficiently bad to stop Joe and Rouse from following them the next day. Their intention was to try to fix rope up to the West Shoulder and Camp 3, but instead they remained tent-bound in what had to rate as a "one-of-the-worst-nights-in-the-world" scenario. Gradually the extreme stress of living there drove them down one by one. Joe was the last to descend: alone, weary and thankful for his life.

In base camp, I sat glued to a telescope that was focused on Camp 2.

"If those tents stay up in this gale, without anyone tending them, then they should be fine when someone is inside," I commented.

Above Camp 2, low-angled snow swept up for a thousand feet to 23,500 feet, almost to the crest of the West Ridge. Though it was obviously easy climbing, we needed to fix rope up it, bearing in mind Brian's experiences much lower down. To do this meant an inevitable night in the tents and then a day's work to see it completed. Pete with Brian and I with John decided to go to Camp 2 and put in the next try. Brother Al had been sick with stomach problems and was to follow a day later. When I eventually panted my way into Camp 2, it was four in the afternoon, and the shadows were already beginning to slant down towards the small dots on the slope below. I dumped my 'sac alongside the orange dome-tent and unzipped the door.

"Shit!" Six inches of snow covered the entire floor.

A tiny gap in the unclosed door had provided the recent storm with all the access it needed. Reluctantly, and with many curses, I set to work to make the place habitable. As I was finishing, John arrived and we both settled into making soup and other drinks. Brian and Pete crunched past outside, going to the box-tent.

"It's interesting that despite all the guys on the trip, I've only climbed with you, Al and Joe," I told John. I had the feeling that people of equal strengths gravitated to each other and then the circumstances of rest-days and action kept them together. It was not what we had expected, or even wanted, but some natural laws were being obeyed.

The night was cold and I slept in my full winter down suit inside my sleeping bag. I'd become accustomed to the luxury of ice-cave living, so the small confines of the tent were barely comfortable. Sometime around midnight, the howl of the wind increased, and our small shelter shook frost down onto our faces. I tightened my hood and tried to ignore it, and I think John was doing the same.

It was still dark when I experienced a familiar, frightening feeling. There was air beneath my back. The tent was lifting. Then it did it again. And again.

"Oh-oh," I thought, "now what?" Ping! Ping! The poles snapped and ice-lined nylon muffled my face.

"John, the tent's gone!"

"I know. What're we going to do?"

"Wait until it's light, I suppose," I shouted over the pounding gale.

We were effectively bivouacking out at nearly 23,000 feet in the middle of a Himalayan winter. It was as dangerous as it was ludicrous, but there was nothing else we could safely do. We lay still, helpless until we could see what we were doing.

At the first hint of light, I scurried around finding my gloves, which had been inside my bag and underneath my back for extra insulation. They were warm and dry. John held up the tent fabric so I could get my boots on. Then I did the same for him.

"My hands have got really cold," he moaned in agony.

I stumbled out into the teeth of the storm. It must have taken twenty minutes for me to put on my harness. The ends were whipping around all over the place, and the buckles were doing a flagellation job on my aching body. All the time the wind howled around us, battering and snatching with invisible punches.

"Get tied in!" I bellowed and pointed down to the box. I jerkily gave him a safety rope down to where Brian was melting water, oblivious to our plight and John's frozen hands. When they heard our commotion, a tent-zipper opened and Brian handed out a big mug of steaming tea. Without hesitation John stuck the affected hand into the liquid and howled with pain. Rising panic had me jigging like a racehorse before a race.

"I gotta go, John," I said. "Will you be okay?"

"Yeah. I'll be right behind you once my hand's warmed up," he replied.

I needed to keep moving to stay warm despite the fact I must have looked like Mr. Michelin Man with all my gear on. Down the ropes I slid. Down, down, down. Snow whipped across my face and goggles, stinging my bare nose. I locked into a deep concentration to make sure there were no careless slips or fumbles. If I were to drop my figure-eight rappel device, I didn't have a spare.

"Keep thinking," I said to myself, over and over. "Come on, concentrate. It's not that bad. If you concentrate."

As I lost height, the wind began to ease off, and I occasionally stopped to cast a nervous glance up to where John should be. There was no sign.

"He'll be okay," I kept telling myself. "He's a real pro. He'll be all right."

I reached the foot of the face and began the slog back across the Lho La. The weather had become worse, but the end of my struggles was in sight. It was uphill for the last ten minutes to the cave, and I required about three stops to catch my breath. I could see Al waiting for me outside the cave entrance and decided I would climb the next section without a stop to show him I was still strong. He received me with warmth and I could feel the power in his control of the situation.

"Sit down, lad," he said. "I'll bring you a drink. You're safe now."

I flashed back to the flapping, broken tent. I'd turned on the walkie-talkie and heard Joe's voice. I'd then managed to splutter over the broken waves that the tent had blown apart and we were descending. No niceties. No "over and out." I just switched off. Al had been looking for me for more than two hours. Finally I was safe.

Once my pounding heart settled down, I became aware that all this epic was being filmed by Mike Shrimpton, who a few days earlier had settled into the ice-cave to record events and instruct people how to use the lighter-weight cameras, as he wouldn't be climbing higher. He'd done really well to get to the Lho La. Most expedition cameramen I'd ever heard of sat around base camp for the better part of the time, and I respected Mike's drive.

An hour later, a very frosted and drawn-looking John fought his way back up to the cave. His hands were feeling fine and his sense of humor still dominated his smile.

"Bloody hell, Aid," he said. "When I heard them poles snap, I knew we were in for some excitement. Brian wondered what I was doing when I put my hands into his tea."

Brian and Pete came down, too. It was as if the mountain had definitely won that round of the game.

While we recovered from our ordeal in base camp, Pete and Joe set off to try to redress the balance. They spent a couple of nights in the tents of Camp 2 and ran out the rope to easy ground just below the West Shoulder. While they were digging around to find a place for a cave, they accidentally broke through into a concealed crevasse. With a bit of exploratory digging, they quickly realized that it would be perfect for a cave and would entail far less work than those lower down.

This step forward gave everyone a much needed boost of moral, and plans were made for higher on the mountain. We needed to complete construction of this new cave, supply it with food and make the big leap across the West Shoulder to what would be our final cave. After all our hard-won efforts, we were getting nearer the possibility of a summit bid.

Brother Al was supposed to have gone up with them, but he found himself getting so cold that he descended to base camp instead. He looked pretty dejected as he walked into camp.

"I got so cold by the time I got to the 'schrund that it scared me, Aid," he said. His face was gaunt and lacked the impishness of recent days. "I need to eat more food just to stay warm."

There was something in his voice that was not typical. A kind of hopelessness pervaded his words. I hoped he'd get some rest and that he wasn't signaling his first doubts about the climb.

After two nights up at Camp 2, Pete and Joe were ready to move into the ice-cave at Camp 3 when our Sherpa cook suddenly collapsed. There was talk of a perforated ulcer and of his losing some blood.

Rouse radioed up to Pete: "I'm afraid you're going to have to come down and treat him, Pete. None of us knows what to do, and if he dies, we'll be in big trouble."

The climber that was Pete suddenly changed to a caring doctor: "Okay, Alan. I'll be down tomorrow. In the meantime give him thin broth, and don't let him dehydrate."

It had to be a big blow to someone who had so recently advanced the climb to have to relinquish his place to someone else. Paul and I volunteered to take his place and accompany Joe to Camp 3.

It would be a long way up the fifty-two rope-lengths from the Lho La, and I tried not to think about it too much. My pack was full of sleeping bags, pads and food  when I attached myself to the first rope.

"I'll see you up there," I said to Paul before I left.

"I'll take a bit longer than you," he said, "but don't worry. I'll get there, Aid." This was the steadfast determination of a seasoned mountaineer. Paul was the oldest member of the expedition, but he knew how to hang in and get the work done.

I decided to mask the intense hard work and boring labor by thinking about Lorna on Bali. I'd received a letter from her, telling of exotic beaches and warm seas. Of pig-roasts and beautiful people. What a contrast to where I was! I hadn't had a bath since Kathmandu almost two months before. Our food was bland and repetitive. As for our group of climbers, one could hardly call them beautiful.

Slowly the exposure built up below me. I turned the big overhang and could then see the long slope leading to Camp 2. I felt like I was getting somewhere.

"Wakey, wakey, youth!" I shouted to Joe when I arrived. He wasn't out of the tent but had a mug of tea waiting for me.

"I'll be glad to leave this bloody tent, Aid," he sighed. "Everything takes so long."

Joe had so much willpower. Just to camp out at those elevations was horrendous, let alone to put in a day's work. He was a very modest person in my company; later, when he wrote about his experiences in his book, *Everest the Cruel Way,* he often chided himself for his laziness. He once wrote about staring across to the North Ridge—scene of early British attempts on Everest—and feeling honored to be part of the history of the mountain: in the company of Mallory and Irvine, who had disappeared somewhere high on the mountain. A strange twist of fate finally bonded him to the mountain when he, too, disappeared, the very next year, on the North Northeast Ridge, with his fate also unknown. I'm proud to have shared a few moments with him.

When I eventually reached the end of the ropes, I'd been going steadily for seven hours. A ski pole marked a small hole leading into the crevasse. I sat on my 'sac and pulled out a bar of chocolate-covered mint cake. Normally I wouldn't touch the stuff, but these were not normal times. The cake almost tasted good.

Joe arrived while I was digging, like a mole in a pile of dirt. The snow was crystalline and easy to scrape from the side walls of the crevasse. I stuck my head out into the air to greet him.

"A bit of a slog, those last five rope-lengths, eh?" I said.

"The whole day was a bit of a slog, but what a great view from up here!" he said, happy to have arrived.

We took turns digging the sleeping chamber and shoveling snow debris out through the hole. It felt much colder than the caves lower down. There was a draft coming up through part of the crevasse, and I was glad of the big one-piece suit I wore. Paul arrived as we were trying to settle into our new home. He was even bigger than normal when encased in his down suit.

"It's going to be a bit tight tonight, but it should keep us warm," he said in his flat, matter-of-fact way.

The steam from heated water rose out of the pan. We were looking forward to some nourishment after the long day. "It's like a bloody London fog in here," I observed. "I hope it doesn't wet our gear."

It was a fitful night at our new altitude and in such cramped quarters. Hot Ovaltine was all we could manage for breakfast, but I forced down some more of the mint cake a little later.

"I'll stay here today and enlarge the cave," Paul volunteered, "if you lads want to go and check out the route."

"That sounds okay to me," said Joe. "Aid, you want to go up onto the ridge?"

"Yeah," I said, knowing that he'd wish to go exploring. "We can carry some rope up there ready to begin fixing."

Out in the cold morning air, the surrounding mountains sparkled like white gems and the sky radiated an intense blue. Unroped, we began slowly, matching our pace with our breathing. My feet felt warm inside the new and innovative plastic boots and double overboots. I marveled at the difference between the modern technology and the old leather boots. Maybe it would be only the better, advanced-design that which would allow Himalayan winter-climbing to survive.

We were climbing up onto a rounded dome which marked the beginning of the horizontal section of the West Ridge. The snow was firm and wind-packed so that our passing was recorded only by tiny crampon holes punched into the surface. I reached a large rock as the ground leveled off and sat down to wait for Joe, who was not far behind. The wind had picked up and was growing stronger by the minute.

I turned my back on it and shouted into Joe's ear: "Let's go as far as is safe in this wind and see what the difficulties are."

He nodded. Before us, Everest rose in a huge, black, wind-blasted pyramid. The crest that stretched in front of us snaked into the middle of it like a white wave. Few people had ever seen it from that position, with the North Face slipping away to the left and the unearthly plunge into the Western Cwm on the right. The view was a just reward for all the calf-straining effort of the past few days.

Our walk across to where the ridge narrowed became more of a stagger as the wind roared out of the south. It pushed and pushed and pushed again. Our whole bodies tilted into it at crazy angles, only to be kicked sideways by an unexpected super-gust. We roped up for safety, and when it became obvious we'd have to cross over the knife-edge to continue, I turned to Joe and signalled a halt. We needed to begin fixing rope, but I was punch-drunk from the wind and knew it was too bad to go on.

Back at the cave, Paul had been working hard. There was more room, but the place was still dismally cold. I reflected on this with the others: "You know, this cave will never be as warm as those at Camp 1 because there's a slight flow of air coming from somewhere. I think the snow is not as dense, too, and that's not helping." We had to make the most of it, though; creating a new one would use up masses of time and energy.

There was a voice outside, and Rouse arrived with a cough: "Any room in there? Phew! It's hard work getting up here."

He slid in beside us. We sat in a circle, like gnomes around a toadstool, watching the stove's weak efforts at melting snow.

It was snowing the next morning. Paul, who had been unable to stomach any food, decided to descend to the Lho La for more supplies. Rouse disappeared to bring more equipment up from Camp 2 but never reappeared. He found the weather so foul that he, too, descended. That second night at almost 24,000 feet had been a poor one for me, and I had developed a drumming headache and felt listless and tired. All day Joe labored at making drinks to revive me, but it wasn't working. I slipped in and out of sleep and now know that I was taking quite a risk to remain there feeling as I did. I was hoping I'd recover and hated the idea of not achieving more before going down.

"I'll see how I feel tomorrow, Joe," I said. "It's a pity someone else couldn't come up here to help you."

We both felt isolated from the rest of the group and I wished my brother would come up and join us. Finally, exhausted from four nights at that height, we descended in poor weather.

Back in base camp, the snowfall wasn't heavy, but the grey skies weighed down the group's morale. Without the radiant heat of the sun, it became depressingly colder. We huddled in the dining tent and tried to keep warm around a single camping stove. It was a pathetic sight.

John and Pete Thexton had been up to Camp 3 on overlapping days, but only Pete had climbed beyond. It seemed as if we were approaching another crisis in our progress up the mountain. The climb from Camp 1 to Camp 3 was so daunting that one really had to "psyche up" for it, and not everyone was managing to get there. Ideally, we needed four people up there to support each other's efforts, but it just wasn't happening.

It was around that time that both Paul and John decided to return to their jobs in England. That was the price of having a "real" job, and I was sorry to see them go. They had added tremendously to the group effort and were going to miss out on a summit try.

Toward the end of January, under perfect blue skies and almost windless weather, I set off back up the long haul to Camp 3. Joe was a few hundred feet behind, and we were in high spirits. It felt as if I was faster than the previous time, and I hoped that the earlier nights spent high would help me feel better once up there. I began to count off the rope-lengths as I climbed: "Three. Four. Five. Ten. Twenty." I was enjoying the freedom to move at speed. Though I was panting heavily, it didn't seem at all painful. Five hours later I jumared into camp. A natural high of bubbling elation welled up in me. Maybe we'd go to the summit this time! Inside the cave, I put on a pan of snow to melt and waited for Joe. A while later, he arrived and grinned when I passed him a hot drink.

"First-class service even at this altitude," he said.

We sat in our sleeping bags and tried to stay warm. I asked Joe about his earlier life in a seminary and how he began climbing.

"We were really naive about the outside world," he said. "One of the younger fathers took us out to an old quarry, and then we began hitching rides up to the Lake District." He laughed as something else came to his mind: "One time I was hitching near the Lakes when this bloke picked me up. He kept giving me sideways glances and then put his hand on my knee. I panicked and asked him to drop me off."

I laughed, as I thought of my own response to something like that. Mainly, punching the guy in the nose.

Joe continued: "About five years later I was hitching in the same place, and guess what? The same bloke stopped again."

"No."

"Yeah."

"So what did ya do?"

"I got in and smiled at him and told him where I needed to go. This time he didn't touch me, but you could see he thought I was game. So he drove me all the way to the Lakes. I smiled again and got out quick. Thanked him and buggered off."

Joe had a poor night and awoke with a headache. Outside the wind howled across the cave entrance, and light snow sped by. We were once again stranded by poor weather.

"I'll go crazy if we have to spend many more nights up here just doing nothing but suffer," I complained to Joe. "Achieving something is worth it, but to lie on your back all day is like being in hospital."

All day we lay. We cooked. And we lay down again. The following morning while I busied myself making breakfast, Joe was on his knees making dry, heaving vomits. There was something about living up at that camp that felt as if we were much higher than the 23,500 feet we knew to be the real altitude. Maybe it's a winter phenomenon.

"It's probably too windy to accomplish much, but we could go up to the shoulder and shoot some film," suggested Joe, who had taken a great interest in high-altitude filming.

"Okay," I said, "but you'll have to load the Bolex in a sleeping bag as I've never practiced before."

Snow conditions underfoot were as good as the first time, but the wind was far worse. It pushed and punched at us constantly, snatching our breath even before we had time to gasp. Slowly we staggered upwards to the crest and rested at the large rock.

Out came the Bolex and a simpler autoload camera. All but one of the turret lenses on the Bolex were frozen solid, despite having been specially "winterized." I took it and got Joe to provide me with a foreground by staggering further along the ridge. It was difficult holding my breath to keep the camera steady, and I was concentrating so intensely that I didn't notice my nose had frozen to metal on the camera. When I took my head away from the eyepiece, flesh tore away with it. I wouldn't do that again in a hurry.

Soon we were safely back in the cave. I voiced some fears to Joe: "You know, if something had happened to one of us out there today, we'd really be in trouble with no one else up here. I wish someone else would come up to help."

"We'll see what happened today when we radio down tonight," he said.

Al's voice came on the radio: "Camp 3, come in, please."

"This is Aid. What happened today?"

"Brian and I tried to come up today, but there was so much snow blowing over the start of the ropes, we were getting buried." The crackling voice continued: "We'll try again tomorrow."

"Is anyone else coming up?" I asked, trying to monitor everyone's health and attitude without asking directly.

"Alan, Brian and me are all here at the Lho La. Pete has broke a couple of ribs through coughing but seems to be okay. What are you doing tomorrow?"

"It depends on the weather. Today was really bloody windy. It was even worse than Patagonia, kid."

I finished and said to Joe: "People are getting knackered with prolonged exposure to the cold. Have you noticed how it sounds like a TB ward down in base camp? Especially at night?"

"Yeah, but we've still got two weeks left before the permit runs out. We could still do it if we pulled together as a team," said Joe, whose determination was what made him so successful a mountaineer.

There was something in the way my brother spoke that made me feel he wasn't giving the whole story—something that rang like an alarm bell in the back of my mind. I didn't mention it to Joe. There was no point. But I vowed to probe a little deeper the next time we talked.

Living in the ice-cave was not what I'd hoped. It was far too cold and drafty to get a good rest. Even though the stoves were fueled by a propane-butane mix, we needed to keep the cylinders in our sleeping bags to prevent them from freezing—along with boots, gloves and other assorted bits of gear.

I turned to Joe who was trying to melt snow, and said: "All this crap we have to keep in our pits doesn't give us much room. There's many other things I'd rather have in my bag."

"Like that American girl you met in Kathmandu," he grinned.

"Certainly better than you, youth. But she's not stupid enough to be here."

And so the banter went.

Come morning, the wind was worse than ever, though it was difficult to believe it possible. I sat in the entrance to the cave with walkie-talkie in hand.

"Al, do you copy? Over."

"I get you strength five, Aid. Over."

"Is anyone coming up today ?"

"Me and Brian got up early, but it's bad out."

There was some uncertainty in his voice. I tried to push him a bit more.

"How bad, Al?"

"The wind is blowing a plume from the summit. What will you do today?"

"We're not sure yet. Before we go sticking our necks out on the ridge, we need to know someone else is coming up here. It feels bloody isolated up here."

Pete Thexton broke in: "This is Pete at base camp. I can hear you both. I will be fit in a few days."

I needed to think and to speak with Joe. In Al's tone, I heard the first sounds of having given up the attempt.

"We'll call back in a half hour," I  said and switched off the radio. "Joe, I think Al's saying he and Brian aren't going to come up."

In the past week I'd been so focused on my own efforts that I'd lost sight of the "big picture." There were only six climbers now on the mountain, and Pete in base camp was sick. I pictured Al and Brian in Camp 1, looking up at a storm-ravaged mountain and comparing it with the comforts of the ice-cave. Maybe I'd be thinking the same if I were in their shoes. Still, I wasn't and so wished to press my own agenda.

Joe was into using guilt and coercion to bring them up to us, but I knew it wasn't going to work. I stated my mind: "If they won't come up, then we don't have a chance. I'll talk to them once more."

I turned back to the radio: "Al, if you come up to here, then we'll try and go along the ridge to the next camp."

There was silence.

Then came Al's voice: "Aid, if you show us you can get there, then we'll come up. Everybody is tired and the weather is bad. I don't see what else we can do."

"How do you mean 'show us you can get there'"? I bellowed into the mouthpiece. "We've *shown* we can get up there!"

He was making me mad. I couldn't see that he was negotiating for the others, too. He knew the mind of everybody below us and was trying to tell me it was all over.

"If you won't come up, then I'm coming down!" As though that was some sort of punishment. "Over and out!"

I turned to Joe: "That's it! We can't do this on our own. Wait till I see our kid!"

I began to pack my sleeping bag. I thought of all the work to get up there. All the trips up and down ropes, lugging heavy 'sacs, digging the caves. Everything for nothing. So many cold nights, lousy food, bed sores from waiting around.

I began the long descent to base camp. It was pretty silly to be mad because we'd failed to reach the summit, to blame other people because they'd had enough of all the hardship. Everyone has his own personal breaking point, and we'd all stretched ours far beyond anything we'd ever done before. In the immediacy of it all, I couldn't see what we had gained: the chance to bond with good climbers whose personal charisma outstrips most people one gets to meet in life; the satisfaction of being able to work with some of the best climbers around; and the teamwork we did achieve. Pitch for pitch, we'd done more climbing than on two alpine winter climbs. Yet there I was, descending and spitting curses into the gale. Useless curses, very strong gale.

When I stuck my head into the cave at Camp 1, Brian told me that Al had already gone to base camp. His face was drawn and tired. He'd done his best. I continued down the ropes and felt stronger with the thickening air and almost-warm temperatures.

From the edge of base camp, I could see a few people sitting around outside, hunched over and drinking tea. Much of my anger had evaporated during the descent. I dumped my pack down onto the ground and sat next to Al with a sigh, "Man! That's a long way down!"

"Yeah," he said, looking dejected. "People are either sick or worn out, kid."

"When the mind gives up, the body ceases to function," I snapped, eyes blazing.

Almost immediately I regretted my outburst. The expedition was over. We must all accept it.

The next week was spent clearing as much equipment off the mountain as we could. I remember one incident which reflects the power of the wind and the puny impact we had upon the mountain. Al was at the Lho La with duffels filled with tents, mattresses and sleeping gear. He had dragged them over to the head of a gully he was about to pitch them down.

His voice crackled over the radio: "They've gone, Aid. Can you see them falling, with the telescope?"

"Not yet. Are you sure they've fallen? There's nothing."

"They slid down over the edge."

There was a silence and then: "Oh, shit, man! I don't believe it!"

"What is it, Al?" I bellowed.

"The bags rolled down the gully for a hundred feet, and the wind has blown them back up!"

A week later we were on our way to the Lukla airstrip. I turned a corner in the trail, and there below me was a smiling face framed by a head of flowing hair. Lorna had returned from Indonesia to meet me.

Since that expedition, I've thought about how people can drive themselves through fatigue and exhaustion, and I've pondered the relationship between body and mind. I had said that the body gives up when the mind allows it to. I had not thought about how the body forces the decision upon the mind. That is what had happened during the last weeks of the expedition. It is a delicate balance between driving oneself to exhaustion and listening to the body as it strives to survive without oxygen, food and heat.

A year later Joe was climbing with Pete Boardman on Everest. He miscalculated the fine balance and paid for it with his life. A few years later Pete Thexton did the same near the summit of Broad Peak; he died of cerebral edema. What happened to Al Rouse on K2 is another story. But all these incidents show that we must never stop watching the delicate balance of our own lives along that fine line.

# CHAPTER
## 16

## DHAULAGIRI

BY ADRIAN

It was difficult to believe that the old airport in Kathmandu belonged to a world-class destination. It reminded me of the Leeds airport in Yorkshire: small, confused and definitely *not* international.

As Al and I rode to the airport in a taxi to collect Jon Jones and Chuck Masters, who were about to arrive from Delhi, I asked Al: "Do you think we'll be able to get the gear through the same as with the winter trip?"

At that time, we'd somehow closed a deal with the customs guy at the eleventh hour. Seventy loads were in jeopardy, and he'd asked Al what was in one of the boxes. From among a mass of tins in the box, he held up a can of corned beef, which was prominently labeled with an unmistakable drawing of a cow.

"All fish, sir," said Al, knowing that beef was not well received in a Hindu country.

"Very good, sir," said the customs guy, his mind on higher matters. "Do you have film? I have a camera."

I gave him the official ten rolls of film, and he then gave us our seventy loads.

Were we going to have a repeat this time?

"No problem," said Al, as the taxi neared the airport. "I've got a box of multi-colored chalk. It's all we need."

We knew the routine. A customs official would look through a bag and then, in chalk, scribble a Nepali letter or number onto it. It didn't matter which, because we'd then copy it with our own chalk. In this way, we'd release our own baggage with few questions asked. The only snag was that they used different colored chalk every day. They thought *they* were sneaky!

John told me later that on the flight from Delhi, both he and Chuck were concerned about the amount of luggage they had.

"How many bags are we allowed?" Jon asked Chuck. "Will we have to pay for extra gear? We might have a problem with importing all our gear. There are supposed to be taxes, but it can't be that much."

Jon paused to let that sink in and then added, almost as an afterthought: "Do you have a spare five thousand dollars you can get hold of if we get hit in customs?"

Chuck is a doctor, but one who's almost always broke. His reply wasn't affirmative.

So with a feeling of impending doom, they deplaned in Kathmandu and were herded into the tiny, crowded baggage-claim area. One of the main problems with this place is that no one tells you what to do. You have to work it out for yourself, and for people fresh from the organized West, it's pretty terrifying.

In order to use the chalk trick, Al and I needed to get inside the baggage-claim area, but it was guarded by an unfriendly soldier. His job was to keep out people like us and to check all baggage for the telltale chalk mark.

I held my Alberta driver's license up to him as though it were a pass card, and without a second glance, we opened the door and dove into the throng. Jon was standing amid a mass of duffles and back-packs. When he spotted the two of us, he visibly brightened.

"How did you get in here?" he asked. "They wouldn't let us out."

"Never mind right now," said Al. "Where's all your gear? Pile it up by this customs table."

Al began hauling a large duffle across the room, and I quickly tried to explain to Jon and Chuck just what was going to happen.

"They want to look in the bags and then mark it once it's been passed," I said. "You lift a 'sac onto the table and get the custom guy's attention. We'll get the rest out with our own piece of chalk. The more we move bags around, the less they'll keep track of them."

Chuck looked bewildered.

"Don't worry, guys," I said. "We've done this before."

Al had already covertly marked a number of bags and was handing a bunch of rupees to porters. Before we knew it, everything was outside and loaded onto a creaking minibus.

Chuck asked Al: "So we didn't have to pay any import tax for that lot of gear?"

Al grinned. "Of course not," he said. "We don't have the money!"

Kathmandu airport is a busy place immediately before a flight departs to the West. Trekkers argue with airline staff over excess baggage. Sherpas say their goodbyes to tourist *sahibs*.

But for Lorna and me, there were only the two of us. The surrounding chaos did not exist. She was on the verge of tears at our parting, and I felt none too brave.

We had spent a month wandering the streets and bazaars of the city. It had gone too quickly. Now she must return to work for a U.S. federal judge. It sounded terrifyingly serious to me. Yet I would leave to go to Dhaulagiri in a couple of weeks, and that sounded terrifyingly serious to her.

I held her tight one last time and said: "I'll come and visit you in Colorado. 'Bye."

I turned and left with a great big lump in my throat.

At 26,810 feet (8,172 meters), Dhaulagiri is the sixth highest mountain in the world, and it was one of the last to be climbed. The mountain's isolated position in western Nepal makes it the first target for all major storms that sweep in from India, so it's often called "The Mountain of Storms."

An imposing spur of ice and rock stretches down the northeastern side of the peak. This was to be our route. It would be a smaller expedition than the one to Everest. There would be only six climbers, most from Calgary. While Al and I had been on Everest, Jon Jones had been busy in Canada, organizing the necessary equipment and money. Jim Elzinga, a tall, blond photography student, was to be joined by Doni Gardner and Dr. Chuck Masters.

My immediate job after Lorna's departure was to order all the local foods and pack them into thirty-kilogram loads. Alan was trekking with a girlfriend in the Dhaulagiri region and would be returning soon to help me.

On my way back from seeing Lorna off at the airport, I called in to see Mike Cheney, an expatriate Englishman who ran a small trekking operation out of a large dilapidated house on the edge of downtown Kathmandu. "Hi, Mike," I said as I entered his spacious but spartan office. "Have you seen Pasang Tenzing yet? He said he'd be in from Khumbu around this time."

"His brother, Nima, told me that Pasang will be here in two days," said Mike, in his precise south-of-England accent. "I sent Nima to your hotel an hour ago."

Nima Tenzing was to act as a climbing Sherpa on our expedition. He came highly recommended. He'd been to Kanchenjunga with Doug Scott and Joe Tasker. He wasn't like the young Sherpas one sees dressed up in bright colors and new Western climbing gear. He was about forty-five years old and no more than five feet tall.

When I spotted him sitting in the shade at the entrance to the Himalayan View Hotel, he leapt to his feet, a huge grin on his tanned face. He wore an old red sweater and faded blue jeans.

"Mornin', sa. Mike say you here," he said, holding out a calloused palm.

"Hi, Nima. How are you?"

"Very good, sa." He never did say *sahib,* as many Sherpas did. It made me think he'd worked in the army.

We sat and discussed what food I would buy, when we hoped to leave Kathmandu for the mountain, and when the other climbing members would arrive. He listened intently, his eyes bright and watchful. Although I didn't know him well, I could see immediately that he was trustworthy and honest. I warmed to his quiet modesty and confident manner. He assured me that when Pasang arrived, they would both pack all the food themselves, leaving me free to take care of any other arrangements.

I had met Chuck only once back in Calgary, and as he was a doctor, we'd spoken then only about drugs and medicine. Now he told us about an incident he'd been involved in while in India:

"We were riding on top of a bus: a Dutch guy, a French hippie and I. The stupid Frenchman pushed a local who was trying to climb up onto the roof and was hanging onto the guy's ankle. Suddenly, a mob formed and started throwing stones at us. They went crazy—shouting and trying to get at us. I was terrified. It was probably just the kind of thing you boys would have liked. Well, I didn't. I was glad when the bus driver took off, with bodies hanging all over the bus."

"Don't worry, Chuck," said Al. "We're going to be using a three-ton truck that belongs to Encounter Overland, and it'll have an Australian driver."

Al brandished a large, shiny—and probably very sharp—Kukri knife and said: "I 'eard that this Indian in Bradford (of northern England fame) was attacked on 'is way 'ome from work. So he pulled out something like this and chopped the bloke in two."

With a two-handed grip, Al slashed the knife down through the air. I saw Chuck wince as if he expected to treat his first casualty.

Later, when we knew each other better, Chuck confided to me that we weren't anything like he'd expected. "I thought you were all going to be hard-core jocks," he said, "and you'd be marching up and down the mountain like Nazis. But, oh, no, you're just a bunch of crazed party winos who happen to climb."

Sometimes Chuck can be very observant.

After a long, dusty day in the back of a truck, we crawled into the small roadside town of Baundanda. It was the point where porters would take over our loads, to carry them for ten days to base camp. The small, tough-looking porters, who had disproportionately large feet, began hefting our loads down from the truck.

"Watch that! It's got glass in it!" yelled Al, but a kindly brown face just smiled back. Then Pasang shouted something in Nepali, and the porter set the load gently on the ground.

To a casual observer, the scene probably would have looked chaotic. Many of our loads were packed in dirty jute sacks, which were then tied into conical wicker baskets woven from bamboo. Pasang called them *dokos*. These were being whisked away to a campsite down by a nearby river. As there were many similar looking bundles that were not ours but were also being carried in the same direction, a few of the members began to show signs of panic.

"Which are our loads? Should I go with them? Who knows which is what?" Questions erupted from Jim Elzinga, who towered a couple of heads above the crowd of noisy Sherpas.

"Don't worry, Jim," Al shouted back. "Pasang knows exactly what's going on, and Nima is already at the campsite to see it's stacked properly."

Although, in theory, it was possible that a load could go astray, it was very unlikely, because most porters are unswerv- ingly honest and also because they have little use for packaged food or high-altitude clothing.

The next morning, we handed out loads and wrote down the porters' names. I always like to do this myself while the *sirdar* —in this case, Pasang—coordinates everything. It gives the porters the feeling that a Westerner is in charge of the proceedings and that they will definitely get paid at the end of their journey. A few crooked *sirdars* have been known to skim cash off the top of wages, completely un- known to expedition members who are told by *sirdars* that the angry porters are just "bad men."

"*Nam ke ho?*" I asked the porters their names.

"Rambadur Tamang," replied a smiling man who was prob- ably about thirty years old. Although his face looked older, his body did not: large veins and sinewed muscles bulged from his powerful- looking legs.

I wrote down his name and the number painted on his load. I gave him a necklace of string holding a disk with the same number, and then I placed thirty rupees in his hands. He accepted the bills with two upraised palms and disappeared to buy provisions for the journey. And so it went until all eighty loads were being transported up the trail.

While walking up the trail, I like to be able to pick out a load and then check my book to see the name of the particular porter carry- ing it. I call the porter by name and follow that with a greeting: "Namaste Phuri! *Ramro manchi!*" It never fails to elicit a surprised smile, as I apparently remember his name.

Our first view of Dhaulagiri came on the morning of the sec- ond day. It had rained all night, and we had decided to sleep in a local tea shop-cum-lodge situated on a pass overlooking the Kali Gandaki River. A heavy mist settled over the valley, but above the sky was clear

*Dhaulagiri soars to 26,810 feet (8,172 meters)*

and a pink glow spread across the northern horizon. The huge bulk of Dhaulagiri stood before us, its snows changing from pink to yellow as the sun rose higher.

"Looks big to me, lad," said Chuck, as he snapped a photo.

"Yes, and it's still nine days away," I replied, watching his face to see his response. He got my message: the mountain is *very, very big*.

We hiked for a few days, heading north to the town of Beni. It was very relaxing to have nothing to do but stroll along the banks of the Kali Gandaki. Every lunchtime, Pasang would organize a picnic, which might consist of tuna, sardines, cheese pastries and an occasional cake.

It was during one of these leisurely halts that I discovered Jim didn't drink tea or coffee. In fact, he didn't like hot drinks at all. He was also accustomed to eating large amounts of meat while in Canada, and meat was in short supply in Nepal. He also could not eat rice—the basis for any Nepalese dish—and appeared to survive on fried potatoes. Given those eating habits, I thought it certain that he would lose a lot of weight.

At the end of our fifth day, we were hiking in a heavy downpour when we arrived at the village of Dhorpatan. There, as in many of the villages, we were directed to the school playing field to camp. Many porters wished to return from there, as we would soon be gaining altitude, and they were ill-clad for the cold. We decided to take a rest day while more porters were found. I don't know if this particular day coincided with a local holiday, but a number of wiry-looking men wandered onto the field and set up a target at one end. They all carried wooden longbows and sharp arrows complete with flight-feathers.

"Hey up, looks like Robin Hood and his merry men are here," joked Al. "I wonder where Maid Marian is ?"

"Some things never change, do they, Al?" quipped Chuck, who already had Al figured out.

The marksmen were good—very good. The range must have been close to 150 feet, and they were consistently hitting the heart drawn on the board.

"Leaves no imagination as to why they use these bows, does it?" said Doni. "Think I'll have a go."

He walked over to the guy who seemed to be in charge, and we could see him select an arrow. When he hit the board with his first shot, our Sherpa kitchen staff all stood up and began to cheer and shout. However, when he centered the heart with the third arrow, all the archers came and shook his hand in amazement.

When he returned, I asked: "How d'ya learn to do that, Doni?"

"Living with the Eskimos for six months," he said. "They make *their* bows out of antlers. I was just lucky."

I didn't think that was luck, but it was typical of Doni's modesty. I remembered his story about a cross-country ski race when he was still at high school. He had overslept in the school gymnasium where all the racers were being housed. No one was around to give him a ride to the starting point, so he hitched a lift and then set out on the race after everyone else had begun. When he arrived at the finish line, after passing many racers, they still hadn't erected the official post. He had won!

The terrain began to change from level open valleys to steeper, terraced hillsides. The trail traced a difficult, winding way up the left side of the Mayandi Khola, a torrent that was a thousand feet below our feet. A slip would certainly be fatal.

We arrived at a dirty cluster of shake-roofed houses nestled in an east-facing hollow: the village of Matel. Our tents were pitched on a series of small dry terraces, from which corn had already been harvested.

Pasang walked over from the kitchen area and said: "Aid, can I buy a water buffalo tonight? They say they can give me a good price."

"How big is it?" I inquired, as I'd never seen a *small* water buffalo.

"Come, see. Over there." He pointed to a huge animal tied by its neck to a tree.

"They asking 1,500 rupees. That is good price."

"But how will we carry it to base camp?"

"Oh, eight porters only, I think."

I thought of eight times thirty kilos of meat being hauled to base camp. Jim would be very happy.

"O.K.," I said. "We'll buy it, but you must find more porters."

He ran off and I think I saw a skipping motion in his stride. Watching from the door of my tent, I soon saw a man with an axe approaching the tethered beast.

"Hey, Al!" I shouted. "Come and look at what's going to happen here. I don't believe this guy's going to axe it."

What followed I can only describe as terrible, as we slipped back centuries into the Dark Ages. The man with the axe crept slowly

*Porters dividing water-buffalo meat*

up to the beast, which was the size of a large cow with a pair of nasty-looking horns. Two slightly moist and patient eyes watched him with growing interest. Then, THUNK! The eyes turned from patient to angry, and the beast swung its huge body around the tree.

"Man, that cow must have one sore head," commented Al, rubbing his own in sympathy.

When the axe-man tried another blow, the buffalo ducked away, and the axe fell to the ground beneath the animal's forefeet. The guy tried to sneak up and snatch it away, like a matador who'd lost his sword. But the buffalo's horns were flashing. After another brave attempt, the man retrieved his axe. We looked on as if it were really only a movie—no one would actually *do* that.

THUNK! Another blow hit its mark. There was a mighty roar, and the crazed beast tore back its head and snapped the rope. We watched in horror as the normally docile animal leapt down a bank, galloped across a terrace and raced downhill with the gait of a cantering rhinoceros. Charging down from terrace to terrace, it was soon out of sight, followed by a whooping contingent of swarming villagers.

"They're nuts—crazy to try to kill it that way," I exclaimed. "And I think I've lost my appetite."

It took two more days to reach base camp beneath the west face of the mountain. We did not pass through any more villages as we climbed up through an area of bamboo and then rhododendron. During the final hour, the trail left the woods, and we exited onto a sloping area of grazing land. The altitude was a little over 14,000 feet, which we all felt was too low for a permanent base camp. All the porters were paid off, except the fifteen strongest. They would remain and help us carry our equipment the final stage to the edge of the glacier.

Beyond us was a dry glacier of grey ice and then a narrow valley with steep-sided cliffs. Because of fresh snow higher on the mountain, there was danger from avalanches in that section, especially later in the day when the sun had warmed the slopes. A plan emerged whereby we would carry our loads through the valley to a halfway staging camp and then move past to where the second base camp would be. We would therefore have to drop back to collect the gear. It would be time-consuming, as well as hard work, but if we didn't do that, we would be too far away from the mountain to stand a chance of climbing it.

I was walking through thick mist with my head down, trying to follow a faint trail in the snow. On my back was a seventy-five-pound leg of buffalo tied onto a pack-frame.

"Man, I don't believe I'm trying to carry this," I panted to Doni, who carried a slightly smaller piece of flank.

"Do you want me to take it for a while?" he offered. "We've come about halfway."

I collapsed in the snow so he could take it from me.

"If this stuff goes rotten before we eat it, I'll be really sorry," I whined, rubbing my shoulders to ease the pain.

It took almost a week before we completed transporting all the equipment and food up to our final base camp. Although it was back-breaking work, it did help us to acclimatize for the eventual climbing.

Our tents were set up on the edge of the glacier and, we hoped, out of the way of most crevasses. Beyond the glacier, the huge north face of Dhaulagiri soared above. There were a few ice cliffs, a rock-band and then the final summit—snow-slopes swept up to the pyramidal peak.

Our proposed route took the left-hand skyline up a vast prow of snow, ice and rock. At the base of the Northeast Spur lay a wide U-shaped pass where we would have to make a camp at 18,000 feet. Jon came over to our group with a photocopy of the route.

"I can show you where the camps are," said Jon, who, as a lecturer in geology, was accustomed to handing out information. "Camp 5 is below the fore-summit. Camp 4 is at 24,600 feet, where the snow ridge abuts the rock, and Camp 3 is perched on that cliff." He described every location with precision and the specific height.

"Jon, I don't think we need to have a Camp 5," Al said and glanced to see my reaction. "Once acclimatized, we should be able to do the final 2,500 feet in a single day."

I agreed, because making a camp higher than Camp 4 would be sheer misery. Why take two days to do what could be done in one?

"Maybe you two monkeys can do a long last day," interjected Chuck, "but what about normal people?"

"Don't you have any speed-ya-up and go-faster drugs in that medical bag?" I joked.

"Used them all up before I came here to be with you crazys," he said, teasing. "If only I'd known what I'd let myself in for . . . ." He shook his head in mock disbelief. Chuck was a real gem of an expedition member. The more I learned about him, the more I liked him.

A week passed before we had all necessary food up on the pass at 18,000 feet. We built tent platforms into the side of a snowbank to shelter our temporary homes from the sharp southerly blasts that swept across the flank of the mountain. It was from this camp that the real climbing would begin.

Our first task was to mark a clear trail across the wide and featureless pass to where the slopes steepened and a broad ridge led up to our Camp 2 at a height of 21,000 feet. We placed bamboo marker-wands—freshly cut during the last days of our walk to base camp—every fifty yards or so and tied fluorescent tape to each one. Without this kind of signpost, a descent in snowy, whiteout conditions would be very serious. There were big crevasses and holes everywhere, just waiting to swallow a lost climber.

After a couple of days, Al and I decided to spend the night up at Camp 2 and then reconnoiter the steepening ridge ahead. The rest of the climbers would carry food and fixed rope up to the camp, but not sleep there until they were better acclimatized.

Our tiny Japanese tent felt quite claustrophobic as Al and I sat facing each other while melting snow for a drink of tea.

"I should have known better than to use a Jap tent on a big hill," I remarked to Al, whose head was squashed against the tent roof. "And the Japs would probably say this was a *four*-man tent!"

That night it began to snow, and the snow piling up onto the tent made it even smaller.

"Man, I'm beginning to suffocate," gasped Al as he sat up in his sleeping bag and beat at the tent to remove some of the offending snow. What was actually happening was that the snow on the slopes above was beginning to push down and squeeze the tent from its platform.

"I'll go out and dig away some of the snow," I said as I began to put on my boots.

That night taught us a valuable lesson about the location of our camp. It was at risk from avalanches, especially after a heavy snowfall, and it would be safer if we dug a snow hole. The next morning we retreated to Camp 1 in a whiteout. The marker wands were invaluable, and I agreed with Al's comment: "Thank goodness, we got one thing right."

The next time we were up at Camp 2, we had shovels and a will to dig. The snow was perfect: not too hard and yet compacted enough not to collapse. We dug a four-foot-high tunnel that went directly into the slope for six feet before we could enlarge the chamber and carve two parallel bunks, each four feet wide. Then we made one more chamber across the back of the cave where three people could comfortably sleep. It had only taken about four hours and was well worth the extra effort. Jim had joined Al and me at this point, and together we hoped to establish Camp 3 at 2,000 feet higher.

The next few days we worked out of the cave. The terrain had become steeper, and it would be safer if we fixed rope up the steep snow and through a number of rocky sections—all the way to the next camp. We would take  turns at leading, while the other two climbers would carry extra rope to fix even higher.

Working with Al in situations like this was pretty straightforward because we had established a system over the years, and I don't mean just a system of fixing rope. We knew how to deal with the complex issues of handing over the lead when absolutely shattered with fatigue and still not needing to lose face or feel that one had not done enough. Or how to support one another psychologically if one of us was having a bad day.

Having Jim there made it more complicated. He was not acclimatizing as fast as the two of us, and we did not have the depth of communication to be able to give him the support he needed. He was pushing himself to very stressful levels, and if either Al or I suggested he take it easy and maybe descend for a rest, he would begin to think we were trying to cut him out of our small circle.

It became obvious to Al and me that Jim would not be able to keep up with us once we moved higher onto the mountain. In fact, it was likely that he could jeopardize our summit try—and maybe even our lives—if he remained in our threesome. What could we do or say? We decided to wait and see.

As the high point of our fixed rope snaked higher towards the site of Camp 3, we decided to save a day and fix the last pieces of rope as we moved up to inhabit the camp. What a hard day that turned out to be! Our packs felt heavy as each of us ascended the ropes to the high point. It didn't take too long for it to dawn on us that the lead person couldn't both fix rope and carry his pack. This meant that one of us had to begin ferrying the extra load as well as his own.

I was leading at this point and struggling with some steep ice that led through a patch of brittle rock. As the day drew on, I began to worry that we were running out of time. What if we didn't make the camp that day? We'd have to carry all our gear back down again. Oh, shit! I didn't want to do that!

I tried to go faster, but couldn't.

Finally, I made the camp with an hour of daylight left, but I had very little energy. I found two small rock platforms that were snow-covered and had horrific drop-offs on both sides. Not a place to sleep-walk! Al soon arrived, but Jim was far below, panting towards us.

"I'll dig away at the snow if you'll go and get your 'sac," said Al.

The thought of descending was unpleasant, but so was the thought of spending the night without a sleeping bag. Down the ropes I went. I could see Jim about 300 feet below, but he was above where my gear hung suspended on a rock anchor.

"Keep it going, youth," I encouraged him as I descended past him. Every few steps he'd lie against the ice and close his eyes.

I shouldered the pack and headed back up for the last time that day. With the rope in front of me, I could let my mind relax. Soon I caught up with Jim, clipped my clamps on the rope in front of him and left him to his own pace.

"Jim looks really whacked," I said to Al a little later.

"So am I," said Al, "but we still need to put up a tent. Jim really should go down, but I don't know how to tell him."

The next day Al and I felt tired, and we sat around eating and drinking. Jim's tent was twenty feet below ours, but we didn't go visiting that day. The priority was to quench the awful thirst that just wouldn't go away. I drifted in and out of sleep while my body struggled to come to terms with the altitude.

The second morning dawned fine, clear and very cold. We hoped to climb the steep slope immediately behind the camp and fix more rope. Jim volunteered to lead this section. That pleased me, first because I still felt tired but also because it meant that Jim must be feeling better. I watched while Al held his rope.

Jim was showing a lot of determination and pushing himself hard. The deep snow caused him to flounder and rest frequently, but still he continued. After a long time and 300 feet of climbing, he reached easier ground. His giant form stood out on the skyline as he anchored the rope. It had been a good effort.

Al and I decided to carry a few items of equipment as high as we could. I packed a tent and Al some food and gas cylinders. Even following Jim's trail was tiring work. Steps would collapse and we'd lose the steady rhythm that is so important in conserving energy.

"Good effort, Jim," we panted. "Let's keep going a bit farther. The angle of the slope's easier now."

We plodded upward on wind-packed snow. The last of our fixed rope had run out, but luckily there was some old cordage just beneath the surface, so we yanked it out. We went 300 feet more, and then I wanted to return. Clouds swirled around us and my head felt light from past effort.

"Let's dump the gear and get down for a brew," I said.

It always amazes me just how much easier it is to descend in these situations. Al holds a scatological theory which he now proclaimed: "Shit always flows better downhill."

When Al went to Jim's tent the next morning, he found him very sick and weak. The snow outside the tent door was brown with vomit. Inside, Jim lay in his sleeping bag with a pained expression.

"My head hurts and I've not eaten for the last three days," he said in a weak voice.

"You should go down while you still can," encouraged Al. "In a few days you'll feel better, and maybe you could come back up with one of the others."

Our worst fears had come true, because if he did not descend at once, his condition would probably deteriorate sufficiently to risk his life.

"Jon," I called into the walkie-talkie. "Please look out for Jim. He's sick and pretty tired. Should be down with you guys fairly soon."

It never occurred to either Al or me that he might need accompanying in his descent. We felt that, as it was fixed rope all the way to easy ground, he would be O.K. and that after descending a couple of thousand feet, he would feel stronger. I also think that beneath the surface we blamed Jim for his own condition and didn't want to lose a moment in our drive towards the summit.

Yet another morning dawned as we laboriously melted snow for hot drinks. The days of constant effort made it more and more difficult for us to leave the secure warmth of our sleeping bags. But we needed to reach Camp 4.

Re-ascending the ropes felt easier, and we were soon at the previous high point. The views from this crest were stunning. Off to the east, snowy peaks stretched forever. Some had to be Annapurna and even Manaslu, but at that moment we could only stare with a kind of glazed-over look. Every step required several lungfuls of air as we made our way carefully from rock buttress to steep snow slope. The afternoon clouds were rising with the heat of the day, and our visibility would soon disappear.

Then we saw what we'd been waiting for: a platform of snow-covered nylon, the past site of Camp 4. I suppose it might seem strange to appreciate other people's debris in such an awesome and beautiful place. One might expect us to have felt anger and remorse at the desecration. However, for us, drawing near the end of our reserves, it was an affirmation that we'd finally reached our destination in a world so hostile and desolate that life itself is threatened. We dumped our loads and scurried back down to our tiny tent more than 1,500 feet below.

It had been a difficult few days. The altitude had had a draining effect on the two of us. Besides that, Jim, on arriving in base camp, had packed his bags and left for home.

Jon later explained to me the reasons for Jim's decision: "Jim suddenly realized something that we all had known from the start: that he was not going as well as you twins. I don't think he could accept going on a second summit team and didn't wish to hang around to see what would happen. I also think it scared him getting sick that high on the mountain."

We two decided a rest in base camp would help us recover quickly, but we hadn't taken the dreaded water buffalo into account. When we strode into camp, Pasang had a mug of tea ready and food soon followed. First we discussed the route, how it looked and how we felt about it. Then Jon told us of the stomach problems he'd had and how supposedly he'd banned the Sherpas from eating any more buffalo meat.

Jon went on: "They're like naughty dogs. They pretend that they're not touching it, but then they secretly go and dig it up when they think we don't notice. I'm sure they've all got bad stomachs but won't admit it. Then they pass it on to us."

We clearly had to be careful in what we ate. It felt so warm down at base camp after being so long on the mountain. Our mail-runner had brought a couple of letters from Lorna, and I spent quite a while replying. That part of my life seemed so far away, almost like a past dream.

Five days passed during which the weather vacillated between fine mornings and misty, snowy afternoons. Guilt at being off the mountain built up the need to move again. On the sixth day, dawn had not yet warmed the eastern sky before Al and I headed back up to Camp 1.

"My stomach hurts like hell," said Al as he headed to one side of the trail to relieve himself.

He returned, shivering slightly with a look of despair on his face. "I'm sure I've got Giardia again," he snapped. "That bloody buffalo and those fucking Sherpas! I'll have to take some more Flagyl. I hate that stuff!"

The powerful antibiotic always made him tired, something he didn't need just then.

Doni and Chuck were waiting in Camp 1. Doni had been at work and had built a couple of amazing Eskimo-looking igloos: a skill he had honed while living in the arctic. It meant that we could all be together when we cooked and ate, and less isolated in separate groups. While Doni made a huge mound of rice in our pressure cooker, I made a corned-beef curry.

Overnight a big storm moved over the mountain, bringing lots of snow and high winds. We wandered between tents and igloos and alternated between eating and sleeping. Major storytelling sessions kept boredom to a minimum. It was a credit to how well we all got on together that not a single harsh word was ever spoken.

Al and I related tales of travel and living off the land in order to go climbing. The tales would go something like this: "And so Al arranges to meet two girlfriends in Venice. One is an ex-girlfriend and the other a present girlfriend. By the way, these girls were the best of friends who climbed with each other all the time. Then Al tries a sly maneuver to hit up on the ex again, and the other girl gets drunk and tries to drown herself. I couldn't believe it—"

"Just 'cause the Italian girl you'd picked up on the beach wouldn't let you in the house 'cause her mother was there," interrupted Al.

"I think you're both bad. That's what I think," said Chuck, who pretended to sit on the bench and judge the cases.

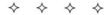

A week later, the storm had passed, leaving a couple of feet of fresh snow. Up high, the roaring winds blew white plumes from the ridge crests, but the sun had returned, at least in the mornings.

We decided upon a simple strategy. Doni and Chuck would break trail to the ice-cave so that we could save our energy as we followed. Then we would be on our own to climb the rest of the mountain.

Halfway toward Camp 2, the slope settled with an alarming WHOOMPH! We all froze, waiting for the slope to begin sliding. Nothing happened, so on we went. Doni, ski poles in hand, powered his way through the snow. It was easy to imagine him doing the same in some big ski race. About four hours passed before we arrived at where the cave should be, but there was no sign of the entrance or of the bamboo wands that had marked it.

By digging and probing, we eventually found a wand that had been avalanched. We worked methodically up the slope from this and found the entrance, where we began digging furiously to create a tunnel we could crawl through.

"This shows just how dangerous this place would be for tents," said Al.

He was right. Any tents would have been lost, and as to anyone inside them . . . .

Doni and Chuck stayed the night and in the morning wished us well. By now, both Al and I were keyed up for what was ahead, and our partings were brief and honest: "Thanks, lads. We'll do what we can."

The wind had blown off much of the snow where we were climbing, and we could move quickly up the fixed ropes. I felt strong and energetic, but I also knew the temptation to rush up this section of the route would make me more tired later on. I needed to conserve the strength I had regained in base camp and not squander it on some kind of high-altitude time-trials.

As I reached the steepening below the camp, I felt some trepidation about whether the tent would still be there. We had not taken it down when we left, and if it had been whisked away during the storm, our attempt would end there. Another 200 feet of rope slid by, and the tent came into view. Our attempt was still on!

After taking off my crampons, I walked around the tent and shoveled snow away from the edges and re-tightened some of the anchoring ropes. This was a strong Gore-Tex tent with two fiberglass poles crossing in the center. A climbing friend, Mo Antoine, had given us the tent with a generous "Let me know how it works." It certainly helps to have all these small associations with friends when one starts to become overwhelmed by isolation and high altitude.

That evening we had a meal of mashed potato and canned meat. We were settling into our sleeping bags when the winds began. First there came a single gust, not too strong, but then another and another. We closed the tent door to stop the flying snow entering. Before long, the wind became constant with sudden, fierce gusts which would flatten the tent onto our faces. Then the poles would spring back up.

"I think we should sit sideways across the tent, Al," I said. "That way we can brace the tent better."

Memories of my ordeal on Everest with John Porter flooded back. Another shredded-tent epic I didn't need.

"Let's call Chuck and Doni and tell them what's happening up here," Al suggested. "Camp 3 to Camp 1. Come in, please."

We could hardly hear ourselves speak above the wind's roar, let alone decipher the weak voices crackling out of our hand-set.

"I think it's Doni," I said. "Doni, the wind is desperate. If the tent goes, we must come down. Please open every hour. If no call, look for our lights. We might need help. Over."

"Roger," came the barely audible answer. "I understand. Every hour. Good luck."

Then silence. And more loneliness. The tent buckled. We held our breaths. The tent sprang back up. I could see Al's face and shoulders hunched in silhouette. I tried to close my eyes and get some rest. Impossible.

Every hour we made the call, and every hour I was more surprised we were still here. Then, at about 5 a.m., I became conscious of a number of lulls in the gale. They crept slowly into my exhausted consciousness like silky fingers, smoothing, caressing. I fell asleep.When I awoke two hours later, all was calm, and the sun had begun to warm the sides of the tent. It would have been easy to believe the night had all been a dream, except that I felt exhausted.

I asked Al: "How do you feel about today? Should we go up or rest?"

"Dunno," he said. "I feel very tired as I hardly slept at all last night. Let's make a brew and then decide."

We ate a leisurely breakfast and melted snow for tea. The sky was a deep blue and it actually felt warm, even though we were at 23,000 feet. Then at ten o'clock we made the decision to go on up. After all, we rationalized, it would probably only take us a couple of hours and we could sleep later.

Although it didn't take us long to climb up to Camp 4, it was already misty when we arrived. The weather seemed to change quickly, and once more the wind showed signs of picking up. How glad I was to be with Al! There were no problems in quickly erecting the tent, even though it was a complicated external-frame- and-box design. We tied it down with so manyguy lines that it began to look like a ship in dock.

"I can't believe this wind is blowing again," I said wearily. "I hate the thought of another night like last night."

Inside the tent I braced my back against the tent door while Al made drinks and food. When I felt too punch-drunk from the wind's beating, we changed positions.

Again I radioed the news down to Doni. This time his voice showed a lot of concern, as we were even farther away from them. The wind pushed and strained and beat against the tent, but everything seemed to be holding. I examined the light coming in between the individual stitching and prayed that the tent hadn't been made on either a Monday morning or a Friday afternoon. All it'd take would be for one strand of cotton to blow apart, and the tent would be shredded in less than five minutes. My tired mind began to wander, and I mused on the idea of how we would never consider rappelling off a strand of cotton. But our lives now depended on just that strength.

"Before we sleep tonight, I want to go outside and check all the tent anchors," said Al as he began to put on his plastic boots. "Being perched on the edge of a cliff is O.K. just as long as you know you're not going to be blown over the edge."

He came back from his mission covered in hoarfrost, with his beard totally white.

"Man, it's cold out there!" he chattered. "And guess what? Two of the tent poles have bent slightly. If we get some real blasters, they could go."

That bit of information was not going to help me sleep. That night was just as bad as the previous one. But *we* had changed. We lay there just accepting our fate. There was no need to worry any more, because we had done all we could do. Our fears became anesthetized by the constant roar and the pressure. We had broken through the barrier that paralyzes the mind and hamstrings the body. On the other side was a level of acceptance and resolute calm. Al's presence next to me gave me confidence. Together we could climb to the summit.

We had already decided to take a day off and rest at this upper camp even if the wind died down at daybreak, which, of course, it did. Staying put was, to some degree, a bit of a gamble because the weather might go bad on us, but it could just as easily work the other way and become more stable.

Looking out of the tent door, we had the most amazing views. There was the Kali Gandaki Rift off to the left, and off to the north were the arid plains of Mustang and Tibet. The East Face of Dhaulagiri was directly below us, and it drew us into conversation about our friend Alex McIntyre, who had climbed it the year before.

"Do you remember that article he wrote, 'The Big, the Bold and the Beautiful'?" I asked Al. "The one about the Bonatti-Zappelli climb? It was a classic piss-take about us. We were the Big. Tut Braithwaite was the Bold. And Alex himself was the Beautiful. He seems to have matured in the last six years, because I thought he had a bit of the-smell-of-death about him when I first knew him. I wonder how they're doing over on Makalu?"

That afternoon the weather seemed better than ever. The usual storm did not appear, so we decided to take a quick look at the beginning of the route so that we could find our way in the darkness prior to dawn. There were a few rock buttresses to weave through and, with footprints to follow, it would speed up the next day's climb. Pleased with our reconnaissance, we rappelled back to the tent and a final big meal.

"We must be acclimatized by now because I actually feel hungry up here," said Al, who tends to judge everything according to his weight and his stomach.

The first part of the next day was a well-practiced affair. Drinks were made in the dark and a few food bars nibbled at. Boots and crampons were adjusted and harnesses donned. We were ready and well-rested.

The stars shone from a cobalt sky. It was easy to follow our pre-made trail with help from our headlamps. This led to a 300-foot snow slope angled at about fifty degrees. I led out the first half of this until all the rope had gone.

"We'll climb together," I shouted down to Al.

The first light of dawn grazed the eastern sky as I reached a small outcrop of rock and sank a lost arrow pin to the hilt.

"I'll bring you up," I called to Al.

He would climb more quickly if he knew I was belayed. Panting heavily, he swung the lead up the edge of the rocks to another good belay. The slope above stretched up for another couple of rope-lengths, and I decided we could climb together again. This simultaneous climbing is something we like to do rather than just unrope and solo. It gives the option of an immediate belay if the leader needs it without all the hassle of re-roping. I wouldn't do it with just anyone, though, because of the risk of being snatched from my steps. I trusted Al to tell me if he were unhappy, and he the same with me.

The angle of slope eased until I could see a sort of gully up to our right. Halfway up this, there was a yellow blob in the snow: the remains of a tent. I thought it must be the Camp 5 that Jon had spoken about. We had been climbing only a couple of hours, and so it seemed pointless to stop there. I stood on the old camp and brought Al up to join me.

"Let's eat something here, seeing as we've just completed a stage," I suggested and he agreed.

Soon we were off again. Across to the right, a shallow relief ridge led up to the fore-summit. Rope-length by rope-length, we neared its rocky crest. Then we reached a point where a huge precipice dropped off to our left, and to our right was a smaller cliff.

"Hold the rope, lad, while I traverse these towers," I said to Al, while making sure I had enough pitons with me to protect the next hundred feet.

With my hands on rock and feet on small patches of snow, I began this key pitch. As I arrived at a point where I would need to descend, the rope came tight. There was no more left. I quickly kicked a couple of footholds and hammered in a small knife-blade. Then with a tiny wire-stopper to back up the belay, I brought Al across.

"This is quite spooky," he said as he arrived. "Do you have a good belay?"

"Don't worry. It's okay."

He took my place on the footholds, and I tiptoed down a patch of ice and resumed the traverse. When I could sink my axe's shaft all the way to its head, I let out a big sigh of relief. The rest looked easier.

Up above and way over to the right lay our route. We climbed together across small rock ledges, swept clean by the wind. When those ended, there was snow and, at last, the final gully leading to the summit. Rising cloud blocked out our view of base camp, and even though we couldn't see the Kali Gandaki, we could see the clouds welling up from its depths.

Then there was the feeling of relief of not having to climb up anymore. We were up!

A glance at my watch showed we had been climbing for exactly six hours. But the job was not yet over. We took a few quick photographs and scuttled back down again. I had that awful feeling of a door closing behind, trapping us. Minutes later we were enveloped in thick mist, with the visibility dropping rapidly. We returned across the slabs, then while we were on the towers, it began to snow.

"Don't panic," I told myself. "Pretend it's Scotland and this is normal."

The traverse went smoothly. Hardly a word was spoken. There was no need. Years of climbing together helped blend smoothness with skill. We descended safely.

Below the Camp 5 platform, a strong wind blew away the clouds but created a ground-blizzard, which made it difficult to see our old tracks. Still descending, we lost height, sometimes taking a belay and sometimes climbing together. A couple of rappels and the storm became less severe. We could see our red-and-blue tent tucked beneath a dark cliff, and then we were next to it. Home!

Only then did I really begin to feel happy about our summit success. The tension that had surrounded me all day began to evaporate. Al was holding the stove as I picked up the walkie-talkie.

"Hello," came an excited voice.

"We just climbed Dhaulagiri!" It was all I could say.

Three days after Al and I stood on the summit, we were ready to leave base camp. Pasang and Nima would take all our luggage back down the way we'd come. They had already ordered some porters, who were due to arrive any day.

Meanwhile, the climbers would take a shortcut over the northern flank of Dhaulagiri and down to Jomsom, a small village situated in the dry upper reaches of the Kali Gandaki Valley. This place had a small airfield with direct flights out to Kathmandu. In theory, we could be back in civilization within days.

Jon and Doni had left the day before while we were still bringing gear off the mountain. This left Chuck, Al and me, until Pasang came up to me wearing a sheepish grin.

"Aid, *sahib*," he said, "our liaison officer wants to go with you. Pinzo can go with him and take his gear. This O.K.?"

He performed the "Nepali head-wag," rolling his head from side to side on his shoulders. Sherpas always do this when there is a level of uncertainty expected in the reply.

"Does he know it's hard work to go over Frenchman's and Dampus Passes?" I asked.

"Oh, yes, *sahib*. He say he is Nepali. No problem."

"It's because he's bloody Nepali there will be one," Al interrupted.

"Pinzo take good care," Pasang pleaded. "O.K.?"

"O.K.," I relented.

Pinzo was our mail-runner. He was a Sherpa and a strong lad. His English was halting, but he had a heart of gold. I didn't know him well then, but in the years since, he's been with us on more than half a dozen expeditions and has become a close friend and confidant.

The morning we left, the clouds hung low over the mountains. We were each carrying around forty pounds on our backs, except the liaison officer, who had about ten. Pasang came out of the cook tent with small packages of chappattis and hard-boiled eggs.

"Here is your lunch," he said, his gold tooth gleaming. "Tonight you are in Jomsom."

We set off slowly, heading for Frenchman's Pass, which we couldn't see because of the mist. The pass was only a thousand feet above base camp but it was rocky underfoot and we couldn't see a trail. When Nima gave us instructions, he'd made it sound very simple. After the first pass, we had to skirt around the upper part of a valley and then over Dampus Pass. Then it was all downhill to the village of Marpha, and Jomsom was a couple of hours beyond.

It wasn't until after Frenchman's Pass that I felt something was wrong. It sneaked up slowly like night turning into a grey dawn. We had lost height in deep soggy snow, and it looked like Scotland, with long hummocky grass and thick banks of cloud swirling around the hills. Visibility was a few hundred yards, with no sign of the next pass.

We wandered around, making wide sweeps across old patches of corn-snow, but still no pass appeared. I turned to quiz Pinzo, who had said he'd been to Dampus Pass.

"The Swiss expedition camp on Dampus and fly everybody to Camp 1," he told me. "I was never this way."

"*Oh, bloody hell!*" said Al slowly after realizing we were lost.

With little choice, we headed down valley but kept a constant lookout for the elusive pass up to our right. The liaison officer was dragging his feet, and Pinzo had taken his pack.

High up on the ridge was a pass of sorts that looked like our only chance of effecting a crossing.

"Shall we go up there, Al?" I asked. Chuck groaned.

"I suppose we've no choice," I added.

My voice must have held a tone of being resigned to a lot of hard work to come, because Chuck groaned again.

"My 'sac is heavy, lads," he said. "I've got all the medical hardware with me."

The afternoon was getting on and the shadows lengthening. The grassy shoulder stretched up and up. I was knackered. My stomach growled with hunger, and the previous weeks of climbing were now telling on my strength. Only Pinzo was going strong, but he had a charge to take care of.

Chuck broached a subject: "We'll have to bivvy."

"No food, either," sighed Al.

I didn't say a thing but just felt sorry for myself. If we'd had food, it would have been a great bivvy, lying out under a clearing sky. As it was, there were many nagging worries.

First, we were lost, and this pass was the wrong one. Second, we couldn't see over it to check the descent. It could be impassable. We might have to retrace our steps to try to find Dampus, but I knew I didn't have the strength. Finally, with no food at all, moving anywhere was going to be a trial of the highest order.

The ridiculousness of it all was not lost on us. We'd climbed one of the highest mountains in the world, and now we might die while hiking home. The shame of it. The ridicule.

We repacked our bags in the morning and staggered beneath the weight. "How can forty pounds feel so heavy"? I asked myself.

The narrow pass was coming closer. Every five minutes, we'd sit and rest. Then we'd walk a few yards more and rest again. We looked pathetic.

Chuck opened his 'sac. Out came an ophthalmoscope. "I don't need that!" he said pitching it into the air. "Or that!" Another instrument flew off. Then a box of drugs hit the dirt. "Two hundred dollars worth!" He was getting excited. "All gone! The lot! Don't need it!"

Chuck was assessing the value of his life. Al and I looked on, shoulders sagging.

"Save the Ketamine," suggested Al. "It's always handy to have a painkiller, if only for recreation."

At the pass, I looked down the steep snow-gully and heaved a worried sigh.

"If this proves impassable, I'll never have the strength to climb back up," I lamented. "We don't have a rope or axes. The L.O. and Pinzo don't even have boots."

I looked at Chuck, whose eyes bugged out so far I could have hung my hat on them.

Al handed his umbrella to the quaking L.O., looked down the chute and said: "Follow me, sir, and don't slip or else . . . ."

Down we went. Heels dug firmly in. A hundred feet. Then five-hundred more.

Then: "Oh, dear! Oh, shit! A cliff!"

Scurrying back and forth, we sought the key to the problem. A none-too-obvious chimney led down and around it. We were clear once more.

Sometimes we'd climb down small waterfalls and at other times a short cliff, but all the time we were losing height. The L.O. looked terrified, but he had guts and kept right on behind us. Then, without any forewarning, a grassy meadow appeared from behind a bend in the gorge.

"We're out!" whooped Al.

Every face broke into a big cheese-eating grin.

Two hours later we entered a filthy little village.
"Double omelette and chips!" cried Chuck.
"One kettle of *chang*!" I called.
"Send out ya daughters!" cheered Al.

We were met by Jon Jones as we reached Jomsom.
"Where've you been?" he asked.
"It's a long story!" we replied.
That night we had a party. There was real bottled beer and food galore. Inside the lodge, the decibels were rising, stories flowing.
At one small table, a mother and son looked on. They were Canadians, drinking in the warmth of success of our "First Canadian 8,000er." You could see the pride on their happy faces.
"More beer!" ordered Doni.
The table was almost full of empty bottles. Our admirers ceased to smile.
"Skin up some joints!" yelled someone. Our admirers were scowling.
"Bring out the Ketamine!" howled Al. Our admirers left.

# CHAPTER
## 17

# Foxhunts & Debutante Balls

BY ADRIAN

Returning from Asia to the fast pace of Western life has never been easy for Al and me. After seven months in Nepal, two expeditions and, between us, a number of loves, we felt extremely close as friends and fellow adventurers, let alone twin brothers. Maybe it was this level of fulfilling closeness that allowed us to make a quick 180-degree change. Al went to Canada, and I left my French girlfriend, Christine, and went to Colorado to be with Lorna.

I never considered myself "in the market" for marriage. I was a free-wheeling hedonist, used to moving around the globe for either work or play. Yet here I was in Colorado, happily making plans to live with Lorna forever. Given my level of naiveté in social matters, I naturally saw no problems in loving and living with her, while climbing where we wished and partying how we liked. Life should to be lived to the full, and that's what we were going to do!

How could I have ever expected that eyebrows might be raised among Denver's upper crust? Certainly my pedigree papers were not all in order. Where had I been to school? What did my father do? Who, in fact, was I? I explained myself as best I could, knowing that the Atlantic Ocean is wide enough to open up many gaps and maybe lose a few facts on the way. Thankfully, these people are wonderfully eccentric and fun-loving. Many of them owned tall, elegant Thoroughbred horses, and they seemed to see me as an extension of these. I quickly learned to accept these folks and jumped with both feet into the fray.

The time around our wedding was divided into two parts: to accommodate the older, more genteel folk and our younger friends. It was on the Friday night before our actual wedding that the major "social blaster" took place: a fancy club, a scrumptious buffet, the average age teetering around the 60s mark. When I entered the room—sporting a borrowed jacket, tie and cord pants—I decided to use a special party-ploy. I was going to be passed around among friends, family and whoever else held pedigree. Therefore, I reasoned—correctly, as it turned out—that my chances of reaching the bar were nil. I would be the only sober person by the end of the evening. The thought appalled me.

On collecting my first Scotch, I explained to the pretty young serving girl: "This party is for me, and this is the last chance I'll get to come to the bar. So when you see my glass is almost empty, please bring me another one. The bigger they are, the fewer times you'll have to do it."

She was a good waitress, but not a good judge of character. I consumed more than I ought. Photos taken in the late evening at that party show me as a disheveled individual with a cheese-eating smile from ear to ear.

Lorna was raised with horses; she was riding by the time she was four. Her mother kept five horses next to her own house. It wasn't long before I had the opportunity to sit astride one and take part in trail-rides along the banks of a nearby canal. It became obvious immediately that I had a lot to learn about this sport, but the chance for a good ol' adrenaline rush kept me trying.

As I chased Lorna around the bends and across the fields, with clods of earth from her horse's hooves whistling past my ears, I let my

*Lorna takes her horse over a jump* (Photo by Alice Koelle)

mind wander. I was a medieval knight thundering into battle. I was an outlaw being chased by the sheriff, or a pony-express rider carrying the mail. These were no backyard ponies. They were real athletes, and I began to relate to their foaming sweat and flaring nostrils. It was truly thrilling. I loved every minute of it.

Soon I was ready to go on the local fox hunt. A black jacket was found for me, and I was loaned an even bigger horse than before. There were maybe fifty riders, elegantly attired and obviously comfortably at home in the saddle. I hoped I wasn't going to blow it and do something wrong.

My horse was quivering with excitement: half a ton of muscle and sinew waiting to spring into action. At that moment, I felt more apprehension than before a difficult climb. I wasn't sure I could hold my horse in check. Her thick, black neck bulged with blood and tension. What on earth was I doing here, anyway? I visualized falling off at thirty miles an hour, with my foot caught in a stirrup. Being dragged along like a piece of dead meat. As my anxious steed strained against me, my arms were bulging as they did on the most difficult rock climbs.

The huntsman's horn trumpeted out a husky peal, and my horse's ears stood to attention. She understood something I did not. We moved forward carefully, but like a wound-up spring. My legs squeezed tightly against the saddle, feet pushing into the stirrups, my balance adjusted for a sudden change of pace. Then it happened. Everyone took off as though all the devils in hell were after them. "Oh-h-h-h!" was all I could get out before I, too, was drawn into the throng. I leaned forward in a hunched-up crouch, wind in my face and ears ringing from a hundred pounding hooves.

This was serious stuff, despite all the pageantry. My instincts told me that people could get seriously injured at this game. I finally found myself so engrossed in the balance and heat of the chase that all fear was gone. In its place was an exhilaration so wild and raw that I didn't want it ever to end. The smell of sweating horses, the snorting of gasping lungs, the blur of brush and trees on all sides: the experience was wildly addictive.

It was probably only my strong instinct for self-preservation that allowed me to survive the first few of these mad chases. Balance helped a lot, but more than anything, it was boldness and daring that were the keys to success. If I had been scared, my horse would have sensed this and would have been unsure and timid. Instead, we believed we could fly. And so we could! It seems that so often our limitations are self-imposed and it was riding that allowed me to examine the subject, safely away from my own image as a climber.

One day in late spring, while I was working as a window-washer in downtown Denver, a special evening came up: my first Debutante Ball. Sarah, Lorna's sister, was to be presented to Denver *Society*. What on earth did that mean? I was to find out, but first had to find my way into the fancy Brown Palace Hotel.

Drawing my old rusting Chevy truck up to the curb by the hotel's valet-parking sign, I collected the clean tuxedo off the gun rack and handed the keys to a youth, who clearly wanted to direct me to the tradesman entrance. He tried not to stare at my hands, which had dirt so ingrained that they would be a giveaway during the course of the evening—I was working class. The youth wasn't prepared for my one-liner: "Be careful with the truck, son." I was through the revolving doors before he deciphered my accent.

The hotel was busy like a Kathmandu bazaar, but with a few differences. The air reeked of expensive perfume and cologne —not incense. What's more, the Nepalese women don't dress so as to allow peeks of slender ankles—through their cleavage! I weaved through the elegant crowd in awe and wished I was already wearing the rented jacket.

In the elevator, the buxom and the beautiful squeezed into the tight space, made even tighter by fellow riders trying not to make contact with me. Their faces maintained the expressionless gaze that you see while riding trains and buses. Did I just imagine that I saw a few noses sniffing discreetly?

Later, transformed into a squire-like figure (I hoped), I met up with Lorna in the private suite her mum had taken so that she could entertain friends and family. Lorna chuckled quietly because it was the first time she had seen me in a tuxedo. The first time for me, too! With a healthy-sized Scotch in one hand and Lorna in the other, I gazed down from the fifth mezzanine floor through a glittering hundred-bulb glass chandelier.

Names and pedigrees were announced over the P.A. system. Elegantly dressed girls were escorted by older males down a wide staircase onto the ballroom floor. Then a band began to play and the dancing began. I'd never engaged in this kind of dancing and had no intention of learning in a place like that, so we began to mingle with the crowd.

Friends and acquaintances passed by with polite nods and the occasional comment: "When's your next expedition?" "Where is it you said you were going? Well, good luck." "I don't know how you do it."

I whispered to Lorna: "I could finance twenty expeditions with what's being spent here tonight."

The partying slowed down and people left for home. We curled up in a hotel room.

The next morning I was back in my dirty work clothes when the spiffily uniformed valet delivered my old truck. An hour later, I was rappelling backwards over a six-floor building with a pail of water swinging beneath me.

*Wedding day for Lorna and Adrian: Fall 1981*

# CHAPTER
## 18

## ANNAPURNA IV: A TALE OF THREE ICE CAVES

BY ADRIAN

After spending the entire afternoon on horseback galloping around nearby wheat fields, I had settled down in front of a warm fire for the evening when a call came from Al in Calgary. He wanted to know if I fancied trying Annapurna IV this winter.

"The Canadian Everest Expedition Committee is sponsoring training climbs to get their members used to the Himalayas," he said. "We could go because no one else could put it together."

"Do they know what a Himalayan winter trip means?" I asked. "Annapurna IV is not much less than twenty-five grand [24,688 feet; 7,525 meters], and in winter it's likely to be harder than Everest."

"No need to tell them that 'cause they have no idea," confided Al. After a pause, he added: "It would be a free trip."

That added weight to his argument. The decision was easy.

"Count me in," I said, "and I'll tell Lorna."

After all the hard work on Everest the previous winter, I didn't really want to repeat that kind of ordeal, but we'd learned a lot during those months and could use the experience to climb something a little less high and less severe. The route on Annapurna IV is a straightforward series of snow slopes and steeper ice steps. The Northeast Face is generally on the lee side, and only during the last days of the climb would there be a serious problem with the wind. The other important factor was that we could use ice-caves for the entire route.

Lorna and I were to be married on the third of October. Soon after that, she and I could visit England and see my parents. Then I could continue eastward to Nepal.

In England, we bounced from party to party and from friend to friend. At the Buxton Conference, a weekend film orgy, John Barry and Paul Moores strode over to us, each clutching a large glass of bitter.

"Hi, Aid. I hear you've just married yourself a rich Californian tart," fired John, pretending not to notice Lorna, who stood by my shoulder. My mouth opened but no sound came out.

"Coloradan," Lorna said, beaming down on him. Her high-heeled shoes made the height difference between them even greater than it already was.

The wild Welshman, Davi, invited us down to his home in Chester. He bought a big barrel of beer as bait. Who could resist? Friends drove up from Wales and down from Manchester. A vehicular medley, ranging from old vans to new Saabs, rolled in for the bash.

The most charismatic friend of all, Al Harris, a virtual living legend, was due to arrive any time. He was famous for many exploits: from slamming his front door into the face of a raiding drug-squad cop, to sitting on top of a haul-bag high up on the Salathe Wall of El Capitan when it cut loose two thousand feet above the scree. He was presently living with a fourteen-year-old girl. He was a crazy guy who was always high-spirited wherever he went.

We were puzzled when he never showed. The next morning, a phone call told us that he was dead. He'd crashed head-on into a minibus while coming to the party. This was a huge blow to the British climbing world. One of their gurus dead! I was numb with disbelief.

The Harrises of this world never die. They ride out the good times and the bad on clouds of sheer joy, showing the timid how life can be lived.

We drove north to Manchester to visit Joe Tasker and Maria Coffey, his girlfriend. I hadn't seen him since we were on Everest the previous winter.

He told us an interesting story: "We were having dinner at Charlie Clark's in London when the phone rang. It was Sir Douglas Busk of the Mount Everest Foundation. He must be about eighty years old by now. Anyway, he questioned Charlie: 'Do you know Adrian Burgess? He's going to marry the niece of an old Oxford roommate, an American. Nothing about financial stuff, but is he a good chap?' "

"Bloody hell!" I sputtered, beginning to hear the faint rattling of skeletons from my past. "What did Charlie tell him?"

"Oh, that you were well-known to be a likable bloke," said Joe.

"Phew!" I exhaled in relief.

"That must be Jerry Hart, brother of Uncle Steve," said Lorna. "They've both been president of the American Alpine Club at one time or another."

"Good job he never called the British Mountaineering Council and spoke to someone like Alex (MacIntyre)," I laughed.

Lorna began to weep when the loudspeaker announced that her flight was ready for boarding.

"I'll write," I said, choking as I spoke. She turned and the walk-way tunnel swallowed her.

My flight for Delhi was to leave two hours later, so I went off to get my boarding pass and then drink my last English beer for some time.

It doesn't take long to organize an expedition in Kathmandu if you've done it a couple of times before, as I had. I met up with the designated leader, "Speedy" Smith, and we made a rough plan for the week. After that, the other members of the team would arrive, with Al among them.

We sat in a small restaurant in the tourist part of town known as Thamel. Note pad at the ready, Speedy jotted down the list I had committed to memory.

"We'll order all the food at the cold-store," he repeated.

"The kitchen we buy in the bazaar and get the *dokos* nearby," I continued.

"*Dokos*?" he quizzed.

"Yeah," I replied. "They're baskets for the loads. Let's get beer."

"Won't that be too heavy?" he asked.

"No, now! A beer, now!" I laughed.

Speedy's job was to look after the finances, and I took care of food and equipment logistics. I suggested he practice his accountancy and pay for the beers.

Next day, armed with the lists, I led the way to a number of shops. We told the shopkeepers what we needed and said we'd be back in a couple of days to collect everything.

"What else do we have to do?" Speedy asked. "Surely there's something more."

"You have to learn to delegate, youth," I said, flattering him, as he looked much older than I. "In two days we'll send all the stuff over to Mountain Travel and arrange for the *sirdar* to pack it up into thirty-kilo loads. Meanwhile, I want to try that Iceberg beer they sell in KC's restaurant 'cause it wasn't out last time I was here."

By the time Al arrived with everyone else, most of our jobs were completed.

"Has he been keeping you busy, Speedy?" asked Al, who looked fresh and unhurried despite two days of flights and airports. He always operates better when he's away from the West.

"Everything appears to have been done, but I'm not quite sure how," said Speedy. "Seems we've spent a lot of time in-side—."

"Organizing!" I added when he stopped short. I winked at Al.

On November 7th, we packed up our tents in the small town of Dumre and begin the first of twelve days of walking. I still didn't know everyone on the trip, so I used the hiking as an opportunity to acquaint myself with them.

Roger Marshall I knew vaguely. He was great fun as he told stories about some of the organizers of the forthcoming Everest expedition. He had secured the permit, but then he handed it over to others when he doubted he could raise sufficient cash to fund it.

"You need friends around you when you're on a mountain that big," he said. "And I wouldn't trust ——— as far as I could throw him. He's a real wanker." He obviously didn't like some of the expedition's leadership.

Carl Hanigan was a barrel-shaped Scottish-Canadian who was a veterinarian in Calgary. When I asked him about his work, he laughed and described an incident in his clinic.

"This old woman brings in her poodle that's supposed to be sick," he said. "It's an uncouth, snappy little brute, but I make little crooning noises as I whisk it away from her. In the back room the bastard tries to take a piece out of my hand."

*Roger Marshall*

"What do you do when that happens?" I asked. I wasn't prepared for his answer.

"Smash its head against the table," he said, pounding down his fist in demonstration. "Then take the stunned thing back to her all quiet and obedient. They never can tell."

We hiked for about five or six hours a day in sunny weather. Along the way there were tea shops that served sweet milky tea and glucose biscuits. We very quickly developed a routine of rising at about 6 a.m., and after a quick breakfast of cereal, porridge, omelette and chapattis, we'd soon be hiking in the cool of the morning. Pema Dorje, our young but highly skilled cook, saw to it that a picnic lunch was awaiting us at 11 a.m., when we strolled into some quiet, grassy glade he had chosen. For the climbers, who carried only light packs, it was a chance to relax and enjoy the journey. Most of the time I'd hike with Al and Roger, and we set up a barrage of nonstop teasing banter.

Roger was a few years older than we, and many people thought we looked like three brothers, especially as we all sported very north-of-England accents. He had stopped climbing for about fifteen years. The reasons he cited for stopping were raising a family and working on a journalistic career. Recently, however, he had begun to tire of what he called "this boring circle of events."

On the morning of our seventh day of walking, it began to rain, and through the swirling clouds, the snowline appeared ominously close. It wasn't long before Al, Roger and I dove into a small, smoky hovel to enquire after hot tea and a chance to stay dry. A young woman dressed in a heavy woolen homespun dress first served us tea and soon after, hot *rakshi*. If we'd been in our own culture, it would have been easy to feel guiltily decadent to be consuming alcohol so early in the day, but the northern hill folk have no such hangups, so we indulged with gusto. Maybe too much gusto.

Her two young children soon began to play with uninhibited joy. Roger pretended to be a dragon, roaring while he crouched forward with a jubilant youngster clinging precariously to his back. Al roared back in opposition as he performed the feline pawing of a big cat. The woman sat to one side, staring through the wood smoke in wonderment. We had taken her home by storm and had forgotten we were supposed to be watching out for our porters who struggled past in the deluge. When we finally re-donned our waterproofs and took to the road, we were all giggles and laughter.

We tucked in behind the porters as they staggered beneath heavy loads up the trail ahead. They were like bundles of plastic and jute with bare toes grasping at the steep, muddy track. It was the cold that brought me to my senses. With snow obviously on the way, the porters would leave and we would be stuck in the village of Chame.

This is exactly what happened. Wintry weather drove off all but the most hardy porters, and we regrouped a few days later. The storm had passed and only thirty of our one hundred and ten porters remained. Pasang, our *sirdar*, had hired some ponies to carry the loads, but with the snow down to 12,000 feet, we were still going to have difficulty transporting everything up 4,000 vertical feet to our proposed basecamp.

It took a whole week to ferry our gear to 16,000 feet and clear the place of snow so we could pitch the tents. Every day there were about fifteen porters who helped us carry the sixty- pound loads. We would break the trail while wearing warm plastic mountaineering boots and they would follow in their smooth-soled sneakers. To help them grip better on the icy path, they tied coarse sisal cord around their insteps. It appeared to work quite well.

During the final day of this strenuous work, I was descending alone, making sure all the porters were safely down. It was a hostile place up on the crest of a wind-swept moraine. The snow lay deep around me, and the trail was slippery and quite steep in places. There were probably only forty minutes of daylight left, and I was anxious to get down before dark. Suddenly, down below I spotted a lone figure sitting on a large rock. Thinking someone might be in trouble, I hurried down.

I was surprised when I saw that the figure was a young girl, casually grinding tobacco leaves between the heels of her hands. She glanced up at me, then calmly continued to empty the mixture into a conical *chilum*. Next she dug around in her pocket for some dry moss, and with two pieces of flint neatly struck a spark into the moss. Then she smoked. It was a simple, timeless procedure but it made me feel stupid and incompetent. Clad in all my fancy Gore-Tex gear, a cigarette lighter in my pocket, I knew that she was totally at home, dressed in her homespun woolen *angi*. We descended together, I to one of Pema's delicious meals and she to a smoke-filled house and a life of hard work.

By the 25th of November, we had moved into base camp, which was placed on a small flat area between glacial mounds. The main frame tent was warm inside when we had the two kerosene heaters going, but we had to be careful to ventilate the place. Outside, it was a different story. There was some sunny weather, but it really didn't heat up the air. The sun left the tents by 2:30 in the afternoon, and by evening the thermometer read -20°C. During the night it was much colder. There was no running water, and snow needed to be melted all the time.

Pema and his cook's helper, Phuri, were doing a great job of feeding us. They had been trained to cook to satisfy the needs of people from the West. They would cook eggs and French fries, pancakes with sausages or combinations of noodle and rice dishes. Pema noticed that some of the food packages for use on the mountain were labeled "Sweet & Sour Chicken." He asked if he could try one. His response defined the boundaries of his taste.

"Ugh!" he gasped. "You should not mix sugar and sour together, sir. One is one, and other is other. Mix is not good taste."

Although the official starting date for climbing, set by the government of Nepal, was the 1st of December, we wanted to make as many preparations as possible to speed up the climb. This involved breaking a trail through deep snow across the glacier and then digging a trench through four feet of powder toward a small rock buttress.

At one point, I was trailing a rope up a surprisingly well-packed slope when there was a sharp THUD! The snow beneath my feet began to move. Startled, I looked up. About seventy feet above, I saw the top edge of a windslab crack off. Instinctively, I began to run up the slope, which was slipping beneath me. The cold hand of fear tugged at my insides, while my breath rasped out in white vapor clouds. Suddenly all was still. I could look back down onto a series of overlapping plates. They were eighteen inches thick and as hard as stone. If my legs had been caught between them, the expedition would have been over for me.

Alan had no such worries. He lay on his back, rolling in the snow with laughter, his voice echoing up the slope: "Ya thought that was it, didn't ya!"

It was a statement, not a question.

"Damned right," I thought, still trying to recover my breath.

Al had seen how localized the avalanche was, but it was I who had to point out the tough edges of the slabs.

Over the next few days, we fixed rope up to a place we called Camp 1, although it was going to be an ice-cave, not a camp. Two more expedition members arrived, Jay Straith and Don Serl. They'd had last-minute business dealings in Canada. They were most impressed with the isolation of base camp and how wintry everything appeared.

They also brought news of the Canadian Everest Expedition and how a special meeting had declared that Al should not be allowed to go. Although Al didn't look overly concerned about this, many of the other climbers were. I suspected they realized how little they knew about this expedition game compared with Al, who daily showed his expertise. The kind of politics involved in that forthcoming expedition helped to show me how much better off we were staying with our "small-expedition" ideal.

Digging the first ice-cave was left to Al and me. Then, while we set the route towards Camp 2, Roger and Speedy enlarged it. The expedition seemed to be gradually taking form; climbers of equal ability and fitness were climbing together. Climbing pairs backed up others, and lead climbers rotated their turns at the front.

If all of the climbers were of the same strength, this would work just fine, but they weren't. After a week's climbing, it became obvious that Speedy was not able to maintain the same momentum as Roger. Despite trying his utmost, Speedy would be exhausted after a long day and would have to rely on Roger to feed and care for him. This created a problem for them both and forced Roger to look around for another compatible companion.

We were four, holed up inside the Camp 1 ice-cave. Two double sleeping spaces faced each other. Roger and Speedy were cooking together, and Al and I the same. WHOOF! Their MSR kerosene stove burst into a yellow ball of flames.

"Shit! Quick, turn it off!" snapped Roger the fireman. The flames subsided.

"Try priming it more before ya pump," said Al the coach.

Pur-r-r. The stove was functioning. WHOOF! No it wasn't. The inside of our white cave was turning black with soot.

"Fucking stove!" said the disgusted fireman. "How come yours works?"

This went on for some time until Al, afraid we were all going to be "napalmed," crouched over and with a few careful and well-practiced actions had the renegade stove humming as its makers advertised. We all laughed. But beneath it all, I wondered what would have happened if we'd been much higher on the mountain, with increased stress and higher stakes.

Al and I went up to pitch a tent at the site of Camp 2. The plan was for Roger and Speedy to live in the tent while they dug a second ice-cave. After they'd moved into the tent, the weather turned foul. This, combined with the fact that Speedy felt tired, turned their efforts to naught.

Carl and Steve Langley then decided to attempt to dig the cave, but while they were trying to find an area of deep snow that would accommodate the cave, a sudden gust of wind flipped the tent and demolished it. They, too, came down.

Days were passing without any upward progress. We twins watched from base camp, distraught by the sudden halt in momentum."

"Shit, man! We're gonna have to go and do it ourselves," said Al, being pragmatic.

He was right. Ice-caves can be built in poor weather, but nothing had happened. We decided to take the initiative and move to the front once more. Roger and Steve decided to join us.

We were in the Camp 1 cave, drinking soup and preparing food, when Sonar and Dar, the two climbing Sherpas, crawled through the entrance out of the frigid evening air.

"We dug a cave, sahib," they told Al.

They had grins from ear to ear. It was the very first time they'd ever dug one. Al had suggested hiring two climbing Sherpas because of our relatively inexperienced team, and now it had paid off. They hadn't needed to be told the importance of the second cave; they sensed it because they were mountaineers. That night was a celebration of a job well done.

The next day we decided the four Westerners—Al, Steve, Roger and I—would move up to the new cave, prepare the route up onto the Plateau and hopefully dig our last cave. There was a new feeling of hope now that the impasse of the second cave had been overcome.

Although we all set off together at around 10 a.m., Al and I quickly pulled ahead, eager to see the Sherpas' handiwork. The cave entrance stood out in the form of dark shadows cast by snow blocks and ice debris. Inside was a small sleeping platform raised above the central standing pit. It felt quite warm as we lit a candle to appraise their work.

"Bloody good effort to find a suitable place and then dig this," I said to Al.

"Yes," he replied. "I'm glad we had these lads along, or else we'd be in real trouble."

There were still a few hours of daylight left, and we decided to climb up the steepening snow slope and seek the easiest way over onto the rounded snow dome which formed the Plateau. It was fun to be out in front again, just Al and I. We came to a fifteen-foot vertical ice-wall that blocked our way. I borrowed Al's axe while he held the rope.

THUNK! What a great sound when you hear an ice-pick fix solid into steep ice! Soon I was over onto easing ground. I drove in a snow picket, tied on a length of rope, and Al came up. We could now see over the convex slope and onto a landscape of wind-carved sastrugi. A blast of cold air swept powder into our faces. We were staring into the prevailing wind as the sun's weak rays slanted down from the west.

"Time to go down, youth," shouted Al. "It'll soon be dark." His words disappeared into the swirling white.

The next morning dawned clear and cold. We didn't hit the wind until we were over onto the Plateau, and then it really began to howl. Strange ice shapes, cut by the erosive power of the wind, forced us to zigzag back and forth.

At the base of a steep ridge, we sought out a place for our final cave. A steep bank of snow lay in the lee of the ridge: a perfect place. One person began to dig furiously to carve out a small hole that would serve as an entrance. Then when the crouched position and heavy panting began to slow progress, someone else would take over. Slowly we burrowed into the ice. Once again dusk chased us back down the mountain to Cave Two.

Constant day-after-day effort begins to wear down a climbers' strength, and we hoped that one more day of digging would complete the cave. The four of us re-ascended our route with the determination that comes with a final effort. The cave began to look more like a tiny home, but the four of us kept getting in each other's way in the cramped quarters.

"Why don't Steve and I go and look for a way up onto the final ridge?" said Al, trying to maximize our efforts. "You and Roger can finish this off in a few hours."

He knew it was better for the two us to split up so that we could keep a close eye on both route-finding and cave-design.

Inside the cave, the howling wind couldn't get at us and we felt secure. However, once out in the swirling, stinging snow, it was a different story. Not only was it difficult to breathe, but it also was difficult to think. Sweat, which built up from the heavy exertion of digging, froze solid in an instant. Our crackling suits became stiff suits of armor.

"When Al gets back we should leave," said Roger during a rest break. "If we were ever to get caught out in the dark in this stuff, we're dead meat."

"Yeah," I agreed. "This cave will sleep three now. I'm knackered from all the digging and I'm pretty wet, too."

Al and Steve returned and down we staggered. The wind was a constant threat. It tugged at us and we became rag-dolls in its grip. All of us lost our footing more than once, making us spin wildly into sharp fins of ice. Our balaclavas were frozen to our beards as breath froze instantly.

Once we were over the Dome and onto the lee slopes, the wind miraculously eased. It felt like a reprieve.

Al summed up our collective fears: "Man! Much more of that and it could get dangerous!"

I thought it was an understatement.

The next day Al, Roger and I descended. Steve opted to remain in Camp 2 to await the arrival of Speedy and Karl. I felt that I needed a good rest after our recent efforts, and this would give the others a chance to get more height and put some food in the last cave. Everything seemed to be working well, and we held high hopes for a summit attempt.

Base camp felt quite warm and comfortable after our week high on the mountain. I mused on how, even given the most horrible of conditions, we humans seem to adapt to almost anything for short lengths of time. We'd been living deep inside the snow, eating sparingly and working hard. Weather conditions had been mentally draining. Yet all this could easily be pushed into the back of the mind as Pema spoiled us with tea in bed and large meals of roast potatoes and canned meat. The luxury of base camp!

A day later our mail-runner arrived with many letters. Lorna had finally received some letters from me, and she wrote that Joe Tasker had phoned to get the most recent news. That was caring of him. Roger didn't get a single letter, and I almost felt guilty for getting so many. Still, he didn't seem to mind.

All day we watched Speedy through the telescope. He was trying to fix rope above the last cave but appeared to be moving really slow and in the wrong direction. What could he be thinking? He was heading towards a very steep ice-cliff which would probably prove to be an impasse.

"Oh hell," I thought, "not more wasted time!"

But there was nothing we could do, and we watched with frustration. The nighttime radio-call confirmed what we had been thinking all day. He believed he'd gone the wrong way, but it had been a sincere try.

The next day was the 20th of December, and we were approaching the shortest day of the year. It was 7 a.m. when I opened the door flaps of the dining tent.

"Mornin', Pema," I said. "Where's Al and Roger?" We were going up to Camp 2 and it would be a long day. Almost 4,500 vertical feet.

"They coming soon, I think," said Pema.

Al entered, blowing into his bare hands and complaining: "My bloody zip froze up. Even down 'ere."

But we were both thinking of "up there." We hung around in the relative warmth of the tent until the sun had risen from behind the massive pyramid of Annapurna II. Then, with a last farewell to Jay and Pema, Al, Roger and I set out across the glacier. Hanging around had been like waiting to leap into an icy pool, but with the direct action of leaving, we immediately felt better. We didn't rush, just took it fairly steady but without stopping.

Halfway towards the first rock buttress, Sonam and then Speedy came past us on their way down. The rest soon arrived. We chatted with them only briefly as sweat began to freeze on our backs, and we went our separate ways. Speedy said something curt to Roger about his hav-

*Approaching the last ice cave on Annapurna IV*

ing teamed up with Al and me. It seemed that there was a degree of envy towards us for getting to try the summit first. Ironically, as I watched their forms becoming smaller, I felt rather envious that they could go down.

At Camp 1, we changed into our down suits and moved on towards the second cave. The sun had long since passed behind the skyline. An occasional strong gust of wind blew spindrift onto our bare cheeks. Every fifteen minutes we stopped and rested while gazing up to the summit, away to our left. Plumes of snow blasted northward, tinted orange by the setting sun. It felt cold. A lone ski pole stood by the cave entrance. On it a small thermometer read -21°C.

"Cold enough to freeze the balls off a brass monkey," said Roger flatly. I don't think he referred to anything nautical.

The cave was very comfortable for three people, and we settled into making a corned-beef stew with rice. We followed this with cups and cups of sweet tea. Roger went outside to relieve himself and came back with bad news: "It's snowing out there."

We discussed this sudden weather change and set out our options. A rest day might be in order. We'd have to wait and see what the morning brought. As it turned out, only an inch of very light powder had fallen overnight, and although it was bitingly cold, the sky was blue. Our route took us up onto the Dome and across the Plateau. I took photos of Al, dwarfed by the final 3,700 feet of the peak, his tiny red form engulfed by cloud after cloud of searing spindrift. The wind had changed direction and blasted from the north. There was no cover, no lee side behind which to cower.

We fought our way across to the final cave. Curses of curses! The wind was blowing directly into the entrance! We had to do something quick just to survive the night.

"Roger! Go in and get a brew on!" Al shouted out at the top of his voice. "We'll have to make a new entrance!" His last words were whipped away as soon as they were formed.

We fought for two hours to cut snow-blocks and curve the entrance away from the wind. When we finally crawled inside, we were both cold and hungry. More than that, though, we felt dejected that the chance of a calm next day was probably nil.

"If the wind continues like this, we can forget tomorrow," said Al.

I agreed with him but felt we should eat and drink as much as possible just to take care of the moment. All that time in the wind had been tiring, and my only wish was to crawl into a sleeping bag and stay warm.

There followed a fitful night for me. Al lay on his back snoring, and Roger's feet were jammed between us. I was too crushed to be comfortable. Finally, unable to bear the discomfort any longer, at 3:45 a.m. I pulled on my plastic boots, complete with two full overboots and went outside. All was quiet.

What luck! I called back up: "No wind!"

Al stirred, grunted and made himself more comfortable in the space I'd just left. What he meant, though, was: "Seems you're up already, so put the water on."

This I did, being careful not to "burn" my fingers on the frosted metal. Pink pads of skin showed through the holes in my silk glove-liners. I tried to sleep lying up against the cave wall, but nothing seemed to work. Finally, when water bubbled in the pot, the others came to life, and I was no longer alone. Even inside the cave, it was much colder than I had expected. Slowly we donned crampons and harnesses. Fingers quickly began to freeze while we fiddled with straps and buckles, and we were forced to keep warming them over the stove. The thermometer read -30°C.

Once moving, we began to generate some heat as we rounded an ice cliff and up the rope we'd seen Speedy fixing. Although the final stretch of rope led left, the route obviously should go to the right. Al led out, over a steep ten-foot step and out of sight. We could clearly see the white vapors of his labored breathing even though he had disappeared from our view.

"My feet are already beginning to freeze," said Roger, stomping up and down to aid circulation. "So let's get a move on." We wasted little time in joining Al.

Above us, there were only three hundred feet of steeper snow before the angle eased. I led out the last of our thin line and fixed it to a "dead-man" so we could use it in descent. The others jumared.

For the first time, I could see the southern plains of Nepal. Over to the west, shadow covered the south face of Annapurna I. Orange light crept down the fishtail of Machapuchare. Below it, a thick bed of cloud hid Pokhara and its picturesque lake.

Al's head appeared, rime already forming around his mouth.

"No wind yet," I said in greeting. He nodded, breathing heavily.

We moved up the crest of the ridge towards the first of a series of rounded bumps. The snow was hard and wind-blasted. Jagged icy fins, carved by the wind, stood in our way, and we spent precious time climbing around them. The sun rose over the rocky summit pyramid and with it came a gentle breeze from the south. Half an hour later, it was strong enough to make walking more difficult. We said nothing, but I began to grow concerned.

A steep step loomed on the ridge above. We formed a huddle to discuss the route.

"We don't have enough gear to climb that rock section!" I bellowed above the noise of the wind. Realizing the need for speed, we had chosen not to weigh ourselves down with unnecessary climbing gear and had nothing but eighty feet of rope and our ice-axes.

"Maybe across the slope on the left," said Al, suggesting an alternative. "Yesterday's wind probably blew a lot of the loose snow away."

He was right. The condition of the snow was better than we'd expected. Al took the lead and diagonalled up toward the skyline, which looked a long way away. We were still managing to keep up a steady pace, but it was proving too fast for Roger.

"I'll untie and follow at my own pace," he said. "Don't worry. I'll be O.K." He dropped the rope's end onto the slope.

At 11 a.m., we were still short of the flat col leading to the long final snow-slope. When we stepped out onto the ridge, it was like stepping onto the wing of a jet at 22,000 feet. The roar was unbelievable. Snow, swirling everywhere, searched for the tiniest hole to penetrate. Speech was impossible. We entered our own worlds of wind, noise and grueling effort. My feet grew cold and the thumb of my left hand began to freeze.

"Keep your hands low," I told myself, sliding my hand down the ski pole that supported me. I could no longer maintain the same rhythm because the force of the wind kept pushing me to the left. To rest, I rammed the pole into the snow and allowed the handle to push into my chest. Al also seemed to be having problems. He crouched, molding his head and shoulders into the slope. Roger crept slowly up the slope below us. I had never felt so utterly alone in the company of others. I was having difficulty in controlling a sense of panic and wanted to rush down to the safety of Camp 3.

After crossing over two minor "bumps" on the ridge, we strode across the broad pass that was so obvious from below. The 7mm rope linking us bowed out in a vibrating arc. The final long slope lay before us. Normally I would have wanted to zigzag up, first left and then right. But it was impossible to face into the wind. We had to keep our backs toward it at all cost, and even then it would snatch our breath away. My nose and cheeks hurt with the stinging cold. If I had not been wearing goggles, it would have been impossible to see.

Two hours passed while we were almost crawling up that slope. Most of the time, my mind was too numb to think. I believe it was only years of experience that allowed us not to succumb to the weariness and so have to descend. At a slightly more sheltered snow-shoulder, we waited for Roger. We had only about 500 feet left to reach the top, but it was steep enough to require the use of a rope.

"How'd ya feel, kid?" I asked Al, who was trying to gnaw on a frozen chocolate bar.

"Pretty tired," he replied, "but we're almost there. How about you?"

"About the same," I said. I definitely felt weary from the constant battering, but I knew we were going to make it.

When Roger arrived, Al took the first turn to kick steps up a steep, narrow crest. His breath came in explosive gasps as he struggled up toward the deep-blue sky. We were all struggling.

Roger led the final pitch, which ended dangerously close to the cornice. I tried to take a summit photo, but the camera, coated in moisture from my breath, iced over.

That was it then. We'd made it!

But we still had to get down and had only two and a half hours of daylight left. It had taken us eight hours of constant effort, with barely a rest, to reach the summit. It was no wonder we felt so tired.

Very carefully we down-climbed facing the slope back to where we had left our ski poles. There was no emotion, only strained and frozen faces. The race against time was on. No moment could be wasted. Our position was serious. The wind seemed even stronger when we faced into it. I raised my left hand, dropped my chin and tried to protect myself.

WHAM! The wind slammed me sideways. I tried to lean down into it and found myself going dangerously quickly and threatening to pull Al off his feet. One word kept on bouncing, revolving through my mind: "Go! Go! Go!"

I began to be afraid. Had we blown it by being so determined? I looked at Al and pointed at my nose. He shook his head. No frostbite yet. Down we hurried, first along the crest and then off to the northern slopes, which were more sheltered.

Roger began to lag behind. His staggering form showed undeniable weariness. We were afraid he might miss the way, so we had to wait. He began to go wrong. I shouted and waved an arm. He saw us and stumbled down. From there, the wind began to ease off. For the first time, I realized that everything was going to be O.K.

At the top of the fixed line, I took a photo of Al and Roger crouched together, big smiles shining through their frost-rimmed beards. The light was failing fast, but it no longer mattered.

We were safe! We'd done it!

That night the ice-cave seemed like a palace. I lay in one corner wearing my one-piece down suit inside my big sleeping bag. I was a dilapidated wreck, but a happy one. Al selflessly began making drinks for us all. It was the unspoken sharing of tasks between us that made us such a tight-knit team.

"Here ya go, man," he said as he handed me a huge mug of tea.

It tasted *so* good! I drank it down and must have fallen asleep. The next thing I knew, Al was tapping my feet and handing me some soup with meat in it.

"Oh, thanks, kid," I murmured, with my eyes barely open.

The next morning we headed on down, across the Plateau, down to Camp 2. Then down again with barely a halt. Camp 1 came into view, and soon we dove inside.

"There's far too much food here," commented Al. "It's always the same. People overload the lower camps as they're trying to acclimatize. Let's take some down with us."

Crossing the glacier before base camp, we were like three schoolchildren about to begin a vacation. There was laughter and joking. The bonds of friendship had drawn tighter.

While we rested in base camp, the others were making their attempt, but only Steve was really strong enough. He told me later that when he was almost crawling up the long final slopes, with the wind trying to launch him from the mountainside, he looked around and Speedy was nowhere to be seen. I could imagine how this would make him panic. He was alone and rather confused by all the buffeting. He turned around and descended. No one else would try for the summit.

Meanwhile, it was time to send down for porters to help clear our base camp and return to Kathmandu. I volunteered to descend with Pema and help him. As we went down the snowy slopes, heading for the green of the forests, we chatted constantly. There was no doubt that he was a bright and hard-working person. He told me it was his wish to climb on a mountain as a high-altitude Sherpa.

"Aid, I want to know how it is to be up in the snow," he said. "When I am old man, I can be a cook again. But I like to try other ideas."I told him that if we had skis, we could be down in the trees in five minutes.

He laughed and said: "I think only falling can be so fast." His big grin and mild manner were very attractive. I liked him.

As we descended into the trees, we continued chatting. Pema was not married, and he joked about Sherpanis and his future prospects.

"One time, so I hear," he began one of his many stories, "there were three Sherpas who liked some girls, but every night their father locked the door of the house. The Sherpas make a plan to get inside to visit the girls at night. One boy goes into *rigi* [Sherpa for potato] field and makes a ringing sound with yak bell. The old man thinks yak is eating his *rigi*, and he goes out to chase it. While he is outside, another boy goes quickly inside and hides in the dark. After old man goes back inside and back to sleep, then the boy opens the door and all three Sherpas go up to play with the girls."

His mischievous grin showed his amusement.

"Weren't the girls angry at that?" I asked, trying to imagine it happening in the West.

"Oh, no, Aid," said Pema. "They thought it good idea!"

After about two hours, we entered the small village of Pisang and found some Tibetan guys who had carried equipment for us before. Entering a low door, I found a poorly lit room where a small fire provided the only illumination. Rugs were pulled out, and we sat near the heat. Butter tea was served to us in delicate porcelain cups. It tasted more like greasy soup than tea, with a slightly rancid aroma from the yak butter. Pema drank with gusto while he arranged for more porters.

"Everything is fixed," he said. "They will find thirty porters and take them to base camp in two days." Then he signaled for us to leave.

It was too late to return to base camp, so we sought out a small woodcutter's cabin in which to spend the night. He and his wife were quite old, with deeply etched faces blackened by wood smoke. He gave us a big, toothless grin and beckoned us to his fire. I sat watching the flames with my legs crossed under me. Pema had explained how it was thought to be very rude to show one's feet to the fire, or to anyone else for that manner. I was learning a great deal from him. Nothing to do with climbing but everything to do with living.

Pema fitted into the situation very quickly and smoothly. He bought some eggs and potatoes, opened a can of meat, and we dined royally. A dirty bottle, half full of *rakshi*, was brought out from an old trunk.

"You wish to drink some?" asked Pema. He obviously did.

"Is it safe?" I asked, eyeing the rather greenish liquid.

"Safer than climbing" was Pema's cheeky answer. We both laughed.

That night, sleeping by the fire, I felt supremely happy. The mountain had been climbed, everyone was healthy and I had been privileged to be asked into some of the local people's homes.

# CHAPTER
## *19*

## EXPEDITIONS: LARGE/SMALL

BY ALAN

The 1982 Canadian Everest Expedition was a mammoth million-dollar expedition, involving 21 Westerners, 35 Sherpa climbers and upwards of 200 porters who carried more than 700 loads of equipment to base camp.

While preparations for that expedition were under way in the spring of 1982, a challenging but much smaller-scale trip for the same time was being planned by Adrian along with Paul Moores, a longtime climbing friend from England; Fred From, an Aussie whom the climbing community knew as Fred From Australia; and Peter Hillary, a Kiwi who is Sir Edmund Hillary's son. The four of them were going to attempt Lhotse, Everest's sister peak, the world's fourth highest mountain, without Sherpa support and without oxygen. Lhotse and Everest share the same base camp, and for part of their route—through the Khumbu Icefall and up the Lhotse face—they were going to be climbing alongside the Canadian Everest Expedition. Their trip would cost about $4,000 a person: $20,000 maximum for the whole venture. The team, known as the New Zealand Lhotse Expedition, included a Brit living in America, a Brit resident of Scotland, an Australian and one New Zealander. Whose flag to take to the summit was not part of the pre-expedition planning.

Roger Marshall, who had the original permit to climb Everest, was the Canadian expedition's first leader. But when he couldn't raise enough money to fund the expedition, he handed the leadership over to George Kinnear.

With George as leader, Air Canada came in as the major sponsor, and Roger became deputy leader. There had been some problems in organizing the expedition, but when Air Canada got involved, everybody was confident that there would be adequate funding.

George managed to raise money, but on a training climb, he sustained serious eye problems and had to hand over the expedition leadership to Bill March. English-born, Bill was a professor of outdoor education at Calgary University. He was one of the old school. He was a good, hard technical ice-climber, but he had only a small amount of Himalayan experience. When Bill became the leader, Roger was again demoted, this time to author of the book. As a journalist, he was certainly capable of writing a book about the expedition; in fact, he had the book contract. As it turned out, I wrote the book, but that story comes later.

Half of the Canadian Everest team was made up of British expatriates. Adrian and I were not initially invited because Adrian was not a Canadian national and I was a landed immigrant, not a citizen. But when Bill March took over as leader, he invited me in February 1982. I had just finished Annapurna IV in the winter and was hanging around Kathmandu and going trekking. Bill sent me an airline ticket and asked me to return to Canada to act as a logistical problem-solver. Thus, I was drawn into the expedition.

I went back to Canada for three weeks of planning sessions. Then I spent a week in England on my way back to Kathmandu. The first contingent of the Canadian expedition came to Nepal in April to get oxygen, climbing equipment and propane gas and to walk the supplies into the Everest region. Bill wanted to feel out the logistics in Kathmandu and get acquainted with the variety of possibilities. Jim

Elzinga, Laurie Skreslet and I were leaders of the three groups of porters. After three weeks of walking the gear into the Khumbu, I went to Ladakh with Roger Marshall for the summer.

The previous spring, a friend, Reinhard Karl, the first German to climb Everest, had been killed in an avalanche on Cho Oyu. I had helped his wife Eva with the logistics of dealing with his death and promised her that I would build a *chorten*, a Buddhist memorial pile of stones, up in the Gokyo Valley under the face of Cho Oyu, to commemorate Reinhard.

After the summer in Ladakh, Roger and I went into the Gokyo Valley so I could fulfill my promise. We found a small grassy shoulder that was covered in flowers and had a fine, clear view of the mountain. We built the *chorten* there: a perfect resting place for the spirit of any climber.

Roger and I spent two fine weeks in the high valleys and had an excellent time getting to know some of the Sherpas we'd be climbing with on Everest.

When we met the expedition in Namche, Bill March came up to me and said: "Alan, can I have a word with you? In private, please."

We went into a tea shop, and Bill told me he was going to kick Roger off the expedition and send him back to Kathmandu! I was astounded that Roger, the original leader, the guy who got the permit and conceived a Canadian Everest Expedition, was now going to be kicked off!

The real reasons for this action have never been detailed. At the time, it was alleged that Roger had brought some illegal substances back into Canada and that his admittedly somewhat renegade behavior had the potential for embarrassing the expedition's sponsors. So Roger was sent down valley, and we headed up.

There were some good people on that expedition: excellent guys and good strong climbers. All of us found that it was very risky picking our way through the Khumbu Icefall with many loads of gear. For seven days after we arrived at base camp, we tried to fix rope on the Icefall from about 17,500 to 19,500 feet. A week into the trip, there was an avalanche that killed three Sherpas.

That was the first accident. The next day, everybody came down to base camp. The body of one of the Sherpas was found, and he was taken down for cremation below base camp. All the team members sat around base camp, wondering and thinking.

Adrian and his group arrived for their Lhotse climb. They acclimatized for several days in base camp.

Then Adrian went up, his first day through the Icefall. After he returned to base camp, he reported that on his way back down he saw four climbers and two Sherpas fixing a ladder in one of the most dangerous parts of the Icefall. He said he also noticed that they had taken in a video camera to film the action.

Too many of them were in the wrong place at the wrong time when there was an ice-shift, a surging of the glacier itself. Big blocks the size of cars tumbled everywhere. One Sherpa went down a huge crevasse and could have been crushed; fortunately, a big ice-boulder also went down and jammed the crevasse.

When the shifting stopped and all was sorted out, the tragedy became apparent: Blair Griffiths, a Vancouver photographer and a really nice guy, was dead: pinned and killed by a block of falling ice.

The second accident within a week! The team pulled off the mountain to reevaluate what was happening on the expedition. Within the first ten days of the Canadian Everest Expedition, three Sherpas and a Western photographer had been killed. In the next two or three days, half of the team decided to go home.

Meanwhile, there was bad weather. The New Zealand team, Adrian and I spent a lot of time figuring out what we were going to do, and what kind of expedition was going to continue—if any at all.

Adrian, Paul, Fred and Peter were just starting their Lhotse expedition. They'd arranged with the leaders of the Canadian expedition to use the Icefall route that had been fixed by the Canadian team in exchange for the Lhotse team fixing rope higher on the mountain. But two or three days after the accidents, the Icefall route, which had not been maintained, was collapsing. The ladders either were being crushed by crevasses closing up on them or were falling into widening crevasses. Fixed rope was buried under three feet of new snow. The Icefall route needs continual maintenance: people trafficking up and down it at least every other day.

About this time, there was a turning point on the expedition.

I'd been drinking *chang* with Adrian and the Lhotse team. When I came back to the Canadian dining tent, I found team members, leader Bill March and business manager John Amatt trying to decide whether to close down the expedition. I protested that we could climb the mountain with the gear already in position, and we should stay.

There was silence. Then John switched into a positive mode. He said he agreed completely and was right behind us and would do whatever he could to help. He would be going back to Kathmandu to handle the media.

At that point, it was either break up or go. I was very serious about how we were going to climb the mountain. The original route was to the left-hand side of Lhotse face: the so-called South Pillar. It is steeper than the South Col route, which we eventually shared with the New Zealand-Lhotse team.

Two Canadians and the four members of the New Zealand Lhotse team opened up the Icefall again. We cut the number of climbing Sherpas to minimize the traffic through the dangerous sections of the Icefall. I chose about a dozen of the best climbing Sherpas and limited the amount of equipment to come through the Icefall: just enough to climb the South Col route.

There isn't a great deal of difference in technical difficulty between the South Pillar and South Col routes. Both involve snow-and-ice climbing at angles of up to about 50 degrees. Some campsites on the South Pillar route would be more difficult because they'd require constructed platform ledges, but on the South Col route, there were good campsites where you could dig into the ice and snow quite easily.

Within a month, we had climbed the mountain. Laurie Skreslet made the first successful summit bid and became the first Canadian to climb Everest.

I was a member of the team that made the second summit attempt. I didn't want to use oxygen, but having been given the opportunity and the privilege of having a support group carry the oxygen up to the South Col, I felt obliged to use it.

I should say I *tried* to use oxygen. There were two systems: a constant-flow system and a demand system. I tried to use the demand system. The idea was that it was more efficient. It was incredibly efficient: I couldn't get any oxygen from the bottle!

On the summit day, I got about 1,500 feet above the South Col, at around the 27,000-foot level. My oxygen had never worked at all. I had just been breathing normal air through the inlet valve. I paced the climb wrong and wasn't able to continue. I'd been carrying the full bottle, but not using it. I hadn't been *able* to use it! I had to turn

*Alan on Lhotse Face*

around. I chose to go back down to base camp. Pat Morrow and Pema Dorje ultimately reached the summit that day.

I discarded the useless oxygen equipment. There was a certain freedom in coming down without it. The view was incredible. I could see Makalu, the world's fifth highest mountain, bathed in pink light: alpenglow on the snow. Everything was crystal-clear. You could almost see the curvature of the earth from that high up.

When I was descending the Lhotse Face on fixed rope, I looked down and saw figures coming up: Adrian and Paul! When I got down to them, they understood very well what had happened and said: "Well, then, Al, come with us!"

My old climbing partners believed that I still had the strength to go up and to summit on Lhotse. They were prepared to share everything!

But I said: "I'm way too tired. I've blown it. I set out carrying a full oxygen bottle. I wasn't using it, but I went at the speed of the Sherpas who *were* using oxygen. It was like setting out to do a marathon at 10,000-meter pace."

So I plodded on back down, went through the Icefall the next day and then on to base camp.

After the expedition, I stayed in Nepal a couple of weeks and went trekking. When I returned to Canada, I had a message from General Publishing in Toronto. The company's vice president wanted to come over and visit with me.

It turned out that Roger Marshall, who had been kicked off the expedition, still had the contract for the book. But it would be difficult for him to write it, because he hadn't been there!

When he came over, General Publishing's vice president asked if I was prepared to write the book. I think I was the only person on the expedition who *didn't* keep a journal! But I had access to all the other journals and tapes. So I spoke to Roger, who said that if I got the book contract, he'd sign it over to me. I promised him I would try to write the true story of the expedition.

I worked with a co-writer, Jim Palmer. He was a lot of a writer and a little bit of a climber. I was a climber and nothing of a writer. By the end of it—shoulder-to-shoulder for 12 hours a day for six weeks—we'd both increased our skills a little. It was an incredible experience for me. Here was a guy I'd met only briefly before, and we became closer than if we'd been on an expedition. We never argued or shouted or raised our voices. We'd discuss different points of view, but we never, never argued for the six weeks. We became great friends.

When a draft of the book went round to be read, the team was critical that I had told only *my version* of the truth!

General Publishing had a contract with the Everest Funding Committee, which had a contract with me, and my contract was to provide something that the publisher would accept. As a result, the expedition committee did not have a right to editorialize, but they criticized me in the media, making accusations and trying to ridicule me. That made me fight back, actually, and tell a little bit more of what I thought had really happened. They replied that the book wasn't true, that it was all sour grapes and that I was using it to attack people.

The publishers were quite happy with the book. It became so controversial that every time it got a review, there'd always be two people reviewing it: one person who would say he hated it and another person who would say it was great.

A follow-up on the New Zealand-Lhotse expedition:

After I saw Adrian and Paul while I was descending from my summit bid, their group camped a little below the South Col. The next morning, the four of them started off soloing up the final couloir to the top of Lhotse at 27,923 feet.

They were within 600 feet of the top when the weather turned. It started to snow. Spindrift avalanches threatened to sweep them off.

Adrian and his group never reached the summit, but they got incredibly high and did very well on a tiny budget. They used no oxygen and no climbing Sherpas. They acknowledge they used some of the Canadian expedition's food and equipment, but then, Adrian helped fix at least half of the rope on the Lhotse Face for the Canadian team.

Adrian, Peter and Paul are still climbing strong. Sadly, Fred fell to his death during an attempt on Everest a few years later.

The Canadian Everest Expedition taught me that I did not ever again want to be involved in a mammoth expedition and that the politics of climbing are more dangerous than the mountains.

Although the style of the expedition appears to me reminiscent of colonial times, when *sahibs* were supported by native staff, most of the climbers meant well. And the team *did* climb the mountain! The expedition made a lot of difference in the lives of a lot of people.

Bill March fought hard to get me on the team and was a good climber in his own right. We got on O.K. after the trip, but I was saddened that we were never close friends again.

The story ends in tragedy for Bill. He came back and had to face the crisis of his wife developing cancer. A number of years later, about 1990, shortly after finishing a run, he suffered an aneuyrism and dropped dead. He was only about 45. Life works in strange ways. Bill strived for the Everest expedition, survived it and became known for it. And then to die after a run . . . .

# CHAPTER
## 20

## THE DOGS OF KATHMANDU

BY ADRIAN

For most people, dogs are "man's best friend," lovable pooches that children play with or those critters that drag you out to go walking on chilly mornings and evening snowstorms. But in Kathmandu they're a different breed . . . if you can find one.

*Canis domesticus* exists in Nepal's capital city, but only behind tightly closed doors. Examples of *canis wildebeestus* are everywhere: sleeping on street corners or in the middle of streets; cruising garbage piles; and hanging out in restaurant doorways.

I knew one who cruised tourists. He'd been given the name Income Tax, because he always caught up with you. He was a sandy-haired mutt with a muscled chest and a curled tail.

We'd stagger out of the Up and Down Bar, and there'd  be

Income Tax: weaving among the taxis and the bicycle rickshaws, with his tail wagging—well, as much as his curlicue extension could manage. A delicate acceptance—a lick of my salty palm—and he'd fall in step behind us.

"Pretty tame for a street dog, isn't he?" Al remarked. "Just don't lie down or he'll be snacking on ya goolies."

To take a dog on a downtown walkabout is easy for the human, but for the dog it's something else. There are dog territories to consider. Every hundred yards or so, there's a different Canine King, whose power has been hard-gained through the difficult game of intimidation and fighting without sustaining injury. Injury and subsequent infection mean inevitable weakness and resulting starvation.

So Income Tax trod carefully until he realized that human accompaniment meant canine immunity. Almost. From behind closed doors and high gates came barking and growls. The "yap-yaps" and "grrs" told of size and attitude, but they never fazed Income Tax. Other street dogs would join in the hike. The dark and the dwarfed came in the game. Saliva dripped and crooked tails wagged. We headed for the Himalayan View Hotel and its wrought-iron enclosure.

"I kinda feel sorry for these homeless dogs," Al remarked. "They can stay in my room if they want."

His brain, muddled by Star beer, emitted a kindness unfathomable in the East. The hotel gatekeeper ran to our calls, swung wide the gate, and Income Tax darted in from the shadows. Feigning innocence, we strode purposely towards our rooms and ignored the gatekeeper's screams aimed at the dreaded scourge that had penetrated his turf. By the time I bade Al a good night, Income Tax and a friend were scuffling around the bottom of Al's bed, making themselves comfortable.

Almost every night we'd run the hounds of Kathmandu. Laughter rang out down the dark deserted streets, and a wave of howls and yelps reverberated through the ancient city. Then one night at a corner, the pack skidded to a halt. Ears at alert, Income Tax led the way through a low doorway and into a concealed courtyard. There were a few growls and some whimpering, and then one of the street dogs emerged with a small puppy locked firmly between his jaws. As we looked on, transfixed in horror, they ate it!

We turned and walked away in disgust. Income Tax jogged over and licked my hand, blood dripping from the side of his mouth. What could you say?

One of the first things new visitors to Nepal always comment on is the noise the dogs make all through the night.

"It's like the city of jackals," growled Chuck Masters before we left for Dhaulagiri. His eyes were puffy from lack of sleep.

" 'The Hounds of the Baskervilles!'—they're out of control!" said Carl Hannigan. And he was a vet, too.

"Do they ever shoot any of them?" someone asked Al.

"Oh, yes," replied Al. "But a few human babies have to go missing first."

We'd just returned from Everest in the spring of 1989 and were staying at the Tibet Guest House, a clean, five-story hotel squeezed into the narrow streets and hovels of Chettripathi, a suburb of Kathmandu. Darkness had forced us to move from cocktail-hour in the Roof Garden to the fifth-floor room I shared with fellow-climber and doctor, Ralph Bovard.

Ralph was from Minneapolis and loved to ski. He'd been asked to come on the expedition at the last moment, and on his arrival at base camp, he was suprised to find that the expedition didn't have a medical kit. So he was known as the Doctor Without Medicine by the Sherpas. Laughter is a brilliant cure for most ailments, and fortunately he had a bagful of that.

Back in the hotel room, music blared from a small boom-box, more beers were ordered, and stories, lies and tales were swapped end-lessly. Suddenly the door burst open, framing the lanky figure of Johann, one of a pair of crazy Swedes who'd been on the mountain with us. Blood ran from his lip.

He explained what happened: "I tripped on a step coming into the hotel last night. Don't remember much, but I've been in my room all day. After a climb like this, no one should be farther than one meter away from a beer. Ralph, can you fix it?"

He was led to the bed, and Ralph went to wash his hands.

"Sir," I said to Johann, feigning servitude, "can I get you some music to listen to while he operates?"

I clamped a headset over his ears and cranked up the volume. Ralph had needles and painkillers and stitching kit laid out on the bed.

"Sir, is there anything else we can do for you?" asked a Dutch trekker who had infiltrated our ranks. He took out a hunk of black hash and broke off a chunk. He held a match to it, and when white smoke curled up, he caught it in an upended glass. He was very adept at this.

"Here you are, sir," he said. "This is a full-service surgery."

He placed the glass over Johann's nose, and Johann's eyes suddenly widened perceptibly. Ralph stitched and tied knots, reshaping Johann's grinning lips.

The patient had just sat up when there was a knock on the outside of the window. To our horror, we saw there the maniacal face of Johann's climbing partner, Mickey, staring into our room. Somehow he'd climbed up five stories on protruding bricks and traversed to our window.

"If he'd ever seen how they make those bloody bricks, he wouldn't have that stupid grin on his face," I said, shaking my head in disbelief. "You guys are outta control."

Just how much I didn't know until someone else had to help them use their key to open their hotel room.

The canine bedlam was not yet in full swing. There were a few barks in the north and the occasional counter from the west. But it was nowhere near as good as it can get.

We decided we should help the nightly serenade on its way. I leaned out of the open window and gave it the best I could: "Wuff-wuff-wuff! Arf! Arf! Arf! Wuffwuffwuffwuff!!" Then I listened. There were a few responses from the streets and a few counter responses, but nothing impressive.

"Here, Aid, let me have a go," said Ralph, moving over for the next try.

I wasn't prepared. He must once have been in a choir or was a reincarnated town crier.

The deep voice of Odin, the chief Viking god, boomed over the city: "WURF! WURF! WURF! WURF!"

They were slow, powerful barks. Akin to a Liverpool barge's foghorn. They boomed like thunder off nearby buildings and echoed down the narrow streets. Then . . . silence. A quiet unknown in that ancient city.

Every single dog had stopped to listen. Not a yap or a yip or a wuff emerged from the inky blackness. Ralph had silenced the whole bloody lot.

We fell about hysterically.

So far I've written only of city dogs: the mangy, rabid curs that prowl the streets in search of food and copulation. But there's another canine type in the countryside: the trekking and expedition dog.

They can be seen hanging around roadheads and airstrips, waiting for tourists. Lukla, the town Everest trekkers fly into, is most popular. When a plane lands, tails start wagging. The dogs appreciate the kindness of Westerners and tag along with them, gratefully accepting their cookies. Soon they become mascots. Sherpas often are able to recognize dogs from previous treks, and they feed them generously.

The first time I saw an expedition-dog was when we were at Everest base camp in winter. He was dark, sleek and handsome and was named Bivouac, because that's what he did at night.

When we went to Manaslu in the winter of 1983, a trekking group returning from the mountains gave us a white dog that had followed them down from a high village. His name was Seti—which means "Big White," though he wasn't very big. He shared a tent with one of the climbers, and when we finally returned to Kathmandu after six weeks, he came with us.

Knowing he'd never survive in the city, we found him a home with an Australian trek-leader who lived in Kathmandu. The last time I saw Seti, he was sitting proudly in the front seat of a taxi, his pink nose sniffing the morning air, on his way to get his doggy-shots.

Probably the best thing that could happen to an expedition-dog is what happened to our mascot on the 1989 Everest trip. He got himself a green card—that is, he moved to America.

Karen Fellerhof, who lived in Salt Lake City, was the expedition organizer and leader. She met a handsome, pure white fellow with the cleanest fur and the keenest senses. The Sherpas would call him in their language: "*Sho! Sho!*" (Come! Come!). And so his name became Shosho.

He stayed in Karen's tent, ate in the kitchen and sunned him-

self on a nearby rock.
When the expedition was
over, Karen took Shosho
back to Kathmandu and
got him a plane ticket.

Shosho now
lives contentedly in a
suburban American
household. He barks at
the mailman and the de-
livery man, but when
there's garbage on the
curb, he can't resist a
quick tear of a bag, a
snuffle through the con-
tents, maybe a chomp on
an old bone—just for old
time's sake, when life
was different.

✧   ✧   ✧   ✧

The story of
Kathmandu dogs would
not be complete without

*Lorna and P.T.*

mention of a special dog named Pasang Tsering (P.T). He was born in
the Kathmandu suburb of Jawalakeil, the Tibetan refugee camp, in the
spring of 1993.

His humans were Tibetan refugees who brought the Lhasa Apso
south to Nepal, where the breed was greatly treasured as a furry little
"temple dog," the guardian of valuable artifacts in Buddhist temples—
a sort of Tibetan answer to shoplifting.

In their own way, the Lhasa Apsos are treasures, too. Their
export is frowned upon, and they never can be bought, only given.

P.T.'s brothers and sisters had all died, either at birth or not
long after. So he lived alone with his mother, both of them crawling
with lice.

Then one day along came a woman who bathed him, bought
him a wicker basket and fed him rice and bread, his usual diet.

Not long after, this woman tucked him inside her shirt, next to her salty skin, which he liked to lick, and woman and dog boarded a plane after passing a big, black, contraband-sniffing Labrador. The Lab paid no attention to P.T.

In the plane, he slept in the basket that was now his home. Twice his human had to move, and twice he went inside her shirt. After a whole day and night, they stood with many other people, and an immigration man said: "Welcome to America!"

It was Lorna who brought P.T. home. As I write this, he is lying on my feet. The words of the Tibetan man who gave him to us ring in my mind: "He will always be with you . . . ."

# CHAPTER
# *21*

## CHO OYU

BY ALAN

Cho Oyu, at 26,750 feet the ninth highest peak in the world, is located west of Everest at the head of the Gokyo Valley. Its name means "Mother Goddess of Turquoise." I first thought of climbing it in 1982, when Roger Marshall and I went ahead of the main group of Canadian Everest Expedition to build a *chorten* in memory of a friend, Reinhard Karl, who had died on Cho Oyu's south face that spring. In the winter of 1984, I became intimate with the goddess's steep northern slopes.

Roger had obtained permission for Cho Oyu's West Ridge. He invited two Czech climbers, Jarik and Dusan; an American, Pete Athens, from Colorado; and me. His permit started on December 1, the first day of the Himalayan winter season.

During September and October of that year, Craig Ballinger and I led guided trips in Nepal. The first one took us into the Annapurna Sanctuary, and the second went from the flat plains of central Nepal up into the Khumbu region and on to Everest base camp. We achieved a basic level of acclimatization from those trips plus a couple of quick trips up Kali Patar, the grassy hill overlooking Everest base camp, which was not so grassy that year because an early storm had covered it with three feet of new snow. I spoke to Roger about Craig, and he agreed to having him join us.

The expedition was relaxed in its organization. Roger saw little point in spending energy on irrelevant issues. We would climb as three teams: the Czechs, Pete and Craig, and Roger and I. Because of the weather, we probably would all be climbing at the same time, but we would be free to move at our own pace with no responsibility for the other teams. Roger believed that climbing Alpine-style in small teams placed the responsibility of survival directly on the individual, and that gave each of us the possibility of maximum personal growth.

We assembled in mid-November in Namche Bazaar, where prior to our departure we stuffed ourselves with the traditional English fare of eggs and chips, washed down with liberal amounts of Nepal's Star beer. At times like that, anticipating possible food shortages on the climb, we indulged in "panic eating": gluttonously attempting to make up any deficit beforehand.

Our drunken lunchtime departure from Namche Bazaar and subsequent arrival in Thame village proved normal. The stagger on-wards to Chagrogpa in the dark was enlivened by the local police, who stopped us to search for illegal buffalo skins in the loads our yaks were carrying. They found nothing. Our Sherpani yak drivers had dropped them in the scrub juniper just minutes before the police arrived. After the police left, glasses were raised to our informer and the reliable tip.

We spent the night in the house of our yak man and continued the next day up the valley. The heavy snows of mid-October were now in evidence. The deep snow created a problem but no serious threat to the yaks.

Some of our best food, which the Czechs had bought, had gone astray down valley, and we survived on numerous plates of potato-and-vegetable stew. We were concerned that we not become weakened this early in our adventure.

The temperature was comfortable during the sunny days, but it plunged dramatically when the sun disappeared behind the western ranges. The wind blew steadily from the west, and the night skies were crystal-clear, holding promise of good weather.

We developed a pattern. One day we would break trail and use our ice-axes and shovels to clear a way, and the next day the yaks would follow that route with our loads.

One day we were crossing a rocky windswept area with the yaks when our yak driver began rushing around releasing our loads onto the snow. It seemed that this wild and inhospitable plateau was to become our base camp. A broken-down stone enclosure filled with the driven snow was to become our home for a while. We had rented a large canvas tent from our *sirdar*, Pasang, and after it was draped over the stone walls, it became our kitchen-cum-dining area. In fact, once the snow was cleared from inside the shelter and a dry tarpaulin laid on the floor, it became quite a comfortable haven in that icy desert.

The first ascent of Cho Oyu and many subsequent ascents, as well, were made from Tibet via the straightforward Northwest Face. All the southern-side routes from Nepal are very difficult and require a lot of fixed-rope and a large team. But approaching the route from Tibet makes an expedition far more expensive.

Mountaineers discovered a compromise, illegal but effective. They come into Nepal with a permit to climb from the western side of Cho Oyu. Then they quickly nip over the high pass into Tibet to the easier Northwest route. Few climbers will admit to this. Nor will I. Therefore, the following description may seem deficient in cartographical detail.

We made one reconnaissance and stowed some food on a pass that was the gateway to our venture. On December 1, precisely the first day we were legally entitled to climb, we staggered northward out of our camp, buckling under the weight of winter Himalayan loads. Pasang grinned as he told us good-bye, probably never expecting to see us again.

The first night we camped at 18,500 feet, the next at 19,000 feet on slopes hidden from the southern sun. Here our teams separated. Pete and Craig went up a glacier to the north, and the Czechs took a glacial branch to the east.

Roger and I started north and, after four hours of effort, corrected ourselves. Roger had only vague descriptions from past expeditions and therefore did not have accurate details about our chosen route. He dismissed such trivialities in favor of higher esoteric ideals. I said that at least we knew we were on the correct side of the mountain, and if we couldn't figure out the rest, we didn't deserve to be there.

Two days later, we had climbed to 22,500 feet and decided to take a rest day. Our tent was a tiny one-man Gore-Tex model that Roger had designed; it had been mistaken for the two-man model back in base camp. We were now clad in thick eider-down, Gore-Tex suits and were wearing two pairs of overboots over our winter mountaineering boots. I had a small thermometer that crawled out of its bulb to show -25C. during the day and then disappeared completely during the night, fearful of registering somewhere below -50C. It certainly felt like winter.

We later learned that because of our error lower down, the Czechs were a day ahead of us and were attempting the summit. We left camp at a leisurely 11 a.m. and climbed the steepening slopes to 24,600 feet, where we found the Czechs' small tent. Roger was noticeably slower at this point, and I wondered if he would be strong enough for the summit tomorrow. I dug out a platform in the snow-slope and put up our tent. Roger disappeared into his sleeping bag and refused all food and drink. I realized that I would be alone on the summit attempt.

Jarik and Dusan arrived back from the summit, jubilant but exhausted. I welcomed them and then dove into our tent to get out of the biting wind and to prepare soup and tea. Roger had his head buried in his sleeping bag and was not communicating except in monosyllabic grunts. I became concerned about his condition.

The night passed slowly. I formulated a plan to go to the summit alone while Roger recovered in the tent. I feared a change in the weather and knew that we were at the limits of our acclimatization and strength.

Pale winter light softened the eastern sky as I cooked soup for breakfast. I had a pounding headache because of the altitude and tried to get rid of it by taking fast deep breaths. Roger once again refused all food and drink, but he crawled out of the tent and determinedly tried to fasten on his crampons.

My headache had gone, and I was read to go. Roger looked at me with tears of frustration in his eyes and told me his eyesight was failing. The news hit me like a solid punch in the gut!

I had underestimated his condition. Eyesight problems are a sign of advanced cerebral edema, which causes pressure on the optic nerve. I reassured Roger, quickly stuffed his equipment in my pack and helped him with his crampons. I told him we had to descend immediately.

Step by stumbling step, I got him down to our last camp at 22,500 feet. After stopping there briefly to eat a chocolate bar, we continued our descent.

We had not brought along a safety rope because of the extra weight. At one point, our route dropped down a steep ice-cliff, and an old piece of fixed-rope was there. Roger slid down the old fixed-line, with his hand locked around the rope. His feet slipped and his weight came onto the fixed-line. Suddenly the snow-stake to which it was attached popped out of the snow. With a reflex action, I grabbed it, thrust it back in place and stood on it.

That day we reached the glacier and in another day were back in legal territory. Roger had a severely frostbitten big toe and three fingers of one hand were black.

Pete and Craig eventually got on the correct route, but they ran into problems above 22,000 feet and also returned.

It had been a magnificent adventure—way up above 24,000 feet in a Himalayan winter, with base camp and security far behind. I felt somehow enriched and vital. I knew that for me this contained the essence of life.

*ABOVE:* **Adrian at 24,000 feet on Everest in winter.** *Photo by Joe Tasker*

❖    ❖    ❖    ❖

*BELOW:* **Nyima Dorgi with Adrian (l.) and Alan.** *Photo by Glenn Porzak*

**Alan Rouse at Camp 2 on the Northwest Ridge of K2**

*ABOVE:* **On a plateau on Annapurna IV in winter.**

✧ ✧ ✧ ✧

*BELOW:* **West face of Lhotse.**

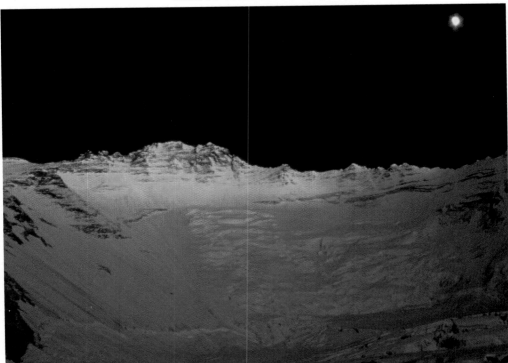

**Twins below Khumbu Icefall—Everest: Spring 1989**

# CHAPTER
## 22

# K2: 1986

BY ADRIAN

I was plodding up a snowy trail on Mont Blanc's Mer de Glace Glacier in the summer of 1985. Behind me, tied onto the same rope, were Lorna and her younger sister, Sarah. We were on our way up to the Couvercle Hut for a day's exercise. I wished to show the two women some of the splendor of the Mont Blanc Range. The sky was a deep-blue, and the steepled Chamonix Aiguilles looked inviting and warm.

Two roped figures came toward us on their way down the mountain. As they got closer, I recognized the long, loping gait of the second person.

"Bloody hell, Burgess! How many bottles of wine do you have in that rucksack?" It was Al Rouse, who was guiding a client.

"None for you—you're working, youth," I replied with a grin. I was happy to see my old friend. It had been a while.

"Will you be in Cham tomorrow tonight?" I asked him. "We're only going to the Couvercle for a night so's I don't have to carry this wine back down."

"Yes. I'll see you in the Bar Nash," he said. "I've got some ideas for a trip I want to talk to you about."

The next evening at the Bar National, I was in the men's room when Jon Tinker, a British alpinist, came in cursing and obviously extremely upset.

"I can't believe R.B.J. bought it. It doesn't make sense," he said to no one in  particular.

"What's that about R.B.J. (Roger Baxter-Jones)?" I asked.

"He's dead! Bloody dead!" said Jon. "A fucking sérac came off on the Triolet. Killed him and his client."

He began sobbing. I stood shocked. Stunned. My zipper jammed half-shut. R.B.J. was a friend and a good climber. One of the "old crew," he'd been around for years.

The next few days were horrible. It was as though everyone wore lead coats. Proud shoulders slumped and once carefree heads sagged forward. Roger's funeral procession streamed through the streets of Chamonix. People shuffled slowly toward the cemetery. Not far away was the old Biolay campsite in the woods where Roger had spent many of his younger days as an itinerant alpinist. Recently he'd lived in Chamonix with his French wife, Christine, and everybody liked and respected him.

Old friends I hadn't seen for years flew over from England to bid him farewell, but the air was too charged for me to be able to enjoy their company. How could we celebrate our lives when one had just been taken from us?

Lorna and Sarah, particularly Sarah, were pretty freaked out by it all. I'd be sitting around a table with friends, drinking a glass of wine, and I'd feel Lorna's hand slide into mine with a reassuring squeeze.

A fun holiday of hiking and climbing had begun badly. For me, it was a repeat of so many losses. I felt numbed.

"All this is really shitty, Aid," said Rouse as he sat down at our table. "But we've seen a lot of it, eh ?"

I remembered sitting in the same bar with him five years earlier. We were both crying. His French girlfriend, Gwendoline, had just been killed skiing.

*'Your kid'—brother Al*

Now I simply nodded, biting my lip. I was full to bursting point.

"Well," said Rouse, "I wanted to ask you if you and your kid [he meant brother Al] wanted to go to K2 with us next year. I've got a permit for the Northwest Ridge."

"Who else's going?" I asked, trying to clear my mind of the present situation. It was not the time to begin questioning the whys and wherefores of what we do. The death of R.B.J. had nothing to do with my future plans. It was as though we each had a predestined life, and interfering in that plan seemed pointless. We each knew we had to climb, no matter what else happened.

"Brian (Hall) and J.B. (John Barry) for sure and maybe Wilks (Dave Wilkinson) and J.P. (John Porter)," said Rouse.

"Why did you get the Northwest Ridge?" I asked. Was the Abruzzi free?"

"It was the only permit I could get next year," said Rouse. "But I bet we could always nip up the Abruzzi if the Northwest Ridge is too hard."

I didn't think we'd be "nipping up" any route on K2, but I was interested. I wished to do a bit more research into the route and to weigh the project as a whole. K2 was a great-looking mountain and I certainly wished to climb it.

"Yes, I'd like to," I told Rouse. "I'll see you in England when I get back."

I knew that the Northwest Ridge remained unclimbed, despite two very determined attempts by an American group in 1975 and a large Polish expedition a few years later. It was quite obviously going to be a tough climb and not suited to an alpine type of ascent. The strength of the team would be important.

It was around Christmas when I next heard anything. A quickly scrawled aerogram informed me of the climbing team. Rouse and John Barry were joint leaders. Later I learned the reason for having two leaders.

Al's serious girlfriend had just left him for someone else, and he was very upset. Consequently, he'd asked J.B. to stand in for him while he collected his life. I could well sympathize with Al. Which dedicated expedition-climber had not had these kinds of problem at some time or another? My brother had problems with Daphne, I with Christine . . . the list was endless. The long absences, the hectic preparations, the withdrawn returns: they all made for relationship problems.

The expedition would have six climbers: brother Al and I, John Porter, Brian Hall, Dave Wilkinson and Phil Burke. Though we'd never climbed with the latter two, we knew them either from the Alps or from Alpine Climbing Group parties. The aerogram said we'd depart for Pakistan sometime in early May. It didn't say how much it was going to cost me in hard cash. I suspected there wouldn't be much change out of $5,000.

The next time I heard was a 4:30 p.m. phone call from England. Rouse's voice came down the line: "Aid, it's Al. I've got some good news!" he said, his voice bubbling with delight. "We've got a sponsor for the trip! Fullers Brewery, man! They'll foot the bill! Curran is going to come and make a film, too."

"That's great," I said. I looked at my watch. It was 11:30 p.m. in England. Then I knew why he was so effervescent—he'd just returned from the pub.

"Have you just been celebrating?" I asked.

"Heh, heh, heh," he giggled. "Fullers sent us a load of cans as samples. Got to make sure their product is worthy of our attention. We'll fly at the end of April. Can you come over a week before to help us pack? Oh, can you tell your clone, too?" He rang off.

So, that was it. We were going. I knew I would never have saved enough by earning eight dollars an hour as a carpenter.

Lorna flew with me to London. She had a lawyers' conference to attend, but after that, she'd join me in Yorkshire. It was great she'd be able to be with me until I left for the mountain. She'd already met many of my climbing friends either in Britain or Kathmandu, and she particularly liked Rouse for his eccentricities. To spend a few days with her away from her own work pressures would be good, especially because we'd be separated for three summer months.

We rode to her hotel in a taxi. The driver was friendly: "Where you going with all that luggage, guv?"

"On a climbing trip—to K2," I replied, thinking he'd be none the wiser.

"Oh, a big one," he said. "It's the second highest, isn't it ?"

"Sure is." I was surprised he'd even know. I doubted that the same would have happened in New York. Climbing has a much higher profile in the U.K.

Rouse's old Victorian house in the Nether Edge suburbs of Sheffield was in chaos. Brand-new climbing equipment, clothing and skis were all stacked up next to half-empty cardboard boxes, empty chip papers smelling of vinegar, and crushed beer cans: London Pride, care of Fullers.

Rouse was in fine form, running about with lists and inventories that spewed out from his personal computer.

"Brian'll give you all your gear," Rouse said. "He's the only one who knows what's going on."

He spun away laughing. He seemed quite happy with his life, and he had an attractive new girlfriend, Deborah. She wasn't a climber, but she looked on the whole chaotic affair with amazement as climbers came and went and more gear arrived.

I met Jim Curran in the kitchen. He had a can of Fullers in hand.

"How am I going to tell you and your brother apart?" he asked. "Do you have any special identification marks?"

"Yeah," I replied. "Al looks like a bachelor. I don't. You know, the way his eyes move but his head doesn't. He's mentally undressing every girl around."

I didn't know Jim very well, but I did know he was one of Rouse's best friends and confidants. I could imagine them sitting in the kitchen in the wee hours of the morning, debating a topic so thoroughly that they'd forget how it all started. He was a warm and thoughtful person with a particularly ironic sense of humor. He'd been to Pakistan before to make a film about Trango Tower. Judging by his tummy, I knew he hadn't climbed anything very difficult for a while, but I hoped he would help to keep the expedition light-hearted.

That night the team met in the Byron House Hotel. It was a favorite hangout for Sheffield climbers, and many an "old hand" could be heard holding forth on anything from climbing ethics to the difficulty of finding a beer in Baltistan. One could expect to hear heated debate on the use of bolts on British rock or the use of oxygen above eight thousand meters, though many an "expert" had used neither and hoped they'd never get into a position where they might have to.

"So, how's the U.S. of A," asked John Barry, as he strode over, his hand extended.

"Hey-up, J.B.!" I responded. "I didn't know they let Southerners in this pub. It's a lot bloody sunnier in the States than 'ere, I'll tell ya. Do ya ever find webs growing between your toes? It's so wet."

"You're not telling me you got that tan from the sun, are you, Burgess?" he joshed. "I bet you used one of those American tanning beds. Probably bleached the hair, too."

J.B. was as sharp as a whip, and though I'd try to return his banter, it was a difficult game. It was good to see him. He introduced me to Jim Hargreaves, a broad-shouldered individual with a bone-crunching handshake.

"Jim was my batman in the service for a while," said J.B. "He'll be base-camp manager and can keep the liaison officer in order."

"Do you climb at all?" I asked him, thinking that the expedition had grown since I'd last spoken with Rouse.

"You won't remember, but you took me climbing once when you were doing some part-time instructing for the army," he said. He had an easy-going but confident attitude. He'd have hard work organizing base camp for our group, because we were a bunch of very opinionated individuals.

The weekend before we left, Rouse threw a party at his house. It was fun to see so many of my old friends, but there were also many people I didn't know. Al had been doing a lot of hard rock-climbing, and many of his young friends were "rock jocks."

Rab Carrington summed up the Sheffield climbing scene for me: "As soon as you get to the outskirts of Sheffield, you can hear the popping and snapping of tendons and the straining of ligaments. The young kids drink only orange juice—in half-pints, just in case even orange juice might be bad for them."

Davi showed up at the party in Gail's fast GTI car, which smelled of fresh-burned rubber. He was in fine form, with every other word a four-letter one, but I noticed his hair had become noticeably whiter. Around midnight Davi and my brother began their antics.

They stood facing each other in the narrow passageway that

led from the kitchen to the dancing room and the toilet. It was a strategic position; their backs were carefully guarded against possible attack, and they could closely examine every young female who passed by. They were making the most of the latter opportunity.

As some unsuspecting young woman headed for the toilet, Davi growled: "Car wash! Car wash!" He and brother Al would bend their knees and straighten them in opposing time. Bend and straighten, bend and straighten. The girls would squeeze past, some with a giggle, some with a jiggle and some with a look of horror. But laughter shook the building. I noticed after a while that some were running the gauntlet more than was maybe necessary.

Our flight to Islamabad on Pakistan International Airlines was set for the 27th of April out of Heathrow Airport. After an evening reception hosted by Fullers and a press conference at the brewery, we were put aboard "The London Pride," a red double-decker bus used by Fullers for their P.R. exploits. The atmosphere was that of an afternoon picnic rather than a departure to climb a new route on one of the world's most difficult mountains. I flipped open a can of real London Pride and turned to J.B.: "Might as well put down what you can 'cause the PIA flight is dry."

For the sake of economy, half of our group went a week early to begin preparations. There were Rouse and my brother, J.B., Hargreaves, Curran and I.

The other person, whom I'd only just met, was Dr. Bev Holt, a well-traveled man of fifty who appeared solid and realistic. He'd worked in South Africa for a while and had his own inventory of medical stories to pit against our climbing tales. Though he didn't go far beyond base camp, he kept us all healthy with his common-sense realities.

"Expeditions are like war," he'd say. "A sick man is a hindrance to everyone. You've got to hit the bugs hard and with everything you've got."

During the flight, we bantered and told stories to while away the hours. We also had time to talk over the climb in great detail.

Rouse told me that Deborah was pregnant, and by the time he returned, he could be a father. I asked him how he felt about that, and he replied: "Dunno, really. It'll take some getting used to, I suppose. I need to climb this mountain first, and then we'll see."

I had the feeling that the expedition's success meant a lot to his career as a climber. In Britain there is room for only a few truly "professional" mountaineers. Bonington and Scott were the most prominent. The rest, like Rouse, were left to scrabble their way up the pile. Tasker and MacIntyre had been in that group, but they were dead, leaving Rouse with a better chance to reach his goal.

As always at that time of year, Pakistan was hot. Islamabad is such a long way from the mountains that it's easy to forget why one's there at all. The British Embassy scene hadn't changed  much from 1980. Several kind people opened their homes to us, and we appreciated their havens of air-conditioning. The Club was still the center of many social activities and the pool a real luxury. There were the same diehards playing tennis in the eighty-percent humidity and diplomats' buxom wives burnishing a tan they'd never get in England. Plus, we had our very own packing shed only five minutes' walk from the bar. No other nation takes care of its mountaineers in Pakistan like the British, and it was a real pleasure to be there.

The day after our arrival, our work began. There were loads to be re-packed into 25 kilos for portage; climbing permits to be checked; local foods had to be bought; and hundreds of postcards had to be signed. The organization of all this was pretty loose, with Rouse assigning tasks from a list jotted on a scribble pad.

"Aid, will you get all the local foods, the kitchen stuff and stoves?" he asked. He expected me to know the quantities, so I sat down and made my own lists.

For others, it wasn't always as easy. Everybody had been on smaller expeditions where logistics are relatively simple, but for a number of people it was their first big trip and they were left scratching their heads with the magnitude of it all.

I knew full well that Rouse didn't want to take a rigid leadership role, but the prestige meant something to him. He suffered the role because someone had to do it, and he had the experience. A large expedition with a large budget and greater hassles: all were, in many ways, the antithesis of what Rouse believed in. But, he had seen it work for Bonington, and he knew it could do the same for him.

Jim Hargreaves had been stuck in the British compound, working like a Trojan for days, so I asked him: "Jim, would you like to see the real Pakistan? I've gotta go to the bazaars in 'Pindi to do some shopping."

We hopped into an old Morris-Thousand cab, whose horn I knew would work far better than its brakes, and began a thirty minute death-defying ride.

"I'll never get used to the way these crazy buggers drive, man," I told him as we plunged into five lanes of tightly-packed, horn-honking traffic. "Not one of these cars would pass a safety inspection, you know."

"About as bad as Leeds or Bradford," he said, chuckling.

In the narrow streets, we wandered from shop to shop. Jim pointed ecstatically at the sights, sounds and smells of everyday Pakistan.

"Just look at all those spices!—sacks of 'em," he marveled. "They sell *everything* here, don't they?"

I nodded toward a juice vendor and his fly-covered fruit-crushing machine set up by the side of the road. I said: "There's enough bugs in that lot to give the expedition the shits for weeks."

Back in the embassy compound, all packing had ceased. Everybody sat around the pool slurping beers and taking the occasional dip. The club manager came over and bought me a beer. He was a stout-looking Yorkshireman called Gordon Hainsworth, whose wife worked in the immigration department.

"Kay mentioned to me the other night," he said, "that there seems to be two distinct groups in your team—them with the muscles and them with the fat. Is there any reason for that?"

"Yeah," I replied. "There's them that drinks masses of beer and them that drinks only a lot."

Then I went out and teased the lads: "Judging by the amount of white flesh around here, the British spring this year was pretty poor." Living in Colorado, I took sunshine for granted, and I didn't want to miss the chance for a dig.

"Curran'll never get a tan anyway," joked J.B., "because the Save the Whalers'll keep rolling him back into the water."

Once the second half of the group arrived, I tried to avoid the packing scene. It was frenetic. Everyone had his own idea of how it should be done. This, combined with the heat and humidity, made for frequent verbal clashes. Tempers were beginning to fray under the stress.

"We've got masses of gear, Aid," said brother Al, shaking his head in disbelief. "Somebody even brought a dartboard, man! What're we going to do with that?"

A week later we were in the small northern town of Skardu, the take-off place for the expedition. A number of us had flown by Fokker Friendship while the rest travelled with our gear by bus up the Karakoram Highway. At the airport, Curran had handed me a movie camera and said, "Aid, shoot some film of Nanga Parbat as you fly past, because I'm going on the bus."

I dutifully mentioned to the beautiful flight attendant what I wanted to do, and she disappeared into the cockpit. She returned smiling: "The captain would like you to come forward with your camera."

Minutes later I wedged myself between the two pilots and their instruments. I don't like flying in small planes at the best of times. They seem so vulnerable. I was terrified I might accidentally flip a crucial switch or back against an important lever. I could see the headlines: "K2 Team Disappears on Nanga Parbat."

The captain turned to me with a grin: "We normally fly to the west of Nanga Parbat, but for you I will change course and show you the South Face."

I must have visibly blanched. He was going to change course without so much as asking permission? After all, it was a scheduled passenger flight. For me, the next ten minutes seemed to stand still. We droned towards the huge mass of Nanga Parbat and began spiraling upwards. Around and around we went, with the Rupal Face tilting, poised to devour us if we flew too close. I could see some of the places we'd climbed six years earlier. To see it in this manner was more chilling than to be climbing it. I stared through the viewfinder, pretending it was just TV I was watching, rather than the real thing. I thanked the pilot for his cooperation and scurried back to my seat.

As we deplaned, he smiled and said: "We used too much fuel flying around Nanga Parbat, or else I would have flown you to K2."

In the K2 Motel, fans whirred and flies buzzed. I struggled with some important calculations: How many porters do we need to carry all the gear to base camp? How much local food should we buy for them? There were porters carrying our expedition loads and others carrying porter-food. It sounded straightforward if you just added the two together, but there were a lot of irregularities to be taken into account. First of all, the climbers ate food—which was carried by porters—on the approach, while the porters carried their own food or bought some from the local villages. Then, after we were into the hike for one week, we would begin to feed the porters. All the food consumed during the walk-in meant that we'd keep laying off porters as we went. At what rate, I had no idea.

"Brian, how do you normally account for all this ?" I asked.

"I let Rouse do it," he said, grinning.

I tried first one way and then another to check my accuracy. The figures did not match at all. "I hate this form of logic," I sighed to the fly trying to take a bath in my half-full tea cup.

How could I apply Western mathematics to a problem I knew should not be approached in this manner even if a figure was reached? There were too many variables that would crop up in a two-week approach walk. What would happen if a storm held us up for a day or a porter dropped a load in the river, not to mention the lack of accuracy when measuring out 22 ounces of *atta* or 2 ounces of *dahl*? Any one of a number of circumstances could sabotage the whole system. In frustration, I did the only thing I could. I guessed. And hoped it was an intelligent one.

Phil and Al went with me to order the food. We checked the quality of *atta*, rice and *dahl* as if we were professionals, rubbing the grains between our fingers and making knowledgeable noises, though we really had no idea.

"This is the normal quality for porters," the shopkeeper assured us, pointing to some rather gritty brown flour.

"It looks pretty rough," commented Phil, watching a few weevils wriggle around in the powder. It was the first time he'd seen coarse *atta*.

"But, sir," continued the grey-bearded merchant, "these are only porters you are feeding. They do not know what fine-quality *atta* looks like."

I was taken aback by his lack of concern for his countrymen. The Muslim brotherhood refers to unity frequently.

"We'll get the next quality up, just in case we have to eat it, too," I said.

"Sir, you are a very wise man," said the shopkeeper.

I didn't feel like one.

After a couple of days, the bus, gear and dust-coated expedition members arrived. They looked as if they'd been hauled through the Indus, dragged across a desert and made to clean General Zia's chimneys.

"Your batman didn't keep you very clean," I said to J.B.

"No," he replied. "Good help's hard to find."

Al Rouse arrived in a Suzuki mini-bus. He'd been delayed by an extra hassle at the Ministry of Tourism and so had travelled the two days on his own. This was typical of Al, and it didn't faze him at all. I suspect the brief respite from our high-energy team and the chance for reflection were very attractive to him.

On the morning of the 12th of May, we all set off by Jeep for the hamlet of Dasso and the start of the trek. This approach to K2 takes almost two weeks with porters. Eventually it follows the gigantic Baltoro Glacier through a gargantuan corridor surrounded by granite spires and snow-clad summits. I've traveled up and down this route three times now, but what makes each approach-hike different are the climbers and their interaction within the group and with the porters.

Only Brian and Rouse had been this way before and knew what to expect, while for Phil and Hargreaves the whole process was new. Al and I were able to take it in our stride because we'd done so many treks, and they all seem to follow the same rough pattern. However, the others were frequently frustrated by the apparent lack of information. They would have liked a brief rundown each day at breakfast, but that was not Rouse's way. He was far too easy-going for that approach.

On the first day, Curran, Hargreaves, Bev and Brian got ahead of the porters and missed a river crossing, which condemned them to thousands of feet of ascent and descent while the rest of us sauntered along a flat, easy trail.

"Bloody hell, man," I said. "There's a lot of up and down the way they're going." I could see them as tiny dots following the thin line of a trail that twisted over the lifeless hillside.

The sun was high in the sky, and we were beginning to fry. At day's end, we all met up again to share our tribulations. Al, John Porter and I had limped most of the way.

"These bloody boots are a piece of shit!" Al barked. "I've got blisters on my blisters!"

All three of us had brand-new leather boots we hadn't bothered to break in. We'd had a cavalier attitude, and we were suffering because of it.

The following day we passed through the crumbling Braldu Gorge where, in wet weather, landslides and tumbling rocks have killed a number of people. Although it was dry and blistering hot, we made steady progress up and then down barren shoulders of friable, flinty rock. When we arrived at the small green oasis of Chango, many porters were hanging around as though they'd finished for the day. There was some discussion, but it was difficult to know what it was about.

Later, our liaison officer clarified the matter: "Some porters are saying they wished to avoid sleeping in Askole because food and sleep is much money there. But Askole men want to stay with their families."

Many of the climbers were tired and hoping the day's walk was over, when Rouse strolled effortlessly by and explained that Askole was better, so we didn't need to waste a day. It didn't make much difference to me, blisters or not, but rumbles of discontent rose from many of the others. People were angry with Rouse, thinking him inconsiderate and aloof for not sitting down and carefully explaining the problem. However, I believe the real reason was that he couldn't afford to have an open discussion in front of the porters, who would then exploit the situation. In that part of the world, strength and decisiveness are highly prized, and a leader always leads from the front.

That night the incident was brought up for discussion once more. It was disturbing to see how animated people became. Brian, in his steadying and relaxed manner, tried to calm everyone down. There were discussions of how fast we should go versus the height gained every day.

Someone asked: "Yes, but what about acclimatization? We can't go up too quickly."

I shook my head and listened in amazement. These people were going to climb K2 and yet were concerned about what I considered a gentle daily elevation gain. I felt that all the rhetoric had more to do with a few people tiring easily because of their lower level of fitness. I could understand Curran needing time to make his film, but I didn't feel the days were very long at all. In recent years, I've walked out in four days, so two weeks ought to be enough.

I began to lose track of time over the next few days. One place began to merge with the next, and I slowly lost my ability to relate the past events in their correct chronology. At one point, while traversing polished rocks high above the swirling Braldu, a porter screeched, did a pretty good impersonation of a Rawalpindi traffic cop about to be hit by a truck, dropped his load and took off back the way we'd come. I never quite figured out what exactly happened, but his load was divided by other porters who seemed to accept this as normal.

At a small stand of trees clinging some hundreds of feet up above the pebble river bed, I realized we'd arrived at Paiyu. The smell of excrement wafted down on the warm afternoon breeze, reminding me of a time in college when a toilet had blocked during a heat wave. A trickle of suspicious-looking water ran down through the trees, winding its way around tin cans and other garbage, most labeled in languages other than English.

A number of years later, I passed the same way and organized the porters into a cleanup crew. I distinctly remember a bony-faced porter poking the smoldering trash in the pink, fading light. He turned to me and in halting English said: "Some people not understand." He was right. Two months later when we walked out, it was the same as ever.

The next day the porters cooked thick, round Balti bread, which they would take onto the glacier. My brother asked to look at one and banged on it with his gnarled arthritic knuckles: "Man, it's hard! Definitely recommended by the British Dental Association!"

Al Rouse, having handed out all the porter-food, came over to inform me: "Aid, we have fourteen porter-food loads too many."

So much for my guesswork. "It was desperate trying to work it out, Al," I said, "but don't be too worried. It could have been fourteen too little."

I grinned, trying to disarm him, but a man with a math degree from Cambridge was not easily amused.

Mountains began to show up in the distance, and it seemed timely to discuss tactics of how to climb K2. Rouse was obviously concerned about how decisions were to be made and who was going to make them. He suggested having three people as a leading core, of which he would be one. I sat back and listened carefully, trying to visualize the pros and cons of each idea as they were presented. Then Rouse suggested that we could have two groups, one climbing while one rested. That seemed reasonable as it's not difficult for four climbers to organize themselves. I don't think anyone could have foreseen the problems it could cause.

In hindsight, I now think it's better to be flexible and encourage people to climb with many different partners. I know that Rouse was concerned that the stronger climbers might push to the front, leaving the less powerful to act in support. He also suspected that that front pair might be brother Al and I. What he didn't foresee—and neither did I—was that if one puts two different ability levels in the same climbing group, then someone is constantly being reminded of their weakness. And that is demoralizing.

On a snowy hillside littered with huge granite boulders, we stopped for the night. We'd reached Urdukas. Across the glacier, giant spires appeared and disappeared as veils of cloud wrapped around the granite towers.

"There's Trango."

"No, that's Uli Biaho."

"So many . . . ."

That afternoon we all played on some boulder problems. Our boots were muddy and the rock was cold, but it brought us together as we shouted the odds and encouraged each other. One shallow corner beat us all, but Rouse kept on trying. He slipped, fell. He heaved, braced, grabbed a sharp flake—and he'd done it! Brilliant! He stood atop the cliff, smiling and panting heavily.

"Not too bad, after all," he chirped.

We didn't know then that it would be his last boulder problem. I've stood at the bottom of that problem since then and said a silent wish.

There followed days of trudging through snow and mist. Occasionally a peak showed itself and vanished quickly, sucked back into the cloud. As I watched, I began to develop a deep respect for our porters. Their thin ragged clothing did not keep them from the worst cold, which came at night when they huddled a circle. Crouched beneath thin tarpaulins, they made broth and ate their hard bread, while helping the weakest to get the warmest positions. They were a hardy, smiling bunch who would often sing all night when things got tough. It was my first acquaintance with the Baltis, and I was reluctant to invade their privacy. But on later trips to the region, I would duck under the tarps and sit with them, sipping salt-tea and inquiring after their health. The powerful spirit of the mountains seems to flow through them.

One day I heard them speaking among themselves in an ancient language other than Urdu. It was Balti. My ears pricked as I recognized the Sherpa words for one, two and three. Turning, I grinned and said: "*Chick, nee, sum.*" My fingers signaled the same numbers. They stopped in surprise and grinned back: "*Chick, nee, sum! Chick, nee, sum!*" Their local language must have traveled all the way from Tibet.

When we arrived at Concordia, the confluence of Baltoro and Godwin-Austin Glaciers and a mecca for Western pilgrims, we couldn't see a thing. Not a peak, not a summit; only swirling snow and the dark figures of porters emerging from the gloom. Our team had lost a lot of its glamourous, swashbuckling attitude. Hunched beneath red-and-white golfing umbrellas, people would arrive in dribs and drabs, put up a tent and disappear inside.

Meanwhile, Jim Hargreaves turned the stacked loads into a tarp-covered kitchen and began his chore of producing the evening meal. The kerosene stoves roared, producing a warm fug as Jim shouted instructions to the two cooks: "Aftab, stop pilacking around and start making *chapatis*! Five for everybody! Abdul, open these tins! No, wash that paraffin off your hands first!"

At first, I tried to help but it soon became apparent that "too many cooks" were going to overturn the broth, so I went to my tent and read.

A cold dawn broke and people scuffled around inside their tents until a shout brought everybody wide awake: "Bloody hell! You can see K2!"

There it was! All 8,611 meters (28,250 feet) of it!—with early-morning sunlight burnishing its tip. Its massive bulk blocked the entire valley, yet we were many hours away. Like a guardian it hung above us. The first time you see K2, something pierces your whole being. No real climber could turn away and not want to climb it. It draws you and tugs at you. Its pyramidal shape represents the perfect mountain.

"The ultimate, the most inspired expression the force of mountain-building has produced on our planet," wrote Günter Oskar Dyhrenfurth, a noted mountain chronicler.

And what did Al Burgess, noted mountaineer and fellow adventurer, have to say? "Hey, Aid, here's my camera. Take a pic for me will you? It's bloody cold out there!"

It was a perfect day to approach base camp. The grey skies and blowing snow had magically disappeared, so that we could finally see our mountain, let it draw us to it and be absorbed by it. Rouse was

*K2: The world's second highest mountain at 28,250 feet*

ecstatic and suggested we go together to search out a good base camp. It was as though he'd never wanted to be away from the mountain since his attempt three years earlier. That's why he seemed to be in such a rush to get the trek over with and stand before the mountain. We chatted away like two children on vacation. He hoped I didn't mind not climbing with brother Al because he wished to spread the greatest experience evenly among the team.

"If *we* all climbed together, the others would be lost," he reasoned. He emphasized the *we* as though it were special. I told him that it was a big mountain, and we'd need to work as a team or else we didn't stand a chance.

As we reached the base of the mountain, a long glacier swept rightwards with a very prominent medial moraine extending like a huge spine down the center. That was The Strip, where most expeditions camp, but our route lay off to the left, halfway around the mountain. Because of this, we opted to have our base camp beneath, and to the left of, a 300-foot-high shaley pedestal: the Gilkey Memorial.

Art Gilkey had died on the 1954 American expedition to K2. His friends' attempt to rescue him is a mountaineering legend. Nowadays it's a burial place and creepy as hell. The first time I went up the scree slope to the rocky pinnacle, there were goosebumps the size of gooseberries on the back of my neck. Bodies from a variety of accidents have been stuffed down rocky fissures and then covered over with small rocks. Staring at a collection of small memorial plaques decorating the walls, while large black blow-flies buzzed around my head, I vowed there and then that my name wasn't going to adorn these ghostly rocks. Hell, this is a bad place! I returned to camp.

The last porters were paid, and they set off to Concordia as if all the devils in hell were after them. We we set about pitching tents and storing loads. Al organized a group to assemble our enormous North Face Super Dome dining tent. Its geodesic construction had the likes of Dave Wilkinson shaking his head in disbelief; I think it was larger than his home in England.

I heard Al curse and throw away a large black bag. "We've carried in about twenty wooden marquee stakes," he snapped. "What the hell are we going to use them for?"

There's a lot of work in setting up a big base camp, and by the end of the day everyone was tired and irritable. The smallest decision seemed to set off an argument or encourage a curt remark. Everyone could feel the tension, so we didn't discuss climbing but rather broke out our final bottle of Scotch and hoped some healing would take place.

When you're closely involved in a trip, it's not easy to see what to do to resolve conflict. Later, after reading both John Barry's and Jim Curran's books about our expedition, some things became clearer to me. Both authors were correct in their perceptions, but both were also biased. John had been disappointed with Rouse and so tended to attack him, while Jim was equally determined to protect him. When you're on the sideline, it's easier to keep everything in perspective, but we all tended to move center field at some time or other to protect our own interests. We'd forgotten that mountaineering is really only a game and began to take ourselves too seriously. How often I heard the comments: "But he's too slow!" or "He's too fast!" or "He carried too little!" or "He never told me what to do!"—and on and on.

It's only natural that one creates one's own reality, based on past experience and present desires, and it's all too easy to make judgments that reflect on the actions of others. However, it's important to remember that all the people on the expedition were good people, despite individual quirks.

The next day while we sat around drinking mugs of sweet tea, Rouse explained his plan to us. We'd have two teams, A and B. Each would take turns at climbing in the lead; the other group would provide support or would rest. I would be in group A, with Rouse, Phil and John Porter. The other group would be brother Al, J.B., Dave and Brian. No one complained at this, and a few were relieved at Rouse's decisiveness.

The first casualty came almost immediately. Brian had been having trouble with an old ski injury to his knee, and the trek to base camp made it worse. After a few days, he realized he wasn't going to be able to climb and became awfully depressed. He had done so much to help put all the expedition gear together that it was a particularly cruel blow. He decided to return home and left with some porters from another expedition.

I was so enthusiastically and energetically helping to carry equipment up to an advanced base camp, which was placed three hours up the Savoia Glacier, that I hadn't had time to miss Brian. But this wasn't the case for Team B. They were struggling to maintain a steady pace without one of their strongest climbers.

Beyond advanced base camp. the glacier rose gently towards the Chinese border and Savoia Pass. There were a few large crevasses showing, but by wearing skis we could make it reasonably safe to go without a rope at our individual pace. We all had touring bindings on our skis and used skins for ascending, which we could remove for the streak back down the glacier. My skies were long: 205-centimeter downhill racers.

"Al, how come I've got these long, heavy skis?" I asked Rouse. "They're not really meant for turning."

He chuckled: "You wouldn't want Curran wearing them, would you? *You* can ski. And they're too long for most of the others. We got them given because they're ex-rental."

"I noticed you and Brian have soft-tipped touring skis," I said.

"Yes," Rouse replied. "We didn't have enough second-hand skis given, so we had to score some extras."

He grinned his impish grin. You couldn't help but like the guy.

Camp 1 was up in a small hanging-cwm that gave access to a 2,500-foot face of snow and rock. The problem lay in choosing a safe way up to it. First, a straightforward snow gully led up between rocks on the left and a tottering ice tower on the right. The snow was heavy and unreliable, so we decided to fix some rope to act as a handrail. Higher, we had to pass beneath an evil-looking spike of ice, which seemed as if it would fall onto us at any time. Gasping, lung-wrenching movement was the only justifiable way to pass this obstacle.

I decided to share a tent with Phil, because I knew Rouse was desperately unkempt in his camping habits and that would drive me crazy. John, on the other hand, was an old-time friend and had read English at university. He frequently waxed philosophical: well above my head, scattering my remaining brain cells like some supercollider experiment.

In Phil, I chose the devil I didn't know, but it turned out great. He is one of those rare people who was a natural athlete from the moment he stepped into a pair of running shoes. In high school, he entered a number of national cross-country events and came third in one of them. Born with a light frame, he rock-climbed at such a high level that our tent-bound discussions on the sport were fascinating.

"Why would you want to rappel a climb first?" I asked.

"Well, how could you practice the moves otherwise?" the innocent replied.

"Isn't that cheating?" I countered, knowing that when I began rock-climbing, it was.

"That's Stone-Age ethics," he said with a grin.

Phil was pleased I took an interest in a sport at which he excelled, especially when we were in a place where I could show my climbing strengths. Although it was his first time at real high-altitude climbing, he pushed himself constantly, but he had difficult time staying my pace. This was hardly surprising, because I was acclimatizing at a faster rate. I often wondered if he thought: "How can that old fart keep going up here when at sea level I know I can run him into the ground?" Being an excellent sportsman and athlete, he maintained a great attitude and I grew to like him even more.

On the 2nd of June we finally moved into Camp 1, nine days after arriving at base camp. The snow was deep powder, which made moving anywhere a tiresome task. No sooner had we established ourselves than it began to snow. I went to John's and Rouse's tent to discuss the situation.

"Should we stay up here or go back to ferry some more food?" I asked.

"The main problem, Aid, is we only have four days' food," said Rouse. "If we stay up here and eat it all, we won't have gained a thing. I suppose we should descend and save the stuff we've humped up here."

We descended. It was quite a while before we finally managed to fix some rope above Camp 1.

Then progress speeded up, and we started to feel as if we were getting somewhere. I remember one day it was Phil's and my turn to be in the lead, while Rouse and John Porter came up behind and helped us carry rope. Dawn arrived fine and clear, and we hoped we'd be able to put in a full day's work. When I arrived at the top of the last fixed rope, the cloud began to swirl around us and snow flurries filled the air. Hell, I couldn't believe the weather was doing that to us!

"It was bloody hard work getting up here," I said to Phil. "I hate to go down without doing something. Whaddaya think?"

"If you want to try and fix some rope, it's O.K. with me," he agreed. "It'll be just like climbing in Scotland. A bit of snow wouldn't stop us there, would it?"

We set out on a long traverse towards a large open gully that split the face. Snow-covered rocks made progress slow and precarious, and I couldn't help feeling excited as I glanced back at Phil's ice-encrusted face. It was more like climbing in the Alps in winter than Scotland. We needed to cross the gully at some point, and we clung to the rocky edges until I decided on the exact place.

"I'm going to cross it here," I panted to Phil. "It might avalanche, so you'll need to be well tied on."

I slotted a "friend" into a nearby crack as additional support.

"I'll tie onto two three-hundred foot ropes, so I don't need to stop in the middle. If it should avalanche when I've a lot of rope out, please hold on tight 'cause I'll go a long way—maybe three hundred feet or more."

He nodded slowly and with precision as he got the picture: "I'm just a human disc brake. Is that it?"

"I'm going to be careful," I said. "Don't worry."

I left him paying out the rope. It was snowing persistently, and the mist obscured almost everything except our immediate surroundings. Hissing snow-slides separated around me, but the main snow mass held firm. By the time I reached the other side and drove a pin into a solid granite crack, I could barely see. Snow got behind my dark glasses and was freezing my eyelids together. I tied off the ropes and slid back to Phil, who was freezing.

"Let's go and get a brew, mate," I said.

Often the hardest part about fixing rope is in reaching the high point before heading off onto new terrain. We'd have to re-break a trail through fresh snow for a few hours before any new climbing could be achieved, and it proved to be terribly tiring. The more rope we managed to fix, the further we had to ascend the next time. That was the kind of position we found ourselves in when trying to reach the main ridge and site of Camp 2.

For Al it was almost too much because he found himself in the lead for disproportionate periods of time, with his two companions trying to keep pace. On the 18th of June, the three of them made a big push forward, with Dave in the lead, and almost made it to the ridge.

The following day was perfect weather, and the trail was still good from the B team's effort. Rouse, John, Phil and I finally led out onto a shallow snow-basin: the elusive Camp 2. Beyond and thousands of feet below, the giant K2 Glacier stretched out for twenty miles into the Xinjiang Province of China. Ahead of us stood the profile of K2's magnificent North Ridge. Somewhere up at 26,000 feet, we hoped to join it for the final day.

It was at about this time that we should have all sat down to discuss future events and the effectiveness of the teams. But we didn't. We all knew who was coping well with the altitude and who was going slower, but for some inexplicable reason we never all sat down to discuss our situation.

I met my brother descending from Camp 1. We were alone for the first time in weeks. He was able to be completely candid.

"How would you feel if every morning you awoke to know you were going to be busting the trail," he said. "I'm drilling myself into the ground trying to keep our group working effectively."

I saw the strain on his tired face and knew things would have to change. But in which direction? The first opportunity to break out of our tight groups came the day after we'd established Camp 2. The other members of my A team were resting, and Al's companions had descended to base camp. I told Al I'd re-ascend to Camp 2, so he wouldn't be wasting his time going up alone.

"If we can break a trail and fix some ropes up to the rocky gullies, then Rouse and J.P. can set to work on it the day after," I told him. I finally felt as though we might be getting somewhere, and climbing in the company of my brother was reward enough for the hard work.

Above Camp 2, the ridge formed a broad hump before disappearing into the banded, craggy face. We set off up the wind-blasted snow and, after thirty minutes, decided to rope up as the face steepened. I then led out 600 feet of rope while Al fixed it to snow anchors as he followed.

"I don't want to begin fixing any rope up above because it's supposed to be complicated route-finding, and I think Rouse knows the way," I explained.

I was more tired than I cared to admit after the past few days of work and, with the perfect weather, didn't want to burn myself out.

We walked into Camp 2 and saw Rouse and John making a brew in the sun. Rouse looked terrible. He'd been vomiting and had almost lost his voice, but his determination was still as strong as ever.

John, on the other hand, looked his handsome, debonair self and could probably have warmed my ears with a few sonnets by Keats if I'd asked him. Some people have described John as the "dark horse" of the trip because he rarely joined in the heated discussions. I didn't see him like that at all. I knew very well how strong and fit a climber he was. He'd done very well when we were all on Everest, and I always thought of him as stronger than Rouse, though he never tried to press the point. During the next couple of days, they led and fixed eleven rope-lengths—1,600 feet—to a height of over 24,000 feet.

The past week had been one of frenzied activity during which a great deal was accomplished, and the two groups had really worked as a team, though it now seems to me that motives varied. John Porter later told me that Rouse had spoken of making a dash for the summit when they were in the lead. This was a classic hare-brained Rouse-ism, born of his determination to climb the mountain. I can imagine John's reaction: 4,000 feet below the summit and Rouse's voice almost totally gone! He asked Rouse how much difference it would make if Al and I were to climb the mountain before he did, as we were in better health at the time. His reply was interesting: "Oh, it wouldn't matter that much. They live in the States now, anyway."

The weather took a turn for the worse, and so did the expedition, though we didn't know it at the time. Back in base camp, epics were being reported on the South-Southwest Ridge and the Abruzzi Spur. Two Americans had been killed when a falling block had triggered a huge avalanche, and Maurice and Lillian Barrard, the French husband-and-wife team, were missing—"missing" at 8,000 meters is synonymous with "dead." On the brighter side, quite a few had reached the summit.

After a week of poor weather, John Porter, worried about losing his job because of his long absence, decided to head home. It was a difficult decision for him to make, and for the expedition it was a great loss. He was, without a doubt, one of the strongest climbers. J.B. and Phil were both performing well but had never been above 8,000 meters, so it would be extra-difficult for them. Dave had a steady head on his shoulders and was a safe, conscientious climber but hadn't been able to find the speed that would be necessary to complete the summit-day safely without spending a night out. Although Rouse was debilitated by his throat infection, I knew he'd bounce back, once rested. While Al and I were both healthy and fit, we were not about to make a break for the summit from 24,000 feet. That would be stupid, and so we committed to more rope-fixing and load-carrying.

The day dawned perfectly clear as J.P. prepared to leave for home. Before heading down, he came up to advanced base with us to collect his personal gear. I could imagine his internal wrenching. When I turned to continue, he held out his hand.

"Good luck, Aid," he said. "I hope you make it." He must have been heart-broken.

We set off, trail-breaking in deep snow back up the mountain. There were Al, J.B., Phil and I. Above Camp 1, the ropes were buried deep, necessitating hours of laborious pulling and step-kicking.

Al, following directly behind me, said: "You're doing a good job, kid. If you do the first half, I'll do the second."

The face slowly sank beneath us as we gasped our way upward. I looked down and saw J.B. making his way determinedly in our trail. The next day he would take the lead.

At Camp 2, I dumped my load of food, turned to Al and said: "I'll be off now, but I'll be back up to stay tomorrow. Good luck!"

When I finally collapsed into our Camp 1 tent, I'd been going for eight hours. I told Phil: "I'm buggered, man. But if we don't keep on pushing when the weather's good, we'll never get up this hill."

"Yeah, I know," he said. "I'm sorry I had to turn around early. I was totally whacked. I'll be better tomorrow though."

"Hey, man! Don't worry!" I said. "You can only do the best you can."

Rouse and Dave had come up to join us, which meant that we were three pairs, each one day behind the next. If everything worked out, I was hopeful we'd get a great deal of work accomplished. The following morning Rouse set out very early. I could hear him coughing in the next tent as he pulled his boots on.

"See you later," he croaked. He still appeared sick but was driving himself hard.

Later, on the fixed ropes, Phil and I passed him as he leaned against the slope, coughing and spitting gobs of yellow phlegm. It was heart-rending to see my friend struggling like that. I went on my way quietly.

Above Camp 2, Al and J.B. were re-plugging steps. Much of the past work had been eradicated by the last storm. They strode into camp later.

"Well done, lads," I welcomed them. "How's the short little legs?" I said, teasing J.B.

"Getting shorter by the day," he laughed. "Your brother's a bloody machine when it comes to trail-breaking."

The next day's plan was for Al and J.B. to ascend to the top of the ropes and pull them out of the snow on the way up. Phil and I would then carry a tent and our gear up onto the snow-dome and establish a Camp 2A, from where we hoped we could speedily fix more rope up to 8,000 meters and our last camp. Rouse and Dave would move up to

Camp 2 and be ready to assist us. Everything was working well, and harmony was established in the face of action.

When I reached the snow-dome, I walked rightward to an area of dry, rocky platforms. It would be the first time we'd slept on rock since base camp. Phil came over the rise and I asked him, with the ring of a real estate agent: "Would you like this house, sir? Or perhaps this little number? Good clear views into China and Pakistan. One of a kind!"

We sat back in the sun while the stove purred away. Up on the buttress, J.B. had stopped at the beginning of the ropes. A bad sign. Al was on his own, hauling out ropes. We watched while he reached the high point. Then they both came over for a social call.

"Pulled 'em all out for ya," said Al, smiling. "Tomorrow you should make good progress." Then down they went.

That night everything seemed to go wrong. Phil complained of a headache and began vomiting out of the tent door. Most of the night he moaned and whimpered, as the ravages of altitude-sickness racked his frame. When morning arrived, I suggested to Phil that he descend to Camp 2 to recover.

"Next time you come up, you'll feel much better," I said. "Can you ask my brother to come up this afternoon?"

I decided to climb up the ropes on my own, with more rope in my pack. Al had made a good trail, and it was quite easy to follow the ropes around small cliffs and up snowy ramps. I found myself enjoying the isolation, with the new ground holding my interest. Unfortunately, it was over after an hour and a half. I stood at the head of the ropes, wondering what to do next.

"Maybe I could fix some on my own," I thought. "It would be a laugh to try anyway."

I loaded up with some wired nuts and "friends" and kicked steps up to the foot of a rock rib. Behind me trailed a couple of ropes. A tiptoe-traverse with crampons scraping took me into another small gully. I looked down the huge North Face, and a tingle of horror crept across my scalp: Don't want to fall here!

I moved up and was forced left again by a sizable overhang. With the rope anchored, I peered around nervously. It was technical ground and I needed a belay. I descended.

While I sat outside the Gore-Tex Denali tent, I could see Al's red form moving up to join me. As he drew closer, I noticed his strong, steady gait. He still had a lot of energy left.

"So fill us in on what's happening, kid," he said.

"Phil's suffering from the altitude. He gives all he's got, but he's had it."

"Yeah. J.B. has a bad cold, too. Everyone is getting tired."

We hadn't had a chance to discuss how the climb was progressing until then and it didn't look good. Our partners had slowly dropped behind and Rouse was still sick. What should we do?

"Every bugger and his dog is climbing the Abruzzi," Al said. "And here we are, driving ourselves into the ground on this difficult route just so we can record a glorious 'High Point.' Let's go and climb the Abruzzi while we still have the time!"

The next morning Rouse arrived at our camp, and we voiced our thoughts. He sat quietly, thinking for a while, and then agreed: "You're probably right. But it's a pity."

The descent off the Northwest Ridge and back to Camp 1, with packs full to bursting point, was hard and unrewarding. Our bodies felt the leaden weight of defeat.

"There's no one here," I told Al as I crawled into my tent. "Phil's personal gear has gone, too. He's obviously gone down. I think we packed it in just in time, kid."

"At least no one got hurt," replied Al.

Back in base camp we discussed our chances of climbing the Abruzzi, which had again been climbed by a variety of people. However, every time the route was climbed, I noticed there were others having epics. The Polish climbers, Kukuczka and Piotrowski, had made a new route on the South Face, but the latter had fallen to his death during the descent. One thing stood out quite clearly: the successful summiteers had all climbed to the summit of at least one other 8,000er prior to K2, a fact many people overlooked.

Al and I wished to climb together on the Abruzzi and told the rest of the team. In our minds the expedition was over, and any loyalty to previous expectations seemed moot. One night Rouse dropped a bombshell when he said: "Although we'll be climbing in pairs—Aid and Al, Phil and J.B., Dave and I—on the way up, I think the strongest should be prepared to wait for the weakest on the descent."

"I don't agree," I said bluntly. "Above 8,000 meters, everybody has to be responsible for themselves. It's insanity to depend upon help from someone when you're that high."

"I take it we can't rely on help from you then," Phil said.

That hurt! How could I tell friends I'd been climbing with for the past two months that they should not try and go to the summit? That there had been enough deaths!

Rouse's suggestion invited the unprepared to stick out their necks in the assumption that help lay just around the corner. I already felt that there were climbers on some of the other expeditions who would not even have made a serious attempt on the mountain if it wasn't for all the other people around. It was a kind of safety-in-numbers syndrome, and I didn't want our expedition to fall into the same trap. To me, it was like buying an insurance policy that couldn't be honored. I could never agree to it, even though the peer pressure made me feel really bad.

For Al and me, speed and safety were synonymous. None of the climbers who had climbed K2 quickly had had any problems. But the slower individuals were always getting caught in storms, and that's when the accidents were taking place.

The day after that discussion I walked across to The Strip with Rouse. I was feeling crummy about the situation.

I began: "You know, Al, if anybody got into trouble really high, of course my brother and I would help them. You know we would. It's just I don't want to go advertising it so that people will get out of their depths by pushing too hard. If you're up there on the final day and Al and I are there, too, then you could join us." I felt like I needed to heal some of the damage that had occurred in the past few days.

"I know, Aid," said Rouse. "It always ends up the same old friends together."

The next day we spread out our gear on the rocks around base camp: a bright-colored melange of red Gore-Tex, blue nylon and yellow fleece.

"How many days' food, kid?" asked Al. "I think four up and one down. How about you?"

"Let's take two substantial ones and three soup-type ones," I replied. "We'll need loads of liquids up high, and I ain't gonna want chicken curry at 26,000 feet."

We packed it all into our lightweight 'sacs and then threw in a couple of extra gas cylinders for good measure.

J.B. came over with a question: "How many days' food are you lads taking?"

He took a look at our small pile. There was something painfully sad about our regrouping after all we'd been through. Phil and J.B. were packing and had their gear strewn about, too. It was like swapping girlfriends with your best friend. It made me feel hollow inside.

The days slid by as the weather taunted us with bright periods chased away by snow flurries. Finally on the 15th of July, we decided to leave, even though the wind still came from the south. We had learned that all really stable weather developed when the wind blew from the north: the China Wind. Even so, it was possible for the wind to swing around quite quickly, and if the weather improved we would be in a better position to make the summit safely and return, still in good weather.

Although we didn't have permission to climb on the Abruzzi, we didn't think anyone would really mind; socially, at least, they were our friends. Rouse foresaw one major opposition party.

"Julie Tullis will go ape-shit if she thinks we'll try the Abruzzi. Kurt (Diemberger) doesn't care, though."

Julie was an English climber, climbing with one of the most famous Austrian climbers of past years, and I felt that Rouse was in private competition with her for the first British ascent. She was nowhere near the climber that Rouse was; she didn't have even half the experience. But we all knew stranger things had happened in mountaineering before. She was very driven to climb K2, and if our group changed routes, a shadow would be drawn across her life. They had been filming the Italian ascent—ostensibly at least—and had opted to remain on the mountain when their group left.

"Let's sneak past their base camp without them knowing," said Al, visualizing a military manoeuvre among the tottering ice towers of the glacier. I think it appealed to his sense of anarchy.

"It wouldn't hurt to avoid their liaison officers," I agreed.

In the late morning, we stumbled over untracked moraine and wove around glacial pools, one eye always on the "enemy." J.B. taught us words like *dead-ground*, and I almost caught myself looking for land-mines. It was fun. But if we'd avoided those antics, we'd have saved two hours of toe-banging hiking.

Three hours later we crossed a small icefall to reach the base of the spur. A group of Koreans greeted us from their tents. We tried out a white lie; we said were checking out the descent for a probable traverse

*Alan on the Abruzzi Ridge*

of the peak. They smiled uncaring, all Eastern politeness and hospitality. The route up to Korean Camp 1 lay to the right of the spur, up snow slopes and the crest of subsidiary ridges.

For Al and me, it was great to move at our own pace—no one else to consider: just the two of us. A lot of the time we chatted while keeping close together on the fixed ropes. Time passed so quickly that we arrived at Camp 1 almost suddenly. There were a lot of tents taking up every available site. We scratched around in the snow, making a lot of noise, until a Korean face poked out of a tiny red tent and bid us sleep in the empty one next to him. He probably thought we'd keep him awake all night with our excavating.

As darkness chased us into our sleeping bags, the other lads arrived and began stomping around with head-torch beams crisscrossing the starry night. I could still hear them cooking as I went to sleep.

To make the best use of the good weather, Al and I left that camp in the grey light of dawn. We hoped to reach the Camp 3 above the Black Pyramid at a height of 24,600 feet and maybe even go to Camp 4 at 26,000 feet. It depended on the condition of the route: how much snow and how difficult it was.

We climbed quickly up frozen snow and crossed a succession of rocky outcrops, always moving together and chatting.

"This route is so well fixed with rope that I'm not surprised Benoit (Chamoux) climbed it in a day," said Al. "Because it's steep, we can gain a lot of height quickly. Look, here's the Austrians' Camp 2 already."

We'd been going for two hours and had arrived at a couple of good ledges poised below House's Chimney, a dark gash slicing a red-colored buttress. Fifteen minutes later we both stood atop the famous feature and could see three Austrians who'd left their camp that morning.

"Let's catch them up for a laugh," I suggested to Al. "They have to be moving like old men to only be there."

After three hundred feet, there were more tents and a Hunza high-altitude porter—working for the Koreans—poked his unshaved face from one of them and asked: "You want some tea?"

"No, thank you," said Al, grinning. "We just had some for breakfast, not long ago."

He turned to me and said: "I know why there are so many dubious climbers on this route. They feel safe because of the numbers and the fixed rope. The good ones have done it and left, but the hangers-on are all still trying."

It wasn't long before we moved in behind the puffing Austrians as they climbed up a rocky bluff with the help of a fixed caving-ladder. At the top, they stopped, stepped to one side and kindly waved us past. We were free to set our own pace once more.

The technical crux of the Abruzzi Spur is a 600-foot-high buttress seamed by icy cracks: the Black Pyramid. With the help of ample fixed line, we soon stood on top of this bastion. A cold wind skimmed across the crest while we donned our red one-piece down suits.

"Have you seen the sky?" asked Al. "I think the weather is changing." He faced south toward a dark cloud that had sprung from nowhere while we had been happily chatting. While he spoke, light snow flurries added weight to his observations.

"Shit!" I snapped. "All that work for nothing! We might as well go down now 'cause tomorrow everybody and his dog'll be descending, and they'll be kicking loose shit down every which way."

We still had time to get to base camp if we didn't dither around, tormented by our decision. I clipped a karabiner and sling onto the rope for safety and began the 7,000 feet of descent.

First we passed the Austrians, who looked bewildered. Why were we descending?

"It's pretty obvious even to a blind man," growled Al under his breath.

Next we came upon Rouse and Wilks.

"The weather's fucked, lads," I called as we passed.

"Shouldn't we wait a bit and see?" asked Rouse hesitantly.

"I prefer to go down while it's not too bad, rather than tomorrow in a full-blown storm," I answered.

Down we went. J.B. and Phil were resting at the platforms below House's Chimney. We told them our plans and left. When we passed the Italian base camp, Cassarotto's wife waved cheerily. He, too, was probably descending from his solo attempt on the South Pillar, and she was all smiles at the prospect of his arrival. They were a kindly pair: he a tall, bronzed hero and she a beautiful bride.

Al and I both felt tired from our two-day excursion. We skirted a few open crevasses and arrived at our base camp by 5 p.m. Although it had been an unfruitful attempt, it had given us a great deal of pleasure. To be able again to move freely together, unfettered by worries of any kind, had drawn us back into the team we had been many times before.

Around midnight, I became aware of a commotion outside the tents. A Polish climber was shouting our names. What the hell was going on? Then I heard the reason, and my heart missed a beat: "Cassarotto is in a crevasse! He fell in last night at five o'clock!"

Everyone was being recruited to help carry him down to where a helicopter could rescue him. The rest of the night was spent slogging up a slippery scree slope and winding our way through a small ice-fall. It turned out that Cassarotto had misjudged a jump across a crevasse he'd crossed many times before, and he'd fallen a hundred feet. From the dark bowels of the hole, he'd radioed his wife and told her he was dying.

Dawn arrived as we reached the scene of the accident. Other climbers were already there. Cassarotto's lifeless body lay on a sleeping mat. The sweat on my back chilled. I shivered and cursed. What a waste! A cruel end to one of Italy's most prominent mountaineers!

It also had a devastating effect upon our group. Our close proximity to death had made it all the more real. We'd been on the mountain for nine weeks, and many were thinking about going home.

Brother Al had arranged to meet Katrine, his German girlfriend, in northern India. He left with Phil on the 20th of July. Since I'd planned to meet Lorna in England on the 7th of August to hike part of the Pennine Way, I knew I'd have to leave by the end of July.

One drizzly afternoon, when heavy, moisture-laden clouds obscured most of the surrounding mountains, Rouse suggested: "Aid, do you want to visit the Poles? Maybe they'll have a few drams of vodka."

We wandered down "The Strip," past the Diemberger/Tullis camp, past the Koreans and met Janusz Majer

"Hello," he said. "Would you like to drink some coffee?"

We went inside. I'd always got on well with Polish climbers, ever since my 1976 visit to Poland, and we spoke of old friends and past climbs. The afternoon passed, and we were invited to dinner. During this time, Rouse was introduced to a girl of slight build but of great determination: Mrufka. She asked Rouse about his plans to climb K2 and what I was going to do. I said that I was to meet my wife in England. Later she convinced Rouse to climb with her on the Abruzzi.

A few days later, I spoke with Rouse as I was leaving. All the expedition's baggage had been sent out with porters, but he was going to stay on and try again.

"I don't know how long I'll wait but I might even catch you up in Skardu," he told me. "If not, I'll see you in England." I never saw him again.

The torrential rainstorms which hit us as we reached Skardu translated into a ferocious snowstorm high on K2. Rouse reached the summit of K2 before, but on the same day as, Julie Tullis. They were less than thirty feet apart when they died, trapped in the storm at 26,000 feet.

The stories of that tragedy seeped back to Britain. Brian Hall phoned me at my parents' home.

He was blunt: "Al's dead. Curran just called from Islamabad. Al climbed K2 but couldn't get down in the storm."

After the initial shock wore off, I found myself sittting over a pint of ale, gazing out a pub window while a Derbyshire gale slanted curtains of rain across the moors. We had been a society onto ourselves, a microcosm of life as a whole. Somehow we'd have to learn to readjust and come to terms with our own lives, lives without our friends.

I could almost see how it happened. I'd been in storms: tired, listless, the body slowly dying.

On the 10th of August, five exhausted climbers put on their icy boots, pulled on their down-filled jackets and staggered out into the howling gale. How many days had they been trapped there? They'd forgotten exactly. Four days. Or was it seven?

At 26,000 feet, oxygen-starved brains had become confused. Each person had withdrawn into himself, trying to conserve the last ounces of energy and heat. They were wild animals acting out of self-preservation. Their mouths were cracked raw from attempting to eat snow. A snowball stuffed hopefully in the mouth simply remained a snow ball. The vital heat was almost gone. Speech was impossible. How useless were even eloquent words, as they then could only be thought. And even that process was quickly slipping away.

Julie had died days before. She was the first. Her nylon-encased body was already half buried by the blizzard. Rouse didn't want to move from his sleeping bag. I could almost see his stubbly chin sticking out from his balaclava, as he rambled on about melting some snow in a plastic bottle. Just another few drops and he'd be ready to descend. The bottle was wedged between his thighs, but the heat was now only in his inner-core. Nothing melted. He wasn't even able to rise to a sitting position.

Diemberger glanced over at him, trying to think. Should they take him? But how? He and his bottle must stay together. His sunken eyes stared at the flapping green fabric. Someone zipped the door shut.The snow rose to their waists. Tortured sinews tugged at sunken boots. It was impossible to move. The snow rushed up to smash into a ragged beard. A tongue licked hopefully at the frozen crystals. There was blood on the snow. Five minutes passed before the body wriggled again. Another try, another collapse.

The Austrians, Alfred and Hannes, lay side by side. Then, unexpectedly, the heat began to rise and, with their eyes closed, a strange comfort seeped into them. At that same moment, the life forces seeped out.

Mrufka, Willi and Kurt barely noticed their passing. Their clocks, too, had begun to slow down. Down they struggled, through the wind-blown powder snow, eyes strained through iced-up glasses. Which way to go, left or right? Then a rope stretched down, out of the mist. They knew this lifeline would take them 9,000 feet lower to their friends—friends who had given up on ever seeing them again.

Only a tiny core of energy controlled each of them. Sometimes they imagined they had clipped onto a rope only to turn and discover the opposite. The various levels of reality had begun to separate. The composite called "self" was coming apart. Sometimes as they descended, they had the feeling that it was happened to someone else, that they were looking down on their own bodies from some safer place. They had become observers.

Mrufka was the most tired, but she dearly wished to escape the maelstrom. She pressed on down, using her only friction device, a small metal plate with two holes in it. The rope passed through it to create a brake that controlled her downward slide. The ropes were so frozen, like steel hawsers, that they constantly stuck. Sometimes she couldn't move at all until she jerked at the rope. Her body began to shake as she sobbed in frustration. It was all happening to someone else. The rope was really jammed. Locked solid, it prevented any further descent. She slowly sank into her harness and a comfortable warmth flooded her body. She never moved again.

Willi staggered half-dead into base camp. Unable to speak, he pointed to the mountain to indicate that Kurt was still up there and needed help. Fortunately, a rescue party managed to get to him in time to save his life.

Only two out of seven survived.

# CHAPTER
## 23

## THE JOURNEY

BY ALAN

It was one of those long summer days in the green pastures of Khumbu Himal, the air thick with monsoon mist and drizzle. In the early morning, the summits of Everest and Cho Oyu dominated the skyline, briefly visible while tattered remnants of cloud clung momentarily to the higher ramparts. In the afternoon, dense monsoon cloud enveloped the few scattered huts, moisture dripping from the cold stone walls and slabbed eaves. The glistening morning dew and dancing patches of red, blue and yellow flowers faded with the freshening breeze and deepening shadows. Fresh mugs of breakfast curd were replaced by afternoon butter-tea and steaming *chang*.

My trekking companions, Tal and Heather, were new to the

Himalaya, but each sensed the magic in the air. Time stilled and flowed backward, and the glasses were refilled.

An old yak herder told us of times before expeditions and trekking, when only the seasons changed and life itself stood still. Then the foreigners came, bringing strange foods, clothes and customs, and they employed the young men to help them climb the snowy peaks. Many of the young Sherpas followed these Western ways, and some went to live in the lowlands, to Kathmandu where the gods of the Indian Hindus lived.

A yak-dung fire smoked and burned slowly at our feet as the old man continued with his memories. He told about when he was young: when the men of his village traveled to the plains of India to buy sugar, cotton fabric and spices; when they carried hundred-pound loads north over the passes to Tibet to trade for sheep meat, wool and rock-salt.

An amiable mood filled the hut, smoke swirled and shadows danced. A sprig of juniper was tossed onto the embers and flared briefly. Shadows sharpened with the flame.

Heather and Tal listened intently, captivated by the old man's simple but direct expression. They were typical of a young generation of world travelers, visiting many regions in Asia in the hope of discovering the truth about themselves and the world around them.

Tal was a physicist from Israel. He believed that change was inevitable and necessary, even if there were pain and hardship along the way. He supported the introduction of Western technologies and felt that adaption to change was the only solution. Heather was a teacher from Canada and was not so sure that things were so simple. She felt there was a certain charm and value in the old ways, in which the rigors of farming and direct contact with nature taught humility and enriched the soul.

As the level of *chang* in the kettle fell, the volume of the differing philosophies rose. Both Heather and Tal were convinced that their opinions held the answers; both were certain that their own reality was the true one. The more they argued, the more fixed became their differing beliefs.

As the old man rocked forward to hear more clearly, I explained the subject of the discussion as best I could. His eyes twinkled with amusement, and he spoke to his wife, asking for more *chang*. His smile widened. He asked if we believed the truth was only what we saw, tasted, touched or heard.

When his question went unanswered, he sat back on his crossed legs, back straight with his chin resting on his chest, deep in thought. He slowly raised his head and began:

"When I was younger, a Sherpa called Nima told me of a trading trip to Tibet. As now, it was the time of the monsoon, a time when Nima and his younger brothers, Pasang and Pema, made their way from Khumbu to Tibet over the long and difficult Nampa La pass. They took with them six of their strongest yaks, loaded with Indian goods. They took seven days from Khumjung, following a glaciated valley, and passed Thame under the shadow of towering peaks and shining summits. They crossed the wide snowfield of the pass and came into the arid land of southern Tibet and the village of Tingri.

"They had completed the bulk of the trade and would be returning with salt, wool and sheep fat. Nima still had one trade to make, but it would have to wait until the village mayor left for his midday meal. Nima had a Swiss watch, a gift from an expedition he had worked on. It had been a forbidden item of trade ever since China conquered Tibet. He hoped to trade it for a carpet or a piece of jewelry that he could sell to tourists in Namche Bazaar.

"He decided to start his brothers and yaks on the homeward journey, while he concluded his watch trade. He was certain he could overtake them before nightfall.

"As the faint light of day grew in the eastern sky, he watched his brothers and animals disappear up the rising trail, creeping south towards the pass. The morning star flickered silver, and a golden glow grew behind the distant peaks. A tinkle of distant yak bells and the low snort of penned yaks and their young filtered through the sharp morning air. Nima turned and ducked into a dark doorway to eat *tsampa* flour mixed with Tibetan butter-tea and to discuss the day's business.

"Time meant nothing to these Tibetans: life passing with the seasons; raising yaks; tending barley fields. Even Nima, who was also a farmer, regarded them as a people from the past.   These days the major part of his income came from mountaineering expeditions.

"The trade moved slowly. Only part of the conversation touched on business; most of it centered on recent news from Khumbu. He tried to speed up the process without upsetting polite custom and rose as if to leave. The men squatting on the floor knew that time was on their side, and they beckoned him back down again.

"Three hours later, Nima left the dark smoke-filled house, the deal completed. He carried a Buddha statuette, wrapped in a thin yellowed prayer scarf, safely inside his jacket.

"Nima hurriedly packed his backpack: a handful of barley flour tied up in a cloth, and a water bottle of local *chang*. Most of his warm clothing and his sleeping bag had gone with the yaks so that he wouldn't be burdened with a load. Although it was later than expected, he believed he could overtake his brothers before they reached the pass.

"He started up the dirt trail past low-built stone houses, with smoke seeping out through the flat dirt roofs. Small children ran around him, touching their tongues with a finger, demanding candies. He felt a stranger to this backward culture, even though his own roots lay in the plains of eastern Tibet.

"As he plodded slowly toward the sunlight in the south, he contemplated the changes that had come to Khumbu in recent years. Many of the old rituals were no longer practiced, many barely remembered. People no longer employed the services of the spirit doctor but went to the Western doctors and new hospital in Khunde. He had heard many old stories of special powers of *lamas*, but his village didn't take them seriously anymore. Life had gone forward in Khumbu these days. A strong breeze blew clouds of dust from the field terraces, and the dark shapes of Tingri melted behind.

"Two hours of steady uphill trail took Nima to the edge of a glacial moraine, a ridge of rocks and boulders leading to the ice of the glacier. A biting wind had sprung up from the southwest, blasting cloud and snow through the pass overhead. A veil of white powder dusted the dirt at his feet and clung to the rocks and clumps of coarse grass. The swirling snow quickly swallowed the shallow trail he left, and his eyes automatically scanned ahead, searching for marker stones.

"He approached the open snowfield leading to the pass. He briefly lost his way. The snow swept across his face, icing his sunglasses and blurring his vision. He was confident of finding the fresh yak trail once he reached the open slopes. He felt hungry and considered stopping to cook the *tsampa* flour, but then he remembered giving the cook pot to his brothers. He tried eating the flour dry, as Tibetans did, but it stuck dryly in his throat. A few swallows of *chang* helped, but made his head spin on a empty stomach.

"He gained the permanent snow, searching in vain for hoof prints. The wind-blown powder had obliterated any trace of earlier passage, and cloud whirled, shadows danced and spun. Gusts of ice crystals stung his cheeks, and grasping at the void for support, he sank hip-deep, falling face down into the ice. A current of fear zapped through his stomach and back. To break a leg or twist an ankle would mean freezing slowly, alone and without help. He struggled to his feet, lonely and frightened and mindful that one mistake, a wrong direction or a misplaced foot, could result in his becoming colder and weaker until his eyes would freeze over, and the life force would be squeezed from him.

"He felt the Buddha statuette press against his chest, its weight sagging heavily inside his jacket. He forced his frozen hands under his arms for warmth, where they touched the shiny bronze figure. The prayer scarf was silken to his chilled fingers. Numbly grasping the Buddha, he took it from his pocket and held it sheltered in his palm. It was four inches of exquisite artistry. Golden light gleamed from its folds, the casting of Guru Rimpoche both beautiful and fearful, generating immediate reverence.

"Without thinking, he took half a step forward. His leg sunk to the knee and he stumbled. The icon shot from his grasp, rolled down the slope and disappeared under the powder. Frantically shoveling with frigid hands, he scraped and dug relentlessly until his arms were deadened. He had no success. He stared at his useless hands and released a deep, heart-rending moan. It was gone.

"He struggled into the rising blizzard, oblivious of anything except the need to reach the pass. He could barely tell which was uphill or down. The slope was not steep, but the snow swirling around his legs confused him.

"A strong diffused light filtered through the maelstrom. The blinding light, shadow, wind and powder howled and circled him, like some malevolent white beast.

"He glanced to his side. One shadow appeared different. It was darker and had more shape, like a figure or the shape of some animal. Was he losing his mind or were his eyes playing tricks? He wiped his sleeve across his glasses, but the more he stared, the more his strained eyes recognized the shadow of a large cat. Spinning around, he saw nothing. It had vanished.

"He shook his head and peered again. There it was again, a shadow off to one side, moving towards the right. He resumed his walk and saw the shadow move away, halting when he stopped, almost beckoning him to follow. He was too numbed and exhausted to feel fear, and he cautiously followed the spectre. He took a few steps forwards, but it moved slowly away. He felt a flicker of hope and comprehension: if this really was a snow leopard returning to the valleys of the Khumbu, it could lead him to the pass.

"In a dreamlike state, he strove to follow the vision. His mind wandered, drifting over the events of the past few days, from the stay in Tingri to the hardship of the journey. He wondered about the small Buddha. He recalled a story about a statue that had been removed from a monastery; it had grown heavier the farther away it was taken. What had happened to *his* statue?

"Wearily he stalked the shadow, stumbling in its wake. Sometimes it stopped, allowing his labored breathing and pounding heart to quiet. The wind rushed by, becoming more powerful with each minute. The shadow stood boldly before him.

"He looked beyond his guide and saw other shadows, some still, some flapping wildly. Staggering forward with the wind buffeting him, he recognized the stone marker, encased in ice crystals and surrounded by wind-blasted and colorful prayer flags. This was the pass. The vista before him swept cloudless to the valleys of Nepal.

"A heaviness washed over him as he turned towards his companion. But the only shadow was the hunched shape of a Sherpa leaning into the wind."

As the old man finished his story, his eyes glowed with the life and fire of younger days. I wondered if he himself had been the Sherpa in the tale. He took a final swig of *chang* and leaned heavily against the hut wall, his chin resting on his chest. His breath became deep and even in sleep. His wife pulled a tattered sheepskin around him and spread the embers out to die.

A thick, heavy silence hung over us. Finally, with alcohol clawing at my reasoning and speech, I voiced the bewildering prospect of experiencing that reality.

Tal's face had a puzzled expression, a look of mild skepticism or disbelief. He asked if we thought the story was true. Heather was sure it was. She'd read somewhere that native American medicine men could transform their physical bodies at will. Had we read the books of Carlos Casteneda?

The fire died, and darkness and cold drew close. Shadows stilled and deepened. Drifting in a realm of alcohol-induced fantasy but self-conscious and speaking almost to myself, I told of an experience in the winter snows and forests of Canada.

I had started a 30-mile ski trip at midday, without food or warm clothing. I ran continually in deep snow until nightfall, and because I was unsure of the way, I was afraid to stop lest I freeze. Uncertain of my strength to run all night without food, I came on fresh bear tracks. My fears mounted.

But I was committed to survive. I regulated and deepened my breathing. My mind wandered. I was stressed and nervous.

As an experiment, I altered my perceptions into those of an animal of the forest. I saw through the eyes of a wolf. That released my human fears, and I loped along in timeless balance with nature.

Since my bladder was full, I stood, moved to the door and ducked into the night. I thought how fallible our observations are, and I wondered how tourists must be regarded by these mountain people.

I live between cultures, sometimes in the West, often in the cities of Asia and many weeks high in the mountains. I know that one place is no more real than another: different and yet the same.

I remember once watching an old lady sitting in the firelight. With a slight movement of her head, the light changed and she appeared as a beautiful young woman!

I know how a slight shift in the way we look and perceive can completely transform the manner in which we live.

# CHAPTER
## *24*

## LHOTSE SHAR: A TIME OF QUESTIONING

BY ADRIAN

The end of 1987 was drawing near as I returned from an unsuccessful attempt to make a crossing of the three Lhotse peaks. Lhotse Main Peak is the fourth highest in the world at 27,923 feet (8,516 meters), and both the unclimbed Middle Peak and Lhotse Shar are over 27,000 feet.

Alan and I knew we had set ourselves an exceedingly difficult task. As I write this, Lhotse Middle Peak and Lhotse Shar still remain unclimbed. We would have been quite satisfied to have climbed any one of the peaks.

On board a Thai Airlines flight from Bangkok to Tokyo, I was agitated by all that had happened in the past few months. A kind of relentless energy was making me restless. I needed answers.

The summer had been a bad one. First, Roger Marshall died in his solo attempt on Everest. I remembered all the times Roger and I spent laughing together, either on the Annapurna IV winter trip or back in Boulder.

Just when I became accustomed to the idea of never seeing Roger again, there was another accident. Dave Cheesmond and Katherine Freer disappeared on Hummingbird Ridge of Mount Logan in the Yukon. Though I'd been out of touch with Dave since we'd climbed Fitzroy, I could still remember the many days holed up in ice-caves, swapping stories that ranged from local sheep hunting to the outrageousness of apartheid in his native South Africa. Katherine and I had worked for the same window-cleaning company; she exhibited exceptional strength, except once when she dropped a bundle of ladders and missed a shiny, black Porsche by inches.

Weeks ago as we prepared to depart for Lhotse, I said goodbye to Lorna. I swore I'd be careful. I meant it.

The walk into base camp, in late-monsoon weather, was the normal wet, steamy affair. We stayed in the same tea-houses where we'd stopped many times before, and many of the faces were the same, just a little more wrinkled. The "sisters of Changma," whom Alan had been going on about all day prior to our arrival at their rest-house, were as cheerful and flirtatious as ever, matching Alan's expectations. Of course, it all led to nothing more than an expensive beer bill the next morning.

Once more I found myself relearning to forget about the West, its values and its heady pace of life.

Alan told me about his past four months of living in London, as an instructor in a Croydon gymnasium: "It's a long time since I lived in a city as big as that, kid. Rather than go back home at night, I'd go out for a beer with a few friends and crash on one of the tanning salon beds."

We sloshed and squished our way along the muddy trails, all the while recounting our experiences of the past six months.

"Have you ever tried to make lentils in a microwave?" asked Al. "Well, they explode all over the bloody place! I tried it a couple of times while I was hanging out at the gym."

He grinned and continued: "You ought to see some of the women who come in there to work out. They'd say, 'Alan, can you hold my ankles while I do curls?' or 'Alan, dear, do you have a good exercise for my thighs?' Bloody right I did! But I had to behave myself."

We needed to realign our ideas after experiencing completely differing lifestyles for the past six months. Fortunately, we had such a central commonality and understanding of each other that it took no time at all for our ideas to merge easily.

Base camp was in a peaceful, pleasant position, with Lhotse Shar stretching up into the stratosphere. It was difficult to conceive it connected by anything other than the imagination, especially when the monsoon clouds floated lazily at 23,000 feet, giving the impression of a false ceiling. For two weeks the weather was typical of the monsoon. Rain and cloud set in shortly after noon, and we all retired to our tents to write letters or read.

These periods of quiet meditation allowed calmness to filter through me. Then I could reflect back to my days in Boulder and see the frantic speed of life I was normally pressured into following. Back in the States, millions of people were driving themselves crazy. I felt fortunate to be able to escape.

One of my expedition-reading books was *Magic and Mystery in Tibet*. It related the Tibetan travels of a famous French lady, Alexandra David-Neel. She spoke of psychic phenomena, of occultists directing and concentrating force-waves of energy to create visible occurrences. The book questioned the whole state of reality as we know it.

I thought of Roger, Dave and Katherine, of living and dying and of the relationship between the two. I wondered if we chose our own destiny. Or has it been long since predetermined? I thought we ought to be allowed to control our own destiny, but maybe that was a stupid human illusion. Climbing big mountains involves self-control— I hoped. I didn't have enough faith to hand that task to chance.

It was all pretty heady stuff. I decided to concentrate on the climbing. One day at a time.

A group of Catalans camped nearby gave me an excuse to go visiting when the typical afternoon mists closed around our tents. They were working on the South Spur of Lhotse Shar and fixing rope in horrible weather. Whenever we visited, they would show us the kind of hospitality that is common in their part of Spain. Their regional sweet-meats of fudge and nougat always came pouring out. Occasionally we'd get into complex political discussions, but these always ended with laughter and remarks against the ruling powers.

Our two companions, Dick Jackson and Joe Frank, were both from Colorado. Dick was one of the Americans we'd met while climbing on McKinley. He had only just recovered from a climbing accident in the Alps, where he'd broken his ankles and his girlfriend had been killed. For him, the expedition was part of putting his life back together; it reflected his deep commitment to climbing.

Joe worked as a geologist in Boulder. I'd spent the summer rock-climbing with him. He was an avid runner and training fanatic who had climbed with Dick on Himalchuli (near Manaslu). His wife, Kathy, was leading a trek to nearby Island Peak in support of the expedition.

Dick and Joe would climb as partners, as would Al and I.

On the 15th of September, the weather began to show real signs of clearing, and our thoughts rose to logistics and action. Even though the snow lay thick and deep on the slopes, we began the exacting task of fixing thin cord along two exposed snow ridges, in order to prepare the way to nearly 22,000 feet. After that point, we would be able to climb quickly toward the summit of Lhotse Shar by way of straightforward snow-slopes.

The 27th of September was an important day: three days after Alan's and my thirty-ninth birthday. We two and Dick were breaking a deep trail towards 23,000 feet. We avoided a few ice-cliffs by their easier right flanks, but still the snow was disconcertingly fragile. Tension built despite the exhausting tedium of plowing a track.

I had just handed the lead over to Al and was about to say: "Should I put an ice-screw in here? I think the snow is pretty iffy."

Instead, I only got to think the words.

WHOOMPH! The snow-slope cracked. I snapped my head up in time to see the fracture line shooting to the left for 150 feet. My three steps to the right made no difference at all, as a five-foot thick section of cold slab threw me backwards. For a blink of time, I hung suspended in a freezing foam of limitless energy.

"This is it! Over! Pity!" I thought.

Then there was a tug at my waist as the rope leading to Alan came tight. I stopped. Snow in my mouth. I coughed it out. My eyes cleared.

"Wow-w-w!" I managed to croak. I stared giddily below me at a hundred and fifty feet of polished, blue ice. The roar of rushing snow filled the air, as the entire snow-slope below us avalanched. Our time had not yet come!

*At 21,000 feet on the Southeast Face of Lhotse Shar*

"Shit, Aid!" said Al. "That was too close!" He dusted snow out of his hair and added: "Time to go down." The decision was made.

The avalanche swept the slope clean—tore it right down the line of our steps, as neatly as tearing off a postage stamp. We descended carefully to base camp to give the snow a chance to settle and improve, but it was also important to give for our minds a chance to adjust.

In the peace of base camp, with its grass and fragrant flowers, we were able to come to terms with our near-demise. We promised ourselves to exercise more caution when crossing large open snow-slopes.

Al expressed our thoughts quite well: "You don't often get a second chance with avalanches, but if we see that the snow hasn't settled, then we should be really careful. These slopes are *so* big. I think they're in a deposit area created by the wind."

"Yeah," I agreed. "Otherwise, we'll be feeding that bloody scavenger." I pointed up at a circling lammergeier, a large Tibetan buzzard known as a "burial bird." Wood for funeral pyres is scarce, so corpses are cut up and fed to them.

There were only two Catalans in base camp. The others were in two groups of four, heading towards the summit only a day apart. Toni, their doctor, came over looking serious.

"I am concerned for the first group," he said. "They are not making radio calls. They should be near the summit now. It's possible they are over the dome, and the radio is not powerful enough."

We promised to keep a lookout through our telescope, but clouds had been obscuring large areas of the mountain.

The following day brought clear blue skies, and we expected to see the victorious Catalans descending. Instead, Toni had been beyond base camp to where he could see the whole face. He brought tragic and alarming news,

"I have seen bodies at the foot of the wall," he said, as tears welled from his eyes.

We were dumfounded. Dead? How could they be? I remembered seeing them as they passed our camp: big smiles and handshakes. They were warm, happy people. Full of life with glowing spirits.

"The second group has found where a big slab has broken," said Toni, shaking his head as if to clear it. "Our group must have set it off. Please, can you help me go and cover them so the birds don't get to them?"

I thought of the lammergeier. They show up only when there's death.

In the frozen air next morning, Al, Toni and I climbed up the snow-cone of avalanche debris toward colored objects scattered about the snow. It was a dangerous place because of threatening ice-cliffs, but we had to go.

Al turned to me with lips set grimly: "Let's move quick, kid. Get the job done and get the hell out of there."

I nodded my agreement. My stomach felt empty and tight. I was scared of what we would find. They had fallen over a 6,000-foot cliff. Forty feet short of some bright red clothing, we both stopped, faced out and caught our breaths: preparing ourselves.

I said to Al, whose face was grey and strained: "They're not people any more. Remember that. Let's go, kid." We turned and began the business of shoveling snow.

Hearing about death and meeting it full on are different experiences. In the first case, one can become philosophical and examine the tragedy from a safe distance. For us there, at that moment, we had no escape. We were brought face to face with the crudeness of death, as a butcher sees his carcasses. It was horrible. I wanted to throw up. We continued to stack blocks of snow around them, leaving just the heads uncovered until Toni arrived with his camera.

"Insurance," he murmured. He sat down: a broken man. These were people with whom he'd shared his life and dreams. He stifled a sob, and I put my arm around his shoulder. Al gently took the camera and finished the film. We descended together.

A week later when we returned to the climb, the immediate feeling of distress was gone, or at least it had been covered by reasoning born of the determination to be safe. A thousand feet above our last camp, I was kicking steps up wind-packed, crusty powder. I felt sure the mountain was in a much safer condition, and I began wading across a gently rising slope. I was sinking in up to my knees. It was hard work.

"What's it like, kid?" Al shouted from the other end of the rope.

"Pretty deep," I called back. "I'll bring you here."

I began to pull in the rope. When he arrived, I said: "This slope seems to have more snow than before. I'm going to probe with my ski pole to see if I can figure out how deep it is."

I made an extra-deep footprint, and getting down on my knees, I pushed the pole into the base of it. It went in easily. Far too easily! When my arm was deep inside the hole, with the pole all the way in to the handle, there was still no resistance from a firmer under-layer.

"It's at least six feet thick, and I can't probe any deeper," I said, horrified. "If we have to traverse all the way across on where its steeper, I think it'll avalanche."

"What we going to do?" asked Al, glumly. "Is there another route we can take ?"

There wasn't. The route was barred by huge ice-cliffs. We couldn't see above them.

"It's the bloody wind that's caused this," I began. "Even though it hasn't really snowed in the past week, it's been really windy, and the wind has blown snow from other parts of the mountain and deposited it all here. I'll bet it's even worse in some of the leeward pockets by the séracs." There was nothing to do, except descend.

The sky showed the darkest blue, but our spirits were darker still. We didn't want to go down, but we didn't want to die, either. It was frustrating to know that it was only 4,000 feet of straightforward climbing to the summit.

Al came up with an idea: "The Catalans have left and gone home. They've already avalanched the most dangerous part of their route, so we could try to get permission from the Ministry to change onto it."

We descended with a new goal in view. Back in base camp we lost no time.

"Joe and I will run to Namche and radio the request for a change of route," said Al. He wore running shorts with a fleece jacket tied around his waist. The weather was perfect. How could we have known what was to follow?

A couple of days later, the sky clouded over and it began to snow very lightly. Between reading, sitting in our tarp-covered stone shelter and drinking tea, Dick and I passed the time comfortably. One afternoon we had visitors from a Royal Air Force group that was hoping to climb Island Peak.

"Hope you don't mind visitors?" a bright-eyed lad of about twenty-seven asked as some of his group walked into our base camp.

"Come on in an' 'ave some tea," I said. "It looks pretty nasty out there."

We sat for a couple of hours while our Sherpa cook, Kancha Nuru (Pema Dorje's younger brother), served tea and Nepali biscuits. The leaders of the group then arrived: an officer and his wife. After a while of listening and watching, the woman asked me: "How come you can still be so happy if you've been here for so long and after what has happened?"

"Oh, I like it here," I replied. "After so many expeditions, you get used to it."

Not long after, they left, with mutual expressions of good luck.

As the cloud sank lower toward our camp, the smell of snow became a harsh reality. Light flakes were followed by the serious stuff: fat, heavy flakes that stick to each other and fall like white autumn leaves. The thin, ragged layers of mist that had floated down from the ramparts of Ama Dablam were no longer visible. We were in for a big storm.

Inches of snow quickly built into feet. The tents required constant clearing because the strong winds continued to throw heavy flakes like wet mud against the nylon sides. At mealtimes, Dick and I waded over to the cook-shelter, escaping our Siberian prisons to chat with the two Sherpa cooks. The fiberglass tarps that made up the roof were beginning to tear with the heavy build-up of snow.

WHOOMPH! WHOOMPH! We beat the fabric to clear the snow. Spindrift filtered through gaps in the rustic stone wall and covered our dwindling food supplies in a thin layer of downy white.

It had been snowing for thirty hours when I went to my tent to hide from the cold and search for a level of comfort in the depths of my down sleeping bag. For some reason, I could not fall asleep. I lay in a mild state of anxiety, listening to the storm outside. Sleeping was normally not a problem for me.

At 9.30 p.m., I sat up and switched on a small flashlight to see how much snow lay on the tent. All was quiet, except the steady hum of the wind. Then it happened. There was a muffled hissing roar, and half of the tent caved in as though someone had sat on it. I put down the book I was reading, *Magic and Mystery in Tibet*.

"Stop fucking around, man!" I bawled out, thinking someone was romping in the snow. No answer.

"Dick! Di-i-i-ck! Hey, man! Di-i-i-ck!"

Still no answer. Only the skittering of snow blowing across the nylon surface.

Then it came to me. That wasn't anyone screwing around. That was an avalanche that had just hit the tent.

The small, yellow pool of light from my headlamp showed how lucky I'd been. A wall of snow had stopped only six inches from my left shoulder. What should I do ? Does lightning strike twice in the same place? Bloody right it does! Always! I began to cut a hole in the back of the tent and squeezed out into the maelstrom, dragging the sleeping bag with me.

I knew that Alan's tent lay on the other side of a huge granite boulder where strings of Buddhist prayer flags stretched out in "The Four Directions." With Alan off to Namche, his tent was empty. I decided to sleep there the rest of the night.

Large white flecks slanted down across my headlamp beam as I waded through the snowdrifts toward Alan's tent. I stopped, searching blindly, almost lost although I'd walked only a few yards. Then I saw them. Two short lengths of golden-colored tent-pole sticking out of a six-foot snow drift.

"Shit!" was all I could manage. Al's tent had been completely buried by a slide like the one that hit my tent. No one had heard a thing.

Shaken, I moved over to Joe's tent. and once inside I stared blankly at the brown walls. If Alan had been inside . . . . It was too much to think about.

Morning came with startling brightness. A blue sky arched over an altered landscape. Mountains, glacier, tents and boulders: all had had their outlines softened by the thick overlay. I began to search for Alan's tent to retrieve his personal gear. In my mind's eye, I could see him under the huge mound of snow. Could I get him out in time? Would he suffocate before I reached him? I began to dig furiously. Snow flew into the now-still air. I could hardly stop myself telling him not to try to move. I was there and he would be all right. It was taking far too long. I could feel his life ebbing away. "Just hold on," I whispered.

The Sherpas looked on with amazement. Had Aid gone crazy, or what?

I took a deep breath of cold air and returned to reality. Alan would have died, I thought. It was a strange and horrible feeling.

A day later Kancha and I left base camp in bright sunlight and very, very deep snow. At times it reached up to the crotch, and sometimes I'd disappear to the waist. We began trail-breaking down to Chukkung, the nearest village. Normally, it was a two-hour hike. I knew Alan would have realized the expedition was over and would send up yaks to evacuate base camp. Our trail would help them get there. Making it was a strenuous task.

After two and a half hours, we had made it almost to the Island Peak base camp. Kancha said it reminded him of climbing in the Western Cwm of Everest. Although we were considerably lower, the wild, snow-covered valley gave the impression of being much higher.

*Adrian and a Sherpa digging out Alan's tent after avalanche*

I knew that once we turned the corner around the flank of Island Peak, we would see the camp of the Royal Air Force team. I hoped
they had already broken a trail for us to use.

The first orange tent appeared in the distance. Tired after our
efforts, we struggled toward it. There was no one around. Then it suddenly hit me, some of the tents had been avalanched. There was torn
canvas, twisted poles, personal items scattered around.

"What is that, sir?" said Kancha, pointing towards a blue sleeping bag laid out in the snow. He looked uneasy. I walked over without a
thought and flicked the bag aside with my ski pole.

"Oh-h-h," I sighed, caught unawares. It was the woman who'd
asked me why I was so happy. She wore a nice new down jacket, and it
seemed as if she was sleeping, except she was too pale. A thought, a
feeling, crept up on me, and my scalp crawled. That could be Alan!

I paced the camp, checking out the damage. They'd obviously
been avalanched as we had. Some tents were partially dug out and others were fine. Kancha had an uncanny nose for death. He pointed at a
tent,

"There, sir," he said.

I wasn't to be caught off guard again. I approached carefully.
Beneath a shard of canvas, a single hand stuck out from the snow. It

looked as though someone had just removed a tray of drinks from it.

"Let's get the hell out of here, Kancha!"

We met Alan that same afternoon. His smiling face seemed even more precious as I explained the happenings of the last few days.

Since I needed to buy a return airline ticket, Al had some advice for me:

"Never buy a one-way ticket, youth!"

# CHAPTER
## 25

## DREAM OF TIBET

BY ALAN

The dream-like quality remained as I recalled the past two weeks: the vision of mountains and snowstorms, the smell of yak-dung fires, the fragrance of burning juniper. All lingered in my consciousness.

Or was it all a dream? A fantasy conjured to nurture a part of me that felt starved? Was it an adventure of the mind taking me away from my usual large, complex expeditions? Did my subconscious whisk me away north of the Himalayas, to the mystical land of Tibet? Or did it really happen: did I really look down on the arid Tibetan Plateau?

Stretching my tired muscles, I lounged under a heavy yak-hair blanket, suspended between sleep and wakefulness. I closed my eyes and put my mind on the path that led to the dream . . . .

We journeyed over the mountains to climb a peak that pierces the clouds above 26,000 feet. I traveled with a Sherpa friend, his wife and his pretty young niece. The journey was much more than just a climb; it was also a sensual jaunt with a doe-eyed Sherpani girl.

To be on the move with these people, camping where darkness found us, cooking noodles and tea over yak-dung fires: all were as essential to my dream-journey as the technical ice-ascent of the peak. A journey needs a destination as a mountain needs a summit, but the sum of the experience is what holds a lasting value.

We packed two large canvas duffel bags with noodles, chili, garlic, tea, sugar, dried milk, dried yak-meat and packaged glucose biscuits. Our camping kit also included a two-man tent, two sleeping bags, two mattresses, a kerosene stove, fuel and cookpots. My Sherpa friend, Dawa, and I had boots, crampons, ice-axes, rope and down-jackets. The girls had Chinese-made tennis shoes and the traditional long woolen Sherpani dresses.

It took us less than an hour to pack. Then we sent the girls ahead. They were giggling and joking with nervous anticipation. Sherpani girls are rarely questioned, but still they had their alibi prepared. If asked, they were taking a gift of food to the monastery beyond the Nepali checkpoint that controls the route.

Meanwhile Dawa and I sat outside a friend's house in a lower village, eating boiled potatoes dipped in chili and drinking clear *arak* liqueur. We were waiting for the cover of night before heading out fast and light to rendezvous with our girls.

After we passed the checkpoint, we followed a sandy trail that glistened in the moonlight, carefully stepping on protruding rocks to avoid leaving signs of large Western boots. At some point, the trail divided, and we missed our rendezvous with the girls.

Dawa said it was time to sleep. He led the way to a deserted yak-house, whose padlock proved no match for his skill as a locksmith. Dung and pine chips gave us a fire to ward off the chill of a November frost. The girls had the sleeping bags.

The next morning as we lay amid straw, dust and the soft light of a Himalayan dawn, the girls found us. We divided the loads more equally, and away we pranced up the forbidden trail like naughty school-children.

It took us four days to reach the glacier that led to the pass over the Tibetan border. They were four days of perfect bliss. We padded along an ascending trail, with juniper hillsides stretching to the snowline, and beyond rose jagged peaks of rock and ice.

I had never met Pema before, but I marveled at her balance as she carried a sixty-pound duffel bag on a headband and propelled herself with the perfect legs of a nineteen-year-old. She had a quick, intelligent smile, and her eyes twinkled knowingly as she recognized my admiring glances.

We spoke little. Dawa spoke English but the girls did not. My knowledge of Sherpa and Nepali was limited to basic needs. Besides, there was nothing to say that the sun and the mountains did not express better.

The nights were cold. Frost shimmered on the scrub juniper. The sky was a coverlet of dancing gems, and moon shadows were cast by mountain walls. Inside our tent, we huddled under quilted down, shyly at first and then with more intimacy. We slept without care for the future, at one with the rhythms around us.

One morning as we climbed a steep glacial moraine, we heard the distant tinkle of yak-bells. Peeping warily from behind boulders, we saw a yak-train approaching from Tibet. Initially it was difficult to tell if the yaks were Tibetan or Sherpa animals, but soon we recognized the plaited hair and sheepskin clothing of Tibetan yak-drivers.

Dawa said we should remain out of sight. He suggested, to the giggling amusement of the girls, that we lie down behind boulders well away from the trail. After the yaks passed, we breathed freely once more. This hiding routine was necessary twice more, but we felt confident that we had not been seen and our presence could not be reported at the down-valley checkpoint.

On the fourth day, we wound between pyramidal peaks on the pass to Tibet. The bright sun cast broken shadows over the ice, and wispy high clouds streamed from the southwest. It was a day for dreaming. One foot followed the other, and shoulders strained under loads in the thin air at 19,000 feet. It was the first time the girls had been this way; excitement brightened their faces, and rivulets of sweat flowed like tears of joy. A pair of eagles soared on updrafts. Higher still, the wind blew streamers from the craggy ridges.

Prayer flags on wands marked the top of the pass. They flapped in the wind, blowing prayers north toward distant rolling brown hills. Since we were exposed to view for miles around, we quickly followed the trail toward a line of sheltering moraines two miles away. A fortress of ice thrust to a summit surrounded by traces of cloud as fine as any prayer scarf. No mystical fair maiden summoned us from its turret, yet its allure drew us inexorably up into its realm. Our small tent held two maidens of our own, more dusky than fair with jet-black tresses and olive skin burned ochre at the cheek bones. More practical than mystical, Pema cooked *thukpa*, a thick Tibetan noodle soup laced with garlic and chilies.

Yangin, Dawa's wife, ducked out of the tent to fetch ice to melt for water, while Pema sat with her back to my chest and I wore an opened sleeping bag like a cloak around both of us. A small candle flickered when Yangin re-entered the tent, and she giggled as she brushed snow from her stocking feet. An easy atmosphere surrounded us. We sipped sweet milky tea, relaxing after a long day, well pleased with our progress.

The next day we went into the shadow of the great peak, along a loose glacial moraine covered with two feet of fresh snow. We followed a difficult, crevassed glacier to a sunny basin of dry warm rocks, where we set up our base camp. I lit our small stove, and Dawa searched among the warm rocks for running water. Pema squatted behind Yangin, humming a tune and deftly combing and braiding the older girl's hair. Life was good. Everything was in its place.

Dawa and I intended to take only two days to climb the 8,000 feet of snow and ice above us. We would camp once on the way up and once on the descent. But before we could begin, we had to build a small stone shelter to house the girls while we were gone. That afternoon we hauled rocks and placed them in a kind of igloo-shape, a construction often used by yak traders. Within a few hours, we built a small but secure stone house.

The plan was for the girls to keep one sleeping bag and sleeping pad, a cook pot and the kerosene stove. Dawa and I would take the other sleeping bag and pad and a small Epigas camping stove. We each had a complete suit of down-clothing, and we could use the open sleeping bag as a cloak to cover us while we crouched cooking or whiling away the nighttime hours. On a venture such as this, sleep was an unnecessary luxury. We would spend most of our non-climbing time making tea and soups to sustain our efforts.

Dawa and I were equally acclimatized and matched in strength, and there was none of the usual Sherpa-*sahib* relationship: the Sherpa doing all the work and the *sahib* taking all the credit. In fact, on our approach trek, Dawa had given me the heaviest load to carry; he considered me bigger and therefore stronger. In return, I got a little more food, commensurate with my size and weight. Once we were above 26,000 feet, I expected him to be a little stronger than I, but there was certainly no competition between us, as is often the case with Western climbers. It was truly a joint effort to climb as fast and high as possible, and maybe we would reach the summit if everything worked for us: weather, snow conditions and our continuing strength.

The next morning we packed food, gas cylinders, rope and a few snow-anchors. Then we started up a precipitous path behind our camp. We intended to climb as high as possible, stash our loads around 22,000 feet and return to base. The next day we would take the tent and sleeping bag and return to our high point, spend the afternoon resting and eating and leave at midnight for the final climb to the summit.

We quickly reached a long snow-slope leading to a small pass on a ridge at almost 21,000 feet. The snow was in excellent condition, firm but not too icy, and our boots did not break its surface.

As we continued up the ridge, I could see Yangin and Pema watching our progress from far below. Sherpani rarely climb and are expected to stay home working in the fields and tending the children and animals. When I asked Yangin if she would like to work as a climbing Sherpa on an Everest expedition, she just laughed. She did not take my question seriously but regarded expeditions as a man's job. In truth, Sherpanis may not be as strong as male Sherpas, but they are much stronger than most Western climbers—female or male.

The snow-ridge stretched up to vertical ice-cliffs more than 100 feet high. They were a formidable barrier. It looked possible to climb left to reach easier ground and a small plateau. We decided we had climbed high enough for one day, so we descended in leaps and bounds back to the girls, who had prepared noodles and tea.

That afternoon, while Dawa lay back in the hot sun and slept, I stretched out on a large boulder and contemplated life. I thought about my climbing partner and knew I was lucky to have such a friend.

At daybreak we muttered hurried goodbyes and started back up the mountainside, deep in thought about the days ahead. Wisps of cloud streamed in from the west, heralding bad weather, but with a little luck, it would not develop until we were out of danger. Returning to our previous high point, I changed into my eiderdown suit covered with Gore-Tex in preparation for the colder conditions higher up. A wind had sprung up and was blasting powder-snow across the slopes, stinging our cheeks and obscuring our vision.

The ice-cliffs loomed out of the rising storm as ominous and invincible as the prow of an ancient galleon. We climbed the fragile ridge to the base of the wall and tied ourselves to ice-screws implanted in the sea-green ice. The storm was worsening, no longer part of some fantasy journey or figment of a yearning spirit, but cold, absolute and dangerous. I knew we must go down.

Under normal circumstances, we would have been prepared to wait out the storm and try for the summit after the bad weather had passed. But I had no desire to be trapped by fresh snow on the wrong side of the Tibetan border, especially with my Sherpa friends, who would be in serious trouble if caught.

There was no time for hesitation or regret. We had to pack our up base camp in the middle of the snowstorm and try to escape before the fresh snow deepened. The two girls wore tennis shoes, which were adequate on hard frozen snow, but now would mean very cold feet for them.

A break in the storm gave us the chance we needed to flee south. The prayer flags marking the pass were stilled by frost and blasted ice-crystals. They gleamed like priceless gems, beacons in that icy waste to lead us home to Khumbu.

When I awoke, my dream seemed far away, deep in the recesses of my mind. Outside the sun was shining and the sky was a rich autumn-blue. Had there truly been a storm over those passes to the north, or was all just a dream? Was the green ice-cliff nothing but a mirage? Was sleeping under an opened sleeping bag with Pema nothing but a fantasy? The tang of juniper smoke and pungent smoke of smoldering dung seemed so real. Was it all imagined?

At times, a dream is all we have and need. At others, hot-blooded action barely seems enough.

# CHAPTER
# 26

## STRIFE ON THE STRIP

BY ADRIAN

Alan was bubbling from bubbly: "Aid, you should have seen the people at the Gore-Tex party! All the champagne was free, and all the waitresses were wearing Gore-Tex bikinis!" He'd just returned from his first visit to the SIA ski show in Las Vegas, where we were searching for expedition sponsors.

"What gear did you get for the Lhotse trip?" I asked to bring him back to the reason for this trip.

"This one waitress," he continued, "had hair so long it hung down to her calves. Then we went to the JanSport party. Great food! Lots of dancing!"

"What about the show, Al?" I tried again.

"Oh! The Jag booth was something else! They had five girls, all modeling swimsuits!"

As it turned out, he *had* found some sponsorship support in the form of free tents, rope and sleeping bags. Dealing with potential sponsors was a new experience, but we had to perfect it if we were to continue to go on expeditions.

Every March thereafter, my old rusted Chevy truck rattled the seventeen hours from Boulder to Las Vegas (known to many of us as Lost Wages). By day we'd prowl the aisles of the show, checking out the latest designs in equipment or speaking with past sponsors. By night we'd check out the parties.

The one that began first every night after closing-time at the show was the Norwegian party. You didn't need a ticket. You just showed up at the hotel suite and dove into the throng, after making sure that each fist held a Norwegian beer. There were always plenty of climbers there. Most were trying to fill up on smoked salmon so they wouldn't need to buy a meal later on. By 8 p.m. that party would wind down, and it would be time to move on.

One time we'd had a full evening of partying, and it was around two in the morning. Al had met a young lady who needed a ride to her hotel, but first he had to drop me off at my hotel.

"I'll drive, Aid," he said, "because you've had too much to drink."

I handed him the keys. I had a bottle of beer in my hand and decided to finish it on the road. Al drove carefully down the Strip, where hotels were lit up by thousands of colored lights. The casinos flamed and shone like nothing I'd ever seen before.

To our right, a big old Pontiac "beater" drew alongside us, pulled back and lurched past again. A window slid down, and an angry guy appeared to be shouting abuse at me. I wound down my window to hear what he had to say. As I searched for a reply, he became pretty animated.

I held my beer bottle up for him to see and spat out in my best Yorkshire accent: "This American beer tastes like piss!"

Chuckling, I closed out the noise and focused on the road ahead. When we stopped at a red light, something warned me to check for the Pontiac.

It had stopped behind us, and both its occupants were racing towards us. I had only seconds to react. I would either get dragged from the truck, or I needed to attack and gain the advantage of surprise.

I leaped out onto the road and went for the guy in front. My hand sunk deep into his soft, fat stomach. It was as though everything had flipped over into slow-motion. I swung again with a clumsy round-house, missed him and the force swung me over onto my back.

"Oh, shit! Now I'm for it!" spun through my mind as I fended off kicks with both feet.

Al told me later that he saw me fall over and thought, "Oh-oh! Our kid's down!" He jumped out to help.

The first guy's face dissolved into blood as Al's fist beat a rapid tattoo on it. I could hardly believe this was really happening! Here were two cars stopped in the middle of a road  that was busy even at two in the morning, and Al was chasing down the road after the second guy, who received similar treatment when Al caught him.

"That didn't take too long," he said, laughing and wiping his bloody fist onto his T-shirt. As we continued down the road, I felt I'd missed out on all the fun.

A couple of lights later, the same Pontiac pulled in front of us at a light. Those guys were not very bright. The impish hand of impulse whisked me out and onto the car's roof. While carefully watching for the red light to change, I beat out a Scottish jig on their heads. Then two leaps and I dived into the truck.

"Have you gone crazy, or what?" Al said, laughing. "There's no way they're leaving that car again." I was enjoying myself.

Another red light, and I repeated the performance. It was interesting the way the roof flexed and dipped—like a springboard. We faced a whole series of red lights.

At the next one, I remained inside but excitedly shouted instructions to Al: "Ram them!"

"Are you sure?"

"Yeah. It won't hurt this truck. The bumper's huge."

THUD! Detroit steel slammed against Detroit steel. It was a satisfying sound. But I wanted more.

"Again! Do it again!"

THUD!

Al threw it into reverse for a third attack, but the driver of the car had had enough. Tires spun and rubber melted as he pulled out and ran the red light—smack into the side of a passing car! There was the tortured squeal of brakes and a shattering of glass.

"Fantastic!" Al roared.

"Nothing like this has ever happened to me before," our female passenger said.

"Oh, really?" I said. But I thought: "Just stick around!"

Al pulled cautiously around the wrecks, and we were on our way to my hotel.

# CHAPTER
## *27*

## EVEREST 1989: THE LAST THREE DAYS

BY ADRIAN

Our expedition had been on Everest for almost seven weeks and still no one had been able to reach the summit. It was billed as an American expedition, but it included climbers from Sweden, Belgium, Australia and New Zealand—and Al and me, landed immigrants in North America who still held British passports.

Al felt tired after staying so high for so long, and he had decided to descend to Pheriche at 14,000 feet, to build up his strength. I felt as though I no longer had a climbing partner, because I'd never considered serious climbing with anyone but Al. I suppose I felt abandoned because I had my eyes so fixed on the summit that I refused to go down for a rest. I knew that Al was not going to get much more rest by going down. After all, he had to walk uphill for a day to reach base

camp again and that was going to take something out of him. I suspected it had more to do with a brief exchange of harsh words when,
part way through the Icefall, he'd told me his decision to go down. It
was almost as if he'd said: "If you feel so bloody strong, then do it on
your own—if you can . . . ." That made me even more determined to
make it.

As always, the weather was playing games with us. First it was
good and then, just when we had maneuvered into a striking position, it
would turn foul and curtail the attempt. The spring season was almost
over, and I didn't want to go home until I knew definitely that the summit was unattainable. I owed it to myself to have one last try.

I found it difficult to sleep that night of the 21st of May, not
because the next day I was due to leave for a summit attempt, but because the Icefall was cracking and groaning so loudly that I was certain
it had begun to heave and surge. That meant séracs were going to topple
and crevasses snap closed.

As I lay awake, the ice beneath my back kept making popping
noises and sending unpleasant vibrations streaking up my spine. I had
been through that Icefall too many times already and felt that maybe
my luck could run out. My racing mind began to invent its own fantasy.
A collapsing ice-tower would squash me like a fly underfoot. Trun-
dling ice-blocks would sweep me away, leaving nothing for a rescue
team to find. I could easily disappear into a crevasse and no one would
know where I'd gone. I felt more and more vulnerable with every tremor
that shook the ground. Still, I needed to sleep to be able to perform at
my best. I rolled around, tossed and tried to curl into a better position.

When early morning finally arrived, my anxiety level was very
high. I found myself frantically searching for any excuse that would
allow me to remain in the warmth and security of my sleeping bag.
Lorna lay silently at my side, wide-awake. I felt she could sense my
tension but seemed unwilling to say anything for fear of intruding into
decisions that were mine, and mine alone, to make.

I knew I wanted to climb the mountain very much. It was not
going high on the mountain that scared me. It was the Icefall. The
creakings of the night took on a nightmare reality. Bad dreams are only
bad dreams, I told myself.

I slipped into my fleece climbing-bibs and struggled to don a jacket. It felt cold, and I could see out of the tent door that a heavy mist hung low over the glacier. I bent over Lorna and we kissed. She was warm and just she herself wordlessly provided every reason not to go.

Maybe I would have faltered, but before I could, she said: "Good luck, Aid."

We might never see each other again, but she hid her fears well. She would be following my progress via walkie-talkie, and the thought of this made me feel less distant.

Kelly and Johann came into the dining tent as I struggled to down a cup of tea.

"God, I slept bad," I said.

There was a long pause. Kelly nodded quietly and said that the glacier was heaving. I wondered what she was thinking. Was it just another time through that horrible pile of ice? Or did she share my fears but simply not voice them?

I couldn't eat a thing, just a sip of tea with a little sugar in it. I simply wanted to start and get it over with, whatever it was. I didn't sense the same urgency in the others. There was nothing more to do, and I left the dining tent by myself.

I felt very alone without Al to chat with. Why hadn't he shown last night from the village below base camp? His presence would have helped me. It almost seemed as if this was a journey I had to complete alone. Maybe, deep inside, I wanted the chance to prove I could climb just as well without my twin. Maybe I was trying to break out of the role as "a Burgess twin" and wanted to be just "Adrian Burgess." I suspect that psychologists would have had me all nicely packaged: "Long-time joined-ego breaks out and creates individual ego." I would have said: "Creates *scared* ego."

A light dusting of snow had fallen  the past evening, which meant there was no trail, not even a footprint, because it was only 5:30 a.m., and I was the first person to leave that day. A thick barrier of cloud sat heavily in the valley and hid the mountain from view. In fact, the mist began to make route-finding very difficult, and I became momentarily lost. I did not wish to get too close to the crumbling ice face beneath the Lho La, so I searched into past memories to recognize the more distinct features of certain ice formations and crevasses. All the marker-wands had fallen over, but I still needed to find the beginning of the fixed line which would then guide me through the early section of the Icefall.

A warm glow slowly began to spread out on the ceiling of cotton wool above me. I cursed not having a camera with me, for 24,000-foot Pumori began to glow a pinkish-red. This neighbor of Everest pierced the low-lying cloud and stood out proud and dramatic in the clear morning sky. It floated alone on a surface of rolling moisture. The chance for a picture was lost as the moment vanished.

It was hard work climbing the many steep steps before me, but it wasn't long before I arrived at a section we called The Popcorn—the beginning of the dangerous section. No light puffs of corn those ice blocks. They lay at odd tilted angles and were anywhere from the size of a large house to that of a small car. Sometimes I'd have to climb over them, often jumping from one to the next. Other times I'd have to squeeze between them. It was oppressive and scary to feel so small and so vulnerable to the will of the vast glacier. The ice had no compassion for me and would as soon crush me as not. Many of the aluminum ladders that spanned the largest crevasses had bent and buckled, twisted by the immense forces that moving ice creates.

I moved quickly through what I considered the most dangerous areas, but I knew my death could come from any number of directions. The raw, dry air stung the back of my throat as I greedily gasped for more. I simply could not go any faster.

I scrambled over the crest of a giant block and faced another passage of extreme danger, The Eggshell. It was here, in 1982, that Blair Griffiths, one of the Canadian team, had perished when an ice-cliff toppled over. At that time, I had been through the same place only thirty minutes earlier.

At the beginning of this year's expedition, The Eggshell was a 200-yard-wide valley of ice that looked fairly innocuous: a smooth, open snow-slope. Then day by day, the surface had slowly cracked into sections until it became unrecognizable as the same place. Thirty-foot rifts had slashed into the glacier; large blocks were sinking out of sight.

Two aluminum ladders took me down into the icy bowels of a large crevasse. The sheer sides of greenish ice began to tower above me as I descended. A slight shift of the glacier at that moment and it would all be over: crushed! I was so pumped with adrenaline that my limbs were shaking. When I finally arrived at the far side, I could barely stand. I doubled over in an agony of violent coughing and retching from my sprint in the cold air.

No direct route was possible through the upper Icefall. This forced a long upward traverse leftwards which took one beneath acutely overhanging blocks until there were still more creaking ice-cliffs hanging off the flanks of the West Shoulder. It was little consolation to know that the worst was over because up ahead was still bad enough. Had I been in the Alps, I'd have considered it too dangerous. The Sherpas said the route at this time was the worst it had been in seven years. A succession of running-the-gauntlet situations finally hit home. I'd taken enough risks for one expedition! I swore it was the last time through for me!

Two Sherpas, who were employed by a small group of Austrians, were packing up their members' tents as I arrived in Camp 1. One of them, sporting a bright-red North Face parka with a hint of a teal "Patagucci" fleece jacket showing beaneath it, looked up, grinned and caught me off guard when he said: "You are one of twins who are friends of Pema Dorje, aren't you? I was in Boulder last summer. What time you leave camp?"

My watch showed 7:30 a.m. "Two hours ago," I replied, feeling that it was a reasonably fast time.

"Yes" was all he said.

I didn't know if I'd passed the test or not. I wanted the Sherpas to feel that I was not just one more Western idiot who had no right to be on the mountain. They are very observant in sizing up a climber. I knew the Sherpa would tell his friends that he'd seen me—and the time, the size of my pack . . . .

In many ways, both Al and I tend to compare our own efforts with those of the Sherpas, who set a standard of performance. If we were to only compare ourselves with Westerners, it would be easy to get an inflated idea of our abilities because, generally speaking, the Sherpas are much stronger. They have a power on the mountains that we feel is worth our aspirations. When I make a summit attempt, I need to feel that I've earned it and it hasn't just been laid out on a plate for me. Otherwise, I'd only be deceiving myself. But the Sherpas would know the truth.

Next came an uphill walk to Camp 2 through the frozen air of the Western Cwm. The sun had crept up from behind Lhotse, and I hurried to get out of the shadow and into its warmth. I could just make out a number of small dots that were descending Sherpas, leaving Camp 2 with loads to carry down to base camp. As they passed me, they mistook me for Al, grinning all the while as though they could just as well have been returning from Namche Bazaar as from a 21,000-foot camp.

I arrived at the camp with enough time to search out a walkie-talkie and make a 9 a.m. radio-call and tell Lorna that I'd made it safely through the Icefall. Roddy was still in bed, and knowing he could easily sleep for twelve to fourteen hours a night, I didn't expect to see him for a couple of hours. Young Rambadur, "Ram" as he was known to us, came out of the kitchen tent with a cup of steaming tea and said: "You very early. Camp 3 going?"

"Oh, no," I replied. "Today here. *Boli* (tomorrow) South Col *jani* (going)."

He nodded, understanding my pidgin-Nepali. While I went to my tent to take off my plastic boots, he prepared some soup with noodles for me.

Soon after, Lhakpa Nuru and Sonam Dendu arrived. They were going with us on the summit day, and both conveyed an air of solid determination as they strode into the kitchen tent.

"Looks like good weather," said Lakpa.

"Yes," I agreed and added mischievously: "I hope no one will be bumping in base camp while we're up here. Otherwise, maybe snow coming." I was referring to the Sherpa belief that sex anywhere near the mountain can change the weather for the worse.

My two Sherpa friends were the two strongest of our group, and they liked to make that point clear to everyone. I, a mere *sahib*, would normally be indulged and waited for, not with impatience but with a look of pity and understanding. However, I also had made my own strengths apparent and had tried to appear relaxed and at ease. Often when Sherpas were climbing around me, I'd hum or whistle, even when I felt anything but at ease. I'd seen plenty of their games, and I knew that the strongest Sherpas tended to act as prima donnas in their own groups and set themselves far above their "clients" in their assessment of abilities.

I enjoyed playing the game with them. I knew they understood my position, but protocol did not allow too many concessions. Why else had they come to me and suggested that I be the one to try for the summit this time? They felt a need finally to get someone to the top and make the expedition a success in most people's eyes.

In many ways, it seemed a last-ditch effort to reach the summit. I hadn't had even one real attempt. Originally I'd wanted to go with a second summit team and try to climb without the use of additional oxygen. But when all previous attempts were thwarted, I had to reconsider the situation. If I wasn't prepared to use oxygen, then maybe I would be expected to give up my place to someone who would. Was I in a position to gamble with the outcome of the work of many other people—especially the Sherpas? They had worked hard, helping carry many of the vital pieces of equipment up to the high camps.

If I failed to reach the top only because I refused to use oxygen, then I would be letting everyone down. It was a difficult decision, but with the possibility of going to the summit, I sacrificed my previous ideals. Another factor was that I didn't want to repeat all the dangerous work in the Icefall for later attempts.

Around eleven o'clock, Roddy appeared and asked: "How was the Icefall?"

"Bloody bad as ever," I said. "I don't want to do it again."

He nodded in agreement. Everyone was becoming more nervous about it.

"Will you go up to Camp 3 today or go to the Col with me tomorrow?" I asked Roddy.

"I'll go up to Camp 3 this afternoon and see you at the col tomorrow," he replied.

He was never in a rush. I couldn't help reflecting on a past conversation with a close friend, Pema Dorje, who said Sherpas feel that if people are always rushing around, full of nervous anxiety to complete all their work, then they are probably subconsciously preparing to die. Certainly not a good omen! It occurred to me that maybe Roddy intended to live forever, as he was so laid back and unhurried. He finally did leave, though, and waving his hand, he shouted across the camp: "I'll have a brew ready for you in the morning."

I sat for a while and watched Roddy disappear over the crest of the hill. I thought it was strange to be attempting the summit with someone I barely knew. I had spent a couple of nights sharing a tent with him early in the expedition. We'd talked of the effects of global-warming and the expected rise in sea levels throughout the world. Heavy stuff, really. Roddy was a private person and seemed quite happy to be doing "his own thing" on the expedition. In a way, it suited me better, because

I wouldn't feel responsible for him, as I probably would if Al were with me.

Johann and Kelly arrived, and we all sat on large rocks in the warm afternoon sun while tea kept arriving from the kitchen. I sharpened my crampons in preparation for the blue-green ice of the Lhotse Face. High above, Roddy was still ambling his way up to Camp 3, and we could see him arrive as the shadows began to lengthen.

We had made a Camp 3 on the Lhotse Face because not everyone could go from 21,000 feet to over 26,000 feet in a day. However, for me—and also for Al—Camp 3 was a cold, depressing place and often windy. We had watched the Sherpas and noticed that the methods they used when they were high on the mountain differed from those of the Westerners. The Sherpas never used Camp 3 if they could help it, prefering to work longer days and live in Camp 2, where the food was better and recovery faster. I liked this method, but one did have to be strong enough to be able to employ it. Not everyone had that strength. The two Sherpas and I would leave early the next morning, climb past Camp 3 to the South Col and rest in the afternoon.

At 4:30 a.m., after a night of deep and soothing sleep, I went across to the huge North Face tent we called the "Superdome" to see if "Ram'" had tea brewing. There was no sign of movement anywhere, so I went over to his tent and roused him. He was quite apologetic. I crawled back into my sleeping bag for another half hour of warmth, until I heard a shout from Lhakpa.

By 6 a.m., the three of us were ready to leave. I checked to see if we had everything and then walked to the edge of the ice to clip on my crampons. Lhakpa went first, followed by me and then Sonam. I had crammed my one-piece Mountain Equipment down-suit into my pack so that I could change into it at Camp 3. We hoped to move quickly up to there. I would be able to keep warm enough in my Thermo-fleece and Gore-Tex shell jacket.

It was early and the sun stayed hidden behind Lhotse. The snow felt crunchy underfoot, and it was cold enough that I was glad to get the blood pumping heat to my fingers and toes. While I stayed on the safer line of the fixed ropes, Lhakpa cruised over to the left where the polished ice held more snow and was a little less tiring. He was a competitive bugger! Mind you, I was catching on to the idea, too. Sonam followed close behind me. I think he was unaware of the games Lhakpa and I were playing.

We took an hour and forty-five minutes to climb to Camp 3. I smiled at my two companions.

"Maybe summit today?" I joked, hoping they wouldn't take me up on it—you can never quite tell with these guys.

"Hey, Roddy Van Winkle!" I called from outside his tent. "How long ya gonna be?" I half-expected he'd still be in his bag.

"I'll follow you when I'm ready" was his yawning reply. He was in no rush and didn't feel the need to compete with anyone. I doubt he even knew the games I was playing with the Sherpas. I was soon ready to continue, after using the second tent to change into my down suit. Lhakpa signaled me not to wait for Roddy. He wanted to continue our unspoken competition—we were having fun.

"The bastard wants to burn me off!" I thought, amused.

Our threesome began to head out toward the Yellow Band, an obvious belt of frail limestone that runs across the Lhotse face at a height of around 24,500 feet. This year had been so dry that more than 200 feet of bare rock was exposed, and it made for strenuous climbing up a choice of maybe five different fixed-ropes all hanging down the same stretch of rock. These were mostly remnants from previous expeditions, but I knew that our own team had added its own set of new ones after I discovered the rotting state of the old ones.

My two Sherpa friends were taking a drink-rest on a comfortable ledge above the difficult section. I grabbed the opportunity to pass them and climb up onto the hard snow above. At this height, my breathing was strained, and it took concentration to keep it regular and deep.

We were three tiny people out on this huge face, and yet I no longer felt the loneliness of the previous day. The world of very-high-altitude climbing belongs only to those who are doing it. Lorna no longer existed in the same way; neither did Al. For the time being, all the bonds that held us to normal life had been severed. What a wild idea: to let the normal world die away and then return to it at a later time.

The route diagonalled up over hard, compacted snow to a ridge of shale-like rock where old tatters of tent fabric and ropes held many a tale of past epics. Even though we were now fully in the sun, it was not warm, and the air had developed a sharp bite.

By the time I reached the friable rock of the Geneva Spur, I was beginning to feel the altitude, yet at these times I always produce so much adrenaline that I never feel hungry.

I came upon two full oxygen bottles, and Lhakpa shouted up: "*Sahib*, please take one up with you. These are ours for second summit group."

They had been left there by one of our group who either had felt tired or had been caught in foul weather while heading for Camp 4. I thought we were being a bit presumptuous to speak of second summit teams when we had been here for more than six weeks and none of our team had climbed Everest yet. I didn't want to overtire myself unnecessarily, but I thought that because someone else had carried the gear that I was to use, I should do the same. Usually Sherpas never ask Westerners to carry anything, but wait to see if they will. I saw this as a kind of test. They had me figured out, knowing that I wished to be considered an equal.

Almost involuntarily, I began climbing again. The extra weight made me strive for more air, and I slowed to a snail's pace. Suddenly the Sherpas swept past me, leaving the other bottle. Before I could ask Lhakpa why, he answered me: "Two more bottles up higher. We'll take them."

They had sandbagged me, subtly pointing out that if I was as fast as they, I should expect no favor. I didn't feel all that strong anymore, but I was damned if I was going to let them see me struggling.

I crested the spur to see them sitting by the two other bottles. Lahkpa had lit a cigarette and was sharing it with Sonam. They appeared completely at home as they gazed out over the 5,000 feet of the Lhotse face. I smiled as I reflected that only Sherpas would consider smoking at 26,000 feet to be a normal pastime. Without stopping, I slowly went my own way along a narrow trail that contoured the uppermost section of the Geneva Spur. I thought it was probably the highest "footpath" in the world.

Climbing at that height causes the mind to get a bit spacey and vacant. It's easy to drift off into rambling thoughts, only to snap back to the reality of the moment and discover that you've been standing still all the time. My lungs were aching with the effort, and I decided to concentrate on this pain so my mind would drift off less. Of course, the danger of this is that you then start to feel sorry for yourself, and it makes it easier to give up.

My companions arrived as I reached the two yellow "Himalayan Hotels," our tents for the night in our highest camp at a little over 26,000 feet. It was still only 1 p.m. I intended to melt ice for drinks during the entire afternoon.

Looking inside the tents, I saw an awful mess. Sleeping bags had not been packed away, and food lay scattered everywhere. Did this mean there was nothing edible and that my summit attempt was off? Without a decent meal and plenty to drink, it would be dangerous to continue. I crawled inside after throwing off my crampons. The Sherpas moved into the other tent, which was about fifteen feet away, and because we could look across at each other, I noticed that soon they had oxygen masks glued to their faces. Lhakpa looked like some fighter pilot with the bubble of his cockpit open. I didn't understand their hurry to begin using oxygen. I felt fine, as long as I avoided fast movements.

As I started to look through the tent's contents, anger rose and affected some of my actions. I began to list the tattered remains of the contents: Sleeping bags, yes; oxygen bottles, quite a lot but some felt heavier than others—some must be partially used; regulators, yes, but I'm not quite sure how they work—I'll study them later; food, scattered remnants. There was a bit of frozen cheese and a chocolate bar, and the rest looked as if it had been attacked by a bunch of sticky-fingered trick-or-treat kids. I remember thinking that this didn't bode well, especially because by then my body had calmed down, the adrenaline had gone, and I was ravenous. Who said high altitude kills the appetite?

The crisis reminded me of "The Three Bears," and I felt like growling into the walkie-talkie: "Who's been sleeping in my bed?"

I had a bloody good idea who. Some of the other parties on the mountain were really not competent to be there in the first place, and our tents were by far the strongest and best supplied. I knew that some people had already been caught up there in a storm. Why didn't they tell us they had used our gear? This turn of events might cost us dearly.

For the rest of the afternoon, I made cold drinks, as that was the fastest way to get the crucial liquids my body craved. I filled a plastic sack with ice chips and handed them to Sonam. I asked if, in exchange, I could share the huge mound of barley mash they had concocted. This deep-brown sludge looks like a colored version of mashed potatoes and has a bland flavor which is then spiced by a hot chili sauce. Most people think it looks revolting. It does, but it's all easily usable carbohydrate. So I closed my eyes and began to eat it. It was the only way to maintain my strength.

At about 5 p.m., I heard footsteps outside the tent. Roddy had arrived.

"Have you seen the two dots just below the South Summit?" he asked. "It must be Carlos and Elisa. Hell, I hope they don't try and go to the main summit, or we'll have more deaths."

He was refering to a Mexican man-wife team who had been climbing with the Polish expedition on the West Ridge and now had made a last-ditch attempt via the South Col. They had been climbing all day and ought to have begun descending hours ago if they did not wish to come down in the dark.

"Oh, man," I sighed. "What with the Yugoslav and Sherpa bodies already up there, we don't need any more accidents."

The two separate accidents I refered to had primarily been caused by over-reaching and not turning back when daylight was almost finished. However, there wasn't much we could do except watch the drama unfold.

Roddy wasted no time in sliding into the tent to help with the melting of snow. Lying back on top of the sleeping bag, eyes closed, it was easy to imagine oneself at a lower height. Only when a movement was necessary did one feel the difference. Strangely enough, my thoughts only turned to the next day and the preparations I must make for the summit. Alan and Lorna did not seem part of the world I had entered. I had become so focused that in a way, Roddy, too, was only incidental to my objectives.

"Tomorrow the Sherpas are going to use two oxygen bottles each," I told Roddy. "What about you?"

"Last time I tried, the first bottle lasted me seven hours," he said. "These smaller bottles don't hold as much, so I'll take two as well."

"Mm," I wondered, "that's going to be quite heavy, and these boys aren't going to carry our spare bottles, that's for sure."

Although Sherpas often are expected to act as guides and do most of the hard work, we knew our situation was different. If we wished to go to the summit, we had to do it all ourselves. The Sherpas' actions and attitude had been made this quite clear.

"Would you want them to?" asked Roddy, his sky-blue eyes twinkling.

Of course I wouldn't! Using oxygen seemed enough of a compromise, and I'd been vocal enough about that in the past.

We checked the settings, and Roddy schooled me in how best to fit the face-mask so that the floppy bladder—a thin rubber balloon that hangs by the chest—did not get in my way.

We planned to rise at 9 p.m., make a drink and leave by midnight. Three hours might seem like a long time to make a drink, but it's sometimes taken me that long at sea level—with a head-banging hangover.

The time came soon enough, and yet it did not really feel all that cold. I didn't feel the need to use any glove-liners inside the tent, which is just as well because I'd somehow misplaced them in one of the many pockets of my clothing. I stepped out into the night, glad to be moving again. Stars twinkled brightly. Not a cloud anywhere.

The attempt was on. Yet, strangely enough, I was not overly excited. I functioned in a robotic fashion.

My crampons took the longest to fit because the two pairs of overboots I wore were bulky—and I'd had to slit the toe and heel so that the wire bale clipped onto the lugs of my plastic boots. That completed, I loaded my pack: two water bottles, two oxygen bottles and a climbing rope. It felt heavy, maybe 35 lbs, and I wondered if I'd be able to carry it all day. While I kept picking it up to test its weight, hoping it would somehow become lighter, I felt a pain in my lower bowels.

"Hell! I need a shit!" I cursed. What poor timing, considering I was all geared up and ready to move. I wobbled for nearly a hundred feet over the stony ground, crampons skittering off the rocks. I can't think why I went so far, except that maybe I was looking for a tree to go behind. After all, strange ideas do occasionally drift into oxygen-starved brains. There were zippers and Velcro and more zippers and flaps. I was starting to panic. Finally everything was aligned and out came the Sherpa mash. I thought that the stuff hadn't changed that much. I shuddered with cold, the kind that freezes the very bone-marrow. I felt drained and suddenly physically wasted. Still, I refused to let any inconvenience lower my mental state.

"Try to ignore it," I told myself. "It can only get better." No one else was quite ready, so with a quick "I'm off!" I left the camp. There was hard, wind-polished ice sloping up to the start of a steepening gully. I walked slowly, very slowly. The main problem lay in the ridiculous weight on my back.

"So this is was what oxygen does," I thought. "It's supposed to make life easier, but the weight makes my legs feel like lead. Should I dump it? I definitely felt better on Lhotse without it, and I was higher then, too." Then I remembered that only ten days before, a New

Zealander, Gary Ball, had done just that, with poor results. I decided to hang in and hope for the best.

Lights flickered in the gully I was heading towards. It was the Mexicans. They were coming down very slowly. Their extreme weariness showed in every movement. I prayed they wouldn't fall. We met as they crossed the bergschrund. Their shoulders spoke of defeat and fatigue as they swayed towards me.

"O.K.?" I asked. "You're down now! Only fifteen minutes left!" I added, trying to console them. They nodded wearily, and I slapped their shoulders, trying to pass a bit of human warmth through many layers of insulation.

I turned to watch them go. I saw the two lights of Lhakpa and Sonam. Roddy was not with them.

"Roddy's crampon broke," said Lhakpa. "We keep going."

His voice was muffled as he tried to speak through the rubber face-mask. I turned without a word and slowly began to climb the slope. Hard snow lay underfoot, making trail-breaking unnecessary. We zigzagged up the slope, in order to rest first one side of the body and then the other. The two Sherpas were looking strong, taking powerful steps—maybe a little hurried, but maybe just finding it easy. The competitive aspects of the previous day were no longer apparent because no one could afford to be too cocky if our strength was to be nurtured.

I'd go for five steps and have to rest. Again and again I cursed the weight. Lhakpa had gone into the lead and seemed to be cruising. Sonam was not far behind. I was no longer the bouncy *sahib*, and my gut felt icy from the diarrhea. In situations like this, all manner of thoughts come into one's mind and spin around in there, refusing to leave. They repeat themselves and then mix up with other new thoughts: a whole kaleidoscope of mental energy. A sudden thought pierced a crack in my conciousness. There was no way I could carry all I had on my back and even go for another half-hour, let alone reach the top. I thought to tell Lhakpa my fears, but he was always twenty feet ahead. Somehow, his respect didn't matter anymore to me. I was left struggling with my own self-respect and had to keep moving at all costs.

Then there was a dry section, where I concentrated on placing my crampons so they wouldn't break on loose stones. We began to traverse right, heading toward a diagonal sloping ramp of snow. I drifted back to all my training in Colorado. There I'd run uphill between 2,000 and 3,000 feet a day for more than two months. During every run I'd try to visualize the last day on Everest: the struggle uphill and the weariness. How we'd go from one point to another and then past it. Now all this seemed of another world, another time. How could I have expected the comfortable world of Boulder to translate to the rigors of life above 27,000 feet? I felt small. I did not feel strong.

Then I entered another stage. It was sort of like coming back to the present, but more acutely focused. There was about a four-inch layer of loose snow covering the harder stuff and I had to consider the possibility of a small snow slide. Maybe it was the presence of danger that made me lose my self-involvement. Sonam had also slowed a little, and it helped to know that he was feeling the pace as well.

There was a small rock-step to scramble over, another short slope, and suddenly we could look down the Kangshung Face into Tibet!

It was still dark as I looked at my watch. In disbelief, I rechecked. It was 3 a.m. We had been going for only three hours! My whole being lifted with that knowledge. I'd thought we were struggling, but the truth was that we had been moving very quickly. I stuck both thumbs in the air for my companions to see, and then we were off again.

The route followed the Nepalese side of the ridge and then switched to the Tibetan side. Snow had collected at this point, deposited by the wind in the lee of the ridge. The steep slope up to the 28,700-foot South Summit lay immediately ahead, and in the gloom I could see a rocky step about halfway up.

Lhakpa took off his pack and sat on it. It was obviously a good place to rest and wait for dawn to bring more light. I felt happy that we were actually having to sit and wait for daylight because we'd come up so quickly.

Slowly the stars began to go out. Dawn was on its way as we started moving diagonally right towards the steep section. None of us had considered using a rope, which was still tucked away in my 'sac. I stopped and waited for Sonam to scramble over the striated layers of friable, orange rock. Looking back down the ridge, we could see that our trail led to a red dot. A person. Roddy! He must have fixed his crampon. So, we were all going to do it!

An initial worry about him being all alone disappeared when I realized there was little we could do other than wait, and that if he had done O.K. to that point, then he was doing fine. Anyway, at this kind of altitude—it was the highest place I'd ever been—each person has total responsibility for himself. No one forces us to place ourselves in these high-risk situations, and we must face the outcome of our decisions. If Roddy had been in trouble, I certainly would have helped him, but I don't believe he would have expected it of me. That goes for me, too, if I overreached myself and got into trouble.

The rock was not easy. I began to wish I'd taken a line further to the right. The drop into Tibet looked awful—more than 10,000 feet of snow and rock—so I focused my energies into action instead of letting nervousness distract me. Sonam was speaking into the walkie-talkie as I topped the buttress. I was caught off guard by what lay before me. The sun was just risen over the Tibetan Plateau and had thrown Everest's pointed, triangular shadow over the still-cold mountains of Nepal. The darkness looked so solid that it seemed one could walk across it to the peaks beyond.

I learned that Alan had made his way up the Lhotse Face, and when he arrived at Camp 3, he was told we were almost at the South Summit. He later told me that tears of joy were on his cheeks after he heard the news. Everyone was taking bets on our summit-arrival time, some saying 9 a.m. and others 11 a.m. Alan said 7:30 a.m. and was only half an hour wrong.

The South Summit is no place to stand around because it feels dizzily high, so we crossed it to the security of a small pass on the far side. There we changed our oxygen bottles and drank some water. One of my water bottles was so frozen that I stood it in the snow with disgust. It's probably still there. Then we tied onto the rope. I felt happier. Every item unloaded from my pack made it lighter. Lhakpa went first, followed by Sonam, then me. We all climbed together, but if one person had fallen, there were enough small spurs between us to act as rough belays.

I photographed the Sherpas as they climbed the Hillary Step, the last problem before the top. Then it was my turn to tackle this famous forty-foot problem. The others had reached easier ground and began to move forward more quickly. I, who still could only move slowly up the difficult section, found the rope tightening at my waist. I suppose I should have shouted at them to slow down, but the face-mask hampered communication. Instead, I began to rush, bridging up a steep corner to a hand-traverse on a blunt-edged flake of rock.

Without warning, I felt myself start to choke and hyperventilate. There was no way I could risk a fall. I tried to breathe more deeply from the clammy mask. It didn't help much, so I lifted the mask off my face and gulped down some ambient air. Whew! My breathing rate went back down to mere gasps. This passed quickly in the reflex of the moment. It was only back in base camp I thought about the absurdity of the situation: forgoing oxygen to use the thin air!

Two smaller rises and that was it! Finished! *No more up*!

It was like stepping up onto a table to stand on the summit of Everest. It was exactly seven hours after we left the tent. Lhakpa handed me some playing-card-size notes of super-thin tissue paper imprinted with small figures of Buddha. We cast them up into the air and they floated on air currents about fifteen feet overhead.

I was looking up from the highest point on Earth. Yet there was so much more above me, and in a strange way, so much more beneath me, too. After the hard work of the past weeks, I felt happy to be finally there.

My two Sherpa companions were beaming with happiness, especially Sonam. He had deserved a chance for the summit because of all his hard work in carrying equipment for the common good of the expedition. He always seemed happy just to be alive.

We took photographs of each other. I couldn't help but chuckle at the way the two of them took off their sunglasses for the brief instant they became models. Then Roddy appeared at the top of the Hillary Step. His movements were smooth and typically unhurried. The edge of responsibility I still felt for him made me sigh with relief.

What now strikes me as important is the way I felt in control of the situation. This is the way I prefer to climb: everything going smoothly, without the epics I'd seen other people often get themselves into. I did not relax my mind from what we still had to do: descend. It had been a trying morning—especially early on—but going down is nowhere near as hard as climbing up.

I'd begun to organize my face-mask, as I'd spent the entire half hour on the summit with my face free and the oxygen switched off. We were just about to leave by the time Roddy arrived. I quickly took a picture with his camera and made him promise to come down as soon as he had taken a panoramic shot. I remembered stories of dreamy climbers sitting for hours on Himalayan peaks, unable to drag themselves away from the momentary joy, only to die up there among the clouds.

Twenty feet lower I turned and beckoned him down. There was no way I was going to let him stand around up there, lest he forget where he was. He waved back and caught up with us as I belayed the Sherpas back down the first step in the ridge. They seemed quite happy that I should do this, which told me they really did have confidence in me, because I had heard many times that to have a roped "member" above them, when they themselves do not have a belay, is very much against their way of thinking. There have been too many times when a foreign climber has pulled Sherpas to their deaths.

    We were back on the South Col by 10 a.m. I didn't even feel thirsty, so I declined to hang out for a brew with the other three. I packed my few belongings and set out down the 5,000 feet back to Camp 2. After forty-five minutes, I met Alan coming up the icy face. We were still thirty feet apart when I suddenly felt the loss at not having him there with me on the summit. Many people may have wondered if something had gone wrong. After all, it was too early to be coming back from the summit. Not Al, though. He knew right away and began to take photos of me before I reached him. I tried to impress upon him the importance of keeping going with all that weight upon his back.

    "It gets easier once you're warmed up," I told him. "Don't be hasty in thinking it's too heavy."

    With that, we parted, he for the summit the next day and I for basecamp.

    When I arrived in Camp, "Ram" was there with Tom Whitaker. They seemed surprised to see me, because it was only two in the afternoon. Fortunately, "Ram" quickly recovered and gave me some hot sweet tea and a shake of the hand. Later, Tom told me that I looked as though I'd just returned from a stroll on the glacier. Considering where I'd just been, I think I must make a good actor.

    I considered trying to get back to base camp the same afternoon—I would have had enough time—but the thought of descending a sun-warmed and melting icefall put an end to that crazy ambition. Thick cloud began to blow up the Western Cwm, and I thought of the others: Al, Pete Hillary, Andy, Jeff and Kelly—all awaiting their chance up on the South Col. If the weather were to change, it would be a cruel and dangerous blow. Everything was set, ready for another summit team. They certainly would not have any problem because they were all strong.

When I awoke at four the next morning, the weather had grown worse. There was more cloud high up, and I knew Al would not be trying in those conditions. What rotten luck! To miss the chance by one day! They still had to get back down, too, and I could guess that the wind would be howling strongly. Still, I was looking forward to a tasty omelette and gallons of tea in base camp and so wanted to get down through the Icefall before the day warmed up.

I set off into the mist enroute to Camp 1. What a mistake to go off alone with new snow obscuring the trail and visibility down to twenty-five yards! Many, many times I stopped on the brink of a strange crevasse—lost! Then I'd look around and sometimes retrace my steps until a familiar shadow put me on route again. What ought to have been a simple walk turned into a far more complicated affair. Yet, through all of it, I was beginning to enjoy being on my own. It was the final part of a personal journey, one I seemed reluctant to relinquish to others. As soon as I reached base camp, I would loose part of that unique feeling by sharing it.

Camp 1 loomed out of the murk, much to my relief, and I raced down through the rest of the jumbled route, heading for base camp. Wishing to hold onto those special feelings of personal identity, I wanted to sneak into the camp unseen, for it was not yet 8 a.m. I could change into some drier clothes and surprise Lorna at the same time.

However, I should have guessed that the sharp eyes of the Sherpas would have spotted me descending the Icefall. I was not really prepared for the warm reception offered me by my friends as I re-entered a different world, where I must share myself with others and where I was "normal" once more.

# *CHAPTER*
# *28*

## DEATH OF A SHERPA: TO A LOST FRIEND

BY ALAN

Looking upward, I saw a body splayed horizontal, with outstretched arms windmilling and clawing at empty air. My Sherpa climbing partner, Ongchu, was falling, caught in time and space, his face twisted, already resigned to death.

The vision vanished. I saw the *real* Ongchu balanced 100 feet above, linked to me by an eight-millimeter nylon rope as I stood vulnerable and unprotected on an ice step, with the slope dropping away to a deep crevasse 600 feet below. Unusually nervous and distracted by the premonition, I screwed an ice piton into the slope and tied into it, even though I knew that should Ongchu fall, it would rip immediately from the ice.

The rope ran smoothly through my hands and shards of ice

tinkled past me, loosened by Ongchu's boots. He disappeared from sight, moving quickly on easier ground, climbing to find a good anchor point for the fixed line. Nothing but a slight breeze and flickering rays of light disturbed my isolation. There was crystal silence and the quiet rhythm of my heart beating.

The faint sound of crampon steel crunched on ice, and an urgent cry cut to my core. My muscles responded as if hit by a high-voltage current. In a terrifying *déjà-vu,* my eyes witnessed what my heart already knew. Ongchu was falling, his body stretched across the ice. Grasping at air, his glove flew away and his red jacket caught a flicker of light. He swept by a mere arm's length to my left, his stare frozen, a scream cut short by a glancing blow to the head. Bouncing down a sharp craggy rock wall, his body flew into the void, before crashing and spinning onto the ice and then plunging with a sickening thud onto the slope below. A streak of blood led to a small bundle which had halted in deep powder snow where the slope eased. Nothing moved.

It was October 31, 1990. I was 200 feet from the Tibetan border on a mountain called Cheo Himal in the central Nepalese Himalaya. My friends and climbing companions, John and Matt, were 300 feet below, silent witnesses to the fragility of life.

Although we had started out as clients and guide, our relationship had become much closer than that. We all came from my home village of Holmfirth, and this expedition had forged strong bonds among us, as mountains have a way of doing. Now we were to share something else that mountains can produce: tragedy. Trembling with shock, I glanced down at the tiny broken figure that was once a proud Sherpa. I thought . . . dead.

Above 20,000 feet and balanced on an ice step in one of the farthest corners of the world is not a place to panic. Fighting down terror and feelings of lightness and floating sensations, I breathed deeply and slowly until I regained physical and emotional control. I knew I had to descend, but I also understood that the slightest lack of concentration could result in my own death.

I rappelled slowly, resisting the urge to hurry back to my companions. They appeared calmer than I, and after talking myself through how to descend, I continued on down.

Jumping across the deep crevasse at the foot of the slope, I landed in thigh-deep powder snow and plunged on down towards Ongchu's body, following the trail of blood and disturbed snow. The body moved and struggled to sit up. Ongchu was still alive! Gasping for air, I reached him and quickly scanned his head and limbs in an attempt to assess his injuries. Blood seeped from a hole in his temple the size of an egg, and he coughed up frothy red spumes from his lungs. One eye was smashed and closed, while the other flickered with desperation and fear. His limbs all seemed intact, almost a miracle as I thought back to the series of thuds his body had made on the ice.

As I watched John and Matt approach, my gaze continued past them to the looming ice cliff that threatened us. If the cliff—the size of a hotel—collapsed, we all would be crushed instantly. I screamed at them to hurry and then apologized. They understood only too well the urgency of the situation and smoothly followed my instructions to cross the slope to the left to escape the threat.

Leaving Ongchu, who was now groaning in agony, I hurried after them and anchored a rope that led to safety 300 feet lower. It was Matt's first day on an alpine ice climb, and even though he demonstrated natural climbing talent, I was reluctant to involve him in additional danger. John, who had already summited a 20,000-foot peak with me the previous year, had considerable experience on alpine terrain and could be trusted to get them both onto safer ground. I told them to wait on the glacier for me, and I watched them head down the rope.

Terrified of the leaning ice cliffs, and even more frightened of the decisions I was being forced to make, I traversed back across the ice to Ongchu to see what could be done.

He lay on his side in the fetal position, moaning softly. His hat and gloves were lost during his fall, and he was beginning to shake from shock and cold. Slowly easing his body around, I managed to get him into a sitting position and pulled my own wool hat onto his head. Resting his head against the snow had stopped the bleeding from the large hole in his skull, but pulling gloves onto his swollen and wooden hands was difficult. His head lolled against my shoulder as I supported him.

"Sorry, sir." A dry moan—half mumble, half pain—whispered from his lips.

"Ongchu! Ongchu!" I said. "Can you hear me?"

His one clear eye moved with signs of recognition.

"We're going down, Ongchu! Down! Can you hear me?"

With a shudder that seemed to come from the very core of his soul, he tensed and made as if to stand. The courage that has endeared the Sherpa people to all mountaineers radiated from him.

His limbs did not appear broken, and he struggled to straighten his legs as I hoisted him to a standing position. How would my courage have stood the test if the situation were reversed?

Suddenly, as if a light had been switched off, the power drained from him, and he slumped back into the snow. I tried again to raise him, but he was too heavy and he curled onto his side. I glanced up at the lengthening shadows on the ice cliff and tried to believe it would not collapse.

I realized it was impossible to take him down the way we had climbed. It was too steep and crevassed. The only possibility was to go directly down the slope under the ice cliff and hope there were no obstacles that proved impassable. I tied a length of rope to his harness and plunged through thigh-deep powder snow. Dragging Ongchu through the snow, I managed to move him only ten feet before he dug in his heels. He was shouting with pain. The harness tugging on his body must have aggravated some internal injury, plus disturbing possibly broken ribs.

Panting heavily, I climbed back up my trail, tears of sorrow and frustration flooding my cheeks. Unsure of what to do next, I traversed back across the ice to the point where our fixed line dropped away over steep crevassed ice. I knew I could never take Ongchu down that way. It was beginning to dawn on me there was little chance of rescue. Even if I could get him down the 400 feet to the glacier, base camp was still 1,500 feet lower, and medical help many days away.

I trudged once more back to my friend. He was very still, but I could hear him breathing rapidly. I squatted on my haunches with my back to the mountain and looked south to the massive bulk of Manaslu. Memories flooded back from our expedition there the previous October, and I could see clearly the point of our final camp and remembered the fearful night Aid and I had spent battling hurricane-force winds. Now it was calm, and the late autumn sun bounced long shadows and sharp rays of light across the ice.

Waves of emotion surged over me. The stark wild beauty of this place contrasted with the warm vulnerable body lying at my side. Yet here was the balance of nature at its most Spartan and everything was in its place. Even death has its reasons. I felt resigned to the outcome: Ongchu was going to die.

My gaze dropped to the snow, and tears of sadness glazed my vision. I struggled to come to terms with my decisions and actions. Maybe I had sent my two companions down too soon? Maybe with their help we could have dragged Ongchu farther down the slope? But suppose we had even got him as far down as the glacier, what then? His head injuries were massive, and without the help that only a hospital can give, he would die anyway. Suppose I had insisted that we all stay together and the sérac had collapsed, killing all four of us! Was it worth the risk? The voices of self-critical demons rang in my ears. But all speculation was irrelevant. All I could do was to deal with the immediate situation.

My memory drifted back to the first time I'd met Ongchu in the streets of Kathmandu, surrounded by the bells of rickshaws, the shouting of street vendors, the smells of open markets and the warm autumn sunshine of early October. Another Sherpa friend had known I was looking to hire a strong climbing Sherpa to help with the expedition and had recommended Ongchu. On meeting him, I knew instantly what a competent climber he would prove to be. Like many of the best climbing Sherpas, in the lowlands he was reserved to the point of shyness but carried a strong barrel chest and compact body with confidence and pride. When I asked him which mountains he had climbed, he looked me straight in the eye and listed a string of high peaks, including a recent K2 expedition. He didn't boast; he simply stated his experience.

Later that day, when I introduced him to the climbing team, I voiced my opinion that the closer to the mountain and the high valleys we got, the more capable he would become. His reserve would evaporate in his more familiar terrain of rock walls and glistening ice fields.

On the "walk-in," he blended easily with the Sherpa cook staff and was always searching for ways to help, whether in the kitchen, putting up tents or dealing with porters. On the mountain, I considered him my equal, not only in climbing strength, but in route-finding and decision-making. We had planned the final assault together and had taken turns leading the steep ice on the climb.

The day we reached base camp, Ongchu and I raced ahead of the main group to look for a good campsite. He spoke little and when he did, it was always deferentially. He called me "sir," which I found unfamiliar. With most of my Sherpa friends, I always joked around, laughing and telling stories, drinking *chang* with them and teasing the pretty girls along the trails. I wondered if Ongchu's shyness with me was partially the result of the kitchen Sherpas' talk; our *sirdar* had been on Everest with the Canadians in 1982 when he was a first-time expedition Sherpa and I was acting climbing leader. Ongchu may have regarded me as some wealthy big-time expedition leader with the potential to hire him on a continual basis. Regardless of his shyness, when it came to matters of mountains, he was both confident and assertive. Some of my best and longest-term friends had taken quite a while to get to really know.

Desperation made me try once again to lift Ongchu. I shouted into his face and turned him over onto his back. A great sigh hissed from his lungs and he shook his head heavily from side to side. He reached down, flung his gloves to the ice and untied the rope from his harness. He had decided not to be painfully hauled around any more but to spend his last moments in the way he chose.

I followed the trail once more to the top of the fixed rope. I thought this time I would leave and force myself to go on down. I lifted the rope to attach it to my harness, and then I stopped. If I could not save Ongchu, then it was important to me how he died. If he felt abandoned, I would always feel guilty and would never know about those last minutes. I dropped the rope and turned back across the ice.

I crouched by his silent body and stared out across the valley. If a person had to die, there was no place more beautiful. Better to slip away here than in some hospital bed weighed down by tubes, blinded by fluorescent light and asphyxiated by the smell of antiseptic. The cold provides its own anesthetic, and while the bodily pain becomes numbed, the mind must still be aware of this brilliant light and deep powerful silence.

After ten or fifteen minutes, Ongchu began to stir again. He half turned and I helped rise to a sitting position. The effort to hold his head up proved too much, and it hung exhausted on his chest. I knew that, like all Sherpa people, Ongchu was a devout Buddhist, and the process of his death was of utmost importance to him. I recalled the stages of dying from *The Tibetan Book Of The Dead*: when a Buddhist *lama* talks to the dying person, literally walking him through the final stages of life and into the state prior to rebirth. My memory of the text was a little rusty, but I figured the process of dying must be the same for everyone.

I spoke softly and as calmly as I could. I told Ongchu not to be afraid, that I was his brother and would be there with him when he started to slip away into the long tunnel with a bright light at the end. I realized I was speaking as much for myself as for him, but hoped he would trust me. I told him not to fight the flow towards the light but to concentrate on it and feel himself as part of that light. I urged him not to be distracted by sounds or shadows but to focus his inner vision on the white glow; to feel the warmth of that light and let it absorb him.

I let his body rest back on the snow, not knowing how far away from death he was. Staring out across the lower valleys, I tried hard to remember what came next and how far I could go with him. A cold wind was freshening and clouds swirled around the high ridges, mixing blasts of powder and streaks of air.

My gaze returned to Ongchu's still form. Mumbling half to myself, I spoke into the rising wind:

"When the white light turns to a red glow and begins to fade, have courage, don't be scared. The darkness will change again to light. Then it's up to you, my friend. Where you're at now, you know better than me."

I felt very human and vulnerable, but I also felt weightless, as if I could almost fly. Maybe death is not so bad. Only the fear and pain of it? I felt that now was the time to go. There was a quiet peace in the air, and I rose to leave.

With a last long stare, seeing only a shape, I turned firmly away and forced myself to keep moving without any backward glance. I took a strong hold on the fixed line and slid over the edge, down the ice, through crevasses and across snow bridges, down to John and Matt.

The three of us regrouped on the edge of a bottomless chasm. We stood in silence and turned to start on down the glacier. Now was not the time or place to explain all the thoughts and actions of the last three hours. Communication was restricted to safety commands and route-finding, as we circled large crevasses and leapt across smaller ones.

I looked upward searching for the body and saw a black crow circling, cruising the rising air. Did I see a black speck move high on the face? My eyes played tricks and my mind jumped around like a kite in a storm. We pressed on down toward our camp.

Our Sherpa kitchen staff had seen only three people returning and, with an intuition born of experience, already suspected the worse. Tired and dejected, we staggered into camp. The expedition was over, and an avalanche would shortly wipe out all trace of our passing.

Two of our kitchen boys were lay monks, and that night they lit candles, burnt juniper and intoned prayers so that Ongchu's spirit could find its way down from the mountain. They believe it is important the spirit knows that the body is dead and that it's time to move on to its next reincarnation.

Now that the expedition was over, we left the stark frozen base camp and descended into the forests, wandering through the warm lower meadows rich with autumn colours. Small streams trickled into rivers that foamed under rough wooden bridges, and fallen leaves formed carpets of rust and ochre. The sound of small birds calling merrily pierced the quiet, while sunbeams filtered through hanging mosses that looked like old men's beards. We strode down the trail through a valley made more magical by contrast with the high places we had left only that morning. We needed to know we were alive and breathed in large lungfuls of joy with primitive passion.

With the passage of time, the emotion of that experience has dimmed, partly because more recent experiences have taken precedence. Six months after the death of Ongchu, I helped rescue a young German climber from a peak in the Langtang region of Nepal. He had fallen and broken both legs below the knee, landing on a snow shelf above 20,000 feet. At first, it appeared a hopeless task, but with hard work and a little skill, we brought him to safety. It was one of the most satisfying times I ever spent on a mountain, and during that rescue I often wondered what would have happened if Ongchu had only broken his legs or had the accident occurred in a less remote area.

It would be easy to become sentimental about Ongchu and to emphasize his charming character and great personal courage, but one of the dangers with sentimentality is in the belief of "bad luck." Ongchu died because he made a mistake, and if we the living wish to continue to face dangerous situations, we must always focus on the problem at hand and not allow that concentration to waiver. The rope Ongchu was descending broke because he had untied a knot that isolated a flaw. He died because his over-confidence broke his focus, and the consequence of that was death. It was a brutal, sad lesson.

In high-standard mountaineering, many people die. Ongchu takes his place alongside many other good friends who also made mistakes. His memory still hangs around in the back of my mind, waiting for those times when I am physically or emotionally vulnerable to remind me that life is a fragile edge and only a passing phase.

# CHAPTER
## 29

## THE WINDS OF MANASLU

BY ADRIAN

It was a misty morning at a Gurung village in the middle of the hill country in central Nepal. Beads of moisture clung to the grass, and thick black mud oozed under my trekking shoes. The relative humidity was a tiny drop under 100 percent. I had the feeling that a loud sneeze would precipitate a major downpour.

"I can't believe he said she was *too young*," growled Alan.

He had been up to his usual tricks during an eleven-day trek to Manaslu: trying to curry the favor of a strikingly beautiful young Gurung girl. Had she lived in L.A., she'd probably have been a model or actress. Obviously she'd been flattered by Al's none-too-subtle charms— or was it the hope of a wristwatch or foam mattress that drew her to his tent?

She had just arrived at Al's tent when our skinny-legged Brahmin liaison officer suddenly materialized out of the shadows, his garlic breath betraying his presence well before he actually moved between tempter and temptress (for innocent she was not).

"She is too young, *sahib*," he said. "A mere girl."

"A *mere girl* is all I had in mind," snapped Al.

But the rendezvous was thwarted.

Al may have been interested in only part of the local beauty, but the other twelve people in our group were absorbing all of it. The Buri Gandaki gorge slices through some of the most awe-inspiring parts of Nepal. Travelers must follow foot-wide trails that snake through crumbling cliffs more than a thousand feet above the grey, tumbling torrent. Occasionally the confines of the gorge are relieved by areas of abrupt widening, where residents of small hamlets survive on crops eked out of leached soils.

A flock of mountain sheep bunched toward a monsoon-fed torrent. Their herders were taking them to the old Hindu town of Gorkha for the festival of Dassain. The lead ram had a lot of courage but few brains. He leaped boldly onto a slimy boulder and then, with the optimism of an Olympic long-jumper, tried to clear the next fifteen feet to the opposite bank.

"Don't worry! We'll look after your women!" Al yelled over the torrential roar as the bundle of wool paddled downstream, plopping from pool to pool.

Members of our group exchanged glances, as if to say: "If it's not girls, it's sheep." They commiserated with the unlucky ram. And with Al: none of the ewes was even passably pretty.

Manaslu is the highest and most northerly in a string of icy giants that includes Himalchuli and Peak 29. It is the world's eighth highest mountain at 26,760 feet (8,157 meters), and is much sought after by those eager to bag 8,000-meter peaks. Often overlooked in the rush to the top is the peak's awesome beauty as it rises over the villages of Samagon and Lho, its wind-streaked twin summits splitting the sky above the valley's golden barley fields.

For local people of Tibetan descent, Manaslu is the abode of both gods and demons: an ever-present reminder of the forces of nature. Manaslu is both protector and destroyer. Its melting snows feed the swollen streams, allowing the people to irrigate their precious land during the short growing season. But its snows also avalanche, often carrying away hundreds of yaks; collapsing ice cliffs occasionally tumble into nearby tarns and flood the entire valley. In the early 1950's, as a Japanese expedition was making an early foray onto the virgin peak, an avalanche swept down onto the meadows and destroyed a convent full of nuns.

Our base camp was only two hours above Samagon, a tightly packed cluster of stone dwellings in which animals lived downstairs and families above. As we passed through Samagon's muddy streets, inquisitive faces peered out of the shadows and thought: More *ninji* (their word for stranger) heading for the mountain.

Samagon Gompa is a monastery of the Tibetan Nyingmapa Buddhist sect. It stands on a hill of aging pines and overlooks the village. Beyond it are the flat, grassy campsites we would use for the night. With Pema Dorje, my longtime friend and *sirdar*, I went in search of the local *lama* to visit our base camp and perform *puja* to honor the mountain gods and exorcise malevolent spirits.

During the subsequent *puja*, thick billows of blue juniper smoke curled up into the ether. A nasal monotone of prayer was punctuated by deep drumming: BOOM! BOOM! BOOM! The *lama* in a yellow silk shirt and purple robes sat before a tray of nine-inch-high *torma* (statuettes made of rice). His long, pointed scarlet hat added dignity to his motionless pose. He chanted in Tibetan. Behind him, the hillside dropped away below the Ganesh Himal, and he appeared to be hovering, barely balanced on the edge of our world. From my vantage point behind him, the spire of Manaslu appeared to grow from the tip of his hat, the ceremonial smoke mixing with the wind-blown plume on the summit.

Then he sat and called down the misplaced energy of our ambition, fixing it within the *torma*. The chanting monk exuded wisdom. He knew the dangers of the ego: he had been trying to still their effects within himself for years. But what surprised him was the powerful egos of the foreign climbers. Never before had he witnessed so much energy focused in individual psyches.

Our Sherpa cooks handed out *chang*. I mulled over the histori-cal fact that the great Padmasambhava, the Indian *yogi* who brought Buddhism into Tibet, had introduced *chang* into religion. No wonder he found so many followers! *Chang* is the basis of many Sherpa and Tibetan customs—mainly revelry. Each of us was handed a *torma,* and on cue we hurled the rice into the air.

The next day the climbing—maybe *walking* is a better word—began. Our expedition was a collection of climbers, each pair doing its own thing. For me, this is the ideal way to travel in the mountains. If anyone doesn't feel like climbing or wants to go it alone, it's all the same to me. All of us accepts responsibility for our own decisions.

With this attitude, each climbing duo established its own camp and carried its food. I can imagine compulsive types wondering: "How on earth did they arrange things? It sounds like chaos."

It's simple. I asked Al how many days' food we should carry. He asked me if we were taking whisky. I said I thought we needed marker wands. He hinted that a local village girl might like to help us carry potatoes up to 19,000 feet. I said I didn't like the smell of aged yak butter. He said he didn't either—if it was on a yak. (What *do* those girls wash their hair in?) So . . . it's *easy* to arrange things.

We pitched our tents at Naike Col, then headed up a series of steepening bumps, each one perhaps 400 feet high. Confronting us was a huge gully, ripped occasionally by sérac falls and the odd express train. The longer we slogged through the deep snow, the more danger-ous our crossing became. Luckily, at increasing altitudes the "worry-factor" is countered by the "pain-factor," along with other inexplicable phenomena that dull awareness of impending peril.

Along the way we met the famous Swiss doctor, Oswald Oelz, a member of the Austrian expedition attempting Manaslu's Northeast Face and friend of Reinhold Messner. He had been a speaker at a con-ference on high-altitude medicine which Al attended in Lake Louise. When our conversation turned to Reinhold's loss of short-term memory, Oelz noted that Al and I also fit into this category: "brain-dead" is what I think he meant. Al said: "Yes, doctor, I really wanted to go to your presentation in Lake Louise, but I forgot when it started."

After snowing the entire month of September, the weather turned fair on the day of the *puja*. The skies were blue, but the slopes were heavy with unconsolidated snow. As we broke trail up to 20,000 feet, we came upon a 15-foot aluminum ladder laid across a three-foot crevasse, guarding a 40-foot-high 70-degree step.

"A bit of overkill, don't you think?—this long ladder on a tiny crevasse?" said Al as he stepped easily across the gap. We agreed that the Japanese climbers who placed the ladder were being extraordinarily cautious.

"Maybe they need to take a wheelchair across it," quipped Al, alluding to the aging leadership of many Japanese expeditions.

Had we realized that the crevasse was opening at the rate of nine inches a day, we'd have been more humble. By our expedition's end, the 15-foot ladder would not touch either side of the crevasse; it resembled an Outward-Bound monkey-bridge problem of "pucker-factor 10" (a new grading for an old problem: fear).

We set up camp on a large flat snow-shoulder at 21,000 feet. Al and I suggested digging an ice-cave, because the large open slopes above looked prone to avalanche. Some in our group dug caves; others chose not to. After helping Al dig our snow-cave, I returned to base camp.

I had been down there less than an hour when a porter, sent down by the Austrians, gave me a note from Ron Matous: "Three of the Austrians' Sherpas and Andy (Lapkass) have been caught in an avalanche above Camp 2. No more information, but will radio at 4 p.m."

"Shit!" was all I could say.

I knew that Andy had been on the big depositional slopes below the North Col. Was Ron preparing us for Andy's death? We all sat around, stunned. This kind of speculation most often turned into reality. We knew that the Sherpas had been carrying a radio and the Austrians always kept a channel open for them. There could only be one reason they had not called. It seemed inevitable: no one was left alive. Our gloom deepened. We talked about someone going out to inform Andy's mother. Hell, I didn't even have her phone number.

Eventually, the radio crackled out information: "Andy and the three Sherpas are alive at Camp 2. The Sherpas triggered a huge slab. Andy was back at the camp and saw the whole thing. The crown was 500 feet across and four-feet thick. They rode it for 1,200 feet and came out on top. Andy went up to help and had to restrain one Sherpa who was having an epileptic fit. They lost their walkie-talkie in the avalanche. They'll come down tomorrow. Over."

"Whew!" eminated from everyone's lips in perfect unison.

"Its time to test out that brew of yours," Al exclaimed, referring to 115 liters of "Ye Olde English Ale" fermenting in two large plastic drums in one of our tents. Our relief was immense and so was our thirst.

On expeditions, home-brewing skills are as important as knowing how to cook. It is not just survival that is desirable during long mountain escapades, but the *quality* of survival. I was reminded of the British Raj which recognized the unique thirst-quenching properties of malt, barley and hops mixed with water and thus concocted Indian Pale Ale. The colonial British also depended upon the quinine in gin-and-tonic to combat malaria. Necessity—and pleasure—are the mothers of invention.

After a few days of rest, we climbed back up, passing the recent sites of the Austrian and Japanese base camps; they had gone home after the avalanche. As we came over the steep moraine, we saw our large Eureka storage tent lying in a broken heap, twenty feet from where it had originally been pitched. What had happened? What could have moved 400 pounds of equipment so far?

The answer became obvious as we pieced together the mystery. An immense ice-cliff had cut loose from the skyline ridge of Naike Peak more than 2,000 feet above, probably triggered by an earthquake. The ice blocks had shot over a couple of large ridges and stopped in the middle of the old campsites. Our tent had caught the wind blast, which hit with immense power.

The idea of a huge plume of snow blasting off the summit was unsettling. Normally in October there are breaks in the persistence of the jet-stream winds, providing windows of summit-opportunity. We didn't seem to be getting these.

Al, Paul, Andy and I decided to see just how strong the winds were up where white snow-devils twirled against the royal-blue sky. We left Camp 2 to go to an exposed campsite that was only a snowbank sandwiched between two ice-cliffs. At 21,000 feet, this site was high enough to give us a shot at the top, if we moved quickly. Since my companions were moving like greyhounds, I reckoned we could safely reach the summit.

How we underestimated those little "puffs" of white snow-smoke! I was the first to dump my 'sac alongside a beat-up Japanese tent. The wind screamed around the corner, flattening me against the slope. I took in the reality very slowly. This was going to be one hell of a night, even if the tents didn't take off into the air.

I've never camped inside a freezer, nor have I ever been inside a freezer while someone beat it with a big stick. But now I know the feeling. Flying frost has a certain charm while one is riding a ski lift, but not while you're trying to sleep in a bucking tent of brittle nylon.

Al can be pensive at times, even slow. But the next morning he was quick and lucid: "This is fucking suicide!"

I agreed.

At Camp 2, the air was still. However, swirling clouds of powder scoured the skyline. Reality could change so easily if we gained 3,000 feet of elevation. I began to wonder just how long a person could sit in an ice-cave and patiently wait for better conditions. I recalled the times I had to calmly sit and wait. There had been many . . . . I had no desire to end the expedition, because the winter winds could suddenly stop, and then within six hours, we could be within striking distance.

So we relaxed in base camp and watched the upper mountain for a drop in the wind. Life was so much kinder in base camp. The food was good and the beer tasty, but it was the people from Samagon that made it wonderful. We received visitors almost every day. Some of the climbers had decided to leave for home and porters gathered outside "Manaslu Lodge," our kitchen-shelter. They looked like characters out of a novel by a Tibetan Dickens: their greased black hair fell over Mongolian features and black fur-lined *chubas* (cloaks) wrapped swarthy bodies. They looked fearsome as they honed the blades of their long swords and pointed daggers, but their eyes sparkled with fun. There was much laughter and joking while they heated a potent mixture of coffee and *rakshi* and offered it to us. They are amazing people. We loved them.

We told stories in a cross of Nepalese, English, and Sherpa, along with a fluid twisting of palms. Communication is their art; they are traders. By comparison, we were babes, but we had the will and it was recognized.

As time passed and the mountain became less important, our

thoughts turned to Kathmandu. I almost said "home," but then I realized that we felt truly at home where we were. This brings up an expedition reality that has caught the media's attention these days: What to do with the garbage? First, it's important to know what *not* to do.

Al summed up what normally happens:

"The expedition leader often just wants to get the hell out of there, so he says to the *sirdar*: 'Please burn the rubbish and bury it in a pit nearby. I'm going down to the village to see about the porters (and maybe drink some beer or *rakshi*). See you later.'

"The *sirdar* usually replies: 'Don't you worry, *bara sahib* (chief). I will do everything.'

"But what the *sirdar* thinks is: 'Thank god he's going out of the way. Now I can settle in lining up this young lass who's just brought up a gallon of *chang* for me. There's no way I'm soiling my hands with that rubbish shit. I'm a *sirdar*, not a bloody Tamang porter!'

"So he says to a couple of the cookboys: 'See that crap over there. Put some kerosene on it—not too much, though, because I'm going to sell the rest down in the village. Make some smoke so the members will see it as they go down. Then pile some rocks on it. I don't know how he expects us to dig a pit without a shovel, and I'm not going to knacker my ice axe doing it.'

"The cookboy thinks: "Wish I could be drinking some of that *chang*. That girl's sister is definitely interested in some fun. We'll set this lot on fire and bugger off. The *sirdar* will be too drunk to notice.' "

There's no easy way of getting someone else to do this dirty work, so we Westerners have to do it. We burned all the empty cans in a juniper fire. A Tibetan girl sifted through the rubbish with us. It was not rubbish to her. It was Western waste and she was there to collect it.

The next day, the three of us sat on a slab of granite and flattened the blackened cans with hand-held rocks. For a day we became Stone Age workers. Then everything was buried in a pit with lime brought in from Kathmandu. It took us little time.

I know why this kind of cleanup is rarely done. Climbers suddenly decide they are on their way home. Home is not where they are. They leave without a second thought for where they have lived for six weeks, because they don't feel that it was a *real home*.

After all, what kind of person would ever leave a pile of garbage stacked against the wall in his own kitchen? Only if we feel we really belong there will we treat it as *home*.

# CHAPTER
## 30

### SHERPA FRIENDS

BY ADRIAN

Pema Dorje was perched on a small 400-foot-high ledge in Eldorado Canyon near Boulder, Colorado, when he abruptly asked: "So, Aid, how much do you pay for your house every week?" The question caught me off guard, because we'd been chatting about my next visit to Nepal.

"A lot of money, Pema," I said, "but Lorna pays most of it. I think it must be over a thousand dollars every month. The bank really owns the house, and we have to pay them back."

"Shit, Aid!" said Pema. "I'm building my house in Khumjung, and I think *it* is a lot. But not like yours. Your house is very nice and mine is like toilet." His round, smiling face squinted as he looked into the sun, and he added: "For Nepal, it is okay."

"I know that everybody in Nepal thinks that Americans are very rich, and many are," I replied and then paused to think of the right words. "But I am quite poor compared to many. I don't have money in the bank. I spend everything to go climbing. After every expedition, I have no money left."

"I understand, Aid." said Pema. "Most Sherpas think 'members' are rich. So they don't mind to take some things when 'members' are not looking. Me, I never do those things. It is not good luck."

I paid out the rope while talking with him. A third climber with us was busy leading. Karl Prochazca was a Czech who escaped from his country while it was still a part of the communist bloc. He'd run through a long railway tunnel with his wife and child to get to Austria and seek asylum. By now he'd become a close climbing friend after phoning me upon his arrival in Denver. A mutual friend in Nepal, Czech climber Miroslav Schmidt, had told him to look me up. It reminded me again of how small the climbing world really is.

Pema was making his first visit to the U.S. and was loving every minute of it. After I met him during the Annapurna IV trip, he had gone on to summit Everest with the Canadians in 1982 and then to summit Himalchuili with a Colorado expedition. It was the latter who had paid for his current visit. Pema had never done any really serious rock-climbing before, but he was a natural. When Karl shouted down that he was safe, Pema began climbing. Although he wore an old pair of rock shoes that were at least two sizes too large for him, he fairly danced up the warm rock and out of sight. He could just as easily have been out searching for lost yaks in his native hills.

The day after a heavy rain, I knew Pema didn't wish to go trudging around in the mud.

"I'll show you 'round the shops, Pema," I'd suggested.

"Good idea," he said and added in his special sing-song way: "Everyone seems to think they must take me climbing. But you—you know different things. I wish to buy a cowboy hat and boots because they are the same idea in Tibet for weddings and I get married next year. Maybe later we drink some beer."

So began our journey around the malls of Denver. When I showed him a clothing store that specialized in western apparel, he

*Pema Dorje*

looked at every boot—and there were dozens. Then at the hats, which he thought were expensive.

He asked the sales attendant the price of everything in the store. Then he said to me: "I wish to see other shops to check prices, please, Aid."

What had I begun? Five stores later we hadn't bought a thing, but Pema knew all the choices and every price. We entered still another store, and Pema went for the kill. He began bargaining with the sales-girl. I hid in a corner and watched, vastly amused. She was polite, though she surely had never had this happen before. She warmed to Pema's honest attitude. He got his deal! Later I told him that he could go shopping for me from now on.

One of the next stores I saw was "Waterbed Warehouse." I

paused, thought a moment and then said to Pema: "Come in here. You will not believe."

"What is inside these, Aid ?"

"It's water. Warm water."

He sat down on the edge of a king-size bed and bounced up and down. The captive waves sloshed back and forth. Pema shook his head in disbelief.

"In Khumjung, they would take a knife," he said, stabbing at the bed with his forefinger. Then he lay out full-length.

"Aid, are these good for bumping?" he asked. His single gold tooth gleamed out from a bright smile.

"Don't ask me, Pema. I've never slept on one!"

We both laughed.

Namche Bazaar is the largest village in the Everest region, but I prefer two smaller hamlets situated a thousand feet higher on the edge of an ancient dried-up lake. Khumjung and Khunde are home to many top-class climbing Sherpas.

Pema's parents' stone house in Khumjung is on an east- facing hillside, about 500 feet from the monastery. The main living area is on the second floor: a compact kitchen, a large main room and a spare room-cum-chapel. Wood is stored downstairs along with potatoes and sometimes a yak or zukyuk.

Nowadays, Pema is well-known. He's climbed Everest three times—and even taken Diana Ross trekking. His clients have been so diverse and interesting that he has a fantastic repertoire of tales which he often tells around a fire and warm glasses of *chang*.

"One time I hear," begins one of his tales, "there was this old lady who has very rich husband. Every year she comes to Mountain Travel for trekking. One time she tries to get Ang Lakpa (the *sirdar*) to sleep with her, but he say: 'No way, I married.' So she look to very strong Tamang porter. He is happy enough for bumping but say she make too much noise. They say all Western *diddi* (sister/girl) do this way. So, after first night she start telling *sirdar* to give the Tamang extra eggs and rice. Then not to have so heavy load. First days porter is very happy, but later he says he is always tired because no sleep. Jimmy Roberts (head of Mountain Travel) ask her if she had good trek. She say: 'Oh, yes, but when I come next year I want same Tamang porter.'

Jimmy say O.K., but he has no idea of porter name. So he will find her other one and *hope she not notice*!"

Pema roars with laughter and shakes his head in disbelief at Western stupidity.

One day in Kathmandu, Pema came to my hotel around 4:30 p.m., which was a good time because it was cocktail hour—as though Pema didn't know!

"Aid, I met this English man in Namche who knows you. He is in Kathmandu tonight and wants to go out for *tomba* (a version of hot *chang*, drunk through a straw). I told him you would come."

"What's his name? How do I know him?"

"Oh, you never met," Pema said, grinning, "but he is from England."

I thought I should tell him that my memory is bad enough, to say nothing of not being able to remember seventy million people. Instead, I tried for more information.

"What's he doing here in Nepal?"

"He's called Mike and has been making some movie in Khumbu. He is from a music group, I think."

I couldn't recall knowing a rock-star, but my curiosity was aroused. We met in the Annapurna Hotel, so I knew the film had an expense account. A round-faced, jovial guy came up and shook my hand.

"Mike Harding," he said in northern accent, likely Yorkshire.

The name took a bit to gather momentum, and then I grasped the connection. Mike was a famous British comedian who had a TV show.

"I saw your brother up in Khumbu," said Mike. "Snores like a chain saw."

"That's 'cause he's not getting laid," I parried.

"No, but he certainly was trying."

Pema bounced around, full of glee when he realized we were going to have a great time.

One Christmas Eve we had just returned from an attempt on

Ama Dablam in the winter. Originally Pema had been one of the four climbers, but after reaching a bivouac on top of the yellow towers, he declared his reluctance to continue,

"I had very bad dream last night," he said. "Al fell down the mountain, and my mother jumped into the Dudh Kosi River without clothes. The *lamas* saw it all."

You couldn't argue with that logic, and so down we went.

During another attempt later, Al, Craig and I were caught in such a strong wind that we could neither go up or down. The wind was ripping off roofs in Khumjung, and we were rumored dead.

Once back in civilization, we had reason to celebrate. Pema took us to the house of his future father-in-law in Khunde, a mile up the track from his own house.

"He is a good man but quite old," said Pema. "When he serves you drink, please take it because then it is good for me."

The old Sherpa was dressed in a traditional sheepskin coat of sapphire blue. His weather-beaten face was full of high-altitude wrinkles, but his eyes were bright and clear. At least they were to start with.

Lorna sat on the floor with Pema's girlfriend, Mingma, and her sister, Mingma Angi. They laughed and giggled together in the dancing yellow light of a roaring fire. Mingma was busy braiding red thread into Lorna's wild, long hair. At intervals, she'd leap up and serve us hot *chang*.

As we were representing the more formal side of the family, it was necessary that we sit on a line of benches with backs to the wall and with small, low tables before us. Stories of climbing and trekking were told and retold. Laughter rang out as Pema entertained us royally. The old man had heated some reddish *rakshi,* which, although it was only for special occasions, he dealt out with obvious relish.

"*Shey, shey!*" he called out, lifting the glasses up to our lips. Then he'd refill them immediately, saying "*Sum, sum!*" This means "three" in Sherpa. It's required that any host must fill all the glasses at least three times, or he will have bad luck. Conversely, a guest must consume the required minimum to be polite. The night progressed in the fashion of a party. Out came more *chang*; out came more *rakshi*.

Rumor has it that I was at the end of the bench, with Al next to me and the two of us were chatting away. Without warning, I keeled forward onto the floor. Out for the count. Al continued to prattle away, oblivious to my plight. When I vomited, he took notice.

The old man was delighted. It was the sign of a good night!

The story goes that Lorna was mad at me and was refusing to sleep with me, but Pema insisted that this was what a good wife had to do—through thick and thin, rain or shine.

An enormous, heavy yak-skin blanket was thrown over me, while Al staggered down the trail to Khumjung, supported between two petite Sherpanis. I awoke in the middle of the night with such a weight on my chest that at first I thought maybe I was dead. Realizing otherwise, I staggered, head thumping like a jack-hammer, towards the toilet. In the dark I misjudged the position of the hole and slipped thigh-deep into excrement. It was not the best of nights.

There is one other very special household in Khumjung: that of Pasang and Chingdoma. Pasang, who had been our *sirdar* on Dhaulagiri, spent most of his time guiding small groups of trekkers in the Everest region.

Chingdoma ran a small tea house at the lower end of the village. She was from an upper-crust family in Namche Bazaar and once had been married to the wealthiest Sherpa in the village, but during the Chinese Cultural Revolution, he failed to return from a Tibetan trading trip—presumed killed. Later she married Pasang, who was quite a bit younger than she.

Chingdoma had real breeding and class, and she was very religious. Whenever Lorna traveled around Khumbu and I was away climbing, she would always stay with Chingdoma. Together they would visit the Saturday market in Namche, collect mushrooms in the nearby woods or walk round the nearby Mani walls.

Chingdoma always seemed to be the brains of the family. I remember once she was having a discussion with Pasang after an American man had given him a big tip: enough money to buy a yak, the symbol of old Sherpa wealth. When Pasang returned with two very small zukyuk half-breeds, Chingdoma teased him reproachfully. Their conversation—in Sherpa, of course—went something like this:

"They look so small, Pasang," said Chingdoma.

"Yes, but two for the price of one!" claimed Pasang.

"Two halves for the price of one, you mean. What are we going to do when the man comes to see what you bought? We'll take these two animals up to your uncle's for the week and borrow the biggest yak we can from him. We'll pretend you bought that!"

While Sherpa men often have dealings with Westerners on treks or expeditions, the Sherpanis tend to be more traditional. Girls in their teens spend a lot of the monsoon season tending yaks in the high pastures. A group of three or four from the same village will live in a small stone shelter with a tarp for a roof. They seem to be quite self-reliant and live off potatoes and yak milk.

Some of the girls carry firewood or help their mothers at small tea shops for trekkers. Late summer is the time of grass-cutting, which is so important to the family that everyone helps. The grass is stored as fodder for their animals during the winter.

Someone like Pema, with his status and degree of wealth, tends to hire people or let his sisters-in-law do this kind of work, while he stays home and makes home-improvements. A lot of *chang* is drunk during this time.

Older women head the households in their men's absence, and the gossiping that takes place is amazing. Tagging along behind a group of Sherpanis as they climb the long hill after the Saturday market, one can learn who is on which expedition; which young girl has become engaged to which highly eligible *sirdar*; and precise information about the updated price of *zee* stones (semiprecious stones held in high esteem by Sherpas and Tibetans: $3,500 per stone at present).

One bright, sunny morning, an ecstatic Pasang was painting the outside of wooden window-frames with paint—red, white and blue!—we had brought from Kathmandu as a gift. Chingdoma was making instant coffee (a drink highly prized by the Sherpas), while Lorna and I pored over a map.

Suddenly Lorna asked: "Chingdoma, you want to go trekking?"

Chingdoma seemed suprised. Older Sherpanis don't go trekking—at least, not the ones she knew, and she knew hundreds.

"Trekking where, Lorna?" She didn't say no.

"Maybe Buri Gandaki, maybe Gorkha," said Lorna. "Pasang can be *sirdar* and Chingdoma 'member'."

"Chingdoma 'member'?" She giggled like a young girl. "Maybe?"

We all laughed, pleased with the idea. Chingdoma explained that she would tell everyone she was just visiting Kathmandu. There would be no mention of trekking; otherwise, the villagers would think she'd lost her marbles.

*Chingdoma*

It was decided. She and Pasang would join us in Kathmandu and accompany us on a ten-day trek from Gorkha to Trisuli Bazaar. We would take a high-level route we had seen on the map. There would be no direct purpose to the trek other than getting to see some wild parts of Nepal. It would be as if a spider had wandered with inky legs across our map and would become known as the "Especial Trek."

Those ten days were a real treat. Pasang hired a small porter staff, so we only had to carry a day-pack with camera and waterproofs. I marveled at Chingdoma, who had told us her hip had been acting up a bit lately. She hiked up and down the long hills in a brisk, gay manner, asking questions of everyone she met and then filling us in on the details.

"Lorna, *diddi*," Chingdoma said. "I tell them we are on hike for Buddha. See many *gompa* (monastery)."

In a country with so few roads, everybody walks almost everywhere they go. But they always have a reason. To them, going hiking for hiking's sake would seem a worthless pastime. Chingdoma always giggled at the idea. She was enjoying the subterfuge.

We arrived at the steep bank of the muddy, swirling waters of the Buri Ghandaki. There was no bridge, only a thin steel cable stretched between large trees on the river banks. A small wooden box hung suspended from a pulley. The whole thing looked pretty shaky, but it was our only choice.

By tossing a sisal cord, I fetched the contraption to our side of the river. Then I gently eased myself into a sitting position in the box. The next thing I knew I was barreling across the wire! With the river a hundred feet below! The huge tree-anchor was hurtling toward me when a horrible realization struck home: I'll break both legs! How stupid of me not to foresee that! I braced for impact, feet high. The cable sagged a tad, then some more. And I glided gently onto the landing platform with a long exhalation of previously-held breath. The wonders of Nepal!

I sent the box back over, and Chingdoma settled herself in for the ride. Although she may have been a bit apprehensive, she didn't let it show. I have a photo of her, mouth open in sheer delight as she swept across to my outstretched arms. It became known as the "Especial Bridge."

Over the years when Al and I would be sitting in the small tea garden of the Mustang Holiday Inn, Pema would breeze in, looking dapper in creased slacks and white shirt. He'd heard we were in town and had called around to drink a beer with us and update us on news and gossip.

Pema would tease Al fondly about his tight, revealing training pants: "So, Al, I see you still have same old trousers and same old change in the pockets!"

Or maybe the hotel gateman would come and fetch us, and there would be Chingdoma, palms held together in the form of *namaste* (greetings).

With sparkling eyes and bright face, she'd say: "*Namaste*, Adrian, Alan. Lorna here? I Kathmandu for big *lama* visit. Tomorrow I go Khumjung. Say Lorna *namaste*."

Her Buddhist energy was radiant.

*How could I ever forget these people?*

# CHAPTER
## *31*

## ALONE & ALIVE

BY ALAN

In the spring of 1991, I came to Nepal with the hope of climbing some peaks without permits. The last major expeditions I'd been on—the American Everest Expedition and the Colorado Manaslu Expedition, both in 1989—were highly organized, with complex logistics and a lot of people to think about. In such circumstances, it was always necessary to consider the sponsors and the media and what everyone else in the expedition was doing. I thought that those pressures didn't allow you to get close to the mountain, only to get high up for a few hours. The big expeditions were two months long, but their meaningful part lasted a very short time—only hours.

I arrived in Kathmandu, where my equipment was stored, and decided to go up into the Langtang region, an area north of Kathmandu with peaks between 20,000 and 23,000 feet. It takes a one-day bus ride and then four days of hiking to get to a place called Kyanjin Gompa at about 12,500 feet. The area is fairly heavily trekked, and there are tea shops and lodges throughout the region. The trekking starts in bamboo forests and progresses up into a region of Tibetans and Tamangs (which means "horse-traders"). The original people of the valley are thought to have been cavalry men for one of the first kings of Tibet. The valley is Tibetan in its culture, like many of Nepal's high valleys.

I arrived in Kyanjin Gompa with two duffel bags. One was full of my climbing gear—sleeping bag, boots, crampons, etc.—and the other was full of food. I hired a local guy named Dendu and told him I was going to go up the valley and cross over a pass heading south into the Helanbhu region. In fact, I had no intention of crossing that pass. I just didn't want Dendu to tell anyone that I was going to be climbing peaks without permits.

The first night out Dendu and I spent in a yak house. The second day we ran into crusty spring snow, and we were falling through to the knee. Dendu had only lightweight shoes, so I offered to pay him off. Before he left to go down valley, I told him I was going up onto the glacier and would spend a few days there. Although he'd seen some of my climbing equipment and I think was on to me, he was very good about it and, as far as I know, never said anything.

After Dendu left, I was totally alone. I was where I'd wanted to be for many months. I was curious to know how I'd react. Initially, I was nervous, not about solo climbing but simply about being alone, having no one to speak to and only my own thoughts. I didn't know how many days I was going to spend on the glacier, and I didn't know which peak I was going to climb.

So I just started. I began by ferrying the loads to the edge of the glacier. I spent one night there, and that first night I was a little nervous. I thought about animals. Other people might think about *yeti*, but I thought *wolf!* . . *bear!* Every time the wind ruffled the tent, I wondered *animal?*! I felt all the irrational fears that we Westerners carry around because we don't live close to nature.

I finally slept and woke up very early. I just sat around. I had no one else to consider. It was completely up to me. There was going to be no motivation from anyone else. I made tea and considered what to do. I decided to go up the glacier. I carried up the first load, knowing that I would come back to collect the second load, but I didn't know if I would come back that day or the day after.

I walked up the glacier. I didn't know what was around the corner. There were mountain walls on each side of the glacier, which was only about half a mile wide. There was a lot of rocky moraine and new snow, so I had to break trail. After about four hours, I reached a branch in the glacier, and I became interested in a peak on the left. Its name, if it had one, is insignificant; it could be any one of many peaks in the Himalaya. It was between 20,000 and 21,000 feet high and had snow and rock ridges.

After four hours, I dumped my load and retraced my trail. It was still only midday. I melted snow and made tea. Then I thought: What am I going to do all afternoon? Well, I can sit around and preserve my strength. But I don't feel tired. Why do I need to preserve my strength?

On big expeditions with a lot of other people, you preserve your strength because you have to climb with those people, and you don't want to have to stop and hold up anyone else. You don't want to be seen as less strong than others. You want to keep up.

But now it didn't matter. If I was tired, I'd just stop wherever I was. I could stop and sleep three days if I wished.

After an hour of sitting around, eating and having tea, I decided that I'd carry up the second load. So I packed a big load and went back up the glacier. This time it took me only three hours to get up to where I'd dumped my gear. I put up my tent and made some more tea. I was getting used to not speaking to anyone. I was having conversations with myself in my head.

At about four that afternoon, I made soup, ate and rested. Then I realized I still had three or four hours of daylight left. What am I going to do? Shall I just sit around? I didn't bring any books to read!

I saw a peak and thought I'd go have a look at its approach. I set off, breaking trail with snow to mid-calf. After two hours, I'd climbed 2,000 feet above my camp. I could see the final summit ridges and the steep technical ground up to the main peak. So I went on another hour and that took me up to the ridge. I realized all the ridges on the main peak were corniced. I wasn't going to climb up *them* by myself. If anything happened . . . !

I hadn't intended to climb that day, anyway. Originally I was going to do this reconnaissance the next day, but now I didn't need to. So I came back down, knowing that I wasn't going to climb that peak. It was almost dark. I ate and drank—and slept. This time I was on the glacier. I felt much easier the second night by myself.

I rested all the next day and just puttered around. I decided to climb the peak next to me, starting at midnight. But after I'd eaten, I thought: Why wait until midnight? It's five in the afternoon. I'll start climbing now. I'll take my sleeping bag, stove, a pan and a bit of food. When I've had enough hiking uphill toward the climb, I'll just bivouac out on the snow. I'll leave the tent where it is.

I planned to sleep on top of the snow, in my Gore-Tex sleeping bag. Two hours later, at seven o'clock, I was at the foot of the mountain, where it steepened. I had nothing else to do so I started moving up. I paced myself and covered a lot of ground because I never stopped. Then I saw an overhanging rock cliff with a flat ledge below it. I went there, I stamped out a ledge and put my sleeping bag down.

I still had an hour of daylight, the snow was melting, and I had no one to speak to . . . . So I started bouldering around on the overhanging rock. It felt really good to stretch my muscles and just play around on the rock. In the evening, a storm came in and it snowed until midnight—about 18 inches. I didn't have a tent, so it snowed straight on top of me as I lay in my sleeping bag. And it didn't matter! If I couldn't climb in the morning, I'd just go down. I had no pressure of any kind, except my own motivation to do what I wanted to do. I realized I didn't need to *achieve* anything. Just *being there* was what it was all about.

The climbing came naturally. It wasn't as if I had to deal with fears of climbing or not climbing. Climbing was instinctive. I just went out and climbed. I could climb at whatever time of day I wanted. I didn't have to follow the normal rules, which at least partially are rules of social conduct.

With the snow falling, I didn't expect to climb the next day. I slept warm, all covered up with only a tiny breathing hole for my mouth. I woke up at about five o'clock, just as it was coming light. I looked up and the sky was perfectly blue. It was going to be a great day! The storm had blown itself out.

I sat up, all covered with snow. I dug out myself and the stove and put snow in the cook-pot to melt. I decided just to sit there. I drank tea, ate something and waited. Finally I stood up and shook the snow off my sleeping bag. I cleaned my climbing gear, put it on and thought: The sun's going to come up. It'll get hot later. I stashed my gear under the rock cliff and looked up at the summit, which was about 2,000 feet above me.

I went across the glacier and started kicking steps up a ridge. It turned to hard ice. I got about 150 feet up this ice, and it felt kind of dicey. The ice was quite green and hard and was not taking crampons or ice tools very easily.

I felt a bit scared: I don't want to fall off! Particularly up here—nobody knows I'm here!

I kept my head and climbed back down again. I saw about a mile away another ridge that looked as if it had more snow on it. So I skirted big crevasses on the glacier and walked to the foot of a couloir. In ten minutes, I was up that couloir and onto the ridge that led all the way to the summit. At one point, I had to traverse the side of the ridge, across the face. I looked down and saw it was probably 3,000 feet into the valley on the other side.

I didn't have a rope with me. I was just very careful to make sure I could reverse anything I climbed up. I didn't want to end up stuck on top of a mountain without being able to climb back down. For the last 30 feet, I took off my crampons and climbed perfectly warm, dry granite rock. And there I was on top of a 20,000-foot peak! With all the mountains spread around me! I sat there for about 15 minutes.

Then I thought I'd better start back down before the snow began to soften. I reversed down the ridge, back down the couloir, onto the glacier and back to my camp. And it was still only about 9 o'clock in the morning. I packed up my gear, and in another hour of fast downhill walking, I reached my tent. Still only 10 o'clock and nothing to do. So I packed the rest of my gear, and three hours later I was back at the edge of the glacier, where the grass and the trail start. I brewed some tea and left some of my extra food on the rocks for the birds, because I didn't want to carry it. Then I set out to walk back to Kyanjin Gompa, with all my gear in one huge pack. That afternoon, another storm came in, blowing snow. I wasn't wearing my Gore-Tex jacket, and the snow stuck to me. But I kept steadily losing height, and by 7 o'clock that night I was back in Kyanjin Gompa.

Now I had to speak for the first time in a week. As I approached a little lodge, I practiced to see if I could still speak okay, because I didn't want to open my mouth and have only a croak come out. I went into the lodge, quiet and unshaven, and I wondered how I could relate to these people sitting all around: these teashop trekkers.

I stashed my gear. It was obvious I'd been climbing. People could sense it. I felt I had a slightly heightened sense—maybe floating a little from fatigue and hunger. I sat on one of the bunks and drank

Mustang coffee, which is a mixture of butter, sugar, instant coffee and a local alcoholic distillation. There were four guys, who turned out to be stock brokers from New York, and they were playing cards and being really noisy. I had to be compassionate and not judge them. They were having a good time, and they didn't know where I'd been. They had no idea that this morning I was on top of a 20,000-foot peak!

At about nine that night, a German guy burst into the lodge. He had on a head-torch, plastic boots, ski poles—he looked like a climber, moved like a climber. His name was Gunther. He said his friend was stuck on Ganchempo Peak at 20,000 feet.

Gunther told their story: The two of them had climbed the peak, but on the way down, his friend, Harold, had fallen and broken both legs below the knee. That was about five days ago. Gunther attempted one rescue with some Sherpas but had barely been able to reach Harold. Gunther had covered his friend with a tarp and left him food and stuff to make tea and soup, but he thought that the next time he went back, maybe he'd find only a body.

I said to him: "I'm a climber. Maybe I can help. What's the situation?"

Gunther replied: "There's a glacier and some steep ice, and Harold's above that on a snow shelf at 6,000 meters (about 20,000 feet). The last time, the Sherpas all started to get headaches. We only just managed to get up to touch Harold last time. No one was strong enough to help me bring him down. I didn't know how we could do it."

I said to him: "Look, this is what we'll do. I've got friends in Kathmandu. Tomorrow I'll radio them and get some Sherpas who are already acclimatized to come up here. I'll request medical equipment, fixed ropes and sufficient equipment to set up a base camp at the foot of the mountain. We can't use Kyanjin Gompa as the base, because it's four or five hours from here to the snowline and then, above that, another four hours to reach your friend."

The next morning I got on the radio to Kathmandu, and the morning after that, a helicopter arrived with three Sherpas who were just off a Cho Oyu expedition and could easily go to 20,000 feet. They brought some rope—not very much: about 800 feet—some ice-screws and some snow-stakes. They also brought big base-camp tents, a stove and more food.

We started walking up to a base camp at 14,000 feet; the helicopter refused to try to land at that elevation. It took one long day, with a heavy snowstorm in the afternoon, for Gunther, the Sherpas and me to get up to 14,000 feet. We'd also hired some local porters, who carried gear to the base camp and then went back down.

The next morning I had a hard time getting the Sherpas to leave early, but I knew that the sun was going to alter the snow drastically. Gunther and I set off, carrying all the climbing rope and ice hardware. The two of us climbed to the beginning of the steep ice, about two hours above the base camp. At that point, Gunther set off to solo up to his friend: to see him and get him ready by the time I arrived. I fixed rope across the 50-degree ice-and-snow slope, so that we could lower him back down it. The rope went diagonally up and across the face. It took two Sherpas a couple of hours to catch up. The other Sherpa was basically a kitchen boy, and he stayed in base camp.

I had soloed out, fixing rope every 60 or 70 feet with an ice-screw. The Sherpas came up the fixed-rope after me, and together we fixed the last 150 feet of rope up to the snow shelf. Harold and Gunther were there.

Harold was still alive, very dehydrated but very pleased. He thought that at last he had a chance of being rescued

I said to him: "Okay, here we are. We've got fixed rope all the way. We're going to start to move you."

One of Harold's legs had a simple fracture. The other had a compound fracture that had broken the skin, but because of the cold, sterile conditions, there was no infection yet. I splinted his legs by sticking ski poles down his legs and lashing them tightly. We didn't have a stretcher, so we wrapped him in a tarpaulin and then I did what is known as a Dutch-lacing: you tie him round with rope, starting with the toes and up to his chest and neck, so that the rope stabilizes and locks his legs together. Then we put a figure-of-eight on a central knot, so that we could begin to lower him down the slope.

I stayed up and belayed him down on a safety rope, while Gunther and the two Sherpas held him away from the slope and kept the rope from snagging. When we got lower, there was more snow over the surface, and we had to pull hard to get him to move down. Occasionally we'd have to jerk on the rope, and then Harold would shout and scream. We had no painkillers—they hadn't sent any first-aid equipment from Kathmandu. If I'd had morphine, I could have given him that, and it would have helped a lot. I kept hoping that Harold would pass out from the pain, and then we could get him down faster. It took us about four hours to get him down to the bottom of the fixed ropes. The snow was deep, and it all was very exhausting. The Sherpas said it was going to get dark and they had to get down themselves.

I shouted at them: "Look, guys! We've got to get him down halfway, because tomorrow I want him all the way off the ice."

I realized that Harold had to spend one more night on the glacier, but at least we got him off the steep ground. Gunther bivouacked alongside his friend. The two Sherpas and I went back down to the base camp, where our sleeping bags were.

The next morning I again couldn't get Sherpas out of bed. They weren't sympathetic with Harold. The only thing they were interested in was how much money they were going to make off the rescue. I climbed quickly back up the glacier and arrived just after the sun came up.

The snow was frozen hard. So the first thing I did was take off the rope around the tarpaulin and put just a single loop around Harold's waist so that I could slide him more easily. Between Gunther and me, we slid Harold as quickly as possible down the snowfield on the glacier. He just skimmed along the surface on the frozen snow. Halfway down the glacier, we came to this enormous crevasse. I belayed Harold into the bottom of the crevasse onto this snow bridge. Then I created a pulley-system on the lower edge of the crevasse and winched him up. At one point, I saw his toes bang into the ice, and he screamed. I felt the pain; it went right through me.

After the crevasse, we began sliding Harold down the lower part of the glacier. The snow was getting soft now. Occasionally on the steeper sections, I would belay him. By about two in the afternoon, we had him down into an area that was warmer and drier, where there were pools of snowmelt water.

As the snow melted in the afternoon, we were sinking in up to our thighs. At that point, I said the snow was way too deep to move Harold any more. I told them I'd run back to Kyanjin Gompa and bring back local porters and a ladder from the cheese factory next door to the monastery. Then we'd lash Harold onto the ladder, using it as a stretcher, and carry him down.

Again I left Gunther with Harold, and I set off and ran all the way back to Kyanjin Gompa. It took me only three hours to get back. I spent all the next day trying to find porters. Finally I had to send down to Langtang village to get porters with boots who would go up into the snow. The following day we started back up. I was hoping that Harold was still going to be okay. The local Tamang men were very compassionate. They understood. They really wanted to help save this man's life. They were running up the hill, shuttling the long aluminum ladder.

We reached Harold and Gunther by midday. As soon as I arrived, Gunther came over to me and said quietly: "I don't think he's doing very well. He's been vomiting black fluid. I think it's a result of the antibiotics I've been giving him. He's very, very dehydrated. I don't know if he's going to make it."

I went over to Harold. The look in his eyes was one of complete trust; he trusted us absolutely to get him off the mountain. Because we'd brought him down to a warmer, less sterile environment, he was starting to get an infection in his open wound on the leg with the compound fracture. We increased the antibotic dosage to counter that, but he was getting very dehydrated. I was very concerned about renal failure. I put my hand on his forehead and felt his fever. I tried to will some kind of stength into him, knowing that all he had to do is survive a few more days. He'd lost so much weight and was so dehydrated.

As we had him sipping water, I told him: "Look, you are going to live! You are definitely going to live! There is no doubt about it! Don't start even to think anything else! I can feel that your fever is already beginning to go down. Let's go!"

Now that we had the rigid ladder, I was able to strap down Harold under his armpits and stretch his legs a bit under tension. On the way down, there was another snowstorm, with snowflakes the size of quarters. Yet it was still warm enough that we were falling in up to the crotch in deep snow. But everybody was so concerned about Harold that we just kept moving.

It was dark when we got down to the main valley, where there was easier ground again. All the porters opted to stay with Harold that night under an overhanging boulder, and they laid a big fire to try to keep him warm. The porters were really into looking after him: a clear example of compassion in people of that region.

I ran ahead to Kyanjin Gompa to radio and get the helicopter for the next morning. By 8 o'clock that morning, the porters had carried Harold to Kyanjin Gompa, and an hour later Harold and Gunther were inside the helicopter and away they went to Kathmandu.

Three days later I arrived back in Kathmandu and got in touch with Gunther, who told me where Harold was—at the Kathmandu Clinic, under the care of a bone doctor who'd been trained in the States. The people at the clinic knew what they were doing. They had antibiotic drips in him to stabilize him so he could be sent back to Germany.

I shook Harold's hand and asked him how he was. He held onto my hand and wouldn't let go. He kept saying: "Thank you. If it hadn't been for you, I would have died. You're a good friend."

I sat and we chatted. I found out that both Harold and Gunther came from Munich.

"Ah, Munich!" I said. "So you must know the Kaisergebirge. Maybe next year I'll come through Germany, call you in Munich and we'll go climbing together. So get that leg better and I'll see you next year!"

I wrote to him later. I never heard from him. He must have lost my address.

In the spring of 1994, I was up in Langtang, for the first time since the rescue. Everybody remembered me as the guy who'd helped rescue the German climber. Apparently Harold had written in the fall of '93 to one of the Sherpas up there and said that things were going fine. I still don't know what the truth is. One guy told me that Harold was perfectly okay, but another guy said that one of his legs had to be amputated below the knee.

That time in the Langtang region in 1991 was a learning experience for me. It taught me that being solitary in the mountains is worth it. It's worth every risk! It also taught me how fragile the line is between ego-driven curiosity and tragedy for the rest of your life. If I had not been climbing by myself, I could not have felt as compassionate toward Harold as I did. Suddenly for him everything had gone wrong. It was an ecstasy-and-agony situation, as if one exists only because the other also exists.

I hope someday I get a postcard from Harold.

# *CHAPTER*
## *32*

## CLIMBING THOUGHTS

BY ADRIAN

After more than thirty years of climbing, it's natural that things have changed. But not as many as might be expected. A day doesn't go by when I'm not out climbing on rocks or ice, or making plans for a future trip.

I live only forty minutes outside Salt Lake City, and I'm happily spoiled by my choices. I can climb frozen waterfalls in the morning, rock-climb on south-facing canyon walls in the afternoon and then maybe ski for an hour before heading to the hot whirlpool at the local health club. Of course, I would rarely string all these things together, but it would be easily possible.

Then there are office-days when files come out, budgets are checked, sponsors are called and manufacturers are contacted.

"We need to lengthen the leg by two inches and widen the articulations in the knee," I tell Titoune Bouchard, who is helping put together some clothing ideas we're working on. I met her in Peru a few days after our Huascaran climb in 1977.

The phone rings, and it's Dave Pompel from Reebok Outdoors.

"Aid," he says, "how does the seventeenth of February look for you to go to Barcelona?"

"Barcelona?" I'm sure I sounded surprised.

"Yes," says Dave. "The International Sales Conference. Can you do your Everest slide-presentation?"

"Sure."

"Oh, and put the twenty-fifth through the twenty-seventh of September on your calender. Reebok U.K. wants you to do a show there at the Harrogate trade show."

"Great! I'll be able to celebrate my forty-fifth birthday in a real pub!"

"You're getting old, Aid."

"Yeah, I know. I can only climb five-eleven."

And so the days go by.

As climbing becomes more mainstream and the number of climbers increases, the separation between climbing disciplines widens. There are people who enjoy climbing on artificial walls and look no further, and there are mountaineers who couldn't climb a piece of rock if a wild yak was chasing them. Then there are others who need the vast spectrum of climbing.

I'm certainly one of the latter group. It's a wonderful feeling to push even a tiny piece of the planet down beneath one's feet. If it's overhanging plastic, it's going to pump the arms like bloated sausages; if it's a steep snow-slope at 27,000 feet, it's going to deaden the legs and make the lungs heave like overworked bellows. Either way, the challenges are obvious.

To travel lightly through large mountains, among the local people with their different religions and codes of behavior: I find this fascinating. But I spoke recently with a well-known Himalayan climber who hated what he called the "bullshit" of getting to the mountain.

After the Gulf War, we were planning a climb in Pakistan, and the American Information Office was giving out gloom-and-doom travel briefings. Any Islamic country was deemed a dangerous place for Americans, and Pakistan was one of them. Pakistani mercenaries had fought alongside Iraqis, even though Pakistan was officially pro-U.N.

People began asking me if we were going to cancel the trip until it was safe, and my answer was always the same: "There's no problem in Pakistan. The locals are great, and the Baltis are wonderful. You just have to look at things their way."

I decided to take a copy of the *Koran* (*Qur'an*) with me and make it available to anyone who wished it. Though the Baltis cannot read it—especially as it's written in Arabic—our liaison officer could, and he would read portions to the cook. When our porters heard that the expedition carried the *Qur'an*, it brought out the very best in them, because although they are simple people, they are honest and devout.

I remember walking into Askole village and pausing next to a huddle of seated grey-haired men. Suddenly, one of them sprung to his feet with a shout: "Leader! Leader! *A salaam aleikum!*" And he gave me a big hug.

I recognized him from three years before. He'd been sitting in the same place and had done the same thing. Then he had been too old to act as a porter, but he reminded me that he had worked for our 1986 K2 expedition.

As I looked into his weary blue eyes, he said poignantly: "*Sahib* is still strong. Now I am old man. Good luck on mountain!"

I shook his hand, bowed my head and said: "*A salaam aleikum.* I worship the greatness in you."

If I'm not traveling, I like to spend weekends with Lorna. Her high-pressured work as an immigration attorney keeps her very busy all week. She comes home with stories of helping famous musicians, eccentric scientists or maybe a well-known horse trainer. I marvel at how she is able to combine the lifestyles of professional and wanderer. How she can feel comfortable attired in the finest of silks or sleeping on the floor of a Tibetan monastery while rats play around her? She puts up with my long absences without complaint. Not many wives would.

On weekends we may go hiking in the high Uintas or rock-

*Adrian near his home in Utah*

climbing in Little Cottonwood Canyon, but at some point we'll definitely ride the horses. The old Union Pacific railway line is only minutes from our house. It's been converted into a hiking-biking-riding trail, the "Rail Trail," which goes eighteen miles in each direction from our home.

Once in the saddle, astride a long-legged Thoroughbred, I'm hooked: an adrenaline junkie. These animals are true atheletes. Never holding back from giving their best, they exhibit an honesty too rarely found in modern sport. Miles are gobbled up beneath their hooves. Flecks of snot and foam fly from flaring nostrils and stick like white paint on my face. Sometimes we'll be moving so fast that I'm sure the horse will roll, as its long, muscled neck reaches forward, wanting to take it to the limit.

✧   ✧   ✧   ✧

In the world of Alpine and Himalayan climbing, you have to be careful not always to try to take it to the limit. It seems to me that the "limit" is a finite place; once crossed, there's no return, just as there is no stopping a horse that is about to tumble. The problem with climbing on very big mountains is that dangers lurk everywhere. Once you've been on a number of expeditions, you begin to recognize when you're "running out of steam." If you always remember that you need enough energy to descend the mountain, accidents can be avoided. It's the small, less obvious dangers that can finish you.

On the first climbing day during an expedition to Gasherbrum II, I was climbing with Paul Moores. We began to move up the icefall as dawn broke. Early morning light sparkled off fresh snow as I broke a trail around small ice-walls and larger gaping holes. We were roped together by a 70-foot length of eight-millimeter rope. Occasionally we'd belay each other if the way looked tricky, but generally we'd move simultaneously.

Everything was progressing without a hitch. There had been no dead-ends, no wasting of time. Within ten minutes, we'd been through the first major obstacle. There was an obvious wide, snow-covered crevasse before me. So belayed carefully by Paul, I wormed my way on my belly. Then I stood and plugged a trail up a gentle rise toward a high crest, where I could see the final part of the route. I was examining the route when an almighty tug snapped me backwards off my feet and I began falling.

I knew immediately that Paul had fallen into the crevasse. I drew my legs and arms together into a ball, trying to create drag in the snow. Still, I didn't stop.

"Here we go!" leaped into my mind just before I halted at the brink of the crevasse. Paul's entire two hundred pounds hung from my waist, pulling me down into a groove at the edge of the crevasse. I lay motionless, knowing that any slight movement on my part and the falling might begin again. I also knew that two friends, Johann and Mickey, were not far behind.

I waited and waited. It seemed an eternity. Where were they? Time was standing still and so, it seemed, were they. Then time resumed and I heard a shout: "Aid! What is it?"

I replied in the kind of squeezed voice that uses air from the very bottom of the lungs: "Paul's in the hole! Get a rope down to him quick!"

Minutes passed. Suddenly the overwhelming weight was gone.

We were lucky. I had a deep crampon gash in my calf, and Paul looked as if he'd gone five rounds with Muhammad Ali. But we were safe.

Paul was shaking as he held out a gloved hand: "Thanks for saving my life, Aid."

I held his hand, grinned and replied: "That isn't why I stopped." Or was it ?

*Pulling Paul Moores out of a crevasse on Gasherbrum II*

# *EPILOGUE*
## Dispatches from K2

*While this book was being prepared for publication, Adrian and Alan Burgess were in the People's Republic of China, with Adrian as leader of the 1994 Reebok International K2 North Ridge Expedition. The route is one of the most challenging on K2, the world's second highest mountain at 28,250 feet (8,611 meters).*

*The expedition included four other climbers from the West—Alan Hinkes, Brad Johnson, Paul Moores and Mark Wilford—and five Sherpa climbers. On April 26, 1994, a truck carrying the expedition's supplies and the Sherpas left Kathmandu, Nepal, on the long overland trip to the trailhead in China. On May 1, the six climbers flew to Kashgar (the westernmost city in China) via Lhasa, Chengdu and Urumqi.*

*Using a solar-powered laptop-computer with FAX capability, Adrian sent—via satellite—regular reports from K2.*

## 17 MAY

Mobile No.492900027    Ocean Region:Indian    17 May'94 15:06 UTC

We arrived at base camp (12,600 feet) yesterday afternoon, after a seven-day walk through arid mountain landscape with 47 camels and a few donkeys. The rivers are now quite low because of cold weather, and we had no problems.

Today the weather is perfect. Our plan is to carry many loads toward our final base camp at 16,600. We purchased two donkeys to help with the loads. Tomorrow we all will carry onto the glacier, with loads between 50 and 70 pounds, depending if human or donkey. The surrounding fauna consists of wild asses, wolves, snow leopards and snow chickens. Why did we bring all this food? The camels have returned. We are alone.

Our flight from Kathmandu to Lhasa took us past awesome views of Everest and Makalu. When we finally reached Kashgar, an important town on the Silk Road, we stayed in a small hotel that reminded us of bygone colonial days. Then we drove by Jeep over some of the most bone-jarring roads imaginable. I didn't know whether to sit on the cushion or put it on my head. This trip took us three days, during which we crossed three passes, one more than 16,000 feet high.

We reached the Chinese Army camp of Maza at the roadhead. It reminded me of a prison in the middle of Death Valley. The soldiers were great, very hospitable. But our truck had not arrived from its long journey from Kathmandu. We imagined every possibility—from crashes to hijacking. All we could do is trust our Sherpas and wait. And wait. They finally rumbled into camp, covered in twelve days' worth of dust and wearing huge grins and dirty Reebok jackets.

So here we are, all healthy and primed to go. But we take one step at a time.

We dream of English beer. Ah, well.

## 20 May

Mobile No.492900027    Ocean Region:Indian    20 May'94 09:35 UTC

We are carrying gear and food up to our final base camp. It will take us ten full days to get into position below the route. Every day we carry about 55 pounds each over rough terrain: loose boulders and rocks, icy stream beds and abrasive dry ice. There could not be better test for rugged footwear. Among us, we're wearing four different styles of Reebok footwear, and we're all happy with our choices.

The mountain has appeared a number of times, always with a strong wind-plume from the summit. The route is awesome. It looks even better than in photos. On first seeing it, everyone was in awe. We're all very excited to be here and cannot wait to get to grips with the real climbing. In the meantime, we get stronger and stronger, just humping loads.

While I'm typing this on a laptop, my brother and Paul are busy setting up a promotional shot for Lagavulin malt whisky. The bottle is dangerously close to my sensitive nose. I may have to sign off soon. The home-brew will not be ready for a month.

## 31 MAY

Mobile No.492900027    Ocean Region:Indian    31 May '94 08:28 UTC

Yesterday we arrived in our high base camp at 16,600 feet and set up the tents. Paul and Mark went ahead three days ago and made a route to Camp 1 (19,000 feet) in only two days. It took 13 days of nonstop load-carrying by all six climbers and five Sherpas to reach high base camp. We all agreed that it was one of the most exacting and arduous times we had ever spent in the mountains.

Every day we carried loads of between 55 and 70 pounds of food and equipment for four hours over glacial moraine, boulder slopes and glaciers strewn with sharp, flinty stone debris. We returned with empty packs, ready for the next day.

All that time we wore Reebok hiking shoes. My brother Alan wore the lighter-weight Cliffhangers, and they held together amazingly well—not a worn seam or hole anywhere.

Last night the weather turned bad, with high winds sweeping across our route and dumping fresh snow. This has forced a few well-earned rest-days until the weather improves. We are very comfortable, with one Ferrino dome-tent per climber and a luxurious cooking/dining tent also made by Ferrino. This last tent is so strong it's like living in a castle at the foot of the mountain.

And what of K2? Its North Face is so close it towers over the whole valley. It's the only real mountain we can see, and is VERY, VERY CLOSE! The entire 12,000-foot wall begins a mile from my tent. It commands our attention. I've never seen anything like it.

# 3 JUNE

Mobile No.492900027     Ocean Region:Indian     3 June'94 5:44 UTC

The weather has been quite good and has enabled quick progress. Yesterday we managed to reach halfway to Camp 2 (21,800 feet). The climbing is on steep, hard and glassy ice set at 50-55 degrees. The ice is so hard that we've been bending steel ice-pitons. Mark and Paul were leading 500-foot runouts on this stuff. Not for the faint-hearted!

Today we have been loading Camp 1 with food, tents, etc., getting ready to move up and live there. The camp is tucked beneath a 20-foot ice-cliff which protects it from avalanches and falling rocks.

Today we watched as three climbers stood at the foot of the face when a big avalanche broke loose 2,000 feet above them. It rumbled down the face but well out of their way—confirming our choice of route. It had a few hearts racing.

Our main problem is trying to keep enough supplies up at high base camp to be able to keep climbing day after day. All of us—six climbers and five Sherpas—carried loads between 50-80 pounds every day for thirteen days before moving up into it. It was some of the most grueling work any of us has ever done. If anybody ever asks me how we trained for this climb, I can only say: "By pretending to be a moving company!"

The Reebok boots were all great. So much use over such rough terrain. What a test!

Two days ago the first batch of beer was prepared and is fermenting nicely under the eye of Phrua, a Sherpa who has done this before on other expeditions. We expect to celebrate the setting up of Camp 3 in a few weeks, weather permitting—that is, if it's warm enough to finish the fermentation.

# 9 JUNE

Mobile No.492900027    Ocean Region:Indian    9 June '94 09:40 UTC

Since our last report, we have had a big snowstorm, which put a foot of snow at base camp. The weather then cleared, and we watched avalanches pour off the mountain in huge blasts. After a day of sunshine, most of the fresh snow had slid from K2's icy flanks, and we went into action again.

Paul and Mark continued to try to complete their task of fixing rope to Camp 2, which meant they slept at Camp 1 and worked from there. The other climbers continued with the less glamorous task of ferrying equipment up to Camp 1. We carry about 25 pounds per person, plus food and drink for the day.

Climbing up to Camp 1 involves traveling up a snow-covered glacier for about two hours. There are crevasses to cross—we have marked the big ones with marker wands and fluorescent tape. A fall into one of these would be fatal, if the climber is unroped. After the glacier, we follow snow and ice slopes angled at 45-55 degrees, much steeper than the most difficult ski slopes. There are a number of unstable and impassable séracs—ice-cliffs from which the occasional "grand-piano" will peel off. We zigzag around these as best we can and then cross two steeper ice sections (70 degrees) to Camp 1.

Meanwhile, Mark and Paul have reached a height of 20,500 feet. The climbing was on hard, glassy ice and could prove to be the most technical climbing on the route.

In late afternoon two days ago, a huge sérac collapsed above and to the right of their position. Mark said he saw a block begin to tilt and very gently tip outwards. It was the size of a five-story building! It roared down to their right about a hundred yards away.

Our route is safe from these dangers, but we get a front-row seat for the action. The avalanche collected a lot of the fresh snow. From base camp, it appeared to scour the lower part of our route. There was no debris at the bottom, and we can only assume it was mainly wind and air-borne powder.

We will always give fresh snow 24 hours to consolidate after a storm and then move quickly through the lower part of the route. Last night the weather deteriorated again, and we are once more awaiting an opportunity for action.

Our home-brew beer is aging in its own keg. Maybe after the next bout of action, we'll sample the K2 Cliffhanger Ale from the highest brewery in China. Yum! Yum!

# 14 JUNE

Mobile No.492900027    Ocean Region:Indian    14 June'94 08:05 UTC

It has stormed heavily since the last message. We're a day of rope-fixing away from Camp 2. All gear, etc., is in Camp 1, waiting to be moved up to the new camp at 21,800 feet. For the past seven days we've had very poor weather, with a foot of fresh snow at base camp and blasting winds. It takes only minutes for any trace of footprints to be whisked away. We stayed huddled in our tents, waiting for an improvement.

In the poor visibility of the storm, we listen to the avalanches booming all around us, wondering where they're coming from and sometimes feeling the icy blast of the wind created by these monsters. Our route is plastered with snow. It will take one full day of sunshine to remove the excess snow and make it safe once more.

The sun broke just through for a few minutes. Mark informed me that the tents at Camp 1 cannot be seen and the entire ledge is filled with snow. It looks like a lot of digging when we finally return to the mountain. You need a lot of patience for this climbing game.

Thank goodness for the big Ferrino tent, which allows us all to get together and sample the freshly-made keg of K2 Cliffhanger Ale. It is very passable.

## 22 *June*

Mobile No.492900027    Ocean Region:Indian    22 June'94 10:21 UTC

The weather has changed 180 degrees. We are now in our seventh day of clear, sunny weather. Yesterday after a concerted effort by the whole team, we reached Camp 2 at 21,800 feet—about halfway up the face. We already have about 70 pounds of equipment in Camp 2 and will move up to sleep there in the next few days.

The route between Camps 1 and 2 is steep ice, comparable in difficulty and length to the major alpine ice-climbs. The 5,000 feet of climbing is so strenuous that we need to take a rest-day between climbing-days. Even so, it is like doing a major alpine climb every other day—something I'd rarely do in the Alps.

I have been wearing the new Reebok mountaineering boot and have good reports about it. It's very warm, as I discovered during the last snowstorm with its cold powder snow.

Our next objective is to reach Camp 3 at 25,000 feet. This means living at Camp 2 and fixing rope beyond it. I expect we'll have more bad weather before we can reach Camp 3. In fact, I'm downright distrustful of K2 weather that lasts more than five days. But we'll see. It's a matter of achieving small but significant goals and then adding them all together to create something more.

Everyone is in good health and good spirits and pushing themselves hard in the team effort. That itself is significant when meshing six such individualistic and highly-motivated persons as the climbers on our team. It must be the promise of a glassful (or more) of the latest K2 Cliffhanger brew! Such is the place where bribery and reward cross.

## 27 JUNE

Mobile No.492900027    Ocean Region:Indian    27 June'94 07:40 UTC

With our loads already at Camp 2, we were getting ready to go live up there when a wet-snow slide flattened a tent in Camp 1 and battered another. Hinkes managed to scramble out of his tent just in time. Once the avalanche was over, I found him dressed only in underwear and buried to his knees in snow that had set solid and trapped him. Not a pretty sight at 19,000 feet!

It was time to rethink how to site Camp 1, so we dug a bomb-proof ice-cave for six people. Now any avalanches will pass overhead, and we'll never again have to worry about smashed tents at this site.

Though the good weather has ended and the barometric pressure is down, we will still be trying to fix rope above Camp 2 in the coming days. Two other expeditions—Spanish and Italian—have come into the area and will be climbing near us. We've had to negotiate with them on the use of our fixed ropes, as it's obvious they would like to take advantage of all our work. The Spanish will carry some rope for us to fix higher. The Italians will fix their own rope. Otherwise, we will remain separate—mainly for safety, as far as I'm concerned.

The mountain boots are working well—somehow they seem to be breathing. They've created a lot of curiosity from other expedition climbers.

# 3 July

Mobile No.492900027     Ocean Region:Indian     3 July'94 08:34 UTC

Paul and Mark fixed 2,000 feet of rope above Camp 2. It goes over much rubble and loose rock. They followed the general direction of the North Ridge but stayed on the right flank most of the time.

Because of the dry season and lack of the usual snow that bonds everything together, crossing this area is like balancing on eggshells. Hinkes, Paul and I, loaded with extra ropes, went back up to the high point, and I was appalled at how unstable everything is. Blocks balance on blocks and various "grand-pianos" teeter, waiting for their final chords. Our main problem with all this is that anything dislodged goes bounding down the steep ice-fields between Camps 1 and 2.

Before we could do any more work, the weather turned foul, and now we've returned to base camp. Most of the materiel, food and fuel we require for high on the mountain is now in Camp 2, so now we travel fairly lightly to that point.

The steep ice between Camp 1 and Camp 2 is a continual irritation to our nerves, with ice-screw anchors frequently melting out and stonefall a constant hazard in the afternoon. Though we have now doubled our ropes in these areas, we are constantly discovering new cuts and nicks in the ropes' sheaths. To be caught out on the steep, watery ice, with a helicopter-like whir and hum signaling a fresh salvo of falling rocks, can make the stoutest calves turn to jelly. Two of our climbers have climbed the North Face of the Eiger, which is renowned for its rockfall, and they tell me the Eiger's nothing compared with what we have to face on an almost daily basis.

So once again we're at the mercy of the weather, and with no more beer, I'll have to brew the final batch.

# *8 July*

```
Mobile No.492900027    Ocean Region:Indian    8 July'94 11:38 UTC
```

Today Brad Johnson and Alan Hinkes reached the site of Camp 3 at an approximate height of 25,000 feet. The route from Camp 2 to Camp 3 takes about six hours on a mixture of rock and ice.

The weather is fair at the moment, but the pressure has dropped and we've had morning cloud. There could be another slight break in the weather, and they will probably descend for a rest tomorrow. They can come down below Camp 2 only in the morning before the rockfall begins.

If the weather picks up again after a few days, then we might be able to try for the summit in the next two weeks. I wouldn't try to forecast a day, but it's getting to that time on the expedition.

What would I give for fish and chips . . . .

## 11 JULY

Mobile No.492900027    Ocean Region:Indian    11 July'94 06:59 UTC

Last night the weather broke, and it snowed a dusting. We'll be waiting in base camp to go back up, set up Camp 3, lay rope to Camp 4 and maybe try a summit bid.

It's been a long, hard grind to this point, what with all the problems low down on the mountain, like ice-screws melting out in the afternoons and the ropes freezing into the ice at nights. Sometimes we'll be jumaring a rope that's sunk into the ice and pulling like crazy to release it, only to discover that once it's free, the anchor we're swinging on is barely in the ice. It's tricky stuff.

The stonefall is another hazard. The rocks are so big that they sound like helicopters as they whir by us. If I ever hear a chopper back home, I'll probably dive under a table.

The situation is not improved by more climbing teams on the same route. They swing on, and use, our ropes and kick off rocks all the time. As if the mountains weren't dangerous enough, you have to see a cavorting Italian to understand the real meaning of danger.

I decided that we have about three weeks of endurance and power left, so I've asked for the camels to collect us at the end of the month—three weeks earlier than planned. This should give us enough time for the summit without allowing it to be too drawn-out an affair.

Natually, we'll need some luck with weather, but it's been an exceptional year in that respect—even if it has turned the mountain into a bowling alley.

## *16 JULY*

Mobile No.492900027    Ocean Region:Indian    16 July'94 05:46 UTC

We've just had a week of bad weather when we couldn't even see the mountain. Today it's begun to clear, so we can again plan to go onto the mountain. I think it will be the last attempt, as one's strength cannot last forever.

The length of the expedition and all the hard work and dangers have finally begun to tell upon our team. A couple of days ago, Paul Moores, Mark Wilford and brother Alan decided they had enough of all the former and asked if they could go out and assure the arrival of the camels. They had all worked really hard, and I could understand their situation. No animosity; just burned out.

So we are now three in base camp. But with the rope out to 25,000 feet, there is still hope. This has been a really difficult climb on a route that is usually tackied by much bigger groups—or "piggy-backed" by small groups following larger ones.

Since we were the first team on the mountain, all the lower-level work has fallen on our shoulders, and subsequent arrivals have been able to take advantage of this. Maybe this is the fate of many Karakoram and Himalayan climbs. where the national tourism/mountaineering department tries to get as many teams as possible onto a climb because of increased revenue.

I'll let you know how things go.

# 21 JULY

Mobile No.492900027    Ocean Region:Indian    21 July'94 06:11 UTC

In the last six days, there has been quite a lot of activity on the mountain. Unfortunately for me, when I went to low base camp to arrange the exit of the three members (the liaison officer will only deal with the expedition leader), I lost the opportunity to spend more time in Camp 2 and go to Camp 3 for acclimatization purposes. This has hampered my personal acclimatization process, and I realized I was not ready to try for the summit when the weather came good.

Brad was also sick in base camp with swollen glands in the neck and sore throat. This left Alan Hinkes as the only person fit and acclimatized enough to try a summit bid. He therefore decided to tag along with the Spanish team, which was also moving up.

The first day (17 July) he went to Camp 2, and then the next day they were moving up fixed ropes for Camp 3 when a major accident occurred. Five minutes in front of Hinkes, a 27-year-old Spanish climber pulled on an old rope and it broke. He fell 250 feet down the slope, breaking his forearm and three ribs and may have a spinal fracture in the lumbar region.

Hinkes eventually continued on to join two other Spanish climbers in Camp 3. The injured climber was evacuated down the mountain by three of his teammates. This was a long, involved rescue operation down thousands of feet on our fixed ropes. They were all lucky that the ropes and anchors were substantial and in good repair. They finally arrived in base camp at 1:30 a.m. on 19 July. The injured climber is in stable condition in base camp.

That same day, two Spaniards fixed rope to Camp 4 (26,000 feet), while Hinkes rested in Camp 3. On 19 July, it snowed in the night, and because of the storm conditions, Hinkes decided to descend to Camp 2. One of the Spaniards went to base camp, and the stronger one remained at Camp 3.

That's the situation at present, except now the weather has become good again, and climbers will begin to ascend again within 24 hours. Because all the climbers have access to fixed rope, no one is in serious danger, unless they screw up like the Spanish lad.

Although climbers may seem to be all over the mountain, it's their personal preference as to where they can best rest. Obviously, there's all kinds of possibilities. So we'll wait and see. We're in touch with all climbers by radio.

## 22 JULY

Mobile No.492900027    Ocean Region:Indian    22 July'94 09:53 UTC

Thought I'd give you some sponsor feedback. Primaloft is brilliant stuff. The sleeping bags we're using on the mountain are very warm, despite not looking that thick; I found them too warm when I was wearing clothing inside them at 22,000 feet. They dry out very quickly. I don't think they weigh any more than a down bag of equal warmth.

I think the most important discovery of the value of Primaloft is in my special inner boots. I have never before worn a double plastic boot that did not sweat on the inside and hold moisture within the inner. This one certainly does not. The other day when our guys and some Spaniards were sitting around, I took the boot off and showed them the lack of moisture. They could hardly believe it. So where did the moisture go? I've no idea unless it wicks out through the ankle. I expected that my feet would always be warm, but always being dry was a surprise.

When I sent past reports, I wondered how specific I should be about the risks on this route. I've tried to be concise, and I didn't want to scare anyone by being too graphic.

One of my concerns is that we have two other expeditions on the route, and they're prepared to take what I consider to be unnecessary risks—or they don't know the risks they're taking, which is worse. This could—and to a degree, has—upped the ante within our group. A bad anchor suddenly becomes not-as-bad when other people don't appear to care. Although our ropes have been nicked by falling rocks, many of the European climbers just shake their heads and continue without correcting the situation. This tends to propel everyone into more risky situations. I've been very cautious about this, but it holds momentum and is not easy to stop.

At this moment, a young Spanish/Argentinian guy is at 25,000 feet alone, because he felt strong and didn't wish to descend. If the weather suddenly changes or he develops altitude-sickness, there's nothing anybody could do. History has shown that this kind of action can be fatal. Live drama can be sickening to watch.

We're all well. Don't worry. I think we're still thinking sanely.

## *26* JULY

Mobile No.492900027   Ocean Region:Indian   26 July'94 04:26 UTC

For the last two days, we've had poor weather in base camp. But for the two Spaniards and Alan Hinkes, there was some luck because the storm was restricted to a height of 23,000 feet and they were looking down on the cloud that we were in.

Yesterday they climbed from Camp 3 to Camp 4 (26,000 feet). This morning they are presently at 26,300 feet and going for the summit in clear weather.

The first part of the route involves a long traverse left across a huge snow-basin at about 40 degrees which holds some avalanche risk. Then they should climb up to the left at 45-50 degrees on snow toward a small gully that leads left onto the summit ridge. They follow that to the top. I'll keep you updated.

The other good thing that's happened in the last few days in that on the 23rd of July in good weather Brad Johnson and I made a climb of a nearby peak of 6,640 meters [21,779 feet]. It was a unclimbed summit and a difficult face 1,000 meters high. We had intended to climb an easier-looking gully, so when we realized we'd forgotten the rope, we didn't worry too much. However, our intended climb had stonefall at 7 a.m., so we were forced to take a more difficult line.

We finally were soloing difficult rock and ice and wishing very much that we had a rope. It took us four and a half hours up and one and a half hours to descend via another route. This involved 500 meters of front-point cramponing down 50-degree ice.

The Reebok K2 boot proved amazingly stable on this kind of ice. A perfect test for the boot!

# 26 July

Mobile No.492900027    Ocean Region:Indian    26 July'94 10:18 UTC

 

The summit attempt was foiled by very deep and dangerous snow conditions. All climbers are returning to base camp. This will be the last opportunity for anyone in our team.

With snow building deeper and deeper at this time of year, it's a good time to leave. As the man said: "The beer's finished. Time to go home."

Tomorrow we move to low base camp. We should be there a couple of days.

THE MOUNTAINEERS, founded in 1906, is a nonprofit outdoor activity and conservation club, whose mission is "to explore, study, preserve, and enjoy the natural beauty of the outdoors. . . . " Based in Seattle, Washington, the club is now the third-largest such organization in the United States, with 15,000 members and five branches throughout Washington State.

The Mountaineers sponsors both classes and year-round outdoor activities in the Pacific Northwest, which include hiking, mountain climbing, ski-touring, snowshoeing, bicycling, camping, kayaking and canoeing, nature study, sailing, and adventure travel. The club's conservation division supports environmental causes through educational activities, sponsoring legislation, and presenting informational programs. All club activities are led by skilled, experienced volunteers, who are dedicated to promoting safe and responsible enjoyment and preservation of the outdoors.

If you would like to participate in these organized outdoor activities or the club's programs, consider a membership in The Mountaineers. For information and an application, write or call The Mountaineers, Club Headquarters, 300 Third Avenue West, Seattle, Washington 98119; (206) 284-6310.

The Mountaineers Books, an active, nonprofit publishing program of the club, produces guidebooks, instructional texts, historical works, natural history guides, and works on environmental conservation. All books produced by The Mountaineers are aimed at fulfilling the club's mission.

**Send or call for our catalog of more than 300 outdoor titles:**

The Mountaineers Books
1001 SW Klickitat Way, Suite 201
Seattle, WA 98134
1-800-553-4453
e-mail: mbooks@mountaineers.org
website: www.mountaineersbooks.org